Rerouting the Postcolonial

D0912744

Rerouting the Postcolonial reorientates and reinvigorates the field in line with current critical theory, reconnecting the ethical and political with the aesthetic aspect of postcolonial culture.

Bringing together a group of leading and emerging intellectuals, this volume charts and challenges the diversity of postcolonial studies, including:

- new directions and growth areas from performance and autobiography to diaspora and transnationalism
- new subject matters such as sexuality and queer theory, ecocriticism and discussions of areas of Europe as postcolonial spaces
- new theoretical directions such as globalization, fundamentalism, terror and theories of 'affect'.

Each section incorporates a clear, concise introduction, making this volume both an accessible overview of the field whilst also an invigorating collection of scholarship for the new millennium.

Contributors: Bill Ashcroft, Anna Ball, Elleke Boehmer, Diana Brydon, Simon Gikandi, Erin Goheen Glanville, James Graham, Dorota Kołodziejczyk, Victor Li, Nadia Louar, Deborah L. Madsen, Jeffrey Mather, Nirmala Menon, Kaori Nagai, Jane Poyner, Robert Spencer and Patrick Williams.

Janet Wilson is Professor of English and Postcolonial Studies at the University of Northampton, UK, and is editor of the *Journal of Postcolonial Writing*.

Cristina Şandru is a visiting lecturer at the 'Lucian Blaga' University of Sibiu, Romania, and works as academic editor for *The Literary Encyclopaedia* and *The Journal of Postcolonial Studies*.

Sarah Lawson Welsh is Reader in English and Postcolonial Literatures at York St John University, UK.

Rerouting the Postcolonial

New directions for the new millennium

Edited by
Janet Wilson, Cristina Şandru and
Sarah Lawson Welsh

Routledge
Taylor & Francis Group

LONDON AND NEW YORK

First published 2010
by Routledge
2 Park Square, Milton Park, Abingdon, Oxon OX14 4RN

Simultaneously published in the USA and Canada
by Routledge
270 Madison Ave, New York, NY 10016

Routledge is an imprint of the Taylor & Francis Group,
an Informa business

© 2010 Janet Wilson, Cristina Şandru and Sarah Lawson Welsh for
selection and editorial matter; individual chapters, the contributors.

Typeset in Baskerville by
Taylor & Francis Books
Printed and bound in Great Britain by
TJ International Ltd, Padstow, Cornwall

British Library Cataloguing in Publication Data
A catalogue record for this book is available from the British Library

Library of Congress Cataloging-in-Publication Data
Rerouting the postcolonial: new directions for the new millennium / edited
by Janet Wilson, Cristina Şandru and Sarah Lawson Welsh. – 1st ed.

    p. cm.
    Includes bibliographical references and index.
    1. Commonwealth literature (English) – History and criticism – Theory,
etc. 2. English literature – History and criticism – Theory, etc. 3.
Postcolonialism – Commonwealth countries. I. Wilson, Janet, 1948–II.
Şandru, Cristina, 1977. III. Lawson Welsh, Sarah, 1966-
    PR9080.R47 2010
820.9'9171241–
dc22   2009025902

ISBN10: 0-415-54324-X (hbk)
ISBN10: 0-415-54325-8 (pbk)
ISBN10: 0-203-86219-8 (ebk)

ISBN13: 978-0-415-54324-8 (hbk)
ISBN13: 978-0-415-54325-5 (pbk)
ISBN13: 978-0-203-86219-3 (ebk)

Contents

Editors

Janet Wilson is Professor of English and Postcolonial Studies at the University of Northampton. She has published widely on New Zealand writing and is currently working on a study of adaptation in contemporary New Zealand and Australian cinema. Recent publications include: *Fleur Adcock* (2007), *The Gorse Blooms Pale: The Southland Stories of Dan Davin* (2007), and the co-edited volume (with Clara A.B. Joseph) *Global Fissures: Postcolonial Fusions* (2006). She is the editor of the *Journal of Postcolonial Writing* and currently chair of EACLALS.

Dr. Cristina Şandru currently works as assistant editor for *The Literary Encyclopedia* (www.litecyc.com) and is a visiting lecturer at the University of Sibiu, Romania. She previously taught at the universities of Northampton and Aberystwyth, at the School of Slavonic and Eastern European Studies at University College London, and Goldsmiths', University of London. Her main research interests are in comparative literature, postcolonial theory and literature, and East-Central European cultures. She has published articles and reviews in *Critique*, *Euresis*, the Routledge series *The New Makers of Modern Culture*, and *English*. Since 2007 she has been an Associate Editor of the *Journal of Postcolonial Writing*.

Sarah Lawson Welsh is Reader in English and Postcolonial Literatures at York St John University, York. She has taught at the Hull, Warwick, Northampton and York St John universities. Sarah's research interests are in twentieth century and contemporary writing, especially women's writing, postcolonial literature, Caribbean literature and diaspora writing. She is an Associate Editor of the *Journal of Postcolonial Writing*. Her publications include the *Routledge Reader in Caribbean Literature* (1996) and *Grace Nichols* (2007) in the 'Writers and Their Work' series (Northcote Press & the British Council). She has published widely on Caribbean and Black British writing and her work has been reprinted as part of the Open University course materials for *A430 – Postcolonial Literatures in English*.

Contributors

Bill Ashcroft is Professor of English at the University of New South Wales, Sydney, Australia. He is a founding exponent of post-colonial theory, co-author of *The Empire Writes Back* (1989) the first text to examine systematically the field of post-colonial studies. Author and co-author of sixteen books, including four second editions, variously translated into five languages, he has also written over 140 chapters and papers and is on the editorial boards of ten international journals. Present research interests include postcolonial utopias and post-colonial approaches to transnational writing.

Anna Ball is a lecturer in postcolonial studies in the English Department at Nottingham Trent University. Her research focuses on questions of gender, spatiality and postcoloniality in writing and film from the contemporary Middle East. She has published on a range of subjects including Palestinian cinema, representations of sexual violence in Arab women's writing and on postcolonial studies post-9/11, and is currently preparing a monograph on the interplay of borders, boundaries and bodies in Palestinian literature and film.

Elleke Boehmer is the author of *Colonial and Postcolonial Literature* (1995, 2005), *Empire, the National and the Postcolonial, 1880-1920* (2002), and *Stories of Women: Gender and Narrative in the Postcolonial Nation* (2005), as well as of four novels. She has published *Empire Writing* (1998), a critical edition of Baden-Powell's classic, *Scouting for Boys* (2004) and *Nelson Mandela: A Very Short Introduction* (2008). She is the General Editor of the Oxford Studies in Postcolonial Literatures. She is currently Professor of World Writing in English at Oxford.

Diana Brydon is Canada Research Chair in Globalization and Cultural Studies at the University of Manitoba where she directs the Centre for Globalization and Cultural Studies and teaches Canadian and postcolonial literatures. She has published on Australian, Canadian and Caribbean writing, edited the 5 volume *Postcolonialism: Critical Concepts in Literary and Cultural Studies* and co-edited *Shakespeare in Canada* and *Renegotiating Community: Interdisciplinary Perspectives, Global Contexts*. She currently works on global and national imaginaries, and serves as a member of the international convening group for a project on "Building Global Democracy" (www.buildingglobaldemocracy.org).

Simon Gikandi is Robert Schirmer Professor of English at Princeton University. He is the author of many books and articles including *Writing in Limbo: Modernism and Caribbean Literature, Maps of Englishness: Writing Identity in the Culture of Colonialism,* and *Ngugi wa Thiong'o,* which was a Choice Outstanding Academic Publication for 2004. He is co-editor of *The Cambridge History of African and Caribbean Literature* and editor of the *Routledge Encyclopedia of African Literature.* His new book, *The Aura of Blackness: Slavery and the Culture of Taste* is forthcoming from Princeton University Press.

Erin Goheen Glanville is in her final year as a PhD candidate in English and Cultural Studies at McMaster University. Her dissertation, entitled "Writing Refugees in Canada", examines refugee narratives as an undervalued part of current diaspora studies and as pedagogical tools for church-based refugee activism in Hamilton, Ontario. She has taught English at Redeemer University, Ancaster, Ontario and is currently co-editing *Countering Displacements: Agency and Creativity,* the proceedings of an international conference she co-organized with fellow members of The Canadian Research Chair Symposium for Diversity in Canadian Literary Cultures in 2007, "Displacements: Borders, Mobility, and Statelessness".

James Graham teaches at the University of Warwick and for the Faculty of Continuing Education at Birkbeck, University of London. His research interests include literature from Southern Africa and the relationship between postcolonial studies and ecocriticism.

Dorota Kołodziejczyk is Assistant Professor and Director of the Postcolonial Studies Center at the English Department, University of Wroclaw, Poland. She has published within the area of postcolonial studies and comparative literature, with the focus on the postcolonial novel, Eastern European novel, magical realism, cultural borderlands, postsocialist transition processes. She is also a translator (Clifford Geertz, Partha Chatterjee, Kwame Anthony Appiah, Gayatri Chakravorty Spivak, Timothy Brennan and Dipesh Chakrabarty) and translation editor (Leela Gandhi, Said's *Culture and Imperialism,* Homi Bhabha's *The Location of Culture*).

Victor Li is an Associate Professor in the Department of English and the Centre for Comparative Literature at the University of Toronto. His research interests include contemporary critical and literary theory, postcolonial literatures, primitivism, and globalization studies. He is the author of *The Neo-primitivist Turn: Critical Reflections on Alterity, Culture, and Modernity* (2006). His current research project, a critique of the representationalist ontology of both pro- and anti-globalization discourses, is titled "Allegories of Globalization." He is the co-editor of *The University of Toronto Quarterly* and is on the editorial advisory boards of *ARIEL, CR: The New Centennial Review,* and *The Journal of Postcolonial Writing.*

Nadia Louar is Assistant Professor of French and Francophone Studies at the University of Wisconsin, Oshkosh. She obtained her Ph.D. from the University of California, Berkeley. Recent publications include articles on Beckett and bilingualism, Jean Genet, Jean Sénac and Virginie Despentes. Her book entitled *Poetics of Bilingualism in the Work of Samuel Beckett* is under review. Her research interests are in twentieth and twentieth-first century French and francophone literatures.

Deborah L. Madsen is Professor of American Literature and Culture at the University of Geneva. She works primarily in the field of Postcolonial American Studies, with a focus on issues of modernity, national rhetoric, and cultural transnationalism. Publications include *Allegory in America: From Puritanism to Post-modernism* (1996), *American Exceptionalism* (1998), *Beyond the Borders: American Literature and Post-Colonial Theory* (ed. 2003), *Understanding Gerald Vizenor* (2009), and *Native Authenticity: Transatlantic Approaches to Native American Literature* (ed. 2010). Her monograph *Contra Trauma: Reading Theory through Native American Literature* is forthcoming in 2010. She is co-editor with Gerald Vizenor of the SUNY Press book series "Native Traces."

Jeff Mather is completing a PhD in English at the Centre for Colonial and Postcolonial Studies at the University of Kent. His thesis is on nineteenth and early twentieth-century British travel writing and China, with a particular focus on imaginings of China's periphery regions. His work also branches into comparative studies, and he is currently working on questions of nationalism and frontier identity in contemporary Chinese literature and culture.

Nirmala Menon is an Assistant Professor in the English Department at Saint Anselm College, Manchester, New Hampshire, USA. Her research explores the role of translations, especially postcolonial translations, from different languages into English and their influence on postcolonial theoretical studies. Her major focus is on the rich resource of language literatures from India (some in original, others in translation). She is working on a monograph that explores the ways in which multilingual literatures can transform and remap postcolonial studies.

Kaori Nagai lectures at the University of Kent. She is the author of *Empire of Analogies: Kipling, India and Ireland* (Cork UP, 2006). She has published widely on colonial discourses of the nineteenth and early twentieth centuries, and has recently completed a Leverhulme research fellowship on artificial language movements in the British Empire. She is the editor of a journal special collection *Dream Writing* (*Journal of European Studies*, 2008) and is currently co-editing a collection of essays, *Kipling and Beyond: Patriotism, Globalisation and Postcolonialism* (Palgrave Macmillan, forthcoming).

Jane Poyner is a lecturer in Postcolonial Literature and Theory at the University of Exeter, UK. She has edited a collection of essays on the South African writer J. M. Coetzee (Ohio UP, 2006). She is currently preparing a monograph on Coetzee for Ashgate (forthcoming, 2008) and is co-editing a volume on Coetzee for the MLA Approaches to Teaching Series. She also has published a number of articles on South African literature and postcolonial theory.

Robert Spencer lectures at the University of Manchester in Postcolonial Literature and Culture. He has published widely on postcolonial theory and literature, in particular on African and Irish literature and the work of Edward Said. He is currently working on a book entitled *Cosmopolitan Criticism*.

Patrick Williams is Professor of Literary and Cultural Studies at Nottingham Trent University, where he teaches courses on postcolonial theory and culture, film, diaspora, and race and nation in twentieth century Britain. His publications include *Colonial Discourse and Post-Colonial Theory* (1993); *Introduction to Post-Colonial Theory*, (with Peter Childs) (1996), *Ngugi wa Thiong'o* (1999); *Edward Said* (2000); *Postcolonial African Cinema* (with David Murphy) (2007). Forthcoming books include *The Routledge Companion to Diaspora Studies* (co-edited with Alison Donnell and John Noyes), and a collection on Orientalism in Routledge's 'Major Works' series. He is on the Editorial Advisory Boards of *Theory, Culture and Society*, and the *Journal of Postcolonial Writing*.

Acknowledgements

Sarah Lawson Welsh

Thanks to Susan Orr and Julie Raby for arranging a period of study leave at York St John University in Summer 2009 and to Saffron Walkling for covering my teaching. To my final year 'Writing the Caribbean' class for keeping things lively and open to debate – you were fabulous.

To Richard, Imogen, Peter and Dan who have put up with a preoccupied partner and parent for far too long. I promise now to pack up my books and come out to play.

Thanks are due also to Alec Samler and Shirley Horsman whose energetic family research turned up Harman Samler (1719–1792), German immigrant, London 'Sugarbaker' (sugar refiner) and unexpected forbear. The irony of discovering an eighteenth-century ancestor and sons so prominently involved in the final part of the triangular trade, the transatlantic trajectories of slavery and sugar, has been sobering indeed.

Finally, this book is dedicated to my daughter Imogen (b. 2001) for sweetness of an entirely different kind.

General acknowledgements

The spelling of the term postcolonial (with the alternative spelling post-colonial) will vary throughout this volume in relation to contributors' own approaches.

The publisher and author would like to thank the following for permission to reprint material under copyright:

Extracts from 'Family Photograph' in *Almost Ashore*© Gerald Vizenor 2006 and 'The Last Photography' in *Interior Landscapes: Autobiographical Myths and Metaphors*© Gerald Vizenor 1990, used by permission of the author.

Every effort has been made to trace and contact copyright holders. The publishers would be pleased to hear from any copyright holders not acknowledged here, so that this acknowledgement page may be amended at the earliest opportunity.

General introduction

Janet Wilson, Cristina Şandru and Sarah Lawson Welsh

Much has been written in the past decades about the effects of colonization on cultures and societies, within the field of both Humanities and Social Sciences, a concentration of interest which has helped consolidate the emerging field of postcolonial studies. This, alongside the emergence of globalization theories and cultural studies, has led to the increasing cross-pollination of these areas of scholarly inquiry, whose exact interrelationship is often contradictory, unequal and therefore unpredictable. Thus, for instance, the encroachment of globalization studies, now often considered to be the dominant perspective through which to consider the contemporary moment, has led in the new millennium to the perception of a 'crisis' in postcolonialism. That postcolonial theory is now an 'exhausted paradigm' was the subject of an Modern Languages Association roundtable discussion 'The End of Postcolonial Theory' in 2006 (Yaeger 2007); while the belief that postcolonial studies is being eclipsed by globalization was the catalyst for the recent collection *Postcolonial Studies and Beyond* (Loomba *et al.* 2005: 8), whose editors advocate going 'beyond a certain kind of postcolonial studies' in order to engage with the imperial formations and ideologies associated with globalization (7). Other critics, however, have noted the collusion between the fields and stress their interrelatedness rather than opposition: thus, Joseph and Wilson find points of overlap through shared cultural concepts such as Bhabha's hybridity (2006: xxv, 36); Krishnaswamy adds deterritorialization, migrancy, difference and cosmopolitanism, and highlights a number of historical and ideological convergences, concluding that 'to be global is first and foremost is to be postcolonial and to be postcolonial is always already to be global' (2003, 2005, 2008: 3).

As the brief overview above suggests, the multiple lines of interaction among these partly overlapping intellectual paradigms have profoundly transformed the field of postcolonial studies. Thus, there was a perceptible shift during the 1990s towards the theoretical and the cultural at the expense of earlier, predominantly literary-critical, explorations; more recently, in response to the conceptual and disciplinary challenges that globalization poses, the discipline has further modulated and refined its engagement with contemporary neo-imperial practices. The temporal horizons of the field are demarcated less by the 'narrative of decolonisation' (Gikandi cited in Loomba *et al.*, 2005: 8) than by neocolonial imbalances in the postcolonial present. Our project – which began at the international conference 'Rerouting the Postcolonial' in July 2007, hosted by the University of Northampton – inserts itself into, and simultaneously interrogates, refines and extends the present contours of postcolonialism, both by tracing new develop-ments in the field and by including ex-centric perspectives on its relationship with theories of globalization and cosmopolitanism. More pertinently, the essays seek to reconnect (and reroute) the ethical and the political with the aesthetic in the context of a recent 'turn to the affective' in cultural criticism as well as a new strand of affirmative utopianism associated with spatiality, mobility and the imaginary. An emphasis on literary texts in some papers reflects the traditional grounding of the field in literary studies and critical theory, even though many of the readings reveal contextualizations and reassessments that current global problems are urgently calling for. The volume also reflects recent culturalist calls for a return to the literary, as, for example, in the conclusion to Peter Hallward's *Absolutely Postcolonial* (2001), or as evidenced by Deepika Bahri's *Native Intelligence* (2003) which foregrounds the relationship between aesthetic concerns, ideology and political responsibility in postcolonial texts.

As intimated above, the postcolonial has moved in recent years from being a historical marker to a more globally inflected term applicable to a variety of regions. Our volume focuses firmly on territories – not as discrete and essential-ized spaces but rather as spaces increasingly defined, perhaps even constituted, *relationally* and/or rhizomatically, through global networks. We therefore include contributions which emerge from ex-centric spaces, but which also present new visions of the global versus the local (what both Brydon and Kołodziejczyk call the 'glocal'), innovative descriptions of the relationship between local, national and transnational forces (Ashcroft's 'transnation'), new insights into cosmopolitanism, underprivileged agencies (refugees and asylum seekers) and, indeed, politically inflected debates about the ethical purchase of postcolonial theory. Such spatiality is inherent in the very semantics of roots, routes and 'rerouting', and, as Brydon herself argues, entirely cognate with Mignolo's concept of 'border thinking' (105 and 110), a very apt metaphor to describe the field's capacity to unravel apparently fixed boundaries, whether mental/imaginary or political.

The collection thus works at the intersection of postcolonial studies, literary studies, critical theory, and globalization studies, and explores new directions within and between each of these disciplines. The transformative ideas of reloca-tion and rerouting are conceptual lynchpins running through a very diverse textual constituency, highlighting the need for new approaches and areas of investigation. The volume probes the tensions between the commonly cited homophones, *roots* (associated with origins, location, place) and *routes* (travel with its attendant mean-ings of uprooting, rerooting, new directions and reconceptualizations of space) (see Clifford 1997, DeLoughrey 2007, Gilroy 1993b). The meta-terms of the title define the major conceptual directions of the volume: 'rerouting' points to the exploration of recent discourses of migration, diaspora, dislocation and the new mobile spaces offered by cosmopolitan travel, while 'the postcolonial' offers new configurations of the field in relation to cosmopolitanism, eco-environmentalism, post-communist concerns, revisionary pedagogies and critical practices. The essays focus on multi-national locations and literatures: from diasporic experience in Scottish–Sudanese fiction to cosmopolitan provincialism in contemporary Polish writing, from global China to post-apartheid South-Africa. Many of them offer comparative analyses of seemingly unrelated locations, thus both widening the scope and increasing the depth of postcolonial literary criticism, and reinforcing an additional recognition: that neat and conveniently unified conceptions of what is deemed 'postcolonial' – such as the anti-colonial centre/peripheries binary – often fail to account for the very intellectual energies that have so far kept the field dynamic and responsive to change.

Beneath the surface eclecticism of the essays there is a common objective of moving the postcolonial to new conceptual and geographical ground, a strong revisionist mode, and a sense of potentially uncharted territory. We have sought to extend the premises and arguments of earlier studies which were rooted in 'conundrums of hybridity and authenticity' (O'Brien and Szeman cited in Loomba *et al.*, 2005: 15) to emphasize how the field is developing under the impact of, among others, globalization, environmentalism, and various transnational formations – whether political and economic (such as neo-liberal ideologies), or cultural (the 'transnation', the 'glocal', the 'cosmopolitan'). In this objective our volume is both a complement to previous similar enterprises (such as Loomba *et al.*, *Postcolonial Studies and Beyond*) and a development of key areas of investigation. Topics and issues commonly associated with the discipline (such as diasporic and minoritarian subjectivities, global networks of power, metropolitan immigrant communities, etc.) are treated in ways that serve to remind readers that the project of postcolonial studies has come to embrace a much larger set of intellectual positions than is commonly presumed, and that it can bring into conversation very diverse scholarly agendas and critical practices.

Most importantly, our contributors reflect critically on the significance of 'postcolonial reroutings' at a time when the term's horizons appear more diffuse than ever before. The volume does not *abandon* earlier postcolonial emphases on routes and roots, but rather inserts these within the contemporary context of cosmopolitan globalization and its numerous (dis)contents. How exactly then, are we proposing to reroute the postcolonial? And which directions might such a rerouting take? Indeed, how do we conceive of the very idea of rerouting, especially in conjunction with previous delineations of the roots/routes dichotomy prevalent in the discipline?

The use of the tropes of roots and routes is not new. Kamau Brathwaite has been interrogating them, creatively and critically, for at least forty years (1987 [1973], 1993, 1999 [1963]). Most recently Brathwaite has been developing the concept of 'tidalectics', a 'geopolitical model of history' inspired by the rhythms and flow of the ocean in relation to the land. Tidalectics is a more fluid and complex model of what might be called 'roots rerouted', which posits the relation between space and time, history and place in terms of an '"alter/native" historiography to linear models of colonial progress' (DeLoughrey, 2007: 2). The work of another Caribbean writer-theorist, Edouard Glissant, has also been influential here in terms of his 'anti-originary Caribbean aesthetic which [...] emphasizes process, crossings and interchange rather than an attempt to retrieve a "pure" ancestral identity' (Thieme 2003: 105). The notion of roots and routes is also central to Paul Gilroy's *The Black Atlantic* (1993b), which shifted critical focus away from a concern with national paradigms and national borders towards a more diffuse, rhizomatic sense of a network of transatlantic connections created by the flows of capital, commodities and people (and people-as-commodities) involved in the Atlantic slave trade. This Black Atlantic culture model, which Gilroy proposes as a counterculture to western modernity, is in part indebted to the earlier theoretical insights of Deleuze and Guattari, particularly their concepts of 'deterritorialization', the 'rhizome', and 'nomadology' (1987 [1972], 1987 [1980]). However, the figures of roots and routes are most closely associated with the work of cultural anthropologist James Clifford (1988, 1992, 1997, 2001), who coined the influential notion of 'travelling cultures' (1992) and whose well-known study of travel and translation in the late twentieth century is entitled *Routes* (1997). Clifford does not use the concept of roots in any fixed sense but sees roots as continually changing, rerouted and reroutable in various ways. Thus in 'Articulations' (2001) he argues that indigenous peoples may route their roots through a number of diasporic trajectories and other movements (e.g. journeys connected to trade and work), thereby complicating the simple binary 'home' and 'away'. Clifford's work has been key to *Roots and Routes* (2007), Elizabeth DeLoughrey's study of what she calls the 'transoceanic imaginary' in Caribbean and Pacific Island literatures. Roots and routes have been invoked by many postcolonial writers (see, for example Nichols's poem 'Wings', 1996: 77–9) and the notions of rooting in and routing through are now so widespread in diasporic and postcolonial discourse as to sometimes seem voided of meaning. Moreover, the use of the term diaspora has arguably become increasingly abstracted and figurative in nature (Procter 2003: 13–14). The essays included in this volume highlight the fact that the apparently dichotomic pair is, in effect, a generative complex of interactions very similar to the rhizomic structure proposed by Deleuze and Guattati, which allows not only for a diverse range of identitarian trajectories, but also for the unexpected and seemingly dissonant configurations of political agency and cultural identification characteristic of the globalized present (see, in particular, Ashcroft, Ball and Kołodziejczyk). These configurations also define some of the ways in which the postcolonial as a discipline is currently being rerouted.

Another area of engagement that runs throughout the volume is the often contested, but highly visible concept of (as well as aspiration to, and ambivalence towards) cosmopolitanism. With its implications of citizenship, civilized conversation, 'conviviality' and heightened political responsibilities, cosmopolitanism is increasingly seen as a term which interfaces the postcolonial with theories of globalization. Much of this volume's theoretical underpinning – as the essays in Section 1 show – stems from a shared ethical concern to reconceptualize cosmopolitanism in order to more effectively address the implications of problems which globalization has brought to the fore and which require 'global' solutions.

All address the urgent need for semantic expansion of this term from its western connotations of education, affluence, elitism and privilege. The occupation of spaces outside national territories in the current global mobilization of peoples requires new discursive modes: Simon Gikandi, for example, draws attention to the limitations (both ethical and political) of the current theoretical vocabulary to articulate the experiences of postcolonial lives lived beyond national boundaries, both in the midst of and, paradoxically, at the margins of the global international system; Erin Goheen Glanville looks in more detail at what the experience of refugees, migrants, nomads and asylum seekers, most often excluded from western cosmopolitan discourses, might tell us about our own convenient amnesias; Dorota Kołodziejczyk formulates an apparently contradictory concept of 'cosmopolitan provincialism', defined by transnational narratives of the local, peripheral and non-metropolitan that cut across monolithic formulations of globalization. In contrast, in considering the multiple spaces inhabited by those who speak more than one language, Kaori Nagai asserts a new reality of '"transnational" cosmopolitanism': noting the double citizenship that the artificial language of Esperanto made possible – between one's own nation and the global dynamic of other nations – she claims that cosmopolitanism offers the staging of a new human space for conversation. Drawing on Tim Brennan's argument in 'Cosmo Theory' (2002), that Esperanto is marginalized in overviews of cosmopolitanism, she posits the movement as a long-forgotten ancestor of current postcolonial theories. Finally, for Robert Spencer, writing on 'Cosmopolitan Criticism', the cultivation of cosmopolitan allegiances is virtually synonymous with the practices of reading and criticism with which postcolonial scholars are preeminently involved.

Nagai's optimistic 'transnational cosmopolitanism' resonates with Spencer's 'cosmopolitan conscience' or self knowledge and his urging – gesturing to Bill Ashcroft's utopian concept of the 'transnation' – of greater risk-taking in our reading practices in order to appreciate how postcolonial literature delineates a 'world cured of divisions put into place by imperialism' (42). New thinking on cosmopolitanism engages with postcolonial arguments on the category of the nation which rehearse either its demise or renewal in relation to globalization (Krishnaswamy 2008: 6–10): thus, Spencer argues that, as 'the engines of globalization' (39), nation-states remain principal sites for the articulation of subjects' rights; while critiques of the nation as 'an *exclusionary*, [...] political formation' (72) are the source of Ashcroft's 'literary transnation'. The transation is a product of movement, reflecting the 'rhizomic interplay of travelling subjects *within* as well as between nations' (79). Ashcroft further distinguishes the 'smooth' space of the transnation, a space of potentiality, from the 'striated' space of the state which it surrounds and interpenetrates. The 'literary transnation', therefore, is not only unbound by nationalism, but has the capacity to embody potentiality: its transformative impetus is linked to the utopian function of literature which embodies imagination's power to envisage a better world.

The increased possibilities for developing interconnected epistemologies of the global and the local, many of them embodying a utopian potential, are explored in other essays: Gikandi reflects on the local as 'already global', while Brydon agrees with Spencer that a 'glocal' sensibility stems from the non-conflictual simultaneous embrace of different systems, localities and traditions (which, as Ball contends, can and *do* also include faith-based practices that are often occluded in standard accounts of what counts as 'postcolonial'). Patrick Williams identifies two such 'glocal' projects: the West–East Divan Orchestra co-founded by Edward Said and Daniel Barenboim, and New Social Movements such as the World Social Forum (Krishnaswamy 2008: 14). Williams's political advocacy of a 'better world' and his vision of postcolonialism as an '"anticipatory" discourse', (as in the case of Palestine) conjoins with similar formulations of the utopian thrust of literature as suggested by both Ashcroft and Spencer.

Like the utopian, the affective signals a less politically driven and more critically reflexive phase in postcolonialism, as globalization suggests the possibility of new theoretical models to link the individual subject to the public sphere. The essays by Victor Li and Nadia Louar consist of case studies which probe the construction of the subject, and, in turning from identity politics to subjectivity itself, testify to the upsurge of affect in postcolonial texts and criticism. 'Smooth' space, the base of Ashcroft's transnation, also comprises the borderless world of Robert Zemecki's Hollywood film, *Cast Away* (2000): this Li analyses by showing the links between the macro-discourse of globalization and the micro-discourse of the neo-liberal subject, best described as "the enterprise of oneself" (60–1). The film shows how globalization, expanding everywhere with its 'disciplinary logic of capitalism', creates flexible and unfixed subjects: when shipwrecked on a desert island, the individual corporeal subject undergoes transformative self-improvement due to the discipline offered by global business practices. Li's stress on the affective component in a Hollywood depiction of corporate culture has affinities with Louar's rerouting of theory towards the affective in her critical category of the unrequited lover as a new model of subjectivity in the work of Jean Senec, and her timely probing of the intersections of postcolonial and queer discourses in relation to earlier anti-colonial writers, canonical and otherwise.

The rise of 'affect' and the utopian turn in postcolonial studies are partly responses to the impact of globalization and the pervasiveness of neo-imperial ideologies. Yet their particular postcolonial embodiment is far from abstract or merely theoretical, as William points out, but rather pragmatic and ethical, articulating a *practical* project that translates, in the terms of Ernst Bloch, the "intention towards possibility that has still not become" (93). As a newly emerging strand of transnational cosmopolitan, reflecting the increased mobilization both within and among cultures and nations, and the need for a more engaged dialogue with the Other, utopianism thus participates in critical discourses which are politically informed. Such a 'utopian postcolonial cosmopolitanism' offers a conceptual basis for a new interdisciplinary framework which is required now that nations and cultures are no longer seen as stable and clearly demarcated entities.

Ways of building such a framework are suggested in many of the essays: drawing together the ideas discussed so far, Spencer, like Ashcroft, reconnects cosmopolitanism with the postcolonial by rerouting earlier critiques of the nation-state and transnationalism. Spencer, Gikandi and Goheen Glanville, we note, show a determination to decouple cosmopolitanism from its association with elite intellectuals, and to broaden its horizons to include readers and critics in general, and in keeping with current developments in transcultural studies, migrant subjects and refugees (Helff 2009: 79). This critical project is not altogether new, but builds on foundations already in place over the past thirty years, as Patrick Williams makes clear in his grappling with the question of 'why reroute'. Yet its potential remains to be fully realized, as several contributors remark; hence Williams's call not only for a rerouting, but also for a rerooting of sorts, as for example in resistance to forms of (neo)colonial exploitation, or his and Brydon's insistence on a 'practical pedagogy' that would inform both our research and academic practices and larger public projects.

One of the new routes of inquiry charted by the volume is postcolonialism's recent foray into unfamiliar locations and contexts. The historical and geographical range of the essays (from Poland to South Africa, Canada to China), as well as their comparative impetus, highlights the ability of such reroutings to go beyond West–East (or, indeed, West–rest) binaries, and not only 'provincialize Europe', but, more to the point perhaps, destabilize grand narratives of both colonial modernity and anti-colonial resistance. Indeed, as Diana Brydon remarks in a key essay in the volume, postcolonial theory's potency resides in its capacity to infuse and diffuse itself into diverse, often seemingly incompatible fields of engagement and geopolitical vistas. Its decolonizing energy – political as well as ideological and cultural – is effective precisely because it disrupts monolithic ideologies and creates 'cracks' in the global imaginary. This is most evident in the essays in Section 2 which explore intellectual and geographical territories that might be considered either obliquely postcolonial (such as China or East-Central Europe), or which forcefully challenge orthodox models of the postcolonial that reject essentialist notions of cultural belonging (Anna Ball's 'rerouting into rerooting', for instance).

As Jeff Mather remarks in his essay on global China, the controversies regarding the country's putative 'postcolonial' status have served to unpack some of the dominant narratives of West–East interaction. An imperial power in its own right, yet in an uneasy relationship with western imperialism, a major non-western player which cannot be comfortably situated within current 'Third World' models, China compels analysts to go beyond convenient political allegiances in order to question the potential impact on their theoretical models of a critical engagement with its complex position. The postcolonial, removed of its primary historical and geographical attachments, can thus come to signify a much larger variety of oppositional practices and gestures of resistance, where the 'Other' may no longer be western imperialism and its exploitative capitalist enterprises (as in dominant postcolonial narratives) but, rather, as in the Chinese or East-European context, repressive nationalist communism. A similar rerouting is shown to take place when a comparative model is used to discuss postcolonial metropolitan literature and post-communist texts produced in East-Central Europe, as in

Dorota Kołodziejczyk's study of provincialism and localism at the shady borders of empires in the novels of Amitav Ghosh and the Polish writer Andrzej Stasiuk. The commonly unacknowledged relation of the Eastern European problematic to postcolonial studies here enables a comparative perspective that places in illuminating dialogue texts which ostensibly have little in common, but which, on close examination, reveal a shared imaginative space, rhetoric and narrative agency. The contributor's own assessment of what such a rerouting of the postcolonial can bring is illuminating: it can stimulate

> the revisionary trend of post-communist discourse from a predominantly national paradigm and inspire [...] a new historiographic and cultural imagery that encourages an exploration of the region's ambivalent self-positioning vis-à-vis Europe, [at the same time] foster[ing] a new understanding of periphery which, among others, actively reimagines itself in a politics of provincialism.
>
> (152)

Also highlighted in Section 3 are different interrogations of the *practice* of postcolonial criticism within institutional locations. The issue of how one 'performs' postcolonial studies, given the disjunction between its objects of inquiry (underprivileged subjectivities and political entities) and the institutional positions from within which their critique is articulated, is anything but new. Indeed, the 'politics of location' has been a contentious issue in the discipline since its inception, and the institutionalization of postcolonial studies in the past decades has added grist to accusations of complicity, privilege and lack of representativity that have been mounted against metropolitan intellectuals. A keynote of the conference, and therefore of this volume, is a retrieval and reassertion of the pedagogical and ethical import of the postcolonial, this time, however, in close conjunction with its aesthetic potential, rather than divorced from it. Many articles take up this challenge, either directly (Brydon, Boehmer, Gikandi) or via new models of textual interpretation (Poyner, Graham). Brydon's essay, arising 'out of dissatisfaction with the current place of postcolonial studies within academic structures' (112), is particularly apposite, as it makes the case for a postcolonial epistemology in which research and education are made to be ethically relevant. Like other prominent scholars of globalization, such as Anthony Appadurai, she exhorts rerouting to 'previous postcolonial concerns with national liberation into contemporary justice, educational, and equity movements, which operate at scales below and beyond the nation state' (Brydon, 111). The kind of politically-oriented, pedagogically-relevant knowledge inquiry that Brydon advocates can be brought about by judicious educational policies, which bring together research practices, curricular choices and concrete postcolonial engagements. The example she offers, of the Human Rights Museum in Winnipeg, Canada, shows how institutional acquisition of knowledge in schools or universities can both inform and be influenced by larger projects of public education, although the problematics of translating memory into words and images, and of determining precisely what types of historical memory are chosen for 'display' and learning, continue to remain controversial.

A more direct reform of prevalent models of postcolonial curricular choices is taken up in Nirmala Menon's discussion of postcolonial canon-formation and its subtending ideological preferences. Menon's article, like Deepika Bahri's recent work on aesthetics, politics and postcolonial writing (2003), is very attuned to the material conditions of production, reception and critical dissemination of postcolonial writings. Menon's case studies demonstrate the continued under-representation of non-Anglophone writers and vernacular literatures in favour of a relatively small range of postcolonial 'cosmopolitan' writers in largely metropolitan-based critical journals. Related concerns are raised by Deborah Madsen, whose *Postcolonial Literatures: Expanding the Canon* (1999) argues for the need to include American, Native American, Chicano, Afro-Hispanic and other marginalized writings within the postcolonial canon. Madsen's article in this volume examines the politics of the disciplinary fields of American Studies and Ethnic Studies, both in terms of the role that postcolonial studies has played in rerouting American studies away from its roots in US nationalism and the white nation state, and in terms of the ethics and future of American Studies and other nation-based academic disciplines. 'Ultimately, both contributors call for the establishment of more provisional, contingent and nomadic textual canons, albeit in different fields'.

What is interesting here is the identification of alternative canons as already existent or at least emergent. Earlier critical considerations of canons and canonicity tend to stress movement away from the narrowness of an English or Eurocentric literary canon (see Gorak 1991; Pope 2003 [1998]) or the role of canonical intertexts and con-texts (Newman 1998; Thieme 2001). Menon's call for a comparative perspective and for studies of works written in original languages still carries traces of this foundational imperative of canon-resistance but, importantly, her piece also moves beyond it, for example in arguing for a rethinking of some of the postcolonial theoretical concepts which act as a kind of 'meta-discourse that assumes a given canon of postcolonial texts' (Madsen 1999: 1). Gupta (2009) cites Rob Pope's *The English Studies Book* (2003 [1998]) as indicative of an outmoded approach to canons and canonicity in its reiteration of colonial–postcolonial binaries and in its anglocentrism. Other recent writing on canonicity is more nuanced in moving beyond binary resistance models. Bahri, for instance, uses the term 'counter-canon' (3) when referring to postcolonial literary production, but also suggests problems inherent in the emergent canon – older texts becoming 'standard' as new ones are admitted. The dangers of homogeni-zation, of a sedimentation of concerns within postcolonial studies, of replicating the exclusions and hegemony of the European canon in the guise of metropoli-tan writers and critics, of foregrounding mobility (geographical and intellectual) and of privileging cosmopolitan models of postcoloniality (see Gikandi, Spencer, Menon), all still require critical attention.

We ought not consider as foregone conclusions the questions: 'Is there such a thing as a postcolonial canon? Is it still emergent? Or is the postcolonial canon, as Damrosch argues (2003: 281), a way of reading texts rather than a grouping of texts *per se*? If there *is* such a thing as a postcolonial canon, what does it comprise? What are its blind spots and orthodoxies? Is there a role for national canons in a globalized, transnational era? Who 'makes' canons and who 'breaks' them? How are canons policed?' (see Gupta 2009; Bahri 2003: 10). As Paul Gilroy observes in *Small Acts*: 'the historiography of canon formation raises interesting issues for the intellectual historian in and of itself' (1993a: 125). However, it also has ethical implications which need to be acknowledged and fed back into critical praxis. Discussing indigenous writing in a US context, Arnold Krupat (1989) distinguishes between an essentialist and instrumentalist perspective. The difference lies in the

> willingness of the former to produce knowledge coercively in the interest of perpetrating an order whose material effect – doubtless undesired, doubtless inevitable, and resolutely denied – is further suffering and degradation for the many. This is what is stake in the argument over literature and the literary canon.
>
> (cited in Madsen 1999: 12)

Our reading choices, as Menon's essay shows, have implications not only for our private imaginative space, but also for how we interact culturally, in the public sphere. They are, as Boehmer's discussion of the ethical import of one's choices of aesthetic modes and tropes intimates, relevant for how the political can be brought to bear on acts of culture. This impact is not necessarily always concrete or activist in kind. Indeed, ethical imperatives and representational choices are often brought together in that space of the 'transnation' that Bill Ashcroft posits, where global and local imaginaries intermingle to produce a 'glocal' sensibility and a 'border thinking' that allows distinct levels of individual and collective identity to become expressed. It is the rhizomatic quality of this 'smooth' imaginative space (as distinct from the ordered, 'striated' space of institutions and governmental categories – see Ashcroft, 79) that the postcolonial citizens of the third millennium inhabit which gives them a choice of subjective identification and political gesture. Yet, as Anna Ball argues in her essay, the choices that the members of these diasporic communities make are not mutually exclusive; indeed, insofar as their identities are polycentric, they can choose to be *both* good Muslim women *and* active citizens of the British polity, rather than seeing these as alternatives. Adherence to faith-based (or other identity-based) communities need not preclude alternative forms of identification; rootedness can, indeed, branch out into multiple routes of action and subjectivity. The rhizome is here being made to approximate the structure of the root and replicate its similar generative, networking potential, in the same way that a rhizomatic postcolonial paradigm would respond to the labels of fundamentalism and essentialism usually attached to faith-based choices and communitarian projects. Faith, Anna Ball shows, is just as integral a part of the diasporic landscape as multiculturalism; in the novels of Leila Abouela, rerooting into faith is, in actual fact, one of the many concrete results of the previous rerouting to the West: Islam happens to the characters because migration and diaspora happened, but one is neither directly determined nor exhausted by the other. The standard exilic narrative trajectory (from national belonging into diaspora and hybridity) is also reversed: rootedness appears as a form of resistance against the leveling encroachment of a non-distinctive multi-culti quilt.

Such a view is a challenge to much postcolonial orthodoxy, coming, as it does, from a theoretical perspective that is more often than not devalued as parochial, restrictive and, fundamentally complicit in structures of oppression. Yet Aboulela, Ball shows, refuses to lend her narratives a particular 'politicized' meaning, systematically precluding the equation of individual life-experiences and choices with wider communitarian symbols. Ball's injunction to take up this challenge and work through the manifold experiences of Muslim communities in the UK – including that of faith – resounds with a particular urgency in the present political and cultural climate, and provides one of the key avenues of the discipline's rerouting.

Such discussions also point, almost inevitably, to the limits of disciplinary thinking in the field of postcolonial studies. Indeed, the postcolonial has become ever more porous in the past two decades, moving away from area and regional studies and a reliance on literary texts, to almost every conceivable field in social sciences, media studies or international relations. Postcolonial insights are becoming increasingly relevant to topical political issues such as post-apartheid South Africa, Muslim diasporic communities, eco-environmentalism and post-communism, to name but a few. Yet many of these preoccupations have created specialist niches, and seldom enter communication with one another. This collection partly aims to reframe the varied geographies and political/cultural contexts discussed above within a theoretical paradigm based on inter- and cross-disciplinarity; in other words, to stage a dialogue between different fields of endeavour and methodologies in order to develop 'better ways of collaborating across disciplinary and geopolitical divides to construct imaginaries better suited to the challenges of the new normative universes we are entering' (Brydon, 115).

Essays such as Graham's discussion of Nadine Gordimer's *Get a Life* in the context of what he calls 'social ecology' provide a particularly well-designed model of how disciplinary work in postcolonial literature, say, can fruitfully intersect with eco-critical concerns and environmental activism. Others, such as Victor Li's compelling film-analysis, show how the power of media-produced neoliberal ideologies can successfully circumvent national frontiers and continue to discipline and transform the individual corporeal subject under their spell. Along the same interdisciplinary lines, Nadia Louar's discussion of Senac and Genet as exponents of the discursive construction of colonial sexualities points to ways in which the disciplines of postcolonial and queer theory can successfully cross-pollinate and produce new configurations of knowledge.

In general the volume responds to the tendency towards sedimentation of concerns within postcolonial studies by deliberately keeping the field of inquiry diverse and mobile, alive to new configurations and reroutings of knowledge. It opens up the field to some new and exciting areas of concern and recognizes the productive synergies which can emerge from a spirit of genuinely interdisciplinary research. Our contributors here successfully expand the project of postcolonial studies both by extending its critical insights and methodologies to new geographical or disciplinary objects, but also by delineating a variety of directions which postcolonial studies may – indeed, must – reroute itself towards if the field is to preserve its dynamism, flexibility, critical force, and, ultimately, cultural relevance. We thus address the perceived need to reground postcolonial studies in a much changed and increasingly mobile contemporaneity, with a view to strengthening and enhancing its theoretical and pedagogical impact in a comparative context that is as mindful of historical particularity and ethical imperatives as it is of aesthetic and literary concerns.

Bibliography

Bahri, D. (2003) *Native Intelligence: Aesthetics, Politics and Postcolonial Literature*, Minneapolis: University of Minneapolis Press.

Bhabha, H. K. (1994) *The Location of Culture*, London and New York: Routledge.

Brathwaite, K. (1963) 'The African Presence in Caribbean Literature', reprinted in K. Brathwaite (1993) *Roots: Essays in Caribbean Literature*, Ann Arbor: University of Michigan Press: 190–258.

—— (1986) *Roots*, Havana: Casa de las Americas.

—— (1987 [1973]) *The Arrivants: A New World Trilogy*, Oxford: Oxford University Press.

—— (1993) *Roots: Essays in Caribbean Literature*, Ann Arbor, MI: University of Michigan Press.

—— (1999) *ConVERSations with Nathaniel Makey*, Staten Island, NY: We Press.

Clifford, J. (1988) *The Predicament of Culture: Twentieth-Century Ethnography, Literature and Art*, Cambridge, MA: Harvard University Press.

—— (1992) 'Traveling Cultures', in L. Grossberg, C. Nelson and P. Treichler (eds) *Cultural Studies*, New York: Routledge,

—— (1997) *Routes: Travel and Translation in the Late Twentieth Century*, London and Cambridge MA: Harvard University Press.

—— (2001) 'Indigenous Articulations', *The Contemporary Pacific*, 13.2 (Fall): 468–90.

Damrosch, D. (2003) *What is World Literature?*, Princeton, New Jersey: Princeton University Press.

Deleuze, G. and Guattari, F. (1987 [1972]) *Anti-Oedipus: Capitalism and Schizophrenia*, trans. R. Hurley, M. Seem and H. R. Lane, Minneapolis: University of Minneapolis Press.

—— (1987; [1980]) *A Thousand Plateaus: Capitalism and Schizophrenia*, trans. B. Massumi, Minneapolis: University of Minneapolis Press.

DeLoughrey, E. M. (2007) *Routes and Roots: Navigating Caribbean and Pacific Island Literatures*, Honolulu: University of Hawaii Press.

Gikandi, S. (2001) 'Globalization and the Claims of Postcoloniality', *South Atlantic Quarterly*, 100.3: 355–75.

Gilroy, P. (1993a) Small Acts: Thoughts on the Politics of Black Cultures, London: Serpent's Tail.

—— (1993b) *The Black Atlantic: Modernity and Double Consciousness*, London: Verso.

Gorak, J. (1991) *The Making of the Modern Canon*, London: Athlone.

Gupta, S. (2009) *Globalization and Literature*, Cambridge U.K. and Malden, Mass.: Polity Press.

Hallward, P. (2001) *Absolutely Postcolonial: Writing Between the Singular and the Specific*, Manchester: Manchester University Press.

Helff, S. (2009) 'Shifting Perspectives: The Transcultural Novel', in F. Schulze-Engler and S. Helff (eds) *Transcultural English Studies: Theories, Fictions, Realities*, Amsterdam and New York: Rodopi: 75–89.

Joseph, C. A. B. and Wilson, J. (eds) (2006) *Global Fissures, Postcolonial Fusions*, Amsterdam/New York: Rodopi.

Krishnaswamy, R. (2003) 'The Claims of Globalization Theory: Some Contexts and Contestations', *South Asian Review*, 24.2: 18–32.

—— (2005) 'Globalization and Its Postcolonial Discontents: Reading Dalit Writing', *Journal of Postcolonial Writing*, 41.1: 69–82.

—— (2008) 'Postcolonial and Globalization Studies: Connections, Conflicts, Complicities', in Krishnaswamy and Hawley: 2–21.

Krishnaswamy, R. and Hawley, J. C. (eds) (2008) *The Postcolonial and the Global*, Minneapolis and London: University of Minnesota Press.

Krupat, A. (1989) *The Voice in the Margin: Native American Literature and the Canon*, Berkeley, Los Angeles and Oxford: University of California Press.

Loomba, A., Kaul, S., Bunzl, M., Burton, A. and Esty, J. (eds) (2005) *Postcolonial Studies and Beyond*, Durham and London: Duke University Press.

Madsen, D. (ed.) (1999) *Postcolonial Literature: Expanding the Canon*, London: Pluto Press.

Newman, J. (1998) *The Ballistic Bard: Postcolonial Fictions*, London: Hodder Arnold.

Nichols, G. (1996) *Sunris*, London: Virago.

O'Brien, S. and Szeman, I. 'The Globalization of Fiction/The Fiction of Globalization', *South Atlantic Quarterly*, 100.3: 603–26.

Pope, R. (2003 [1998]) *The English Studies Book*, London and New York: Routledge.

Procter, J. (2003) *Dwelling Places: Postwar black British Writing*, Manchester: Manchester University Press.

Thieme, J. (2001) *Postcolonial Con-Texts: Writing Back to the Canon*, London and New York: Continuum.

—— (2003) *Post-colonial Studies: The Essential Glossary*, London: Arnold.

Yaeger, P. (2007) 'Editor's Column: The End of Postcolonial Theory? A Roundtable with Sunil Agnani, Fernando Coronil, Gaurav Desai, Mamadou Diuf, Simon Gikandi, Susie Tharu, and Jennifer Wenzel', *PMLA*, 122.3: 633–51.

Section 1

Theoretical reroutings

Cosmopolitanism, transnationality
and the neo-liberal subject

1 Introduction

Janet Wilson

The essays in this first section articulate significant shifts within postcolonial theory made in response to the persistent manifestations of empire and imperialism in the current global era; first, through expanding the concept of cosmopolitanism into a more inclusive and ethically nuanced term with implications for an improved citizenship; and, second, through supplementing and modifying current postcolonial-based theories of the global such as transnationalism and neo-liberalism. A counterpoint is provided by Patrick Williams's emphasis on the discipline's simultaneous 'rerooting' – through a reinvigorated engagement with resistance and liberation, areas that have historically constituted postcolonialism's strength – and 'rerouting' into new areas of inquiry, such as postcolonial film and the 'ethical scandal' (92) of Palestine. Notably, such explorations reveal an emotional softening of the often strident polemic of earlier theorizations and arguments, a stress on the affective in subject formation, and a forward-looking utopianism energized by the engagement with globalization and based on *praxis* – producing a 'positive pedagogy of practical, resistant, "concrete" hoping' (94).

The focus on a politics or ethics of identity in revisionist cosmopolitanism takes its bearings from Kwame Anthony Appiah, Paul Gilroy and Tim Brennan. Simon Gikandi, in discussing cosmopolitanism in relation to the claims of locality, takes issue with the term's inherent universalist, transnational ideals, arguing that differences and inequities persist. Gikandi's challenge to the canonical view of cosmopolitanism as identified with the elite and privileged subject comes from reading the term under the sign of its own anxieties, namely the fear of being part of the 'rootless' crowd (27). His subject is the 'Other' of cosmopolitanism, the postcolonial migrant of the south who has relocated in the European or American metropolis, and whose alternative narrative defines a third zone – inscribed as global – between the metropolis and ex-colony. Gikandi's theorizing of cosmopolitanism as 'a redemptive narrative of globalization, which is in contrapuntal relationship with the condition of being stateless' (26), anticipates the concerns articulated by Spencer and Nagai, who also look to cosmopolitanism for a renewed dialogue between the postcolonial and globalization and for mediation of the relationship between roots (denied or repressed) and routes (paths taken); it also prefigures the interpretative framework of Anna Ball's and Erin Goheen

Glanville's essays, which discuss modes of underprivileged diasporic experience. Gikandi's claim that postcolonialism is 'authorized by a signature gesture of displacement' (23), which, in turn, is 'an essential condition of the modern subjectivity' (24), is pivotal not only to the project of rerouting, but also to other reconceptualizations of cosmopolitanism currently taking place (see, for example, Schulze-Engler and Helff 2009, Werbner 2008).

Gikandi considers what it means to think of the refugee rather than the intellectual as the quintessential figure of life outside national boundaries, arguing for the necessity of a discourse to articulate the experience of such lives lived across the nation, beyond *ethne*. More urgently, he asks why refugee diasporic subjects who belong to the 'global tribe' often reinscribe archaic loyalties to *ethne* and their original homeland, so contradicting 'fluid' or 'hybridized' forms of postcolonial identity (as, for example, in the case of the 17-year-old Islamic Somali migrant living in the US who returned to Somalia to fight for the Muslim cause). He observes that the trust in what Virginia Wolf called 'unreal loyalties' by migrant refugees stems from the same fear as that of the intellectual elites who historically made them their 'Other': that of being rootless. Such adherence to local loyalties, he argues, does not necessarily negate the obligations traditionally associated with cosmopolitanism (as articulated by Ulf Hannerz, Kwame Anthony Appiah, and Arjun Appadurai), that of engaging ethically with and understanding the Other. In fact, as Anna Ball also argues, many second- or third-generation migrants (including those from under-privileged backgrounds) successfully negotiate the competing allegiances of global, multicultural identity and 'rooted' (in faith, tradition, local community) subjectivity. One reason for this is that the local, Gikandi points out, has in fact become globalized due to the effect of mass migration and the reinscription of locality in global spaces – a transformation echoed by Diana Brydon's concept of the 'glocal' or by Dorota Kołodziejczyk's formulation of 'provincialism'.

In his democratizing and localizing of the term 'cosmopolitan' through defining the spaces inhabited by the 'not quite' cosmopolitan subject who may also be described as global, Gikandi draws on a concept of transnationality that is at variance with Bill Ashcroft's notion of the transnation, a space within and beyond nations, 'without boundaries', where utopian transformation can occur; while his questioning of the privileged, elite cosmopolitan adds to Victor Li's critical reading of the neo-liberal globalized subject who reprogrammes himself in order to reenter corporate capitalism as morally improved. Indeed, Gikandi's unease about his own western, privileged subject position, and consciousness of the non-representativeness of cosmopolitan elites who deem to speak for others seems to demand a response such as Patrick Williams provides in his essay: it is what the postcolonial critic *does* that has the greatest implication for the building of a better world, an idea echoed in Diana Brydon's call for a renewed postcolonial pedagogy.

Robert Spencer, in contrast to Gikandi's concern with mobility and questions about the relationship to the Other in global space, suggests that literature makes cosmopolitans of us all in other words, the encounter with postcolonial literature and literary criticism will engender a more morally aware cosmopolitan citizen-ship. He identifies three 'schools' of cosmopolitan thought – the sceptical (Said and *Orientalism*); the celebratory (Bhabha and Appadurai); and the socialist (Gikandi, Neil Lazarus, Brennan) – which, while not necessarily as clear-cut as this clas-sification may suggest, nevertheless distances the concept as currently conceived from earlier divisive discourses of anti-imperialism. Spencer suggests that cosmo-politanism implies a politics that is both more far-reaching than nationalism or localism, but less overbearing than traditional forms of universalism; he also differentiates the concept from neo-liberal globalization, emphasizing its potential as a method for reading postcolonial texts whereby politically-conscious critics and readers might 'unmask the textual concealment of injustice' (42). His concept of a multivalent postcolonial cosmopolitanism is thus an essentially dialectical understanding which requires 'reconciling local attachments with global alle-giances' (40). In anticipating a new form of community – and hence the opportu-nity for postcolonial critics to articulate not what the discipline is against, but what it is *for* – Spencer's position intersects with Williams's and Ashcroft's emphasis on the utopian possibilities emerging out of the engaged creative act and with the utopian dimension which Kaori Nagai identifies in advocating the civilizing influ-ence of the 'international' or 'auxiliary' language of Esperanto.

Nagai examines the historical roots in the first decade of the twentieth century of the artificial language of Esperanto that defined a newly emerging public sphere as multinational/lingual, and relocates it as a 'new bilingualism' within the present condition of what she terms 'transnational cosmopolitanism'. Her claim that speaking Esperanto, a language not one's own, is 'the art of being cosmopolitan without losing one's nationality' (50) shows affinities with Spencer's argument that cosmopolitanism begins at home, with Kwame Anthony Appiah's concept of 'cosmopolitan patriots' and Mitchell Cohen's 'rooted cosmopolitan-ism' (40). Nagai reroutes this transnational movement, which has been largely neglected by postcolonialists, by situating it within the humanistic discourse of the 'brotherhood of man' and simultaneously reading it as a paradigm of local cosmopolitanism, which offers a way of reconciling competing identitarian alle-giances. Its affinity with postcolonial versions of cosmopolitanism recalls for Nagai Bhabha's vernacular cosmopolitanism situated 'on the border, *in between*' (56), as well as Ashcroft's utopian concept of the literary transnation; for, as she points out, Esperanto stages a cosmopolitan space, 'a utopian yet quintessentially *human* space' (58), where conversations can occur.

In Victor Li's essay, it is the affluent neo-liberal subject – both propagator and beneficiary of global capitalism, and so akin to the privileged cosmopolitan elites whose ascendancy Gikandi challenges – who comes under scrutiny. Li's example is Robert Zemeckis's Hollywood film *Cast Away* (2000) whose hero, in learning how to survive on a desert island, reinscribes the cultural and social ideology of capitalist globalization. Li demonstrates that the self-reformation and education undertaken by Chuck Noland, a FedEx efficiency expert in systems manage-ment, have parallels in advice manuals from business sociologists, entrepre-neurial philosophy and New Age thinking. Noland's redefined role as castaway requires flexibility and adaptability to uncertainty, enhancement of his human capital through reproduction and reconstruction, and the development of a new emotional subjectivity in keeping with the 'soft skills' of the corporate market: finally, he reenters the corporate world as a more caring, flexible and adaptable subject. As Li admits, cultural texts such as Zemecki's film, whose 'redemptive' scenario conspicuously lacks any 'Other' – the Friday of the ur-ancestor, *Robinson Crusoe*, or of postcolonial 'Robinsades' such as J. M. Coetzee's *Foe* – lack a point of entry for a postcolonial analytics that draws on theories of resistance (see Krishnaswamy, 2008: 13–14). Yet Li defends the critical return to the more affective, intimate domain of the individual as one way of detecting the film's bio-political investment in self-reliance and self-improvement as outward expressions of neo-liberal governmentality. In arguing that postcolonialism should engage with neoliberal ideology in order to account for globalization's influence on subject formation, he addresses a key preoccupation: the need to formulate a viable subject position from which to articulate politically resistant agency.

In contrast to other terms denoting global movements such as diaspora, migrancy and multiculturalism with their attendant discourse of loss, Bill Ashcroft in his essay articulates the idea of the transnation as the space occupied by local, mobile subjects, whose experiences in an increasingly globalized world assert the ambiguous relation between the nation and the state. Yet the 'transnation' is not an abstract 'object in space' but, rather, a migratory, even diasporic aggregation of flows and convergences, which describes the contingency and variable cultural positions of ostensibly 'national' subjects. It extends 'beyond the geographical, political, administrative and even imaginative boundaries of the state' (73), and can be located both within and beyond the boundaries of the nation (as in India and China). It thus differs from formulations of the 'transnational' or the 'international' because it works *across* rather than *among* states; at the same time, it is distinct from the categories of 'diaspora' and 'cosmopolitanism', for it encompasses subjects that may be locally rooted (in nations, ethnicities, religions, families or tribes), yet simultaneously impervious to state boundaries, moving in and out of national borders, and thus strangely 'cosmopolitan' and 'global'. Ashcroft locates a utopian potentiality in the transnation's deconstruction of bounded ideas of nationhood and statehood, and its prefiguring of a rhizomatic postcolonial subjectivity, one predicated on travelling both *within* and *across* given national and cultural boundaries. The transnation's transformative possibility is also embodied in the utopian function of literature, which enables the imagining of a different world: Ashcroft asks if the colonial language 'releases the writing subject from the myth of a fixed identity' (82), illustrating his premise that utopia is the constant horizon of a present rooted in the past with an analysis of the process of naming and unnaming in Jumpha Lahiri's novel, *The Namesake*. This, he argues, invests the subject with '*the potentiality of subjectivity itself*' (83), for names implicate the operation of memory (a 'smooth' space which flows through the 'striated' space of history) and the past adumbrates a future that transforms the present.

'Outlines of a Better World', the title of Patrick Williams's concluding article, signals kinship with Ashcroft's concept of the utopian literary transnation, with Nagai's acclaim of an essentially utopian cosmopolitan space, and with Spencer's anticipation of a new form of community as postcolonial readers and critics search for alternatives to hegemony and imperial rule. But utopianism, for Williams, in reviewing the case for postcolonialism's rerouting, is not simply something to hope for or aspire to; it can – indeed, it must, if it is to preserve its ethical purchase and political force – find ways of inserting itself in the complexities of the present. As part of this process he advocates a more vigorous engagement with the Palestinian question (currently underrepresented in postcolonial studies), and, drawing on the rhetoric of the Palestinian poet Darwish Mahmoud, urges its reconfiguration as a form of praxis.

Williams moves away from his initial scepticism about the call to reroute, noting the defensiveness of the field which subjects itself to such self scrutiny, and some critical reactions to it, that is, 'uprootings' or strategic rejections such as Walter Mignolo's 'decoloniality', a new approach which self-consciously distances itself from postcolonialism (88). He suggests areas of cultural production where postcolonial analysis could usefully be applied, notably the visual media: photography, television, political cartoons, and film. But his strongest assertion of the need for rerouting is with reference to 'the paradigmatic status of Palestine in the current moral and political landscape' on the one hand, this might require something like sartre's materialist (and anticolonial) ethics' (92); on the other, postcolonialism can simply function as an '"anticipatory" discourse' to shape, intellectually and morally, 'the outlines of a better world' (93). Williams cites Ernst Bloch's concept of 'concrete utopia' as something to be built, as one possible response to the current dystopian situation in Palestine. His essay concludes fittingly with a 'difficult synthesis' of 'hope as resistance (rerooted postcolonialism) and hope as utopian function (the New, the Not-Yet of rerouted postcolonialism)' (95). Williams's emphasis throughout on what postcolonialists do and how they do it shows a way forward rooted in praxis, a project of rerouting which in many ways echoes Brydon's own similar call for a transformative, rhizomatic paradigm, one which can accommodate and respond to the growing complexity of contemporary global pressures.

Bibliography

Krishnaswamy, R. (2008) 'Postcolonial and Globalization Studies: Connections, Conflicts Complicities', in R. Krishnaswamy and J. C. Hawley (eds) *The Postcolonial and the Global*, Minneapolis and London: University of Minnesota Press: 2–21.

Schulze-Engler, F. and Helff, S. (eds) (2009) *Transcultural English Studies: Theories, Fictions, Realities*, Amsterdam and New York: Rodopi.

Werbner, P. (ed.) (2008) *Anthropology and the New Cosmopolitanism: Rooted, Feminist and Vernacular Perspectives*, Oxford: Berg.

2 Between roots and routes

Cosmopolitanism and the claims of locality

Simon Gikandi

I will start with a digression which nevertheless foregrounds the knot I will try and untie in this discussion of the relationship between cosmopolitanism and the production of locality, the limits of what have come to be known as globalization, and the crisis of transnationalism after colonialism. These topics have been addressed from different perspectives by other contributors to this volume, such as Bill Ashcroft, Diana Brydon, and Robert Spencer, but now I want to reflect on what it means to be a postcolonial subject in the metropolitan cultures of the modern west.

In a single afternoon, strolling down the streets of the cities that I love, Nairobi, Johannesburg, Accra, I pretend to be a postcolonial flaneur. I see myself as an incarnation of Baudelaire's painter of modern life, the informed spectator of the manners of the urban class. I'm often tempted to become one with the crowd, especially in the markets and the railway stations, and although my passion and profession, unlike that of the Parisian flaneur, is not to become one with the masses, I seek to move with the ebb and flow of the crowds, 'in the midst of the fugitive and infinite' (Baudelaire 1986: 9). I adopt a pose suspended between the rank of the insider and the detachment of the tourist, the pose of the heroic pedestrian who, in Walter Benjamin's terms, demands elbow space in the crowd and refuses 'to forgo the life of a gentleman of leisure' (Benjamin 2006: 188). Although I walk as one with the crowd, I'm also detached from it. It is only later in the evening, when I visit the haunts of the leisured postcolonial class, at book launchings, galleries, and symposiums, that I stop being a passionate spectator and become one with other connoisseurs of global culture, the cosmopolitans, natives who share the cultural discourse of the intellectual class in the other spaces I inhabit – London and New York – away from the crowd.

But when I board the British Airways flight to London and New York, I find myself in the strange company of Somali, Ethiopian and Sudanese refugees on their way to new lives in North America under the sponsorship of Refugees International and other global charities. These are the outcasts of the civil wars in Eastern Africa and they are encountering the modern metropolis for the first time. Beneath the new garbs provided by international charity, they carry with them the feel and look of the countryside and this is what brings out the simple truth that my liberal sensibilities find hard to countenance: I have nothing in common with these people; we do not share a common critical discourse or set of cultural values. They are not the postcolonials with whom I have spent the last weeks, but strangers caught in the cracks of the failed state.

Suddenly I feel like Walter Benjamin's flaneur; these refugees threaten my identity as a cosmopolitan, a connoisseur of modern cultural goods. Tourists are tolerable because what excites them about Africa is banal. I can afford to be condescending. Fellow cosmopolitans, the passengers who sit next to me reading the familiar *International Herald Tribune* or the *Economist*, are comforting reminders that you belong to a global cultural circuit. But refugees frighten me because they are signs of a dislocated locality, a mote in the eye of cosmopolitanism, of that postcolonial identity which derives its legitimacy from the mastery of the culture of modern Europe.

Where do these people, the rejects of failed states, fit into our fascination with identities constituted across boundaries? When the former residents of Kakoma camp or of the Lokichoggio made famous by *The Constant Gardener* (Le Carré 2000, Meirelles 2005) arrive in Canada, do they become cosmopolitan in the same way as the African elites who move and shake things in the corridors of the American or European university and boardroom? Do they become cosmopolitans in the same sense as the intellectual class; or does their entry into the metropolis as refugees denote a different relation with their adoptive countries? And what does it mean to think of the refugee, rather than the intellectual, as the quintessential figure of life across or outside boundaries? And how do we tell the stories of those who are not yet quite cosmopolitan even when they inhabit the spaces that have come to be inscribed as global?

Within the domain of what now goes by the name of postcolonial theory and criticism, seen as a broad attempt to account for subjects produced in the interstices of the European metropolis and the former colony, there is perhaps no more pressing question now than the development of a vocabulary for explaining the experiences and writings of lives lived across boundaries, outside nation, beyond *ethne* and what Virginia Woolf famously described as 'unreal loyalties' (1938: 78). The rerouting of postcolonialism is authorized by a signature gesture of displacement – the unhomely moment which, in Homi Bhabha's majestic phrase, is 'a paradigmatic colonial and postcolonial condition', which nevertheless 'negotiates the power of cultural difference in a range of transhistorical sites' (1994). To account for the lives of subjectivities performed across boundaries, languages, and traditions, postcolonial scholars have turned to theories of globalization (Appadurai 1996), of cultural difference and empire (Said 1994), planetarism (Gilroy 2002, Spivak 2005), and even liberal cosmopolitanism (Appiah 2006) as a way out of the narrow bonds of nationalism.

Indeed, it often seems that the very legitimacy of a postcolonial cultural politics depends on the unabashed claim for the idiom of transnationalism. And more than any other mode of theorizing, postcolonial criticism derives its authority from a certain claim to displacement as the essential condition of modern subjectivity. For many postcolonial critics, displacement is a form of recognition; it is a point of entry into what Appiah has called 'the global tribe' (2006: xiii). Here, the rejection of local or national loyalties is often posited as the journey towards ideas and institutions premised on a set of universal moral obligations and loyalty to a common humanity, not nation or *ethne*. All these forms of identity would appear to represent the triumph of plurality over singularity.

And yet this aspiration for a common human humanity, one informed by rights and responsibilities to all human beings irrespective of their cultural or other differences, constantly comes up against a set of problems that are inherent in the project of identity itself. First there is the question of aggregating difference: If identity is predicated on the differentiation of the self from the Other, how can some forms of difference be considered more legitimate than others? Isn't the invocation of difference also the foundation for the community-building projects that have led to postmodern genocide across Africa and South-Eastern Europe (Gourevitch 1999: 95)?

Second, there is the nature of the journey that the would-be cosmopolitan subject must make in order to transcend parochial loyalties and become transnational. Appiah describes and celebrates the adventure and ideal of cosmopolitanism – the movement of self-willing subjects away from 'segregation and seclusion' to shared cultural conversations – as the only serious path to human civility and comity (2006: xx). He recognizes that the problem of estrangement – the 'foreignness of foreigners, the strangeness of strangers' – is real enough, but he resists those who might exaggerate the significance and order of magnitude of these problems (2006: xxi)? In the process, he also seem to minimize the fraught and painful nature of the routes that take subjects out of cultural otherness into the ideals and institutions of cosmopolitanism, the journeys from the impoverished and marginalized sectors of the global south to the ideals and institutions of western Europe and the United States. In striving to position ideals and institutions that are closely associated with Europe as the common goal of a divided humanity, Appiah seems to identify the cosmopolitan as the privileged subject of cultural goods and vocabularies that are only accessible to elites. Yet cosmopolitanism, as Ulf Hannerz has reminded us, is also 'a matter of varieties and levels' (1990: 239).

In regard to the politics or ethics of identity, a central idea of cosmopolitanism is that 'we have obligations to others, obligations that stretch beyond those to whom we are related by the ties of kith and kind, or even the more formal ties of a shared citizenship' (Appiah 2006: xv); a condition of cosmopolitanism is the 'willingness to become involved with the Other, and the concern with achieving competence in cultures which are initially alien' (Hannerz 1990: 240). Within this logic, the route to cosmopolitanism is structured by the desire, if not the need, to understand the Other and establish a set of common values. But, surprisingly, routes and journeys across boundaries and encounters with others do not necessarily lead to a cosmopolitan attitude. Increasingly, the journeys that lead refugees from the war zones of the global south, processes often prompted by the collapse of those archaic, yet real, loyalties that make cultural elites uneasy, do not lead to freedom from those loyalties but to their entrenchment.

How else does one explain the actions of young Somalis who leave the comfort of American suburbs to go and fight for Islam in a state that now is nothing but a remnant of the collapsed heap of whatever was imagined to be the modern nation state? Consider the following story from CNN:

> Last month, 17-year-old Burhan Hassan told his family he was catching a ride to school with a friend. He then vanished.
>
> His mother spoke to her son just a few days ago over the phone. To her shock, she says, he told her he was no longer in the United States.
>
> 'Mom, I'm in Somalia! Don't worry about me; I'm OK', the mother quoted her son as saying ...
>
> Hassan is one of more than a dozen young men of Somali descent – many U.S. citizens – to have disappeared from Minneapolis over the past six months, according to federal law enforcement authorities. Authorities say young men have also disappeared in Boston, Massachusetts; Portland, Maine; and Columbus, Ohio.
>
> (CNN, 12 December 2008)

For those of us who have striven to master the institutions and ideals of modern Europe and have assiduously cultivated our identities as postcolonial cosmopolitans, the actions of people like Burhan Hassan trigger deep anxieties. Why would they want to return to those places that now stand as empty shells of modernity, places where the only loyalties that matter are the most basic and archaic – not those of nation or tribe, but *Jes*, the clan – the sign of an unmodern disorder.

The desires and values of Burhan Hassan, like those of the Islamists he emulates, those who want to return Somalia to a deeper sense of itself outside the tutelage of modernity and the infrastructure of colonialism, seem to be at odds with everything that we postcolonial cosmopolitans hold dear. Indeed, even in the metropolitan spaces in which we perform our postcolonial identities and their requisite gestures of arrival, the existence of a mass of people who seem to hold on to what we consider archaic cultures (those who wear bhakas in classrooms, or slaughter sheep in the tubs of suburb houses, or 'circumcise' their daughters in hidden alleys) seem to disturb the temporality of postcolonialism and the terms of its routing. Among the lower strata of migrant populations what we see is not the façade of cosmopolitanism or multiculturalism heralded by postcolonial elites, but signs of a radical attachment to older cultural forms which seems to mock the politics of postcolonial identity, as Anna Ball and Erin Goheen Glanville stress in their articles on the refugee diasporic subject in this volume.

It would be easy to dismiss people who are attached to the romance of the places they have left behind and seek to recreate locality in the metropolis as archaic; we may throw up our hands in frustration at the refusal of refugees and migrants to take advantage of the cultural goods offered by the modern west, choosing instead to cling to parochial traditions and habits. We assume that they do not meet the primary criteria of cosmopolitanism; that their investment in Woolf's 'unreal loyalties' has locked them up in narrow structures of identity; and that the ties they cultivate are defined by kith and kin, not others. Above all, we seem to be troubled that their adherence to entrenched cultural or religious beliefs negates the dictum that true cosmopolitanism is predicated on the valuation of differences and obligations to others.

Yet, I'm not entirely convinced that this adherence to local loyalties necessary negates the sense of obligation or even understanding of others. What we have here is a palpable clash between the desire to secure locality and the claims of universal being and becoming. What appears to be a strict adherence to old loyalties could be seen as the reflection of the prescribed journeys that bring refugees to the modern west, journeys which preclude the process of education and acculturation, the *Bildung* of modern life that makes liberal cosmopolitanism possible. Unlike elites whose engagement with metropolitan cultures begins even before their arrival in Europe or North America, most refugees encounter this world for the first time in the camps when they are being primed for life in those still far away places. For many refugees the idiom of cultural difference does not acquire reality or value until they arrive at the holding centres in their new countries. Quite often, what appears to be the refugees' refusal or inability to take advantage of the cultural goods of cosmopolitanism reflects anxieties and fears in the face of radical alterity.

I want to argue, then, that a discourse of cosmopolitanism remains incomplete unless we read the redemptive narrative of being global in a contrapuntal relationship with the narrative of statelessness and, by reproduction, of locality, where we least expect it – in the metropolis. The refugee is the Other of the cosmopolitan; rootless by compulsion, this figure is forced to develop an alternative narrative of global cultural flows, functioning in a third zone between metropolis and ex-colony, producing and reproducing localities in the centres of metropolitan culture itself. Missing the very states they fled in the first place, refugees do not want to be cosmopolitan because they have no idiom for this experience; instead they set out to demarcate a zone of ethnicity and locality. Yet they are global because they cannot return to their old spaces of identity and must somehow learn to live outside both the nations that have rejected them and those that have adopted them.

In making this argument, it is not my intention to rehabilitate the discredited postcolonial state or to argue for the phenomenological value of rootedness, to claim, after Simone Weil, that to be rooted is 'perhaps the most important and least recognized need of the human soul' (2001: 43). What I propose is that we read cosmopolitanism under the sign of its own anxieties, the fear of being one of the rootless crowd, and avoid the temptation to turn it into a free floating signifier of the moment of postcolonial arrival. My argument is, of course, framed by an earlier discourse on exile and the value of rootlessness. For some of the most distinguished thinkers of the modern period, from Hannah Arendt to Edward

Said, the characteristic figure of the twentieth century was the refugee and exile. Both represented the underside of modernity and the failure of a discourse of reason and rights.

Reflecting on the mass dislocation of populations in Europe after the First World War in the *Origins of Totalitarianism* (1951, 1973), Arendt posited the stateless as the most obvious symptom of the decline of the culture of human rights. A reflection on the condition of refugees produced by every event since the First World War, Arendt noted, confronted students of modern politics with an unprecedented category of the stateless person forced to 'live outside the pale of the law' whose lives could not be 'renormalized' (286). Her description of the stateless in Europe at the beginning of the twentieth century might as well refer to the world of refugees produced by the postmodern civil wars witnessed in South-Eastern Europe and Africa after the end of the Cold War:

> What is unprecedented is not the loss of a home but the impossibility of finding a new one. Suddenly, there was no place on earth where migrants could go without the severest restrictions, no country where they would be assimilated, no territory where they could found a new community of their own. This, moreover, had next to nothing to do with any material problem of overpopulation; it was a problem not of space but of political organization. Nobody had been aware that mankind, for so long a time considered under the image of a family of nations, had reached the stage where whoever was thrown out of one of these tightly organized closed communities found himself thrown out of the family of nations altogether.
>
> (Arendt, 293–4)

Here, the question of rights was connected to the loss of familiar localities and the unreal loyalties scorned by Woolf and others. Indeed, for Arendt, the stateless persons crossing the boundaries of Europe after the treaty of Versailles represented the limit of modernity and formed 'the most symptomatic group in contemporary politics' (238).

But social theory has not always considered homelessness to be the tragic fate of the stateless. Indeed, in the period after the Second World War, the question of statelessness came to be transformed, especially in the thinking of European intellectuals in exile, as a new and better condition of being, outside the prison house of nation, philology and tradition. For example, Theodor Adorno considered exile to be transcendental, an existence outside the reified world of modern life and the prefabricated houses characterized by what he called the culture industry (1998: 120–4). Adorno insisted that the predicament of private life was evident in the fact that the place of dwelling, the house as the arena of subjectivity, was an impossibility:

> The traditional residences we grew up in have grown intolerable: each trait of comfort in them is paid for with a betrayal of knowledge, each vestige of shelter with the musty pact of family interests. [...] The house is past.

The bombings of European cities, as well as the labour and concentration camps, merely proceed as executors, with what the immanent development of technology had long decided was to be the fate of houses. These are now good only to be thrown away like old food cans. The possibility of residence is annihilated by that of socialist society, which, once missed, saps the foundations of bourgeois life. [...] Today [...] it is part of morality not to be at home in one's home.

(1984: 38–9)

Still, the retreat into radical subjectivity that enabled Adorno and others to embrace exile as what Said has called 'a redemptive motif' was circumscribed and haunted by the very institutions it sought to transcend (1990: 364). In other words, confronted with an expansive map of displacement and 'an impersonal setting', exile could not be made to 'serve notions of humanism'; on the contrary, invocations of the aura of exile could not mask the horrors that enabled it:

Is it not true that the views of exile in literature and, moreover, in religion obscure what is truly horrendous: that exile is irremediably secular and unbearably historical; that it is produced by human beings for other human beings; and that, like death but without death's ultimate mercy, it has torn millions of people from the nourishment of tradition, family and geography?

(Said 1994: 257–8)

And yet, increasingly, in thinking about more recent dispersals of masses of people, we no longer seem to think of our world of refugees as 'unbearably historical'. A prior language of describing displacement and statelessness as a threat to human rights has all but diminished as our focus has shifted to the redemptive narratives of global trade, transnationalism, and cosmopolitanism. Quite often, the new discourse of cosmopolitanism emerges in the process of differentiating the order of refugees from those of autonomous migrating subjects. Thus Appiah makes his case for the redemptive narrative of cosmopolitan movement by drawing sharp distinctions between 'the old migrants' and 'older diasporas' that 'began in an involuntary exile' and the celebratory stories of a cosmopolitan that 'flows from the free decisions of individuals or groups' (1996: 22).

My argument, however, is that global cultural flows are still dominated by those coerced migrants rather than the free-willing cosmopolitan subjects. The figure of the refugee may not be as visible as that of the postcolonial flaneur, but the refugee's presence in the heart of the metropolis challenges the redemptive narrative of postcolonial arrival. At the centre of this challenge are two issues: First, there is the growth in scale of violence and statelessness as conditions of postcolonial identities. Second, there is the cultural blockage that refugees face as they try to enter the orbit of cosmopolitanism.

Ultimately, there is an inherent tension between the self-identity of postcolonial elites and the people they claim to represent. For one thing, postcolonial elites are, by virtue of their class, position or education, the major beneficiaries of the project of decolonization. As a matter of fact, one of the common reasons why postcolonial elites end up in the American or European metropolis is because they were beneficiaries of the nationalism they would later come to scorn. Indeed, quite often, these elites profited (directly or indirectly) from the inequalities and corruption of the postcolonial state. At the same time, however, the growth of elite diasporas has been accompanied by mass migration of the poor into the West and it is the presence of this latter group that compels the elite class to differentiate itself from what Antonio Gramsci would call 'the preceding economic structure' even when they are products of 'the developments of this structure' (1957: 120). Since they cannot claim legitimacy from any association with the moral or political economy of nationalism, postcolonial elites come to 'see themselves as autonomous and independent of the ruling social group' (120).

It is this claim to autonomy and independence that makes cosmopolitanism an important term for mediating the relationship between the roots that are denied or repressed and the routes that are taken. For from its very beginnings in the eighteenth century to the present, cosmopolitanism has been pegged on the autonomy – that is, the independence – of the intellectual elite from the ruling class, especially in moments of crisis. As Thomas J. Schlereth has noted in his study of cosmopolitanism in the age of Enlightenment, one of the distinguishing characteristics of the cosmopolitan ideal in the eighteenth century was 'an attitude of mind that attempted to transcend chauvinistic national loyalties or parochial prejudices in its intellectual interests and pursuits' (1977: xi). The desire to be a citizen of the world, the hallmark of cosmopolitanism since Diogenes, was prompted not by the love of the Other but by a negative imperative, what Moses Hadas aptly termed 'a rebellious reaction against every kind of coercion imposed by the community upon the individual' (1943: 108).

The point I want to underscore here is that the larger universal claims of cosmopolitanism only make sense as an 'abstract faith' which becomes, in turn, what M. H. Boehm once called 'a compromise with nationalism, race consciousness, professional interests, caste feeling, family prude, and even with egotism' (quoted in Schlereth, 1977: xiii). But this compromise is an important conduit for understanding the tension between roots and routes that characterize the lives of postcolonial elites; for, when it is considered in a structural sense, the cosmopolitan ideal is caught between the desire to valorize one's culture, home, and social position as essentially good, while at the same time trying to perform one's ability to be tolerant of the strange and different. Tolerance here is performed for all sorts of contingent reasons including one's desire to maintain social status or to legitimize one's role as a native informant. After all, even when we find the cultural practices of others repelling, our performance of understanding and tolerance is essential to our identity as liberal cultural subjects (see Cheah and Robbins 1998).

Let me provide an example. W. E. B. DuBois was an intellectual whose cosmopolitan credentials were continuously challenged by the spectre of race. From the very beginning of his career, DuBois's project was nothing less than the imagination of the black as a universal and cosmopolitan subject. All his major works were attempts to transcend the prison-house of race and to think through the possibility of the being and becoming of the black as human. Dubois's agony, expressed most powerfully in *The Souls of Black Folk*, was generated by the existence and persistence of race as the barrier between the self and its assumed universal identity, especially its striving 'to be a co-worker in the kingdom of culture, to escape both death and isolation, to husband and use his best powers and his latent genius' (1990: 9).

And yet, in spite of his universal and cosmopolitan aspirations, DuBois's project would not make sense except within the particularity of American culture. All his cosmopolitan desires – his Anglo-Saxon intellectualism or Pan-Africanism, for example – were founded on an unquestioned claim to an American identity and his adoption of European high culture as the national homeland of the modern subject. Forced into the slot of cultural difference by racism, DuBois still needed the spectre of the Other to enforce his cultural standing. He could find this difference in the hills of Tennessee, the streets of Philadelphia, or in West Africa. This is how DuBois described the natives of Liberia that he encountered on a 1923 trip:

> Then we came to the village; how can I describe it? Neither London, nor Paris, nor New York has anything of its delicate, precious beauty. It was a town of the Veys and done in cream and pale purple – still, clean, restrained, tiny, complete. It was no selfish place, but the central abode of fire and hospitality, clean-swept for wayfarers, and best seats were bare. They quite expected visitors, morning, noon, and night; and they gave our hands a quick, soft grasp and talked easily. Their manners were better than those of Park Lane or Park Avenue. Oh, much better and more natural. They showed breeding. The chief's son – tall and slight and speaking good English – had served under the late Colonel Young. He made a little speech of welcome. Long is the history of the Veys and it comes down from the Eastern Roman Empire, the great struggle of Islam and the black empires of the Sudan.
>
> (1984: 126)

Here, DuBois was using the language of primitivism not only to understand Liberian difference, but also to measure his worth as cosmopolitan subject. He certainly valued Vai difference and history; but he also recognized that this was not his world, that it could only be embraced as a picture of the Other that was not himself. DuBois's celebration of the Liberian primitive was a form of distancing himself from cultural others while using them to maintain a cosmopolitan identity. Dr DuBois was not about to abandon the vestiges of civilization to become a primitive: 'No. I prefer New York. But my point is that New York and London and Paris must learn of West Africa and may learn' (128). If he had stayed longer and looked around Monrovia, DuBois would perhaps have discovered that he had much more in common with the Liberian intellectual class than Vai and Cru sailors. If he had spent time at Liberia College, founded by his mentor, Alexander Crummell, he might have found an intellectual class engaged in the same project as members of the Talented Tenth in New York. He would have discovered that what aligned him to this intellectual class was not race or caste, but what one scholar has called 'an intellectual and aesthetic stance' (Hannerz 1990: 236).

An intellectual or aesthetic stance is crucial to understanding the degrees of global identities for it leads to the final question that interests me. Who qualifies for the term cosmopolitan? Writing at the height of the oil boom in Nigeria, the culture of petrodollar, Udoji and Wonyosi, Ulf Hannerz wondered whether 'cosmopolitanism' could be applied to traders from Lagos who went on shopping sprees to London. He argued that these shopping trips did little to change the traders' relationship to their local spaces or, indeed, their horizon of expectations. When Lagosian traders and smugglers crossed borders, Hannerz argued, they hardly went 'beyond the horizons of urban Nigerian culture'; what they were engaged in was a process of 'assimilating items of some distant provenience into a fundamentally local culture' (238). Was the process of globalization that was essential to the lives and characters of Nigerian traders in London the same as the cosmopolitanism of the intellectual elites who claimed to speak on their behalf? Or, as I asked at the beginning of this essay, Do African refugees become cosmopolitan when they cross boundaries even when it is apparent that many of them are incapable of, or simply disinterested in, the intellectual and aesthetic stance that cosmopolitanism presupposes?

These complicated questions and the level of generality that I have adopted here does not necessarily lead to solid claims or conclusions. Still, there are two processes involved in the series of entanglements that I have been working with: those between roots and routes, refugees and elites, and globalization and cosmopolitanism. The first process involves the differentiation of globalization from cosmopolitanism. Globalization emerges out of networks of trade, of culture, and experiences, in which the distant is assimilated into the familiar and local to facilitate exchange. Furthermore, globalization does not demand that we engage with the Other in any substantive sense. Indeed, African street traders in New York or Paris do not necessarily conceive a radical disjuncture between their deep engagement with the modern city and their commitment to their local cultures. The Senegalese Mourid traverse the modern economy at the heart of the western metropolis with apparent little interest in the cultural complexes around them, leading scholars to describe them as vernacular cosmopolitans (Diop 2000, Werbner 2006). There is no doubt that the Mourid are intensely global, but it is doubtful that they have cultivated a stance that would be described as cosmopolitan in the sense the term has been used by its leading proponents.

The second process that I'm interested in, then, is the inscription of cosmopolitanism as a state of mind and an aesthetic practice, a cultivated sensibility that underscores one's detachment from the local and ethnic and a willingness to engage with the Other. Here I'm in general agreement with Hannerz when he describes cosmopolitanism as 'a stance toward diversity' (239) and Appiah when he insists on sustaining 'communities of difference' (2005: 105). Cosmopolitans are the flaneurs of our age, walking the cities of the world, convinced that their identity can only be mirrored through their engagement with others, sure of their mastery of global cultural flows and their secure place within it. Still, as Hannerz again is quick to note, the cosmopolitans' engagement with the Other is enabled by their own privileged position within global culture. Unlike the refugees who opened my discussion, cosmopolitans are not stateless; they move freely across boundaries; they are autonomous subjects; they can choose when to engage with the Other and when to retreat. Above all, they function within a discursive formation, what Alvin Goulder once called 'a culture of critical discourse' (quoted in Hannerz, 1990: 246). This critical discourse, of which terms such as cosmopolitanism and postcolonialism constitute a core vocabulary, is facilitated by the media and institutions of interpretation among elites in different countries. From Lagos to New York, from Bombay to Cape Town, cosmopolitans are those who share a critical discourse that is aesthetic in the sense that it seeks to transcend its 'prosaic materiality' (de Man 1996: 90). In this aesthetic sense, cosmopolitanism becomes a form of phenomenalism in which members of a certain class can share tastes and competences across national boundaries.

Where does the local fit into all this? One of the errors that perpetually surrounds discussions of the local is to equate it with parochialism and fundamentalism and thus to see it as a form of retreat from global cultural flows or to seek its meanings or value codings in phenomenological rather than epistemological terms. Arjun Appadurai, to cite one famous example, views locality 'as primarily relational and contextual rather than as scalar or spatial' one with 'a complex phenomenological quality' and a 'sense of immediacy' (1996: 178). But I'm not convinced that a phenomenological quality differentiates the local from the global or the provincial from the cosmopolitan. In fact, an earlier claim was that cosmopolitanism, too, is defined by phenomenological properties, what Appadurai would call 'a structure of feelings that is produced by particular forms of intentional activity and that yields particular sorts of material affects' (182).

Still, one of the most perplexing and intriguing phenomenological aspects of global movements is the survival of locality outside national or ethnic boundaries. Locality is no longer simply produced through rituals of kinship or the production of endogamous identities contained within narrow boundaries. On the contrary, locality itself has been globalized, its boundaries dilated by the mass migrants that initiated my discussion. And thus the narrative of globalization and 'native cosmopolitanism' comes to be saturated by images of what appear to be localities functioning side by side with the insignia of globalization such as cell phones and televisions, or, alternatively, of localities produced and reproduced in the metropolitan centres. In this context, Appadurai argues that at the heart of the project of creating local knowledge is the difficulty of producing and reproducing locality 'under conditions of anxiety and entropy, social wear and flux, ecological uncertainty and cosmic volatility' (181). But if the production of locality is always surrounded by anxiety and entropy, how does one explain its attraction in an age of globalization? Why are people in failed states retreating from the centre to the region? Why are migrants recreating or simulating localities in the European and American metropolis?

There is an even more troubling question: Why do we now confront the production of localities within metropolitan, urban centres, neighbourhoods that have been produced by refugees and others within the most cosmopolitan cities in the world? In Seattle and Minneapolis, Cardiff and Nairobi, one encounters neighbourhoods of Somali refugees and the first thing that one notices is how they have sought to produce Somaliness and to reproduce a Somalia identity abroad (see Farah 2000). Logic would seem to go against this reconstruction of locality; one would think that one of the reasons Somalis are refugees in the world, leaving aside the question of military dictatorship and the collapse of the Somali state, is because they could not agree on definitions and degrees of Somaliness. Yet, once abroad, two generations of Somalis are involved in the work that ensures the presence of the very Somaliness that was the cause of deterritorialization in the first place. How do we explain the persistence of the *ethne* where one expects it to collapse in the face of cosmopolitanism?

We could argue, with Appadurai, that it is precisely because of their displace-ment that Somali refugees seek ontological mooring in an imagined Somali *ethne*. They reconstruct a 'local teleology and ethos' in the metropolis in order to deal with rootlessness; here local knowledge is 'substantially about producing reliably local subjects as well as producing reliably local neighbourhoods within which such subjects can be recognized and organized' (1996: 181). We could debate the means and ends of this project, but listening to local Somali talk radio in Seattle, or Amhara call-in shows in Washington DC, or attending Kikuyu or Yoruba Pentecostalist churches in London or New York, one is struck by how the imagination and circulation of locality creates, in a strictly phenomenological sense, secure and reliable neighbourhoods.

By the same token, cultivating a cosmopolitan identity is also an attempt to deploy the resources of intellectual culture to produce and reproduce a subjectivity that is reliable and recognizable. Indeed, if the postcolonial elite has become a major component of American and European high culture, it is precisely because of its mastery of this culture as a tool for cultivating a reli-able postcolonial identity. To invoke postcoloniality is to claim to be a citizen of many cultures and nations; but it is to claim rootlessness in order to position oneself in multiple cultural spaces and to have access to the goods that come with them. But by positioning itself as the stand-in for both metropolis and ex-colony, postcolonial cosmopolitanism conceals its own peculiar, particular, and often privileged entry into the world cultural system. By claiming to speak for others, postcolonial elites elide the circumstances by which the majority of the ex-colonial enters the world system, as refugees or illegal aliens, and how the process of entry and its terms of engagement generate a different narrative of global cultural flows.

Bibliography

Adorno, T. W. (1994) *Minima Moralia: Reflections from Damaged Life*, trans. E. F. N. Jephcott, London: Verso.

—— (1998) *Dialectic of Enlightenment*, trans. J. Cumming, New York: Continuum.

Appadurai, A. (1996) *Modernity at Large: Cultural Dimensions of Globalization*, Minneapolis: University of Minnesota Press.

Appiah, K. A. (2002) 'Cosmopolitan Patriots', in J. Cohen (ed.) *For Love of Country: Debating the Limits of Patriotism*, Boston: Beacon Press, 21–9.

—— (2006) *Cosmopolitanism: Ethics in a World of Strangers*, New York: W. W. Norton.

Arendt, H. (1973) *The Origins of Totalitarianism*, New York: Harcourt Brace.

Baudelaire, C. (1986) *The Painter of Modern Life and Other Essays*, trans. J. Mayne, New York: Da Capo Press.

Benjamin, W. (2006) *The Writer of Modern Life: Essays on Charles Baudelaire*, ed. M. W. Jennings, trans. H. Eiland, E. Jephcott, R. Livingstone and H. Zohn, Cambridge, MA: Belknap Press.

Bhabha, H. (1994) *The Location of Culture*, London and New York: Routledge.

Cheah, P. and Robbins, B. (eds) (1998) *Cosmopolitics: Thinking and Feeling Beyond the Nation*, Minneapolis: University of Minnesota Press.

DuBois, W. E. B. (1990) *The Souls of Black Folk*, New York: Vintage Books.

—— (1984) *Dusk of Dawn: An Essay Toward an Autobiography of a Race Concept*, New Brunswick, NJ: Transaction Publishers.

de Man, P. (1996) *Aesthetic Ideology*, Minneapolis: University of Minnesota Press.

Farah, N. (2000) *Yesterday, Tomorrow: Voices from the Somali Diaspora*, London: Cassell.

Gilroy, P. (2002) *Against Race: Imagining Political Culture Beyond the Color Line*, Cambridge, MA: Belknap Press.

Gourevitch, P. (1999) *We Wish to Inform You That Tomorrow We Will be Killed with Our Families: Stories from Rwanda*, New York: Picador.

Gramsci, A. (1957) *The Modern Prince and Other Writings*, New York: International Publishers.

Hadas, M. (1943) 'From Nationalism to Cosmopolitanism in the Greco-Roman World', *Journal of the History of Ideas*, 4.1 (January): 105–11.

Hannerz, U. (1990) 'Cosmopolitans and Locals in World Culture', in M. Featherstone (ed.) *Global Culture: Nationalism Globalization and Modernity*, London: Sage Publications.

Le Carré, J. (2000) *The Constant Gardener: A Novel*, New York: Scribner.

Said, E. (1990) 'Reflections on Exile', in R. Ferguson *et al.* (eds) *Out There: Marginalization and Contemporary Cultures*, New York: The New Museum of Contemporary Art, 357–74.

—— (1994) *Culture and Imperialism*, New York: Vintage.

Schlereth, T. J. (1977) *The Cosmopolitan Ideal in Enlightenment Thought: Its Form and Function in the Ideas of Franklin, Hume, and Voltaire, 1694–1790*, Terre Haute, IN: University of Notre Dame Press.

Spivak, G. C. (1999) *A Critique of Postcolonial Reason: Toward a History of the Vanishing Present*, Cambridge, MA: Harvard University Press.

—— (2005) *Death of a Discipline*, The Wellek Library Lectures, New York: Columbia University Press.

The Constant Gardener (2005), dir. F. Meirelles, Los Angeles: Focus Features.

Weil, S. (2001) *The Need for Roots: Prelude to a Declaration of Duties Towards Mankind*, New York, Routledge.

Woolf, V. (1938) *Three Guineas*, New York: Harcourt.

3 Cosmopolitan criticism

Robert Spencer

My purpose here is to show that the gradual elaboration of cosmopolitan perspectives and solidarities (in Martha Nussbaum's terms 1997), the expansion of our knowledge and of our sympathies, and thus of our capacity for citizenship) is to a large extent the very *raison d'être* of postcolonial literary criticism.[1] There are four questions to be asked about cosmopolitanism. The first is: What is it? A provisional answer is that cosmopolitanism is both a disposition – one characterized by self-awareness, by a penetrating sensitivity to the world beyond one's immediate milieu, and by an enlarged sense of moral and political responsibility – *and*, it is very important to add, a set of economic structures and political institutions that correspond to this. The second is: Why is cosmopolitanism necessary? Cosmopolitanism is called into being by the global reach of problems whose solution requires both democratic global institutions and, in order to make these legitimate and effective, global allegiances and solidarities. These problems include underdevelopment and exploitation; ethnic nationalism; environmental degradation; the abuse of human rights; the unequal distribution of resources; the proliferation of deadly weapons; and, of course, the US's overbearing political and military supremacy, along with the threats posed by many lesser militarisms.

The third question is: What does cosmopolitanism look like? One needs to refer here not only to the transnational aspirations of national liberation movements following the Second World War (Boehmer 2002, Lazarus 1999, Parry 2004, Young 2001), but also to contemporary political theorists working on, for instance, the Global Peoples' Assemblies envisaged by Richard Falk and Andrew Strauss (2000 and 2003), as well as numerous thinkers' and movements' proposals for democratizing the United Nations and the European Union, for strengthening international law, discharging trade deficits, preventing the accumulation of debt and engineering sustainable development (Mertes 2004, Monbiot 2004, Sands 2005). By cosmopolitanism I mean not so much an outlook or form of conduct, but something more substantive: a system of transnational relationships embedded in structures and institutions.

My concern, however, is less with the institutional forms that such cosmopolitan arrangements will take than with a fourth question, which postcolonial literary critics might help to answer and on which I endeavour here to offer some

suggestions: Assuming that some form of political and institutional cosmopolitanism is both necessary and feasible, how are cosmopolitan sentiments to be engendered? How, in other words, are we to move from the uncosmopolitan present to
the cosmopolitan future?

Cosmopolitanism is thus a vital aspect of the reorientation or rerouting of
postcolonial studies. A set of values as well as political and institutional objectives, cosmopolitanism provides a cogent alternative to the logic of exclusion and
hierarchy that characterizes ongoing forms of colonial rule and, to some extent,
the nationalist and related projects that have arisen to combat colonialism. My
claim is that it is now worth exploring encounters with postcolonial literature
as one way of encouraging cosmopolitan citizenship and therefore of extending the discipline's traditional emphases. The theory of cosmopolitan criticism
should demonstrate how reading postcolonial literature can engender the critical
consciousness and the global solidarities that are required to imagine, inaugurate
and sustain cosmopolitan political arrangements.

There are several 'schools' of thought on cosmopolitanism in postcolonial
studies: I will call them, perhaps too schematically, the sceptical, the celebratory
and the socialist schools. They are comprised of scholars whose work in each
case shares distinctive characteristics. Interestingly, thinkers in all these schools
are adopting increasingly nuanced, multifaceted conceptions of cosmopolitanism
and so are moving towards a common position, which I shall shortly attempt to
theorize. The object of the exercise is not to separate the sheep from the goats but
to assess the variety of positions held by postcolonial critics on cosmopolitanism
and to identify some common ground.

The first, sceptical, school dominated the postcolonial field after its inception.
It includes thinkers who are so concerned about the dominance of western ideologies, political institutions and economic arrangements that they tend to dismiss
all efforts to produce knowledge about other cultures and societies, let alone to
instate cosmopolitan institutions or espouse universalist ideals like human rights,
as inevitably coercive.[2] Such thinkers present local identities and communities as
the natural units of affiliation and action. This early form of postcolonial work
was more interested in deconstructing the cultural and epistemological authority
of colonialism than in elucidating the relationship between colonialism and capitalism or in asking how to move beyond these things.

Edward Said's *Orientalism* (1985) is in many ways the discipline's opening
salvo. If for Michel Foucault any discourse that claims privileged access to the
unvarnished state of things is deceitfully masking its own partiality, then likewise
for the Said of *Orientalism*, a book that relies on Foucault for its methodology,
what passes for knowledge of the so-called Orient is actually a self-interested
myth, a pretext for the exercise of colonial power. My worry is that *Orientalism*
harps on so relentlessly about the East–West divide and about western scholars' inability to say anything accurate and constructive about the Arab world
that it implies that these divisions are insuperable. It therefore undermines
any basis for the sort of cosmopolitan solidarity that the later Said advocated
more overtly (Spencer 2006). An excessively sceptical epistemology yields to a

relativist political philosophy. As Satya Mohanty points out, this complicates efforts 'to make decolonization a meaningful project involving cross-cultural contact and dialogue' (1997: 145). Despite Said's intentions, this is how *Orientalism* was initially received and how the discipline of postcolonial studies subsequently developed for several years.

I think there is now a much greater awareness among postcolonial scholars that the placing of undue emphasis on difference and identity has not done enough to challenge imperialism and imagine alternatives to it. Taking the place of these earlier preoccupations has been a more topical and, in general, salutary stress on the anti-imperialist potentialities of diasporas and hybrid and multicultural populations. Therefore the postcolonial field's second school of thought on cosmopolitanism, which has more or less eclipsed the first, celebrates the advent of a condition in which borders between peoples and regions are rapidly being dismantled. Its most prominent exponents in postcolonial circles are writers like Homi Bhabha (2004) and Arjun Appadurai (1997). For these thinkers the experience of migration, along with the increasingly cosmopolitan character of culture, are outstripping the culture of the nation, which is where exclusionary and oppressive practices are traditionally spawned. Appadurai is 'convinced that the nation-state, as a complex modern political form, is on its last legs' (1997: 19). So too, apparently, are dreams of ethnic purity, 'communities of sentiment' circumscribed by national borders, as well as the similarly passé belief that the world is divided up into powerful states and comparatively powerless ones. Globalization for Appadurai constitutes 'a complex overlapping, disjunctive order that cannot any longer be understood in terms of existing center-periphery models' (1997: 32).

But is there not a danger that this way of thinking overlooks persistent conflicts and inequalities? When Bhabha speaks unguardedly of 'the negotiation of colonial power-relations' (2004: 292), does he not mischaracterize the relationship between colonizer and colonized as grievously as Said did in *Orientalism*? Bhabha sometimes runs the risk of reducing the so-called 'colonial encounter' to a sort of get-together between interlocutors, not (as it unquestionably was) an unequal conflict between combatants. Statements like Bhabha's surely invite a corrective dose of what Bertolt Brecht famously called *plumpes denken* or crude thinking: an unsophisticated but entirely salutary reminder that colonial domination, though it may once in a while be the cause of what Bhabha calls ambivalence, mimicry and hybridity, as well as other forms of cultural cross-fertilization, entails additionally the systematic exploitation and unnatural curtailment of hundreds of millions of human lives. All talk of negotiation or of what Sara Suleri calls the 'intimacies that obtain between ruler and ruled' (Suleri 1992: 3) ought, in other words, to be juxtaposed with reminders of colonialism's intrinsic propensity for violence such as Adam Hochschild's 1999 claim that between 1890 and the beginning of the First World War, Leopold's colonization of the Congo caused somewhere between eight and ten million deaths.

Like the stress on cultural relativity that preceded it as the discipline's dominant mode, the celebration of hybridity and globalization is hardly invulnerable to criticism. Indeed the third, socialist, school is characterized principally by its impatience with this sort of idiom. Timothy Brennan (2006), Benita Parry (2004), Arif Dirlik (2002) and Aijaz Ahmad (1995) avoid like the plague the glib and precipitate rhetoric that Michael Mann has described as 'breathless trans-nationalism' (1995: 117–8), Tom Nairn as 'departure lounge internationalism' (2000: 148), and Andrew Smith as 'the "free-air-miles" sentiment in postcolonial theory' (2004: 245). For the socialist school this celebration of globalization and cosmopolitanism pays insufficient attention to the fact that colonialism was and is characterized at least as much by violence, conflict and exploitation as it is by interactions and 'third spaces'. Globalization, in other words, is volatile and uneven. Furthermore, continuing inequality and poverty are more salient features of the current dispensation than cultural hybridity. As Simon Gikandi and Erin Goheen Glanville argue in this collection, not all (or even a significant minority) of the world's citizens are exemplars of free movement between places and identities, but are more often victims of situations in which mobility is not an option or in which actual mobility is usually coerced and traumatic. From this point of view, cosmopolitanism amounts to what Paul Smith (1997) has called a 'millennial dream' embraced by gullible academics heedless of the profoundly uneven access to the privileges of travel and cultural eclecticism.

In addition, the nation state is neither obsolete nor expendable. Despite its anti-state rhetoric, capitalism requires a limited role for the state only in the area of social provision; it invents ever more tasks for the state to perform in criminal-izing dissent, maintaining 'security', hampering trades unions, surveilling citizens, removing regulations on businesses while inflicting them on the poor and unem-ployed, transferring vast sums of public money into private hands via a perma-nent arms economy, and, as the current economic depression is reminding us, subsidizing and occasionally bailing out supposedly self-sufficient corporations.[3] Nevertheless, nation states, Brennan points out, also offer an opportunity to subject unaccountable sources of power to the rule of law, to provide welfare and other social services, to regulate economic activity and to distribute its proceeds fairly (2003). Hasty announcements of the end of the nation state and celebrations of a new *trans*-national order overlook the fact that nation states are the engines of globalization and that for impoverished citizens excluded from the oases of affluence that characterize neo-liberal globalization, nation states therefore remain the sites at which they must direct their political energies and of which they must take charge if they are to redress their grievances (Brennan 1997, 2006: 126–44, 205–32).

It might be objected that the complex accounts of cosmopolitanism actually formulated by thinkers in the postcolonial field do not resemble the discrete schools of thought that I have been describing. It is true that I have exagger-ated the unanimity of these schools and the extent of the differences between them. For though there undoubtedly are differences of emphasis, all the critics mentioned so far have adopted multifaceted positions on the question of cosmo-politanism. No critic is so jejune, for example, that he or she mistakes a world in which thirty thousand children under five die every day of preventable diseases and in which uncounted millions of people fall victim annually to the practice of human trafficking for a utopian cosmopolis of equality and free movement. Furthermore, despite their distaste for the term, critics like Brennan and Parry are not opposed to the goals of cosmopolitanism. Rather, they are sceptical about the sort of premature cosmopolitanism that dooms itself to failure by not first tackling the undiminished power of capitalism and capitalism's indispensable conduit, the nation state. The point of cultural and political work for Brennan is 'to build a cosmopolitanism worthy of the name' (1997: 309).

It would be a mistake, therefore, to think that these different theoretical schools have nothing in common with each other. All things considered, we are faced not with insurmountable differences, but varying emphases. In fact, postcolonialists are currently refining a variety of cosmopolitanism capable of reconciling seemingly contradictory objectives. Combined as they are in the work of the figures mentioned thus far, those preoccupations point to a unified, albeit multifaceted and distinctively postcolonial cosmopolitanism. This united position is conscious of the need to think and to campaign at the local and national levels, whilst at the same time thinking and campaigning at the level of transnational institutions and arrangements. In other words, we do not have to choose between the local and the global, for we can and must do both at the same time. Indeed, as Alejandro Colás (1994), Fredric Jameson (2000) and Neil Lazarus (1997) have all argued, we have to work *through* the national *towards* the global, establishing the rights, autonomy and distinctiveness of the former in order to then guarantee and extend these at the level of the latter. Cosmopolitanism, you might say, begins at home. It involves reconciling local attachments with global allegiances. Thus, Mitchell Cohen has talked of a 'rooted cosmopolitanism' (1992) and Kwame Anthony Appiah of a 'cosmopolitan patriotism' (1997, 2006). In her article in this collection on the Esperanto movement, Kaori Nagai calls this 'the art of being cosmopolitan without losing one's nationality'.

We must learn to think, feel and act locally at the same time as we think, feel and act globally. Likewise, we must think of a way in which we can face up to and work politically within our uncosmopolitan present (a time, as Parry and others rightly point out, of immense enmity and inequality), without losing sight of the desirability and feasibility of a cosmopolitan future. This ability to reconcile different emphases should also characterize our approach to cultural diversity, advocates of which all (to varying degrees) acknowledge that the most effective way to guarantee the flourishing of cultural difference is with forms of law and with common values and institutions. Notwithstanding their disagreements, what has hopefully emerged from a consideration of existing approaches in postcolonial studies is a distinctively *dialectical* understanding of cosmopolitanism: one that combines diversity with commonality; political action at the level of the nation state with political action at a global level; and hard-headed awareness of the insufficiently cosmopolitan present with cognisance of the necessity and desirability of a cosmopolitan future.

If cosmopolitan institutions are to be legitimate, sustainable and effective – indeed, if citizens are to will them into being in the first place as instruments of popular sovereignty – then cosmopolitan values, principles and ideals must perforce be encouraged. As Raymond Williams once argued, the task of constructing an emancipated society is 'one of feeling and imagination quite as much as one of fact and organization' (1989: 76). In other words, it is a cultural as well as a political undertaking that entails not just the regulation of economic activity and the perfection of institutions, but also the reimagining and even the invention of new forms of human relationship. Reading postcolonial literature is obviously not the only way of creating citizens who are far-sighted enough to acknowledge obligations to people in distant countries as well as in possession of the kinds of critical awareness required to distrust parochial ideologies and institutions. Plainly, literary reading is not even among the most promising of such methods, given the possibility of reading postcolonial texts in ways other than those which I shall recommend, and given also the significant obstacles of literacy, education, time, capital and inclination that lie between the vast majority of people and the experience of literary reading. One needs to stress, too, as Nirmala Menon does in her essay in this volume, the ways in which postcolonial texts are often filtered and marketed by academic institutions and publishers. These processes of mediation are at best selective and tendentious. We have access in the West to a tiny proportion of the literary output of the rest of the world. Moreover, we are often subliminally encouraged to read those texts that do reach us in ways that flatter rather than challenge our preconceptions (Harrison 2003, Huggan 2001, Lazarus 2005). It would be Pollyannaish to claim too much importance and value for literature or to argue that encounters with postcolonial texts invariably result in constructive forms of moral and political engagement. But it should at least be conceded that literary texts are not negligible things. The wide world is rarely encountered on the spot and the usually unfamiliar experiences and aspirations of its inhabitants are hardly ever learnt about in face-to-face encounters. In fact, the interpretation of texts, as Edward Said had cause to remark in a related context, 'is what the knowledge of other cultures is principally based on' (Said 1997: 164). The world and its peoples are met with and learnt about chiefly (though of course not exclusively) via texts of one kind or another, and there is a need to recognize that cosmopolitan behaviour can be acquired in spite of this mediated involvement with the global sphere and even *as a result of* that involvement.

In other words, knowledge of other cultures and the capacity to reflect critically on one's own can be consequences of reading literary texts. This is only partly a result of the fact that what we call postcolonial literature allows a diversity of voices from unfamiliar situations to contest one's preconceptions about such places. It is also, crucially, a result of literature's distinctive and distinctively valuable ability to arouse in its readers a critical attitude or disposition. Literary texts are where voices are dramatized, reflected on and appraised. Characters' voices are opposed and disputed by other characters, while the authority of authors and their narrators is rendered moot by their narratives' manifestly partial (in both senses of that word) quality and, of course, by the patently fictional nature of the world they describe. This is another way of saying that the voices one attends to in literature are invariably ironized, contestable and imperfect: openly susceptible to and therefore actively soliciting the critical and evaluative rejoinders of their readers. So, too, is one's own viewpoint contested by alternatives. Through encounters with different and unfamiliar perspectives, readers of postcolonial literature can acquire the kind of self-reflexiveness required to relativize and to evaluate their own sometimes partial or even parochial outlook. It is in literature that readers participate in what the philosopher of hermeneutics Hans-Georg Gadamer calls 'the conversation that we ourselves are' (1979: 340). Works of postcolonial literature are thus sources of critique, discussion and discovery. They provide a fascinating deviation from orthodox ways of understanding and representing the postcolonial world. Each encounter with them constitutes what Said, referring to musical performance, calls an 'extreme occasion' (1991: 17–8), a chance to engage in the sort of penetrating enquiry, the imaginative exploration and the prolonged self-scrutiny so often regarded as uncalled-for (but actually sorely required) in other practices, vocations and areas of life. It is the extremity of the literary occasion – by which I mean its bestowal of a peculiarly risky, provocative but also invigorating form of experience as well, alas, as its frequent marginality in the face of corporate and other pressures – that makes it what Said, after Adorno, calls *autonomous* of 'the ordinary, regular, or normative processes of everyday life' (1991: 20).

Our readings ought to achieve, in their analysis of form just as much as in their analysis of content, an accentuation of literary texts' capacity to unmask the logic and actuality of imperialism whilst simultaneously envisioning imperialism's replacement. Literary analysis, as Fredric Jameson argues in *The Political Unconscious*, has both a functional and an anticipatory aspect (1996: 296). If the primary responsibility of the politically conscious literary critic is to unmask the ways in which exploitation and injustice are sublimated and concealed by texts (as well as to show how texts themselves sometimes lay bare these things, something Jameson fails to mention), then an ancillary but nevertheless still indispensable objective of his or her work is to reveal the ways in which literature can also point beyond the status quo. For Jameson the 'Utopian idea [...] keeps alive the possibility of a world qualitatively distinct from this one' (1971: 111). Utopia, a key motif in the tradition of Marxist aesthetics (Bloch 1996), is a term that Bill Ashcroft in his essay in this volume wants postcolonial critics to revive so that they will have some way of describing those moments in postcolonial texts or, better, in those texts' relationships with their readers that serve to delineate a world cured of the divisions put in place by imperialism. In analyzing such works we must heed Jameson's oft-repeated calls for 'the renewal of Utopian thinking' (1989: 110). I am therefore commending a method for the analysis of works of postcolonial literature that combines an emphasis on their critical dimension (that is, on their capacity to dramatize and incite opposition to imperial practices) with an emphasis too on their frequently neglected normative aspect, by which I mean their equally crucial ability to outline – or at least to implore, contemplate or, however obliquely, foretell – alternatives to imperial rule. These alternatives take shape either in certain relationships depicted by the works themselves or, more commonly and without doubt more effectively, in the relationships engineered between the characters and events portrayed and the works' readers.

Plucking books from the pile at the edge of my desk as I write, or running my eyes along the adjacent shelves, is sufficient survey to demonstrate the myriad ways in which works of literature might accomplish the twin goals of dramatizing imperialism whilst foretelling alternatives. The style, form and genre of these works of literature are as diverse as their provenance. They all stress what too many theorists in the postcolonial field, whose work on matters to do with imperialism and with resistance to imperialism addresses culture in a broad sense and is hosted in the main in university departments of literature, are sometimes tempted to forget: that the analysis of literature is the central purpose of our work because such works provide their readers with a source of self-knowledge and cosmopolitan conscience.

Postcolonial scholars' immediate preoccupations, though not their ultimate objectives, have been affected quite profoundly by the Bush administration's belligerent response to the terrorist attacks of September 2001 (Lazarus 2006). Patrick Williams in this volume applauds the discipline's increasing attention to enduring forms of colonial exploitation such as neoliberalism, the 'war on terror' and the unremitting violence meted out to the Palestinians. In what Derek Gregory insists on calling 'the colonial present' (2004), Iraq's assailants have unwittingly done us the service of demonstrating that the world as it is currently organized is not a chrysalis from which cosmopolitanism will simply issue forth. Indeed, as the Italian political economist Giovanni Arrighi has claimed, 'the new imperialism of the Project for a New American Century probably marks the inglorious end of the sixty-year long struggle of the United States to become the organizing center of a world state' (2007: 261). The architects of that destructive conspiracy have discredited the assumption that we come after colonialism and not in its turbulent midst and they have unmasked the folly of understanding imperialism in exclusively cultural and epistemological terms.

Our task is to find ways of thinking the absence (or rather the latency) as well as the urgent desirability of the cosmopolitan condition simultaneously: of conveying the undiminished power, divisiveness and exploitativeness of imperialism whilst articulating the need, hope and the currently germinating potential for the effective supersession of imperialism in the shape of cosmopolitan arrangements. Postcolonial studies is waking up to the enormous threats posed by capitalist globalization, as well as to the equally sizeable opportunities offered by a world in which identities and allegiances are being complicated, mixed and broadened by the migration of labour and the globalization of trade and communications (Krishswamy and Hawley 2008). Our priority should be to think through a situation in which the imperial globalization of capital has not yet been matched by a comparable and countervailing globalization of institutions, values and allegiances (Brecher *et al.* 2000, Gilroy 2005, Mertes 2002). The faculty of self-criticism and the sheer expansion of moral and political awareness brought about by engagements with postcolonial literature can help in this task. Accordingly, we need a critical practice that takes seriously George Steiner's insight that '[t]o read well is to take great risks. It is to make vulnerable our identity, our self-possession' (1967: 29). In this sense, the ethical and political aims of postcolonialism are arrived at, as Elleke Boehmer contends in her essay in these pages, by passing through rather than skirting round or avoiding the specific challenges and complexities of the aesthetic.

The rerouting or reorientation of postcolonial studies that the present volume announces and gets underway necessitates among other things the deliberate cultivation of cosmopolitan allegiances. Rerouting, if I might be excused the pun, therefore entails the pulling up and examination of one's roots. By espousing the use of the adjective 'cosmopolitan' to describe such work I want, of course, not to replace postcolonial literary criticism but to spell out the discipline's normative potential. We need, in other words, to place alongside the well-known narrative of what postcolonial theory is *against* an equally persuasive account of what it is actually *for*. If the discipline of postcolonial studies is to reroute itself then this is not because its characteristic emphases are mistaken or outmoded, but on the contrary because its distinguishing resistance to colonialism requires more than ever the encouragement of complex, provisional and itinerant loyalties. 'Roots', as the narrator of Salman Rushdie's novel *Shame* reminds us, 'are a conservative myth, designed to keep us in our places' (1995: 86). Hence resistance must be as global as the system it seeks to countermand. The exaltation of rootedness or belonging, though occasionally it may serve in the shape of anti-colonial nationalism to defy the depredations of colonialism, is not the outlook engendered by most products of postcolonial writing. Nor is it a long-term alternative to those depredations. The postcolonial critic must learn to tread in the steps of postcolonial literature, which frequently combines an acute attentiveness to the havoc brought about by imperialism with a utopian desire to move beyond it. When asked to justify our work we should recall what the Palestinians' laureate said of Edward Said: 'he is a reader who reflects on what poetry has to tell us in times of disaster' (Darwish 2005).

Notes

1 On the nature and possibilities of global citizenship see Gerard Delanty (2000), Richard Falk (1996), William Smith (2007) and Janna Thompson (2001).
2 The political philosopher Will Kymlicka's books *The Rights of Minority Cultures* (1995) and *Politics in the Vernacular* (2001) voice a common fear that the grand trans-national designs of cosmopolitanism are incompatible with respect for cultural diversity.
3 The nation state is still, as Eqbal Ahmad (2006), David Harvey (2005: 64–86) and Leo Panitch (2000) note, the structure that guarantees and protects corporate profits.

Bibliography

Ahmad, A. (1995) 'The Politics of Literary Postcoloniality', *Race and Class*, 36.3: 1–20.

Ahmad, E. (2006) 'Notes on American Intervention in the Third World', in C. Bengelsdorf, M. Cerullo and Y. Chandrani (eds) *The Selected Writings of Eqbal Ahmad*, New York: Columbia University Press.

Appadurai, A. (1997) *Modernity at Large: Cultural Dimensions of Globalization*, Minneapolis: University of Minnesota Press.

Appiah, K. A. (1997) 'Cosmopolitan Patriots', *Critical Inquiry*, 23: 617–39.

—— (2006) *Cosmopolitanism: Ethics in a World of Strangers*, London: Allen Lane.

Arrighi, G. (2007) *Adam Smith in Beijing: Lineages of the Twenty-First Century*, London: Verso.

Bhabha, H. K. (2004) *The Location of Culture*, London: Routledge.

Bloch, E. (1996) *The Utopian Function of Art and Literature: Selected Essays*, trans. J. Zipes and F. Mecklenburg, Cambridge, MA: The MIT Press.

Boehmer, E. (2002) *Empire, the National, and the Postcolonial, 1890–1920*, Oxford: Oxford University Press.

Brecher, J., Costello, T. and Smith, B. (2000) *Globalization from Below: The Power of Solidarity*, Boston, MA: South End Press.

Brennan, T. (1997) *At Home in the World: Cosmopolitanism Now*, Cambridge, MA: Harvard University Press.

—— (2003) 'Cosmopolitanism and Internationalism', in D. Archibugi (ed.) *Debating Cosmopolitics*, London: Verso: 40–50.

—— (2006) *Wars of Position: The Cultural Politics of Left and Right*, New York: Columbia University Press.

Cohen, M. (1992) 'Rooted Cosmopolitanism', *Dissent*, 39: 483–7.

Colás, A. (1994) 'Putting Cosmopolitanism into Practice: The Case of Socialist Internationalism', *Millennium*, 23: 513–34.

Darwish, M. (2005) 'Homage to Edward Said: Counterpoint'. Online. Available HTTP <http://mondediplo.com/2005/01/15said> (accessed 22 January 2009).

Delanty, G. (2000) *Citizenship in a Global Age: Society, Culture, Politics*, Buckingham: Open University Press.

Dirlik, A. (2002) 'Rethinking Colonialism: Globalization, Postcolonialism, and the Nation', *Interventions*, 4: 428–48.

Falk, R. (1996) 'The Making of Global Citizenship', in B. van Steenbergen (ed.) *The Condition of Citizenship*, London: Sage.

Falk, R. and Strauss, A. (2000) 'On the Creation of a Global People's Assembly: Legitimacy and the Power of Popular Sovereignty', *Stanford Journal of International Law*, 36: 191–220.

—— (2003) 'The Deeper Challenges of Global Terrorism: A Democratizing Response', in D. Archibugi (ed.), *Debating Cosmopolitics*, London: Verso.

Gadamer, H.-G. (1975 [1979]) *Truth and Method*, trans. J. Weinsheimer and D. G. Marshall, London: Sheed & Ward.

Gilroy, P. (2005) 'A New Cosmopolitanism', *Interventions*, 7: 287–92.

Gregory, D. (2004) *The Colonial Present: Afghanistan, Palestine, Iraq*, Oxford: Blackwell.

Harrison, P. (2003) *Postcolonial Criticism: History, Theory and the Work of Fiction*, Cambridge: Polity.

Harvey, D. (2005) *A Brief History of Neoliberalism*, Oxford: Oxford University Press.

Hochschild, A. (1999) *King Leopold's Ghost: A Story of Greed, Terror and Heroism in Colonial Africa*, London: Pan Macmillan.

Huggan, G. (2001) *The Postcolonial Exotic: Marketing the Margins*, London: Routledge.

Jameson, F. (1971) *Marxism and Form: Twentieth-Century Dialectical Theories of Literature*, Princeton: Princeton University Press.

—— (1989) 'Imaginary and Symbolic in Lacan', in *The Ideologies of Theory, Essays 1971–1986*, vol 1, Minneapolis: University of Minnesota Press: 75–115.

—— (1996) *The Political Unconscious: Narrative as a Socially Symbolic Act*, London: Routledge.

—— (2000) 'Globalization and Political Strategy', *New Left Review*, 4: 49–68.

Krishnaswamy, R. and Hawley, J. C. (eds) (2008) *The Postcolonial and the Global*, Minneapolis: University of Minnesota Press.

Kymlicka, W. (ed.) (1995) *The Rights of Minority Cultures*, Oxford: Oxford University Press.

—— (ed.) (2001) *Politics in the Vernacular: Nationalism, Multiculturalism and Citizenship*, Oxford: Oxford University Press.

Lazarus, N. (1997) 'Transnationalism and the Alleged Death of the Nation State', in K. Ansell-Pearson, B. Parry and J. Squires (eds) *Cultural Readings of Imperialism: Edward Said and the Gravity of History*, New York: St. Martin's Press: 28–48.

—— (1999) *Nationalism and Cultural Practice in the Postcolonial World*, Cambridge: Cambridge University Press.

—— (2005) 'The Politics of Postcolonial Modernism', in A. Loomba, S. Kaul, M. Bunzl, A. Burton and J. Esty (eds) *Postcolonial Studies and Beyond*, Durham: Duke University Press: 438–48.

—— (2006) 'Postcolonial Studies after the Invasion of Iraq', *New Formations*, 59: 10–22.

Mann, M. (1995) 'As the Twentieth Century Ages', *New Left Review*, 214: 104–24.

Mertes, T. (2002) 'Grass-Roots Globalism', *New Left Review*, 17: 101–10.

—— (ed.) (2004) *A Movement of Movements: Is Another World Really Possible?*, London: Verso.

Mohanty, S. P. (1997) *Literary Theory and the Claims of History: Postmodernism, Objectivity, Multicultural Politics*, Ithaca: Cornell University Press.

Monbiot, G. (2004) *The Age of Consent: A Manifesto for a New World Order*, London: Harper Perennial.

Nairn, T. (2000) *After Britain: New Labour and the Return of Scotland*, London: Granta.

Nussbaum, M. C. (1997) *Cultivating Humanity: A Classical Defence of Reform in Liberal Education*, Cambridge, MA: Harvard University Press.

Panitch, L. (2000) 'The New Imperial State', *New Left Review*, 2: 5–20.

Parry, B. (2004) 'The Institutionalization of Postcolonial Studies', in N. Lazarus (ed.) *The Cambridge Companion to Postcolonial Literary Studies*, Cambridge: Cambridge University Press: 66–80.

Rushdie, S. (1995) *Shame*, London: Vintage.

Said, E. W. (1985) *Orientalism*, Harmondsworth: Penguin.

—— (1991) *Musical Elaborations: The Wellek Library Lectures*, New York: Columbia University Press.

—— (1981 [1997]) *Covering Islam: How the Media and the Experts Determine How We See the Rest of the World*, London: Vintage.

Sands, P. (2005) *Lawless World: America and the Making and Breaking of Global Rules*, London: Allen Lane.

Smith, A. (2004) 'Migrancy, Hybridity, and Postcolonial Literary Studies', in N. Lazarus (ed.) *The Cambridge Companion to Postcolonial Literary Studies*, Cambridge: Cambridge University Press: 241–61.

Smith, P. (1997) *Millennial Dreams: Contemporary Culture and Capital in the North*, London: Verso.

Smith, W. (2007) 'Cosmopolitan Citizenship: Virtue, Irony and Worldliness', *European Journal of Social Theory*, 10: 37–52.

Spencer, R. (2006) 'Edward Said and the War in Iraq', *New Formations*, 59: 52–62.

Spivak, G. C. (1990) *The Post-colonial Critic: Interviews, Strategies, Dialogues*, London: Routledge.

Steiner, G. (1967) *Language and Silence: Essays, 1958–1966*, Harmondsworth: Penguin.

Suleri, S. (1992) *The Rhetoric of English India*, Chicago: University of Chicago Press.

Thompson, J. (2001) 'Planetary Citizenship: the Definition and Defence of an Ideal', in B. Gleeson and N. Low (eds) *Governing for the Environment: Global Problems, Ethics and Democracy*, London: Palgrave: 135–46.

Williams, R. (1989) *Resources of Hope: Culture, Democracy, Socialism*, London: Verso.

Young, R. (2001) *Postcolonialism: An Historical Introduction*, Oxford: Blackwell.

4 'The new bilingualism'

Cosmopolitanism in the era of Esperanto

Kaori Nagai

In recent investigations into the question of cosmopolitanism, the word 'Esperanto' uncomfortably floats in the margin, although the language itself rarely becomes the object of study; it is instead evoked as a byword for artificiality, non-historicity, or the emptiness of universality. For instance, Robert Pinsky's essay 'Eros against Esperanto', despite its title, does not discuss Esperanto, but the language is used to criticize Martha Nussbaum's take on cosmopolitanism, which he sees as too 'universal' and devoid of local and historical content (1996: 86). Pinsky describes Nussbaum's 'error' as 'like confusing a historical tongue such as English with a construct like Esperanto' (85), and thereby highlights the authenticity and suitability of English as a world language. Also Gayatri Spivak, when asked if her notion of 'transnational literacy' might be useful to 'examine the history of universal language movements', distances herself from 'planned reforms like Esperanto', by 'clinging to Ferdinand de Saussure's wise words': 'In language [...] everybody participates at all times, and that is why it is constantly being influenced by all. This capital fact suffices to show the impossibility of revolution' (2001: 16). She thus understands Esperanto to be a kind of non-language, not suitable to keep pace with ever-evolving human life. As Spivak's authority for her claim about artificial languages is Ferdinand de Saussure, she would not be too pleased to hear that he is remembered by Esperantists as a supporter of their movement. According to Théophile Cart (1855–1931), French Esperantist and Professor of Linguistics, and a former student of Saussure, in writing Saussure's obituary: 'he was very sympathetic to our movement, and firmly certified the possibility of an artificial international language, and approved of Esperanto' (Cart 1913: 107; my translation). Ferdinand's brother, René de Saussure (1868–1943), was also a renowned Esperantist and reformer of the language, illustrating the kinship between modern linguistics and Esperanto, both of which regarded languages as belonging to living human beings to be spoken and lived through, rather than as the dead 'fossils' which nineteenth-century philology took them to be. Early sympathizers of the Esperanto movement also include celebrities like Tolstoy and Max Müller, while Edmond Privat (1889–1962), a Swiss peace activist and trusted friend of Gandhi, was a leading Esperantist who acted as President of the Universal Esperanto Association. Despite having over one hundred years of history, and having created surprising international networks, including both

Esperantists and non-Esperantists, Esperanto, as a rule, lacks any serious consideration of its local and historical contexts and this has ensured that the language will safely remain a metaphor.

According to Timothy Brennan, in his article 'Cosmo-Theory', the 'important range of inquiries has been lost' in our scrutiny of cosmopolitanism, and Esperanto is just such a forgotten earlier paradigm (2001: 666–7). Not much effort, therefore, has been made to locate the language as a culture of cosmopolitanism. This article thus seeks to turn a retrospective gaze upon the early history of the British Esperanto movement in the first decade of the twentieth century, as well as to draw attention to the selective remembering within post-colonial studies. Our amnesia – or inability to think – of the space in which Esperanto existed as a vital model of cosmopolitanism is interesting considering that the Esperanto movement was one of the earliest world-wide transnational movements and earliest 'post-colonial' theories, which consciously addressed the relationship between nationalism and internationalism. It emerged in the late-nineteenth century as a response to accelerating globalization and diasporic forces, and put itself forward as a powerful criticism of the linguistic and cultural imperialism of major European languages. In particular, Esperantism shared with post-colonialism a sense of *hope* – Esperanto meaning 'the one who hopes' – and a utopian vision of world peace and justice. It may, then, be interesting to ask why, with all the uncanny similarities in intent and purpose, post-colonial studies have overlooked 'Esperanto' as an object of study, and *why*, indeed, we are made to feel uneasy when Esperanto is even mentioned?

Esperanto is a constructed language designed to be easy to learn and master. It has a regular and phonetic spelling system, and the vocabulary is taken from roots common to the chief European languages; its grammar can be reduced to sixteen rules without any exception. The Esperanto movement originated in Eastern Europe in 1887, when it was first promulgated by the Jewish eye doctor Ludovic Lazarus Zamenhof (1859–1917). Zamenhof was born in the polyglot town of Bialystok in Russian Poland where, among the different nationalities, at least four languages – Russian, Polish, German and Yiddish – were spoken. He came to regard the misunderstanding arising from the absence of a common tongue as the cause of racial animosities, and thus set out to create an international language to break down the linguistic divides. As a young man, Zamenhof was a fervent Zionist, and Esperanto can also be seen as another Jewish search for a homeland, equivalent to the revival of Hebrew by his contemporary, Eliezer Ben-Yehuda (1858–1922). Both dreamt of the liberation of their people and of a land of union, to be materialized through the creation and dissemination of a living language. The difference was that in Zamenhof's 1907 scheme the Jewish race, which he came to understand as 'neither local nor ethnological, but only ideal' (17), was to achieve its national unity, *not* in the geographical Zion but in Esperanto-land [Esperantujo], an international space which opens up every time his artificial language is spoken, as well as in a kind of Judaism reformed to emphasize the love of and co-existence with its neighbours. In fact, by 1887 Zamenhof had discarded the idea of Zionism as 'a beautiful and impractical

dream' which 'would never solve the eternal Jewish question' (17): the publication
of his international language marked for him a significant moment of rerouting/
rerooting the Jewish nation. Through Zamenhof's language, the Jews could
choose to live among their neighbours as friends in whatever cosmopolitan situation they found themselves. Esperanto, which H. G. Wells called 'the natural gift
of Jewry to mankind' (1918: 65), was the art of being cosmopolitan without losing
one's nationality, and was passed onto a new flux of cross-cultural migrants, who
were increasingly finding themselves in a similar position to that of the wandering race.

The emblem of Esperanto is a five-pointed green star [*verda stelo*]: it represents
five continents (Europe, Asia, Americas, Oceania, Africa) and hope, symbolized by the colour green. In the early Esperanto publications, this green star of
hope is often seen above the sky illuminating, and thereby making visible to the
imagination, the globe (Figure 4.1). A cover illustration from a 1907 issue of the
Internacia Socia Revuo [International Social Review] depicts the globe guided by
the Esperanto Star as the Mother Earth, feeding children of different races with
her multiple breasts, and combating the shadow of death caused by social and
racial inequality (Figure 4.2). We may even go so far as to say that the Esperanto
movement with its 'planetary consciousness' is one of the earliest instances of the
'world-wide-web' phenomenon, occurring long before the internet was invented.
People learned Esperanto to feel globally 'connected' and to tune in to the news
coming from all parts of the world, linguistically separated and thus otherwise
unreachable. Esperantists sought pen pals from all over the world, and philat-
elists learned Esperanto to enhance their collections of stamps and postmarks. It
is important to remember that the question of world language was at that time
closely tied up with technological innovations of faster and more efficient means

Figure 4.1 Rondiranto: the illustrated monthly of the Bulgarian Esperantists (March 1904).

Figure 4.2 The cover illustration of *Internacia Socia Revuo* (January 1907), illustrated by
Adolphe Willette.

of international communication, and early Esperantists also included many
stenographers, engineers and telegraph/postmasters, who were an integral part
of networks of communication.

The Esperanto movement made great strides in the English-speaking countries
in the first decade of the twentieth century, despite the widely-held prediction
that 'the English-speaking peoples, above all others, would never join hands with'
Esperantists (*Glasgow Herald*, 13 August 1907: 7). It is interesting to observe that
many of the 'post-colonial' areas became touched by this movement. The earliest
Esperanto movement in the British Empire started in the French-speaking part of
Canada, in the city of Montreal, as early as 1901. Their magazine *La Lumo* [The
Light] featured articles in three languages (Esperanto, English and French), and
its objective was to bridge a large gap between 'two great families, the French
and the English' through Esperanto (April 1902: 51). Esperanto also attracted
some attention in Ireland, in the midst of the Gaelic Revival. The Pan-Celtic

Association, which started in Dublin and aimed to create a transnational union between the five *Celtic* Nations (Ireland, Scotland, Wales, Brittany and the Isle of Man), advocated Esperanto in 1902 through its official organ *Celtia: A Pan-Celtic Monthly Magazine*, as a means to end 'our present degradation and slavery to the English language' (August 1902: 115). Furthermore, the first British Esperantist was an Irishman, Richard Henry Geoghegan, who learned Esperanto as early as 1887, and translated Zamenhof's *Unua Libro* [First Book] into English. He later emigrated to America, and sent the information on Esperanto to the Pan-Celtic Association. Its secretary, E. E. Fournier d'Albe (1868–1933), became a fluent Esperantist, and promoted Esperanto as the official language of the Pan-Celtic union. India was also touched by the movement, especially through the efforts of John Pollen (1848–1923), an ex-Indian Civil Servant and Irishman, who conducted a series of propaganda tours of India as well as of New Zealand and Australia. The first Esperanto Congress in the British colonies was held in Adelaide, Australia in 1911. Groups were also formed in places such as Egypt, Persia, Malta, Gibraltar, etc., and South Africa and Palestine were two places in which Esperanto was strongly advocated as a solution to their language problems.

Significantly in Britain the Esperanto movement officially began in 1902, immediately after the end of the Boer War. A space for Esperanto suddenly opened up when the sense of imperial disintegration set in and met with the spiralling processes of modernization and internationalization. A new *neutral* language was urgently needed to foster sympathy and understanding between different parties, and for many this new language *had to be* something other than English. Not only was it felt that English 'would smother all other existing languages, and thus pave the way for one universal vehicle of thought' (Gilles 1902: 21), but its complexity and inaccessibility – its irregular spelling and difficult pronunciation – became a metaphor for the Empire's inability to bring together different races and nations in peaceful consensus. 'Down with the Union Jack and up with the green flag of justice', wrote the *Pall Mall Gazette*, reporting the Cambridge Esperanto Congress, 'all's right at last with the world' (13 August 1907). In this context, it is interesting to note that the Esperanto movement in Britain owes much of its formation to William T. Stead, the champion of small and oppressed nations who waged a vociferous crusade against the Boer War. Stead readily lent his name and support to this new international language, which many dismissed as a laughing-stock; 'Were it not for [Stead]', as J. C. O'Connor, one of the British pioneers and another Irishman, put it, 'for his generous help to, and for his whole-hearted advocacy of our propaganda, we would be today as those who cry, cry vainly, in the silence of a mighty wilderness' (1903: 45). In October 1902, Stead began to publicize the language through his famous journal the *Review of Reviews*, which encouraged Esperantists scattered all over Britain to form local groups (Lawrence 1930: 182). The journal reported monthly the news and progress of the Esperanto movement, and Stead even allowed the use of its office for Esperanto classes to take place (Whyte 1925: 67). Stead's support of the language was not surprising, for Esperanto seemed to him to be an ideal medium to achieve his cherished goal: world peace through international arbitration. Therefore, *Concord*, the journal of the International Arbitration and Peace Association, became another outlet through which Stead campaigned for the cause of Esperanto: 'though Esperanto is simply a language, and has nought to do with any political or social association whatsoever, yet, as "Hope" is its name, "Concord" is its attendant' (*Review of Reviews* 1905: 326). Stead never really learned to speak the language, though his private secretary Eliza Ann Lawrence did, and she became a key player in the British Esperanto movement. Stead's assistance swiftly led to the formation of the British Esperanto Association in 1904, which was established as a 'Federation embracing all the Esperanto Groups in Great Britain, Ireland, and the Colonies', and which successfully hosted the third Universal Esperanto Congress in Cambridge in 1907. The association was secretly a subversive society for it palimpsested onto the 'English-speaking' British Empire the federation of many-tongued nations meeting in Esperanto, resisting an Anglo-Saxon linguistic imperialism which sought to colonize other languages. Moreover, it extended its networks to include nations outside the Empire – Russia, Eastern Europe, China, Japan, Latin America – all speaking to each other in the Other's language, that of Hope.

Esperanto became affiliated with a wide range of world peace movements such as vegetarianism, theosophy, anti-war protestors, women's movements, anarchists, socialists, the community of the blind as well as the world scouting movement. For instance, according to the *Vegetarian Messenger and Health Review*, the organ of the Vegetarian Society in Britain, 'Inasmuch as Esperanto seeks to unite the nations of the civilized world, and in this way makes for the spread of a larger humanity, it claims the sympathy of vegetarians' (July 1911: 223). Its president, Professor John Eyton Bickersteth Mayor (1825–1910), a classical scholar at Cambridge and famous vegetarian, surprised everybody by mastering Esperanto in a week when the Universal Esperanto Congress came to Cambridge in 1907, and became an enthusiastic supporter of the movement. Mayor was of the opinion that Esperanto was 'far better than any "pidgin English"' to 'bring divided nations into relations of brotherly sympathy' (1907a: 227). By bringing people together and engaging them in conversation, he believed that 'many differences [would] be smoothed down', for 'you cannot know and hate' which is 'the gist of Esperanto' (1907b: 325). In this sense the Esperanto movement formed part of what Leela Gandhi calls 'affective communities', the anti-colonial affiliations of certain marginalized subcultures in late-nineteenth century Britain and Europe, which cherished particularly utopian visions of the world (Gandhi 2006). Indeed, a significant overlap between the Esperanto movement and Gandhi's affective communities – her own examples include vegetarianism, spiritualism, animal rights and homosexuality – in turn underlines the conspicuous lack of interest in the 'language question' in Gandhi's otherwise brilliant book. Her emphasis is clearly on privileged moments of friendship between English-speaking intellectuals, or the ties made through non-verbal and marginalized regions of body and sexuality, but Gandhi seems oblivious to the fact that there were organized networks, alongside and across her affective communities, which consciously problematized the linguistic barriers which could only be overcome *orally* – choosing to speak Esperanto and not to eat meat coincided as one and the same ethical choice to be hospitable to others.

If our post-colonial remembering of the earlier forms of cosmopolitanism tends to play down 'the Conflict of Languages' (Wells 1904), or what Laura O'Connor calls 'the "eat-or-be-eaten" logic of linguicide' (2006: 5), which was so prominent in contemporaneous discourses on internationalism, and if it only looks for a model which is serviceable to us, we might try to identify those aspects of the language question which are apparently too outdated now to be taken seriously. For instance, a recent trend of post-colonial studies draws our attention to emerging global and 'transnational' conditions of the modern world, which blur the boundaries between nation-states and national identities. For instance, Bill Ashcroft, in his article in this collection, talks of the 'transnation' as an 'in-between space which contains no one definitive people, nation or even community, but is everywhere, a space without boundaries' (77–8). If this 'transnational' cosmopolitanism is our new reality, which post-colonialism now deals with, Esperantism always meant double citizenships between one's own nation and cosmopolitanism, rather than a blurring of the borders between the two. The original agenda of Esperantism was the creation of a *bilingual* cosmopolitanism in reaction to the monolingual imperialism of the colonizing powers. Though Esperanto was commonly described as a *universal* language, Esperantists strongly objected to the suggestion that it aimed to become universal by supplanting existing languages: the language was intended by its inventor as an international *auxiliary* language, that is to say, it was to become everybody's second language. Some Esperantists therefore consciously rejected the adjective 'universal', preferring 'international', which 'means "as between nations"' (Rembert 1903: 99).

Esperanto first came into being in the late-nineteenth century, when dialects and local norms were fast dying out as national spaces were being unified, while at the same time dead languages were being 'galvanized' and 'dragged back to the world of the living' by new nations; as Albert Léon Guérard put it in 1922, '[as] one nationality after another achieved consciousness […] it must needs assert itself through the revival of its ancient speech' (1922: 52). The international space of Esperanto was conceived by analogy with a nation-state – 'Esperanto-land' – with its own flag and national anthem. Esperantist bilingualism demarcated a clear border between 'national' and international spaces, which were nevertheless freely traversable by the bilingual body of each individual, while carving out an autonomous space for small nations. This original model of Esperantism came under internal scrutiny by the end of the First World War, and soon after the death of Zamenhof. In 1921, Eugène Lanti, a French Esperantist, founded the 'Sennacieca Asocio Tutmonda' [World Non-National Association], which proposed to abolish all the distinctions between nations, and which became an influential Workers' Esperanto movement. This more 'universalizing' offshoot of the Esperanto movement can be seen as a reaction against the 'bilingual' model of Esperantism and nationalisms, which it rejected as being still complicit with capitalism.

In its spirit the Esperanto movement reminds us of Paul Gilroy's 'planetary humanism' which calls for global solidarity against racism and racial essentialism. Esperantism's strategy of promoting cosmopolitan 'conviviality' – 'the process of cohabitation and interaction' (Gilroy 2004: xi) – is through 'conversationality'. The *blinding* differences of race, class and nationality which repeatedly material-ized as both visual and aural images were to be dissolved through Esperanto, for its fantasy of vocal uniformity, assisted by the actual ease of pronouncing the language, made it possible for the physical and speaking bodies of individuals to enter into a communal space without being branded with their 'identities'. As John Pollen testified:

> As to the peculiar accent of different classes and countries, it is wonderful how they disappeared when Esperanto was spoken. You could not tell a Cockney from an unspeakable Scot, nor a guttural German from a liquid Italian. All pronounced Esperanto without betraying the country of their origin.
>
> (Vane 1911: 53)

Or, as a Slovak Hungarian with a casual knowledge of Esperanto, who attended the third International Congress of Esperanto held in Cambridge in 1907, observed:

> During my former stay in England I had many occasions to have dealings with the English people and to observe them, but they remained to me mere existences – incomprehensible and strange. At Cambridge I made the acquaintance of many English people, but – wonderful surprise – all these English were just the same kind of people as everybody else. Whence came this marvellous change? [...] Esperanto alone, with its neutrality, had brought about the strange, unexpected miracle.
>
> (Long 1912: 42)

Esperanto, invented by a contemporary of Freud, is another and more thought-out version of 'psychoanalytic' cosmopolitanism – a 'talking cure', which offers itself as a practical solution to 'foreignness' within and without ourselves. Note that the English with whom the foreign guest could not communicate are firstly perceived as if they were 'mere existences', before they regain humanity through verbal communication. The objectification and de-humanization of foreign others is a marked feature in the Esperantic 'primal scene'; they are then magi-cally dissolved into humanness through the use of Esperanto. Esperanto, a pros-thetic tongue shared by everybody, aims to put a stop to the 'vacillation between the archaic affirmation of wholeness/similarity [...] and the anxiety associated with lack and difference', which, according to Bhabha, perpetuates the return of fetishes and stereotypes (1994: 74).

Esperantism also acknowledged the deep psychological need to nurture our own roots, homes, and languages, and tried to reconcile this with the reality of internationalism. It was for this reason that Zamenhof found Hillelism (the name given to the teaching of the Jewish Rabbi Hilell) an appealing philosophy, which he saw as the ideal solution to the Jewish question:

> Hillelism is a teaching which, not tearing a human being away from his fatherland, or from his language, or from his religion, gives him the possibility of avoiding all untruth and contradiction in his national-religious principles and of communicating with human beings of all languages and religions on a neutral-human basis of mutual brotherhood, equality and justice.
>
> (Zamenhof quoted in Boulton 1960: 100–1).

Zamenhof was keenly aware of what some post-colonial scholars have been striving to theorize, namely the relationship between the local and the global, or, to use Kwame Anthony Appiah's phrase, the art of becoming 'cosmopolitan patriots' (1998), in which the love for one's roots and locality and the love for humanity intersect and foster each other. Esperanto was primarily born out of Zamenhof's distress at the plight of the Jewish people who were 'shut up in a Ghetto' and 'separated from [their] fellow-Jew[s] as well as from [their] Christian neighbour[s]', because of their 'jargons' which none but themselves understood: 'the walls of this Ghetto were largely constructed out of dialect' (Zamenhof 1907: 16). His international language, by destroying the 'walls' of national animosities, aspired to transform this prison-like space into a home.

In this sense, Esperantism has much in common with Homi Bhabha's 'vernacular cosmopolitanism' which he defines as '"domestication" of the universal', or cosmopolitanism's turn 'towards the "domestic" to reveal it as an uncanny site/sign of the native, the indigenous' (1996: 48). Esperanto worked to 'domesticate' or create a home space in order to bring to light the 'uncanny' voices of 'all speechless and oppressed people' (Zamenhof 1907: 16), hitherto suppressed. The only difference between them is in rhetoric, which, however, perhaps tellingly conveys the disparity between what is at stake in Esperantism and the post-colonial version of cosmopolitanism. Bhabha, like Ashcroft, sees 'vernacular cosmopolitanism' as being 'on the border, *in between*', and the interaction and transformation between the global and the local are seen as 'the performance of translation' (1996: 48). For Zamenhof, by contrast, the border which separates is captured by the image of walls, or sometimes by censorship: the border is never a place to be inhabited, except as the ghetto or detention centre. Zamenhof knocks down the wall to create a door, through which the bilingual body of the individual freely traverses, and to make both sides a welcoming home: if there is a paternal figure in each Esperantic space, it invariably takes the figure of host and hospitality. Living in-between must be the aesthetics and ethics of those who have never really lived in a border, or of we post-colonial and post-modern 'monolingualists' who are yet to *learn to* discern the difference between the global and the local, inextricably intertwined as we are in a single English language.

In our attempt to reroute/reroot the post-colonial – hardly the first or last – the tale of Esperanto, a project marginalized and even demonized in the recent history of the English language, serves as a cautionary one: What if post-colonial studies were to rewrite history to our advantage once again, erasing marginal voices such as the Esperanto movement from former colonial/post-colonial struggles, because they are considered irrelevant or obsolete? This does not mean, however, that I consider Esperanto as an ideal solution to the language problem. I believe that Esperanto as an international tool of communication has indeed become 'outdated', but this is *not* because English has now become the world language. Remember that Esperanto was a modernist invention created at a time when there was no radio, no TV, no internet. It was built on the faith in the power of human languages alone to evoke a vision of the universal in our collective imagination. 'Cosmopolitanism' could, therefore, only be achieved by abolishing linguistic as well as cultural barriers through constant interaction and translation between different languages. In this sense, Esperantism, with its bi- and multi-lingualism, reminds me of another modernist project, Walter Benjamin's 'Task of the Translator' (1999), which aspires to extract 'pure language', the 'ultimate essence' within a language, which is 'weighed with a heavy, alien meaning': the task of the translator would be 'to release in his own language that pure language which is under the spell of another, to liberate the language imprisoned in a work in his recreation of that work' (1999: 80). Our relationship with language, however, has since changed as a result of the advance of visual media such as real-time television (Virilio 1994): language no longer has the same power to evoke visions in the imagination, and the English language is now the world language in that it provides the most popular 'subtitles' to the images which are now the new world language. New solutions to language problems need to be found by taking into consideration ever-advancing technologies of images as well as words.

Our fear of Esperanto probably resembles most closely our fear of genetically modified crops, for we believe that our thoughts, dreams and literatures are flowers of our languages, and we should not 'artificially' tamper with their growth. However, one may ask: How many of the national languages in our garden are *not* selective breeds, reformed, unified and purified of local dialects and other irregularities? And, more crucially, to what extent would English be 'natural' for a foreigner who is learning it as a second language – that which would immediately mark you as a foreigner, an 'unnatural' and machinic addition to your host country? Behind its self-proclaimed organicity, seen in its celebration of 'hybridity' and 'world' literatures written in, or translated into, English, What 'unnatural' dealings with others has post-colonial cosmopolitanism concealed? All things considered, the world without a language like Esperanto would be a very poor place. What better reminder do we have of what Jacques Derrida calls the Anglo-American *mondialatinisation* (globalatinisation) (2002: 50) than Esperanto, a language based on major European languages to counter the powers of colonization associated with those languages? Our cosmopolitanism has much to learn from Esperantism, of which the basic principle is that true cosmopolitanism starts from a commitment to learn to speak a language which is not our own. Esperanto might not solve problems of miscommunication, but at least it stages a cosmopolitan space as a place where a conversation between different parties would and should take place. Such a utopian yet quintessentially *human* space should never be underestimated.

Acknowledgements

I am very grateful to the Leverhulme Trust for funding my research project on the Esperanto movement. I would like to thank Geoffrey King and Viv O'Dunne of the British Esperanto Association for helping me with my research in the Butler Library in Barlaston, and also Angus Wilkinson for teaching me the basic grammar, and about Esperanto literature; also Pasquale Zapelli, Roy MacCoy, Ionel Onet, Julia Noe, Ralph Schmeits, and Heidi Goes of the Universal Esperanto Association in Rotterdam, who, during my research in the Association's library, kindly tolerated my 'English' invasion and took the time to answer all my questions. Finally, I would like to thank Rob Moerbeek, without whose guidance I would have never found my way in the library of the UEA.

Bibliography

Appiah, K. A. (1998) 'Cosmopolitan Patriots', in P. Cheah and B. Robbins (eds), *Cosmopolitics: Thinking and Feeling Beyond the Nation*, Minneapolis: University of Minnesota Press: 91–114.

Benjamin, W. (1999) 'The Task of the Translator', in H. Arendt (ed.) *Illuminations*, trans. H. Zorn, London: Pimlico Press: 70–82.

Bhabha, H. K. (1994) *The Location of Culture*, London and New York: Routledge.

—— (1996) 'Unsatisfied: Notes on Vernacular Cosmopolitanism', reprinted in G. Castle (ed.) (2001) *Postcolonial Discourses: An Anthology*, Oxford: Blackwell, 38–52.

Boulton, M. (1960) *Zamenhof: Creator of Esperanto*, London: Routledge and Kegan Paul.

Brennan, T. (2001) 'Cosmo-Theory', *The South Atlantic Quarterly*, 100.3: 659–91.

Cart, T. (1913) '*Ferdinand de Saussure (1857–1913)*', *Lingvo Internacia*, 18.3 (March): 107.

Derrida, J. (2002) *Acts of Religion*, ed. G. Anidjar, New York and London: Routledge.

Gandhi, L. (2006) *Affective Communities: Anticolonial Thought, Fin-de-Siècle Radicalism, and the Politics of Friendship*, Durham and London: Duke University Press.

Gilles, S. (1902), 'Esperanto versus Modern Languages', *La Lumo*, 2 (February): 20–1.

Gilroy, P. (2004) *After Empire: Melancholia or Convivial Culture?*, Abingdon: Routledge.

Guérard, A. L. (1922) *A Short History of the International Language Movement*, London: T. Fisher Unwin.

Lawrence, E. A. (1930) 'The Early Days in Britain', *International Language*, 7 (August): 182–3.

Long, B. (1912) *The Passing of Babel or Esperanto and its Place in Modern Life*, London: The British Esperanto Association.

Mayor, J. E. B. (1907a), quoted in 'Professor Mayor, Esperantist', *Vegetarian Messenger and Health Review*, 4.9 (September): 227.

—— (1907b), quoted in 'Speeches at the Public Meeting of the Vegetarian Society's 60th Anniversary, Oct. 14th, 1907', *Vegetarian Messenger and Health Review*, 4.12 (December): 325.

O'Connor, J. C. (1903), 'England' (A letter to the Editor), *La Lumo*, 2.3 (March): 43.

O'Connor, L. (2006) *Haunted English: The Celtic Fringe, the British Empire, and de-Anglicization*, Baltimore: The Johns Hopkins University Press.

Pinsky, R. (1996) 'Eros against Esperanto', in M. C. Nussbaum with Respondents, J. Cohen (ed.) *For Love of Country? Debating the Limits of Patriotism*, Boston: Beacon Press: 85–90.

Rembert, A. (1903) 'International not Universal', *La Lumo*, 2.7/8 (July and August): 99.

Spivak, G. C. (2001) 'Questioned on Translation: Adrift', *Public Culture*, 13.1: 13–22.

Vane, F. (1911) 'World Scouting and Peace', *The Anglo-Russian Literary Society Proceedings*, 62: 46–55.

Virilio, P. (1994) *The Vision Machine*, trans. J. Rose, Bloomington and Indianapolis: Indiana University Press.

Wells, H. G. (1904) 'The Conflict of Language' in *Anticipations of the Reactions of Mechanical and Scientific Progress upon Human Life and Thought*, London: Chapman and Hall: 83–94.

—— (1918) quoted in 'Zamenhof Memorial Meeting in London: Notable Tributes', *Esperanto Monthly* (June): 65.

Whyte, F. (1925) *The Life of W. T. Stead*, vol. II, London: Jonathan Cape.

Zamenhof, L. (1907) 'Esperanto and Jewish Ideals: Interview for the Jewish Chronicle with Dr Zamenhof', *Jewish Chronicle* (6 September): 16–18.

5 Globalization's Robinsonade

Cast Away and neo-liberal subject formation

Victor Li

The economic sphere, far from being devoid of emotions, has been on the contrary saturated with affect. [...] Emotional capitalism realigned emotional cultures, making the economic self emotional and emotions more closely harnessed to instrumental action.

(Illouz 2007: 23)

The title of this collection, *Rerouting the Postcolonial*, calls for a redirection or reconsideration of existing postcolonial critical approaches in order to respond to the changed conditions of an increasingly globalized world. Acknowledging such a call, I wish to argue that an adequate critical response to capitalist globalization would have to analyse not only its magnitude, scale and planetary implications, but also its relation to the more intimate domain of 'soul-making', as Gayatri Spivak once dubbed it. Any attempt at constructing a postcolonial counter-discourse to the neo-liberal ideology that drives globalization must try to understand how globalization has affected subject formation. How is the 'big picture' of globalization, the subject of much public attention, related to the private, individual subject at the other end of the scale? How can we, as David Harvey has urged, link the 'macro' discourse of globalization to the 'micro' discourse of the corporeal self? (2000: 1). Following Harvey's lead, I suggest that we can find in a popular Hollywood film a clear illustration of how the self is shaped by the ubiquitous neo-liberal ideology of globalization.

The box-office success of Robert Zemeckis's *Cast Away* (2000) is in part due to its depiction of human endurance and ingenuity in the face of natural adversity. In portraying a heroic castaway, the film resembles a 'Robinsonade', a narrative genre named after Daniel Defoe's classic tale of shipwreck and survival, *Robinson Crusoe*. Like Robinsonades, the film's focus on the theme of isolation and survival makes it appear to be more a work about humanity abandoned to nature than humanity shaped by society. Yet, as we shall see, *Cast Away*, like its famous precursor, is thoroughly informed by the ideological structures of its society. However isolated and bereft, the individual apparently cannot escape society's grasp. A critical reading of the film will show how the discourse of globalization is linked to the formation of a neo-liberal subject best described as 'the enterprise of oneself' (Gordon 1991: 44). I will argue, moreover, that the film's representation of subject formation not only obscures its neo-liberal provenance, but also hides America's forceful imperial presence in the world by portraying the (American) castaway's island as unpopulated and unvisited, thereby obviating the need to colonize a resistant indigenous people or combat the threats posed by others. Political economy and national interests are thus elided so that the film can focus solely on the theme of human survival, of one man's heroic struggle against the natural elements, and his desperation and despair.

Cast Away may seem, on casual viewing, to be about the subject's exit from globalization rather than its formative relation to the latter. In his review in *Sight and Sound*, Danny Leigh describes the film as a 'fable of loneliness and salvation' (2001: 38). Like Defoe's *Robinson Crusoe*, *Cast Away* portrays a man, Chuck Noland (Tom Hanks), stranded on a desert island traumatically separated from the life he knew as a globe-circling, trouble-shooting systems analyst for FedEx. Like Defoe's eponymous narrator, Noland manages to turn survival into self-renewal; his isolation enables his progress to self-reliance and self-understanding; his involuntary exile from FedEx's 'world on time' provides him with space to reflect on that world's enthrallment to systems efficiency while neglecting affective human values. Yet Noland's island life, like Crusoe's, is neither an escape from, nor a repudiation of the world. His isolation does not result in a regression to a 'natural' state of being; rather, again like Crusoe, he remains tied to the ideology and culture of his society. In his General Introduction of 1857 to *Grundrisse*, Marx criticized those interpretations of Robinsonades that regarded them as stories about the return to a natural life rather than the formation of bourgeois subjectivity:

> The individual and isolated hunter and fisherman [...] belongs to the unimaginative conceits of eighteenth-century Robinson-Crusoe-stories. These do not express [...] simply a reaction against over-refinement and a return to the misunderstood natural life [...]. What we are here faced with, rather, is the anticipation of 'bourgeois society'.
>
> (1973: 83)

Similarly, Peter Hulme's observation of Defoe's novel is also true of *Cast Away*: 'The parable of the self, remote from social and political concerns as it may seem, has very decisive social and political effects' (1986: 196). In the traces of the social and the political – obscured by the story of human endurance and survival – the articulation of globalization discourse to subject formation can be located. What the film shows is not the subject's exit from globalization, but his reconfiguration or redefinition by globalization's neo-liberal ideology.

We are first introduced to Chuck Noland as he attempts to spread FedEx's gospel to Russian workers who are clearly in need of its message of enterprise, speed, and efficiency. Everywhere in Moscow bronze plaques of Lenin are eagerly taken down in anticipation of economic liberalization. The triumph of global capitalism can be seen in Noland's take-charge managerial role in reshaping the Russian workplace and in his rewarding the young Russian boy who shows initiative in delivering Noland's FedEx parcel with visibly branded consumer goods such as a Snickers bar and a Panasonic CD player. The 'evil empire' of communism, it seems, has been toppled by the power of commodities in an ironic fulfillment of Marx's prophesy in *The Communist Manifesto*, that the Great Wall of China will be breached not by cannons but by goods.

Noland's first words capture perfectly the spirit of what David Harvey in *The Condition of Postmodernity* has described as the 'time-space compression' of global capitalism:

> Time rules over us without mercy, not caring if we are healthy or ill, hungry or drunk, Russian, American, or beings from Mars. It's like a fire; it can either destroy us or it can keep us warm. That's why every FedEx office has a clock – because we live or die by the clock. We never turn our back on it. And we never ever allow ourselves the sin of losing track of time.
>
> (*Cast Away*)

Later, Noland complains that the FedEx parcel he had mailed to himself from Memphis, Tennessee, has taken too long to reach him in Moscow: 'Eighty-seven hours is a shameful outrage. Eighty-seven hours is an eternity'. This early opening scene thus foregrounds one of globalization's central tenets, namely that technology has shrunk both space and time, making the globe a more interconnected place. Noland's lecture on the 'time-space compression' of globalization unknowingly echoes the words of Marx, one of the early theorists of globalization:

> [W]hile capital on one side strives to tear down every spatial barrier to intercourse, i.e. to exchange, and conquer the whole earth for its market, it strives on the other side to annihilate this space with time, i.e. to reduce to a minimum the time spent in motion from one place to another. [...] There appears here the universalizing tendency of capital, which distinguishes it from all previous stages of production.
>
> (1973: 539–40)

One of globalization's road warriors, Noland is clearly ruled by time. As a FedEx efficiency expert he not only has to serve the world on time, but his personal life is sacrificed to the service of time as well. His Christmas Eve dinner, for example, is interrupted when he is paged for another overseas assignment. Before he departs, Noland and his girlfriend, Kelly Frears (played by Helen Hunt), consult their respective calendars. 'You've got to be here for New Year's Eve', pleads Kelly. FedEx may be able to move 2.9 million pieces of mail daily all over the world, thus demonstrating what Noland describes as its 'perfect marriage of technology and systems management', but its success as a global company exacts a personal price in the form of a not-so-perfect relationship.

This demanding, pressurized world of deadlines and time-space management disappears when the FedEx plane crashes somewhere in the South Pacific and Noland, as the sole survivor, washes up on an uninhabited island.

William Broyles Jr's screenplay could not have scripted a more appropriate exit from globalization for its mobile transnational worker. Yet the remote island, far from being globalization's antithesis, remains tied to it. For *Cast Away* is not a negation of contemporary globalization but a fable of its reformation, thus resembling its eighteenth-century literary precursor, *Robinson Crusoe*. Like Defoe's novel, Robert Zemeckis's film focuses on the project of *Bildung*, the education and formation of the self. Pierre Macherey's description of *Robinson Crusoe* can also be applied to *Cast Away*:

> [I]n *Robinson Crusoe*, the fable and the image (the island) are the pretexts for a *lesson*: that history of the formation of a man, or rather his reformation (since it is a question of a second life, which takes shape against the distant ground of the first).
>
> (1978: 200)

The lesson of reformation, the chance at a second life, is implied by the film director's comments:

> *Cast Away* celebrates the idea that no matter how many obstacles are thrown into our paths, we will find ways to accept them. The story is not so much about the survival of a human being, but rather the survival of the human spirit and an illustration of the idea that surviving is easy, it's living that's difficult.
>
> (Zemeckis, 'Statement')

Zemeckis's distinction offers us an insight into the portrayal of the lifeworld's critical response to economic globalization. Living is more difficult and more important than surviving, the film insists, because self-realization is more essential than material or economic well-being, and self-understanding is more valuable than a purely instrumental rationality. Paradoxically, however, as I will argue, it is precisely the project of self-reformation and self-care, made possible by Noland's isolation from the demands of globalization, that also enables him to reenter the global economy as a better, more valuable citizen-worker. For in fact Noland remains a subject of globalization *on* or *off* the island. His very surname, one suspects, is a pun on the inescapability of globalization, a witty contraction of the John Donne tag: 'No man is an island'.

Like *Robinson Crusoe*, *Cast Away* portrays a difficult initiation into a new life. Mircea Eliade's description of the regenerative power of initiatory rituals fits Noland's redemptive experience:

> Even if the initiatory character of these ordeals is not apprehended as such, it remains true nonetheless that man becomes *himself* only after having solved a series of desperately difficult and even dangerous situations; that is after having undergone "tortures" and "deaths," followed by an awakening to another life, qualitatively different because regenerated.
>
> (cited in Novak 1983: 43)

Noland's island serves as the site of such an initiation; yet it does not yield the fable of natural innocence that Rousseau saw, for example, in *Robinson Crusoe* when he recommended it as the best book to commence Emile's education. Nor does it provide the allegorical signs of capital accumulation and possessive individualism that modern critics like Ian Watt (1957) have discerned in Defoe's novel. Instead, the island is a scene of instruction that problematizes Noland's unquestioning allegiance to time-space management and efficient productivity. Noland is educated into a new subjectivity not by the complete erasure of his former managerial *habitus*, but by being redefined and reoriented towards a more flexible acceptance of uncertainty, and a greater sensitivity to the value of human affect and emotion. His complete trust in systems management is transformed into a humbler and wiser recognition of the power of contingency; yet he remains capable of ingenious adaptation to change. Noland learns to question the meaning of a life ruled by the discipline of labour and time; yet, in true managerial fashion, he remains disciplined and rational enough to plan his escape from the island by calculating the number of lashings he needs to construct his raft and determining precisely the height of the tides and the direction of the wind. He may acknowledge the meaninglessness of a life ruled by the clock, yet he faithfully counts the number of days he has spent on the island, inscribing on a rock, before he makes his escape, the precise number: 1500 days. Initiation into a new life is thus not a rejection of capitalism's global subject but a renewal of human capital, that is, the retooling or reskilling of Noland.

It is interesting to note that *Cast Away*'s narrative of the profound transformation of an individual life resembles what business sociologists Jerald Hage and Charles H. Powers promote as 'role redefinition', the necessary transformation of routine scripted roles to more flexible and adaptable selves in a constantly changing and uncertain global environment. 'In post-industrial societies', they write, 'people periodically redefine roles in creative ways in order to be more adaptive to circumstantial conditions and more responsive to the needs of others' (1992: 198). Such a human resource view of role redefinition and adaptation to change as a form of self-enhancement supports Colin Gordon's Foucauldian description of the neo-liberal idea of the individual as a strategy of accumulation, as 'an entrepreneur of himself or herself':

> The idea of one's life as the enterprise of oneself implies that there is a sense in which one remains continuously employed in (at least) that one enterprise, and that it is a part of the continuous business of living to make adequate provision for the preservation, reproduction and reconstruction of one's human capital.
>
> (1991: 44)

A key feature of this neo-liberal enterprise of the self is the 'congruence it endeavours to achieve between a responsible and moral individual and an economic-actor' (Lemke 2001: 201). Neo-liberalism promotes the view that the proper conduct and care of the self should be regarded as seamlessly connected to the economy.

Noland's resourceful and inventive adaptation to the changed circumstances of his new island home can thus be seen as a subjective correlative of the new global economy's embrace of uncertainty as the opportunity for innovation and profit. The management guru Tom Peters, for example, has argued that:

> The times demand that flexibility and love of change replace our long standing penchant for mass production and mass markets, based as it is upon a relatively predictable environment now vanished. [...] Chaos and uncertainty will be market opportunities for the wise; capitalising on fleeting market anomalies will be the successful business's greatest accomplishment.
>
> (1987: 245)

Commenting on Peters's work, Pat O'Malley points out that 'uncertainty – in the shape of the entrepreneurial reliance on practical experience, inspiration and foresight rather than statistical calculation or the expert planning of economists – is central to profitability and good economic governance' (2000: 463). According to such an entrepreneurial philosophy, Noland's self-reliance and pragmatic adaptability to challenging conditions of change and uncertainty can only serve to enhance his value as a global professional. Neo-liberal globalization also calls for greater emphasis on the role of affect and emotion. Hage and Powers argue, for example, that in a post-industrial, globalizing economy,

> the growth in knowledge, the process of complexification, and the appearance of more creative minds with complex selves will call on people to be much more responsive to others, much more interactive. [...] [H]eightened levels of emotive communication are essential because societal change necessitates role redefinition; customizing roles can only be accomplished in an environment of interpersonal trust, and interpersonal trust is predicated on emotional communication and commitment.
>
> (1992: 93, 108)

Another sociologist, in a study of how New Age thinking has been embraced by 'soft capitalism', summarizes the new managerial philosophy thus:

> Most generally, the idea is to transform the values, experiences and to some extent the practices of what it is to *be* at work. The New Age Manager is imbued with new qualities and virtues [...]. These have to do with intrinsic wisdom, authentic creativity, self-responsibility, genuine energy, love and so on. The significance of work is transformed in that it is conceived as providing the opportunity to work on "oneself." It becomes a spiritual discipline.
>
> (Heelas cited in Thrift 1998: 53)

Such a role redefinition, which is also an enhancement of human capital, occurs to Noland as he is transformed from a compulsive perfectionist into a more caring person in whom instrumental rationality is now balanced by emotional communication and commitment. The man who used to believe that we must never commit the sin of turning our back on time, now realizes that the greatest sin is to turn our back on others. Thus we see him towards the end of the film apologizing to his colleague Stan and to his girlfriend Kelly for not giving them enough of his time.

Noland's new emotional self is also evident in his personalized delivery of the talismanic FedEx package he kept with him throughout his ordeal on the island. To the package he attaches a personal, affect-laden note: 'This package saved my life. Thank you.' This may be service with a personal touch, but it also resembles the strategic use of affect advocated in a book appropriately titled *Emotion Marketing*. The authors, Scott Robinette and Clare Brand, both Hallmark executives, note that people 'are emotional creatures who have a deep rooted need to connect with each other and the world around them'. They point out that:

> By using a more personal, emotion-driven communication, Hallmark reduced costs, increased sales and built customer loyalty. [...] A strong emotional competence will transcend consumers' rational thoughts and appeal to their hearts. And the heart, after all, is where purchase decisions are made and bonds between company and consumer are established.
>
> (cited in Schacter 2001: M1)

Along the same lines, in an article on management trends, we learn that business schools are emphasizing the importance of emotion and human relationships, often using Shakespeare's plays as teaching texts:

> Top managers are increasingly expected to supplement traditional technical and financial know-how with "soft skills" that make them adept at human interaction. That has corporate development programs and business schools scurrying to impart abstract notions like self-awareness, empathy, creativity and relationship-building.
>
> (Woodruff 2001: M2)

If 'soft skills have hard consequences for the bottom line', as the article also notes, then Noland's new emotional subjectivity will stand him in good stead as he reenters the corporate world.

The film does not, of course, forcefully foreground the neo-liberal agenda I have just described. The enterprise of the self is presented with its economic or market aspects obscured or muted. On the island, Noland's enterprise is not seen as economic productivity or capital accumulation but as the reformation or redemption of the self. With reference to Robert Zemeckis's distinction between the survival of the human being and the survival of the human spirit, it is spirit not matter that ultimately counts in a concern seemingly unrelated to cultural and economic globalization. Nevertheless, Noland's lessons learnt during his island ordeal are the same ones that neo-liberal versions of governance value and human resource experts promote. John Richetti's comment on *Robinson Crusoe* thus applies equally to *Cast Away*: 'The long haul toward the island and back eventually is a journey into "nature" to bring back an acceptable version of official ideology' (1975: 27).

As a parable of initiation and rebirth, *Cast Away* paradoxically sees privation as the condition of renewal, and helplessness as an opportunity for securing better control. What one can call Noland's 'de-globalization', his isolation from the world, is, at the same time, what enables his 'reglobalization', his reentry into the world as a better citizen-worker, more flexible and adaptable, more empathetic and caring. According to the film's narrative logic, then, Noland's helplessness is the paradoxical precondition for his redemption. This paradox also informs the film's commitment to visual realism. Mimetic faithfulness to the depiction of Noland's isolation and despair was carried to great lengths during the film's production. The film was shot under difficult natural conditions on a remote Fijian island and, for over an hour, depicting Noland's stay on the island, no sound track was employed – a commitment to verisimilitude rather daring for a mainstream film. The film's realism even demanded the shutting down of production for a year to enable Tom Hanks, who plays Chuck Noland, to shed 60 pounds. But its realistic portrayal of helplessness is made possible only because of its resourcefulness and inventive control. Representing helplessness requires highly organized and disciplined practices: Tom Hanks's supervised weight loss, transporting film equipment to a remote location, filming in high surf, or using muslin and Griffolyn bounces to direct natural sunlight during daytime shoots (see Holben 2001: 38–53). Thus, just as Noland remains tied to the neo-liberal discipline of the self even when he is marooned on his uninhabited island, so too the film never relinquishes its control over the construction of that self even when it faithfully reproduces a scene of helplessness.

In their book *Empire* (2000), Michael Hardt and Antonio Negri, drawing on Gilles Deleuze's work, describe the new political order of globalization as a society of control which produces a new subjectivity that is not fixed anywhere but that modulates and flexibly extends everywhere, carrying with it the immanent disciplinary logic of capital (2000: 23–7, 329–32). Chuck Noland, on his remote island, is not outside but still fully within this expansive and flexible regime of subjectivity. Or, to put it another way: You can take Noland out of the global, but you can't take the global out of Noland – not even on his desert isle.

A postcolonial analysis seeking to uncover resistance to neo-imperial domination will not find a point of entry into *Cast Away*, whereas an approach such as Hardt and Negri's, informed by Foucault's work on biopolitics and Deleuze's on societies of control, can critically detect in the film's investment in self-reliance and self-improvement signs of neo-liberal subject formation and discipline. Noland, for example, is emphatically not shown preserving or enhancing his human capital at the expense of the natural environment or other human beings. The recognizable postcolonial paradigm which critiques the exploitation of nature or the oppression of others does not appear. In fact, unlike *Robinson Crusoe* or contemporary revisionary Robinsonades like Michel Tournier's (1997) (*Friday*) *Vendredi* or J.M. Coetzee's *Foe*, *Cast Away* does not portray political struggles, forms of resistance, or conflicts over recognition. Problems of race, gender, or sexuality do not present themselves on Noland's island. No Friday or Susan Barton materializes to trouble Noland's self-redemption. The absence of a Friday figure is especially noteworthy. Both Robert Zemeckis, the film's director, and William Broyles, author of the screenplay, obviously took a risk in not having Noland engage in conflict with a threatening Other; but by surrendering the opportunity for dramatic intensity through the portrayal of human conflict, the film is able to concentrate on Noland's individual struggle and redemption, thereby avoiding being viewed as a political allegory that examines the workings of power and domination.

By contrast, the presence of Friday in Robinsonades like Coetzee's or Tournier's immediately raises issues of domination, conflict, and violence. In Coetzee's *Foe*, for instance, Friday, though seemingly subjugated or domesticated by Cruso and Susan Barton, remains nonetheless a stubbornly resistant figure whose enigmatic muteness defeats all attempts at communication with him, retrieving information from him, or turning him into what Cruso or Susan Barton would recognize as a fully human subject. As the latter remarks: '[T]he story of Friday [...] is properly not a story but a puzzle or hole in the narrative' (Coetzee 1987: 121). The civilizing mission has clearly failed in Friday's case. Friday's silence frustrates all hermeneutic enquiries and obstructs all efforts at representing it. Derek Attridge points out further that 'there are indications -- which could never, for us, be wholly legible – that Friday is in fact *subverting* the master discourse with his multiply interpretable graphics' (2004: 87). Gayatri Spivak has notably described Friday as 'the unemphatic agent of withholding in the text', the native who will not 'yield his "voice"', 'the curious guardian at the margin who will not inform', the figure who will resist codification by marking the limits of western or metropolitan knowledge regimes (1999: 190).

If Coetzee's Friday resists epistemic capture by Cruso, Susan Barton, Foe, and even the reader, then Tournier's Vendredi (Friday) resists Robinson's view of what the island of Speranza should be: first, by negating it, and then by reconstructing it. A new beginning becomes possible after Friday's careless smoking causes an accidental explosion that destroys the orderly world Robinson had so carefully and conscientiously constructed and cultivated. The sober, methodical order imposed by the Englishman gives way to the 'entirely different realm' of the 'laughing, exuberant, uninhibited native of a warmer clime'. The narrative continues:

> having released him [Robinson] from his earthly bonds, Friday would now show him the way to *something else*, substituting for an existence he had found intolerable a new order which Robinson longed to discover. A new Robinson was sloughing off his old skin, fully prepared to accept the decay of his cultivated island and, at the heels of an unthinking guide, enter upon an unknown road.

> (1987: 180)

Revising the master–servant relationship of Crusoe and Friday in Defoe's text, Tournier also reverses the original's pedagogical trajectory; it is Friday who now instructs Robinson in the art of living.

Cast Away's uniqueness as a revisionary Robinsonade consists of Friday's absence. In fact, no human being, predatory animal, or even footprint disturbs Noland's solitude. Instead of Friday, Noland has Wilson, a fetishized volleyball, painted in Noland's own blood, with a face resembling Bart Simpson's; instead of Susan Barton, Noland has a picture of Kelly Frears. Both volleyball and picture are inanimate and mute; they are subalterns who can truly neither speak, question nor challenge Noland's enterprise of the self. Focusing on Noland's struggle for self-redemption, the film not only omits the brutal competitiveness of the global market, but also screens out the political, social and cultural conflicts that riddle our world. We are left, then, with a film ostensibly about one man's heroic struggle for survival, the similarity of which to the neo-liberal ideology of self-governmentality and the formation of a new global subject equipped with new values and virtues we have traced. The film's message of self-improvement thus perfectly represents a 'soft' capitalism that has no desire to colonize or antagonize, and that relies for its power on the lure of goods and the language of care, improvement, and rights.

Yet, despite its indirect representation of still influential neo-liberal ideas of globalization, *Cast Away*, released in 2000, cannot but appear anachronistic in our post-9/11 world. Its view of globalization as nationless, antagonism-free, and universal – what Hardt and Negri in their book, also published in 2000, describe as the borderless, smooth space of Empire – can no longer be maintained, because the borderless, one-world appeal of 'soft' capitalism hardened into the striated, nation-based fears that pushed the military forces of America and its allies into Iraq and Afghanistan. In fact, *Cast Away's* very refusal to represent conflict with the Other is, arguably, the film's repression of the troubling reality of military force and neo-imperial domination that exists in our world, a reality that soft capitalism too would rather ignore, deny, or wish away. The absence of Friday on Noland's island is thus the fearful political unconscious of the film.

It may be the case that postcolonial theory's emphasis on resistance to the neo-imperial power of nation-states cannot fully address the film's neo-liberal biopolitics which skilfully articulates the idea of self-improvement and development to the global spread of 'soft' capitalism. Taking its cue from Foucault, Deleuze, or Hardt and Negri, a critique of neo-liberal globalization that astutely exposes the links between the enterprise of the self and the enterprise of capital must nevertheless turn again to postcolonial theory's focus on resistance if it wishes to account for the film's political unconscious, its deliberate disavowal of conflict or competition with the Other. In her contribution to this collection, Diana Brydon has persuasively argued that postcolonial theory must rethink its engagement with contemporary global imaginaries and subjectivities. The thrust of my essay clearly supports such a rethinking or rerouting. But, at the same time, I find it important to affirm dialectically that the necessary rerouting of postcolonial theory through an analysis of neo-liberal subject formation requires an equally necessary return to its central axiomatic, which insists that the continuing existence of oppressive asymmetries of power calls for oppositional strategies that will speak truth to power. What is needed, therefore, is a postcolonial criticism supple enough to deal with both 'soft' global capitalism as well as the hard fist it finds increasingly hard to conceal.

Bibliography

Attridge, D. (2004) *J. M. Coetzee and the Ethics of Reading*, Chicago: University of Chicago Press.

Cast Away (2000) Dir. Robert Zemeckis, with Tom Hanks and Helen Hunt, Dreamworks/ Twentieth Century Fox.

Coetzee, J. M. (1987) *Foe*, London: Penguin.

Defoe, D. (1965 [1719]) *The Life and Adventures of Robinson Crusoe*, ed. A. Ross, Harmondsworth: Penguin.

Gordon, C. (1991) 'Governmental rationality: an introduction', in G. Burchell, C. Gordon and P. Miller (eds) *The Foucault Effect: Studies in Governmentality*, Chicago: University of Chicago Press.

Hage, J. and Powers, C. H. (1992) *Post-Industrial Lives: Roles and Relationships in the 21st Century*, Newbury Park, Calif.: Sage.

Hardt, M. and Negri, A. (2000) *Empire*, Cambridge, Mass.: Harvard University Press.

Harvey, D. (2000) *Spaces of Hope*, Berkeley: University of California Press.

—— (1989) *The Condition of Postmodernity*, Oxford: Blackwell.

Holben, J. (2001) 'Sole Survivor', *American Cinematographer*, 82.1: 38–53.

Hulme, P. (1986) *Colonial Encounters: Europe and the Native Caribbean, 1492–1797*, London: Methuen.

Illouz, E. (2007) *Cold Intimacies: The Making of Emotional Capitalism*, Cambridge: Polity.

Leigh, D. (2001) 'Review of *Cast Away*', *Sight and Sound*, 11.2: 37–8.

Lemke, T. (2001) '"The Birth of Bio-politics": Michel Foucault's Lecture at the College de France on Neo-liberal Governmentality', *Economy and Society*, 30.2: 190–207.

Macherey, P. (1978) *A Theory of Literary Production*, trans. G. Wall, London: Routledge and Kegan Paul.

Marx, K. (1973) *Grundrisse: Foundations of the Critique of Political Economy*, trans. M. Nicolaus, New York: Random House.

Novak, M. E. (1983) *Realism, Myth, and History in Defoe's Fiction*, Lincoln: University of Nebraska Press.

O'Malley, P. (2000) 'Uncertain Subjects: Risks, Liberalism and Contract', *Economy and Society*, 29.4: 460–84.

Peters, T. (1987) *Thriving on Chaos: Handbook for a Management Revolution*, New York: Knopf.

Richetti, J. (1975) *Defoe's Narratives: Situations and Structures*, Oxford: Clarendon Press.

Schacter, H. (2001) 'Get emotional with customers', review of *Emotion Marketing* by Scott Robinette and Clare Brand, *The Globe and Mail*, 18 April: M1.

Spivak, G. C. (1999) *A Critique of Postcolonial Reason: Toward a History of the Vanishing Present*, Cambridge, Mass.: Harvard University Press.

Thrift, N. (1998) 'The Rise of Soft Capitalism', in A. Herod, G. Ó. Tuathail and S. M. Roberts (eds) *Unruly World? Globalization, Governance and Geography*, London: Routledge, 1998.

Tournier, M. (1997) *Friday*, trans. N. Denny, Baltimore: Johns Hopkins University Press.

Watt, I. (1957) *The Rise of the Novel: Studies in Defoe, Richardson, and Fielding*, Berkeley: University of California Press.

Woodruff, D. (2001) 'Shakespeare seen to teach "soft skills"', *The Globe and Mail*, 8 Aug.: M2.

Zemeckis, R. (2000) 'Statement on *Cast Away*'. Online. Available http: <http:www.movieweb.com/movie/castaway/index.html> (accessed 6 July 2001).

6   Transnation

Bill Ashcroft

In February 2008, a month when all Chinese travel back to their families for the Lunar New Year celebration, more than *one million* migrant workers were stranded by snowstorms. Waiting for days at train stations for the possibility of a rare train to their home village, many of them did not move from the queue to eat or relieve themselves. This number of people is more than the populations of a third of the member states of the United Nations. But they were *migrants* and they were *inside* their own country. Forced to live and work in a space between 'home' and the nation-state, they were now stranded. They were, to all intents and purposes, a diaspora. They were away from home, within the nation, and this fact may force us to rethink the concept of the nation-state.

It may also force us to think about the place of post-colonial studies in a world in which the Chinese continental empire is one of the world's richest countries. Should we, and if so, how should we, include China? This astonishing displacement of people is one instance of the message India and China have been sending for some time: that the nation is not the state – it is a transnation. Although China is an empire operating as a nation and therefore it may not yet be the time to include China in post-colonial literary studies, very few cultural engagements with *Chinese* imperialism are either in circulation or available for study. But if the theoretical techniques of post-colonial studies are to take on the challenge of global culture, it is time to consider the message of that bitter winter: no nation is synonymous with the state – and before national borders have been crossed, the national subject is already the subject of a transnation.[1]

This is particularly interesting in these global times in which the nation has been roundly disparaged. The cultural turn in globalization studies in the 1990s was driven by post-colonial discourse, and a strategic feature of this intervention was the critique of the nation. The nation (by which most critics have meant the nation-state) has been a common target for post-colonial studies as an *exclusionary*, rather than inclusive, political formation. Newly independent nations have, with numbing regularity, perpetuated colonial power by reinstating the administrative structures of imperial control. But globalization widened the attack on the nation. Whereas, in the old global order, the nation was the reality and category that enabled the socialization of subjects, and hence the structuring of cultures, in today's globalized world, the nation has become a near-absent structure. At least this was the case until the global financial crisis of 2008. Suddenly, with corporations dissolving and the share market plummeting, it was the nation-state and national governments that were called to the rescue.

Since then the nation-state has reasserted its global viability as an economic stabilizer. However, the nation as an open *cultural* site, a transnational site, needs to be reconsidered principally because of the effects of the two mega-cultures: India and China. It is these two societies that will assert the prominence of economies in the twenty-first century. And the phenomenon of their emergence may also force us to reconsider the importance of the nation as a cultural phenomenon, a horizontal reality – distinct from the vertical authority of the state. In this horizontal reality culture still escapes the bounded *national* society, *exceeding* the boundaries of the nation state and operating beyond its political strictures through the medium of the local. This excess is the transnation.

'Transnation' appears at first to be an old term based on the idea of the transnational. But I coin the term to refer to much more than 'the international', or 'the transnational', which might more properly be conceived as a relation between states, a crossing of borders or a cultural or political interplay between national cultures. It is also distinct from the categories of 'diaspora' and 'cosmopolitanism' which fail, on the whole, to account for subjects who may at various times identify with the nation, ethnicity, religion, family or tribe, who may know nothing of the workings of the state except for their experience of local officials. They may travel beyond national borders or stay within them, and yet never be in contact with other cultural subjects. But their experience provides the constant theme of the ambiguous relation between the nation and the state. Transnation is the fluid, migrating *outside* of the state that begins *within* the nation. This 'outside' is geographical, cultural and conceptual, and is possibly most obvious in India where the 'nation' is the perpetual scene of *translation*, but translation is but one example of the movement, the 'betweenness' by which the subjects of the transnation are constituted. The transnation is a way of talking about subjects in their ordinary lives, subjects who live in between the categories by which subjectivity is normally constituted.

The idea of a 'transnation' disrupts and scatters the construct of centre and periphery, which continues, after Wallerstein (1974; 1980), to maintain its hold on our understanding of the structure of global relations. If we think of the 'transnation' extending beyond the geographical, political, administrative and even imaginative boundaries of the state, both within and beyond the boundaries of the nation, we discover it as a space in which those boundaries are disrupted, in which national and cultural affiliations are superseded, in which binaries of centre and periphery, national self and other are dissolved. This is because, most noticeably in the case of China and India, the nation is already a migratory and even diasporic aggregation of flows and convergences, both within and without state boundaries. Motwani has made a compelling, if provocative, claim for the migratory adventures of Indian peoples since about 8000 BC, migrations as far as Mexico, Turkey, Bali, as well as the obvious migrations to South East Asia (2004: 40). His investigations challenge the very profound and resilient linking of Indian identity with the geographical Bharat (the ancient term for the Holy land of the Hindus). For him, the Indian people have always been migratory and explora-tory; flow rather than stasis is their main cultural characteristic.

The alternative to this is the argument linking identity firmly with place. Kapil Kapoor 2004 makes such a geographical argument very forcibly, contending that 'The Indian identity begins and ends in geography' – that the land called Bharat [Hindu Holy Land] is its cultural and spiritual 'mother' (see Pal and Chakraborty 2004: 30–1). This is a very pronounced restatement of what we might call the centripetal view of national identity, one firmly grounded in the belief of the simultaneity of Hindu religious practice and Indian identity, and in this respect one pole of a continuing argument about the nature of cultural identity itself. According to this, the Indian diaspora is detached from the great mother and therefore from home, marking a people in a state of perpetual not-at-homeness. This argument fails to recognize that internal diaspora discussed by Anjali Gera Roy (2005), such as the Punjab diaspora in India, which may imply an alienation *within* the great mother. The great centrality of the Hindu self is already a travelling self. Subjectivity is always a matter of flow, of locations, or of subject *positions* rather than subjectivities (Hall 1990: 226)

Transnation and diaspora

If the transnation is not synonymous with what we understand as the 'transna-tional', it also distinguishes itself from diaspora. A route for post-colonial studies has long appeared to lie in the dispersal and constant movement of diasporic populations who adopt English as a form of cultural articulation. Ironically, the theoretical reappearance of the nation may provide us with a way to cut through the arguments surrounding the concept of diaspora. I say ironically, because this is a community understood as fundamentally absent from the nation, crippled by absence, loss and alienation. But the constitution of the nation as already in some way transnational circumvents this.

The definition of 'diaspora' has been a site of contestation since the 1970s. In the very first issue of the journal *Diaspora* William Safran defined diaspora thus:

> The concept of diaspora [can] be applied to expatriate minority communi-ties whose members share several of the following characteristics: (1) they, or their ancestors, have been dispersed from a specific original 'centre' to two or more 'peripheral' or foreign regions; (2) they retain a collective memory, vision or myth about their original homeland – its physical location, history and achievements; (3) they believe that they are not – and perhaps cannot be – fully accepted by their host society and therefore feel partly alienated and insulated from it; (4) they regard their ancestral homeland as their true, ideal home and the place to which they or their descendents would (or should) eventually return – when conditions are appropriate; (5) they believe they should collectively, be committed to the maintenance or restoration

of their homeland and to its safety and prosperity; and (6) they continue to relate, personally or vicariously, to that homeland in one way or another, and their ethnocommunal consciousness and solidarity are importantly defined by the existence of such a relationship.

(1991: 83)

This definition, because of its scope, has provided something for every theorist to attack ever since. Thus, James Clifford and Paul Gilroy questioned the notion that diasporas are dispersed from a centre, citing the circulatory movements of indigenous groups in the Pacific and the Black populations in the Atlantic; the collective memory of an original homeland has no meaning for the black diaspora in the Americas; the idea that they cannot be fully accepted does not apply to the 'third wave' of professional transnational immigrants. The commitment to a homeland decreases rapidly for the second and third generation diaspora. Indeed, according to prevalent definitions of diaspora, one of its characteristic conditions is that of absence and loss, of alienation and not-at-homeness. Yet clearly this experience of exile and loss does not adequately describe the experience of all diasporic subjects, nor of any subject all the time. Nor does it accommodate the most pronounced feature of global culture – the rapidly increasing ability to travel back and forth between 'homes'. Thus the concept of diaspora has been a constant source of argument, and a rapidly changing phenomenon, for the last thirty-five years. Definitions of diaspora have had to keep constantly on the move to keep pace with their subject (see Braziel and Mannur 2003, Joseph and Wilson 2006). In rejecting the habitual assumption of diaspora studies that diasporic populations are characterized by absence and loss, I may appear to overlook the very great number of people who have been exiled from a sense of home. In Paul Gilroy's terms, we may appear to be in danger of assuming that all migratory populations are 'convivial' rather than 'melancholic' (Gilroy 2004). But, on the contrary, whether refugees in the most perilous of circumstances, or middle class cultural producers who feel at home in global travel, whether convivial or melancholic, all subjects of the transnation reveal at least some level of ability to move between the structures of the state. We can't deny the fact that the state can arrest this capacity, that millions of people have been trapped by the hysteria of xenophobia and 'border protection'. But the mobility of the transnation *need not* be a permanent condition of displacement, loss and exile. On the other hand, exile, as a condition of displacement, begins *within* the nation, it does not begin once borders have been crossed. The mobility and in-betweenness of the transnation injects the principle of hope into the equation.

Transnation and cosmopolitanism

As chapters by Robert Spencer, Simon Gikandi and Kaori Nagai in this volume indicate, the term 'cosmopolitanism' is growing in popularity. There can be little doubt that cosmopolitanism is being reinvented as the latest

Grand-Theory-of-Global-Cultural-Diversity and many post-colonial theorists have enthusiastically followed Appiah and Bhabha's adoption of this notoriously slippery concept, first because it is a much more politically acceptable term for multiculturalism, but also because it appears to have at its centre a profoundly attractive ethical dimension. Indeed, Appiah's book, subtitled *Ethics in a World of Strangers* (2007), seems to be entirely about ethics – ethics that are very culturally situated. 'Cosmopolitan ethics' have a venerable history, For Kant (1795), cosmopolitanism is a 'universally philanthropic' policy that would ensure peace among nations and grant individuals the right to international hospitality or 'the right of a stranger not to be treated with hostility when he arrives on someone else's territory' ('Perpetual Peace'). Ulf Hannerz defines the cosmopolitan in a way that seems little different from Levinas's view of ethics, when he says: 'A more genuine cosmopolitanism is first of all an orientation, a willingness to engage with the Other. It entails an intellectual and aesthetic openness toward divergent cultural experiences, a search for contrasts rather than uniformity' (1996: 103). This is directly reminiscent of Levinas in *Totality and Infinity* when he suggests that 'to *receive* from the Other beyond the capacity of the I' is 'to have the idea of infinity' (1969: 51). Levinas's definition of ethics as a relation to the Other has become the cornerstone of most discussions of ethics in literature and this dimension of human relations is critically important to post-colonial studies.

The ethical dimension of cosmopolitan theory is its great strength and I admire its utopian orientation. But it constructs cosmopolitanism as an attitude of mind rather than a subject position. It is 'a perspective, a state of mind [...] a mode of managing meaning' (Hannerz 1996: 102). If the ethical defines the cosmopolitan, then it is located in an empty space, a *polis* that is not 'of the *cosmos*', but of nowhere, a protean term amenable to almost any meaning. Attractive though the ethical dimension is, it doesn't solve the problem of who can be allowed into the cosmopolitan club, nor does it resolve the incipient problem of cosmopolitan theory – the attempt by the (mainly) US academy to reinstate the imperial metropolis at the centre of post-colonial discussion.

Cosmopolitan is a useful adjective but a failure as a noun. Hong Kong and Shanghai may be described as 'cosmopolitan spaces'; But who is 'the cosmopolitan'? Within the cultural space of the 'cosmopolitan city', Which category of its citizens may be constituted cosmopolitan subjects? Which narrative of identity in the transitional, open and exogenous space of the world city frames a cosmopolitan subject? Many other cosmopolitanisms, such as approaches to 'cosmopolitan pedagogy', may be instrumental in creating cultural openness in readers, but do they create 'cosmopolitans'? Most theorists have decried the lingering connotation of urbanity, sophistication and wealth that the term carries with it, although Appiah believes the term can be 'rescued' (xiv). But none of the many attempts to define the term has managed to entirely rid itself of the fact that the person who is able to travel freely, to experience and participate in other cultures for long periods, who has the time to engage with the Other in a 'cosmopolitan' way, must almost inevitably be a person with considerable material resources.

This issue becomes clearer when Hannerz himself engages in a boundary-marking exercise, recounting the story of

> Lagos market-women [who] board London-bound planes with loose-fitting gowns, which enable them to travel with dried fish tied to their thighs and upper arms. The dried fish is presumably sold to their countrymen in London; on the return trip, the women carry similarly concealed bundles of frozen fish sticks, dried milk, and baby clothes, all of which are in great demand in Lagos. London is a consumer's [...] paradise for Nigerians.
>
> (1996: 103)

Hannerz remarks, quite correctly I think, that these are not cosmopolitans and their activities 'hardly go beyond the horizons of urban Nigerian culture, as it now is' (103). But these are examples of the subjects of most interest to post-colonial studies, subjects who are localized but mobile, working in and through the structures of the state, subjects who demonstrate agency within the apparently momentous movements of global flows and capital. Clearly, cosmopolitans are not defined by a particular subject position but by an orientation to the Other and to diversity. Cosmopolitans, although they tend to be footloose, are not *necessarily* immigrants, travellers, expatriates or exiles; they are not necessarily diasporic subjects, they almost certainly aren't refugees or labour migrants, and, according to Appiah, are generally not anthropologists. Yet these are the people who inhabit the transnation.

When Breckenridge *et al.* propose in the introduction to *Cosmopolitanism* that 'cosmopolitanism be considered in the plural as cosmopolitanisms' (2002: 8), they mean that cosmopolitanism should not be identified with 'the singular, privileged location of European thought' (2002: 9). This attempts to shake off the baggage carried by the concept, such as John Stuart Mills's contention in *Political Economy* that 'capital is becoming more and more cosmopolitan' (cited Robbins 1992: 171). It is an attempt to exorcize the ghost of the *flaneur*, to open cosmopolitanism itself to plurality. Yet they also declare that '[r]efugees, peoples of the diaspora and migrants and exiles represent *the* spirit of the cosmopolitical community' (2002: 6). Cosmopolitanisms have *one* spirit and one community, one apparently not represented by those who do not cross borders of one kind or another. Yet we do well to remember that distances and differences exist within localities.

The subjects in the transnation

People are different, and differences multiply the more people we meet, placing an ethical responsibility on us to be open to difference. But even more interesting is the extent to which people appropriate and maintain difference within themselves, by negotiating different subject positions. While the concepts of 'third space' and transculturality are tried and tested in post-colonial studies, the Lagos market women mentioned by Hannerz indicate that the subjects of the transnation occupy a perpetual in-between space, an in-betweenness that is negotiable and shifting, demonstrating the actual agency of people as they navigate the structures of the state. Subjects in the transnation are not necessarily transnational subjects. But they occupy what Fanon calls 'the zone of occult instability where the people dwell' (1963: 182–3).

'In-betweenness' is perhaps best exemplified in that most essentialized of subject positions – the indigenous. We can see this by addressing one image, an image that encapsulates the desire of the indigenous subject to escape the boundaries of indigenous representation – Brenda Croft's *Irrisistable* (irresistible). As she says:

> I am aware that as I look through magazines they are not of me, for me. The models are white and pure, or black and foreign, and/or exotic, not from here not of me. I turn on the television and the advertisements make me feel that I have travelled to some other country, I am not at home.
>
> (quoted in Perkins 1996: 92)

Ironically, for Croft, the sense of being 'at home' lies in a space of in-betweenness outside predictable stereotypical representations. In-betweenness is not a state of suspended subjectivity, and not really the 'Third Space of Enunciation', but a state of fluidity, of porous boundaries, of travel between subject positions. Even in this most reified, apparently 'located' and therefore static of subject positions, the ubiquity of travel, both spatial and metaphoric, becomes apparent.

'In-betweenness' circumvents the problematic, organic nature of that most contentious term: 'hybridity'. It also gets closer to the actual contingent and liminal state of all contemporary subjects. But it still suggests location without acknowledging the activity of subjects in their interstitial subjectivity. I prefer the term elaborated by James Clifford (2000): 'articulation'. Rather than an organic hybrid:

> The whole is more like a cyborg, or a political coalition. The elements are more contingent. A body could have three arms or one arm depending on the context. It can hook elements of its structure onto elements of another structure often in unexpected ways [...] the whole question of authenticity or inauthenticity is set aside. There is no problem in picking up and rehooking to your structure something that had either been blown off, forgotten, or had been taken off for tactical reasons. You can reconstruct yourself.
>
> (Borofsky 2000: 97)

When we use the term articulation, then, we don't fall into the trap of thinking of 'in-betweenness' as being lost or undecided or absent, as being *unheimlich*. Clifford showed how the people of the Pacific have perfected the art of cultural articulation, but it is true of all diasporic subjects in this radically moving and migrating world. Reconstructing yourself includes 'hooking on' or discarding nationality, tradition, modernity, religion in ways that confound accepted notions of identity.

After Appadurai (1996) we are inclined to use the terms 'fluidity' and 'flows' when describing global culture and even diasporic subjectivity itself. But the idea of 'articulation' returns us to the rather spasmodic and contingent way in which subjects 'hook on' the various subject positions they may occupy, returning us to the very powerful element of individual agency in the process. Articulation may better explain the ways in which those Lagos market women navigate the contingencies of identity by *articulating* different subject positions strategically, not as cosmopolitans, but as navigators.

The space of the transnation

So the concept of 'the' transnation I am proposing is composed not only of diasporas, but of the rhizomic interplay of travelling subjects *within* as well as between nations. This space within and beyond the state might best be described by Deleuze and Guattari's term 'smooth space'. The distinction between 'smooth space' and 'striated space' seems odd at first, but they explain it with a very concrete image: the contrast between a woven textile and felt. A textile fabric is composed of interwoven vertical and horizontal components, warp and woof, a delimited and organized structure that Plato used as a paradigm for 'royal science', 'the art of governing people or operating the state's apparatus' (2004: 475). Felt, on the other hand is a supple solid, more like an 'anti-fabric'. It is an entanglement of fibres rather than a weave, one obtained by rolling the block of fibres back and forth, entangling, rather than weaving them. It is 'smooth' without being 'homogeneous'.

Smooth space, for Deleuze and Guattari, in contrast to 'striated space' or ordered space,

> is a space of affects, more than one of properties. It is haptic rather than optical perception. Whereas in the striated [space] forms organize a matter, in the smooth [space] materials signal forces and serve as symptoms for them. It is an intensive rather than extensive space, one of distances, not of measures and properties. Intense instead of Extensio.
>
> (2004: 528)

One negotiates with smooth space by engaging with it immediately, being affected and transformed by it so that one's perceptions become indistinct from the very forces and matter that constitute smooth space. One's body becomes indistinct with smooth space's body; there are no organs and discrete functions but the flow and gathering of forces.

Yet smooth space is not separate from striated space. Smooth space takes form when the striated space of government institutions, fixed concepts and essentialized peoples are broken into their composing forces, caught up in a swirling whirlpool that is capable of mixing these forces in new ways to produce monsters that may *defy* the categorizing machines of the institutions of striated space. It is the possibility for the emergence of new and different kinds of subjects and spaces that makes smooth space a space of potentiality, a space where a people and a nation yet to be known may emerge. Smooth space indeed expresses a great intensity or depth that is beyond the measures of governed divisions, like the division of labour between thinking and acting, theory and practice.

So what is the relation between smooth space and striated space when we use these terms to describe the nation? Let us think for a minute of Nehru – a man determined to bring India into the striated space of modernity, to establish the nation as the functional equivalent of the state. And what happened? History declares his unambiguous success. But if we think of the smooth space of the nation circulating around the striated space of the state, India continued its heterogeneous life – as a *trans*nation – regardless of nationalism, regardless of internationalism, in what we can understand as an alternative modernity that had little to do with the state's management. A good example of this is the *harijan* or 'untouchable' Dr B. M. Ambedkar, who was instrumental in framing the Indian Constitution and in particular confirming Article 17, which abolished Untouchability. But there is a dual irony here: a person from the margins of national society participates in framing state legislation; but that legislation has little effect on *attitudes* to caste in the nation.

Dr Ambedkar shows us that smooth space is not separate from striated space, because as a *harijan* legislator he embodies their conjunction and contradiction. The smooth space of the nation exists alongside, between, even within the striated space of the state. But it is not necessarily liberatory. 'Never believe that a smooth space will suffice to save us' (2004: 500), urge Deleuze and Guattari, and we see this very clearly in the case of the Untouchables. Smooth space may be the space of habit, prejudice and hostility. Yet by its very existence the smooth space of the transnation challenges, because it mostly ignores, exceeds, surrounds and interpenetrates, the striated space of the state. It is not in itself liberatory, but it is the medium of liberation, because it is the medium of the glocal.

Hardt and Negri offer a much more utopian view of what I would call the transnation and Deleuze would call 'smooth space'. This is the collectivity they call 'the multitude'. The multitude transcends geographical, historical and class boundaries, but is the collectivity in which the utopian hope of liberation is completely and optimistically focused. Another way of putting this is that the multitude, whose province is the local, is both the field of operation of globalization and the origin of its transformation, and hence the agent of the potential destruction of Empire because Empire cannot exist without it.

> The movements of the multitude designate new space and its journeys [...] establish new residences. Autonomous movement is what defines the place proper to the multitude. [...] A new geography is established by the multitude as the productive flows of bodies define new rivers and ports. The cities of the earth will become great deposits of cooperating humanity and locomotives for circulation, temporary residences and networks of the mass distribution of living humanity.
>
> (Hardt and Negri 2000: 397)

This is all well and good. It is positive and utopian and *Empire* has been a major intervention into the discourse of globalization. But the multitude and the absolute outside are almost imperceptibly, because so comprehensively, universalist, and are therefore suspect. Hardt and Negri's theory is a product of their own material location at the centre of Empire. The concept of the multitude and the disappearance of the outside can be retained only by discarding the necessary relationality of subjects, their relation to each other and to particular national formations, however oblique and transitory they may be.

The concept of the 'transnation', however, while incorporating the separation of state and nation, and endorsing the utopian potentiality of the state's transformation, accommodates the constant, ubiquitous, oppressive and combative discourse of particular nation-states. It emphasizes the fact that the transnation is a product not only of the nation, existing as a kind of 'smooth space' running through it, but also a product of movement, displacement, relocation. The transnation is both global and local. It not only interpenetrates the state, it interpenetrates the multiplicity of states in their international and global relations. The terms 'global' and 'local' are usually placed in a binary relation, even when the global is seen to be something under constant transformation at the local level. The transnation, by seeing the *movement* of peoples in globalization as a fundamental feature of spatiality, accentuates the *circulation* of the local in the global.

Literatures in the transnation

While the nation has reasserted itself in global economics, it has never really been under any threat in the identification of literatures. National literatures, despite the historical baggage of nationalist, nativist and chauvinist ideologies, still hold sway in the institutionalization of the discourse. But there is in literature a dimension that may coincide with the transformative impetus of the transnation, and that is what Ernst Bloch refers to as its utopian function. Literature, according to Bloch, is inherently utopian because its *raison d'etre* is the imaging of a different world. 'It is utopia in the very precise sense that its connection to this reality is like that of fulfillment to lack'; its temporal point of reference is the future, and to Bloch 'literary activity becomes a special form of dream work' (1978: 7, 10; cited by Zipes 1989: xxxiii). J. M. Coetzee puts this in a more sombre, but no less utopian way in *Age of Iron*, when he describes man as 'the only creature with a part of his existence in the unknown, in the future, like a shadow cast before him. Trying continually to catch up with that moving shadow, to inhabit the image of his hope' (1990: 155). It is through narrative, through the stories we tell, that we best inhabit the image of this hope, and may best imagine a radically changeable world. This doesn't mean, of course, that literary works are inevitably optimistic or even hopeful, but that their orientation to the future gives shape to the possibilities conceived in the human imagination. 'Utopia', after all, refers to 'no place' rather than 'good place', but it is the place that defines the imaginative reach of literature.

In the context of the transnation, then, we are compelled to ask the question: Is a dimension of the utopian function of literature released when the boundaries of the nation are breached? Certainly post-colonial theory in its critique of the nation has seen the transformative possibilities of a literature unbound by nationalism, even if that sometimes involves a different kind of categorization in region or race or forms of colonial relationship. But there is considerable interest among philosophers in the capacity of literature to embody potentiality. For Casarino, 'to write of a liberation beyond measure is to love potentiality' (2002: 79). To love potentiality means, among other things, to write, to experiment with forms and narratives that allow subjects to surpass their limits. Conversely, one, could say that 'to write is to love potentiality, which is to imagine a liberation without measure'. This is the utopian dimension of writing, of literature – its horizon of absolute potentiality – liberation without *telos*. What is expressed in writing, according to Agamben, is 'an absolute writing that no one writes: a potential to be written'. Thus, he stresses, 'pure actuality, that is, the actuality of an act, is (also) pure potentiality, that is, potentiality of a potentiality' (1999a: 216). Or, as Blanchot puts it: 'To write is to surrender to the interminable' (1982: 27).

Curiously, the presence in literature of its utopian dimension, of pure potentiality, may be more attractive to philosophers than literary critics. But in post-colonial literatures the issue of language and its transformative potentiality becomes prominent, leading to the politically unaskable question: 'to what extent does a common literary language – the colonial language, the language of power and subjection – become the space of potentiality because it releases the writing subject from the myth of a fixed identity?' To what extent does the language become the medium by which the past transforms the present? These questions are 'unaskable' because they seem to undermine the necessity of resistance. But, on the contrary, they show that the most effective resistance is the transformation of the imperial discourse in whatever form it takes. The question then becomes: 'to what extent are these potentialities realized in the transnation, which in its perpetually articulated subjects and the possibilities of its smooth space reveals itself to be a scene of potentiality, even of pure potentiality?' Theoretically, the combination of literature and transnational subjectivity should lead to an exorbitant potentiality. The reasons such literature doesn't always achieve this lie both in the institution of literature and in the constant pull of political, ethnic and cultural identification. It is not just the framework of the nation that resists the horizon of possibility in the literary text.

But something crucial happens to the concept of time in the literature of the transnation. The utopian potentiality of literature is towards a future without dimensions. But in the displaced post-colonial world of diasporic subjectivity utopia is the constant horizon of the present, the horizon *that is at the same time* the horizon of the past. This is beautifully demonstrated in Jhumpa Lahiri's novel *The Namesake* (2003), which revolves its narrative of diasporic subjectivity around the question of names; they invoke the interpenetrating issues of language, identity and representation. The story hinges on a Bengali couple's naming of their son born in America. The Bengali tradition is to ask the grandmother to name the child, but the letter with her chosen name has gone astray, and before they can discover the name, she dies. This moment encapsulates that critical moment of severance that exists as the moment of absence and loss, or the moment of release and new birth. While waiting for the real name to arrive, the father, Ashoke, gives the son the pet name Gogol, after a copy of Gogol's stories that had saved Ashoke's life in a train accident.

The problem of naming seems to sum up the ambivalence of identity. The absence of a name is the point of potentiality at which the diasporic subject can either be recognized as cut adrift, absent from the nation, or launched into the possibility of new life. Gogol is the name that invokes a past of great meaning to the father. It is a meaning he refuses to or fails to share with his son, but it is a meaning that refuses to invoke a tradition, a culture, a shared identity. When the boy begins school the parents want his official name to be Nikhil, but Gogol knows himself as Gogol and that becomes his official given name. But the growing boy's dissatisfaction with the name he had preferred as a child leads to his renaming himself in a way that will announce his individuality, his belonging to the present of American culture. But the name he chooses is the traditional name originally given to him by his parents – Nikhil. The name he chooses as the signifier of his emergence into home is the very signifier that confirms his connection to the past. But it is a past he has reconstructed by choosing a name. Rather than being determined by the name he articulates it, 'joins it on'. Nikhil is a Bengali name, but it is the Indian version of Nicolai, the given name of Gogol. It also means 'universe' or 'cosmos' in Bengali, the signifier of an unbounded potential, or, could it be, of a transnational subjectivity. The past thus becomes the medium of transformation, the medium of the future.

Nikhil's name is predicated on an unnaming and in this sense the name itself can be seen to embody the continual potentiality for unnaming. The name is not just the subject, but also the subject's fixity in family, nation and ethnicity. The name stands for the illusion of an irreducible identity that locates *this particular* subject, *this particular* subjectivity and no other. But when the name is imbricated with unnaming, when the sign is both the name and the unnaming, it invests the subject with an absolute potentiality that is *the potentiality of subjectivity itself*. This potentiality is paradoxically represented in the choice of the name that has been chosen. It is the transformation of the past into the future as an absolute potentiality.

The name in this narrative cannot help becoming a metaphor for subjectivity, but it does so by implicating the productive and significatory operation of memory. Memory is that medium in which utopia can either dissolve into nostalgia or become the mode of transformation. Memory is the smooth space that flows through and around the striated space of history, the space of the nation state and all structures of fixed identity. Ironically, memory, through the medium of literature, becomes the vehicle of potentiality rather than stasis. This is the potentiality of return, when the past adumbrates a future that transforms the present.

This space of transformation, this space of literature, lies in the smooth space of the transnation. There is a conjunction between the concepts of transnation and transformation that exceeds the term 'diasporic literatures', or even the term 'cosmopolitanism'. This is a conjunction of dissolving borders, both of space and time. Just as the transnation can no longer be conceived of as lying beyond the borders of the nation but also of extending within, so a post-colonial reading shows us that the utopian dimension of its literatures is not simply located in its capacity to cross borders, or even to imagine a borderless future, but in its capacity to dissolve the boundary between past and future through acts of memory that paradoxically imagine a different world.

Note

1 'Nation' is one of the most contested terms in post-colonial studies and the use of the term 'nation-state' invites us to consider the nation and the state as synonymous. The distinction I am making, however, is between the *occupants* (and border crossers) of the nation-state, the historical, multi-ethnic cultural complex that we may call the nation, occupying the political, geographical, legal *structures* that constitute the state. The concept of the transnation exposes the radical distinction between these two entities.

Bibliography

Agamben, G. (1999a) *The Man Without Content*, trans. G. Albert, Stanford, CA.: Stanford University Press.
—— (1999b) *Potentialities: Collected Essays in Philosophy*, ed. and trans. D. Heller-Roazen, Stanford: Stanford University Press.
Appadurai, A. (1996) *Modernity at Large: Cultural Dimensions of Globalization*, Minneapolis: University of Minnesota Press.
Appiah, K. A. (2007) *Cosmopolitanism: Ethics in a World of Strangers*, New York: Norton.
Bhabha, H. K. (1991) 'Conference Presentation', in P. Mariani (ed.) *Critical Fictions: The Politics of Imaginative Writing*, Seattle: Bay Press: 131–48.
—— (1994) *The Location of Culture*, London: Routledge.
Blanchot, M. (1982) *The Space of Literature*, trans. A. Smock, Lincoln, NE and London: University of Nebraska Press.
Bloch, E. (1986) *The Principle of Hope*, 3 vols, trans. N. Plaice, S. Plaice and P. Knight, Minneapolis: University of Minnesota Press.
—— (1989) *The Utopian Function of Art and Literature: Selected Essays*, trans. J. Zipes and F. Mecklenburg, Minneapolis: University of Minnesota Press.
—— (1978) 'Literatur ist Utopie', in G. Ueding (ed.) *Literatur ist Utopie*, Frankfurt am Main: Suhrkamp: 1–32.
Borofsky, R. (ed.) (2000) *Remembrance of Pacific Pasts: an Invitation to Remake History*, Honolulu: University of Hawaii Press.
Braziel, J. E. and Mannur, A. (eds) (2003) *Theorizing Diaspora: A Reader*, Oxford: Wiley Blackwell.
Breckenridge, C., Bhabha, H. K. and Pollock, S. (eds) (2002) *Cosmopolitanism*, London, Durham: Duke University Press.
Casarino, C. (2002) 'Philipoesis: A Theoretico-Methodological Manifesto', *Boundary 2*, 29.1 (Spring): 65–96.
Clifford, J. (2000) 'Valuing the Pacific' (interview-essay), in Borofsky: 92–101.
Coetzee, J. M. (1990) *Age of Iron*, London: Secker and Warburg.

Deleuze, G. (1994) *What is Philosophy?*, trans. H. Tomlinson and G. Burchell, New York: Columbia University Press.

—— (1998) *Essays Critical and Clinical*, trans. D. W. Smith and M. A. Greco, London and New York: Verso.

Deleuze, G. and Guattari, F. (2004) *A Thousand Plateaus – Capitalism and Schizophrenia*, trans. B. Massumi, London and New York: Continuum Books.

Fanon, F. (1963) *The Wretched of the Earth*, New York: Grove Press.

Featherstone, M. (ed.) (1990) *Global Culture, Nationalism, Globalization and Modernity*, London: Sage.

Gikandi, S. (2001) 'Globalization and the Claims of Postcoloniality', *South Atlantic Quarterly*, 100.3: 627–58.

Gilroy, P. (2004) *After Empire: Melancholia or Convivial Culture*, New York: Routledge.

Grosz, E. (2001) *Architecture from the Outside*, Cambridge, MA and London: MIT Press.

Hall, S. (1990) 'Cultural Identity and Diaspora', in J. Rutherford (ed.) *Identity: Community, Culture, Difference*, London: Lawrence and Wishart: 222–38.

Hannerz, U. (1996) *Transnational Connections: Culture, People, Places*, New York: Routledge.

Hardt, M. and Negri, A. (2000) *Empire*, Cambridge Mass.: Harvard University Press.

Joseph, C. A. B. and Wilson, J. (eds) (2006) *Global Fissures, Postcolonial Fusions*, Amsterdam/New York: Rodopi.

Kant, I. (1795) *Perpetual Peace: A Philosophical Sketch*. Online. Available http: <http://www.mtholyoke.edu/acad/intrel/kant/kant1.htm> (accessed June 2008).

Kapoor, K. (2004) 'Keynote Address', in Pal and Chakraborty: 29–38.

Lahiri, J. (2003) *The Namesake*, Boston and New York: Houghton Mifflin.

Levinas E. (1969) *Totality and Infinity: An Essay on Exteriority*, trans. A. Lingis, Pittsburgh: Duquesne University Press.

Motwani, J. K. (2004) 'Indian Migratory Adventures: Global and Ancient', in Pal and Chakraborty: 39–68.

Pal, A. and Chakraborty, T. (eds) (2004) *Theorizing and Critiquing Indian Diaspora*, New Delhi: Creative Books.

Patke, R. (2002) 'To Frame a City: the Singaporean Poet in the Postmodern City', in W. Lim (ed.) *Postmodern Singapore*, Singapore: Select Books, 106–17.

Perkins, H. (1996) 'Strange Fruit: the Photographic Art of Brenda Croft', *Art Asia Pacific*, 3.1: 90–3.

Robbins, B. (1992) 'Comparative Cosmopolitanism', *Social Text*, 31/32: Special Issue, *Third World and Post-Colonial Issues*: 169–86.

Roy, A. G. (2005) 'Geographies of Displacement and Resettlement', in C. Vanden Driesen and R. Crane (eds) *Diaspora: The Australasian Experience*, Delhi: Prestige Books, 104–18.

Safran, W. (1991) 'Diasporas in Modern Societies: Myths of Homeland and Return', *Diaspora* 1.1 (Spring): 83–99.

Wallerstein, I. (1974) *The Modern World System: Capitalist Agriculture and the Origin of the European World-Economy in the Sixteenth Century*, New York: Academic Press.

Wallerstein, I. (1980) *The Capitalist World Economy*, Cambridge: Cambridge University Press.

Zipes, J. (1989) 'Introduction: Toward a Realization of Anticipatory Illumination', in E. Bloch.

7 'Outlines of a better world'

Rerouting postcolonialism

Patrick Williams

Attempting to address a question such as 'rerouting postcolonialism' almost inevitably arouses mixed feelings, not least a sense of déjà-vu (Haven't we been here before, and more than once?). But the mere fact that the concept of the postcolonial continues to be routinely misrepresented, if not straightforwardly travestied, means that there is still – regrettably – work to be done in terms of analyzing, and, if needs be, both critiquing and defending it. In something like an unfashionably dialectical spirit (though some might see as it simply the outworking of mixed feelings already confessed to), this essay will argue both that postcolonialism definitely does *not* need rerouting, and at the same time most definitely *does*, in the hope of an eventual synthesis which, in the words of the Marxist philosopher Ernst Bloch, to whom we shall return later, is best characterized as 'Not yet!'. The candidates for both sides of the argument are numerous, and only a very few can be dealt with in a paper of this length.

One immediate response to calls for 'rerouting postcolonialism' is to query the presumed necessity: 'What are we rerouting *for*?', 'Do we *have* to?', etc., with the accompanying anxiety that this rerouting represents yet another manifestation of that syndrome known as 'The Permanent Self-defensiveness of Postcolonialism'. Although critique, both internal to the field as well as from outside it, has been an ongoing part of the life of postcolonial studies, it frequently seems that those working in the field are all too ready to believe that there are problems that need to be apologized for, remedied and atoned for somehow.

Another slightly sceptical reaction would be to wonder how far calls for re routing are above all symptoms of intellectual fashion, rather than anything more substantial. The demand that theory needs to be new – regularly renewed, ideally permanently self-renewing – has something of the feel of Walter Benjamin's view of capitalist commodification as 'the always-new in the context of the ever-same' (1997: 72), and carries with it the same dangers of evanescence and superficiality as the process of the consumption of commodities: Some years ago, a respected colleague declared that he 'could not conceive of life without Postmodernism'; the fact that he was able to move out of postmodernism and into other areas in quick succession – and subsequently out of theory altogether – did not, however, bring life to an end.

There is also the question of different geographical and institutional perspectives and priorities creating different pressures to reassess or reroute postcolonial studies. Clearly, the situation within US universities is not the same as, for instance, in India, Australia or even the UK, with regard to the kind of well-known criticisms voiced by Arif Dirlik (1994) and others on the putative insufficiencies of the field, those who work in it (inappropriately using their ethnic or cultural background to gain advancement), and the manner in which they carry out their work. (Dirlik, in the meantime, is so keen to dispense with postcolonialism altogether that he claims we are living in a 'post-postcolonial world' (2003)). As ever, disagreements are rife: on the one hand, the problem with postcolonial studies is that it is insufficiently Marxist – as indicated for example by Dirlik, as well as Neil Lazarus and his contributors (2004) – or, on the other hand, the problem is that it is altogether too Marxist: Donald Wehrs attributes all the many and grievous faults of postcolonialism to its inability to rid itself of its Sartrean, and, to a lesser extent Fanonian, heritage (2003: 763).

Another problem is that, despite being in many respects one of the newest collective forms of theory, postcolonialism is seen as already out-dated ('not so much PC as passé...') and numbers of books and conferences, of which E. San Juan Jr's *After Postcolonialism* (2000) can stand as representative, flag the fact that they are 'moving beyond' the postcolonial. Against such premature dismissals, however, it is important to remember the words of an important internationalist and anti-colonialist of the early twentieth century: 'Those who cannot defend old positions will never conquer new ones' (Trotsky 1926: 222), and the necessary defence of older positions marked out by postcolonialism might constitute something like 'rerooting the postcolonial'. (In that respect, Elleke Boehmer's call for the elaboration of a postcolonial aesthetics could be seen both as something of a rerouting, and also as a rerooting, in its foregrounding the 'old' and – for many – ideologically suspect category of the aesthetic.)

Obviously, preliminary scepticism regarding the necessity of rerouting postcolonialism is not the same as complacency about the unquestionable adequacy of the field. On the contrary, self-scrutiny is essential, and the question of *how* we do what we do is fundamental (though whether that then leads to any rerouting is a separate issue), and is a theme to which we shall return.

I would now like to consider briefly one or two areas where rerouting is being called for, in order to argue against the premise. The first of these is the concept of resistance. The conference outline notes 'the shift away from resistant and counter discourses' within postcolonialism, and in some quarters that finds a certain resonance. Robert Young, for example, has recently attacked the idea of resistance as 'part of postcolonialism's triumphalist narrative' (2008). In a very different context, the African filmmaker Mweze Ngangura, director of *La Vie est belle* (1987) starring Papa Wemba, has argued that African film-making should abandon its militancy and concentrate on films which entertain their audiences. The target is particularly the first generation of African directors like Ousmane Sembene and Med Hondo who never gave up their militant stance, but Ngangura's critique also acts as a warning to younger directors tempted to emulate them (Ngangura 1996). Among the problems with this argument is the fact that audiences in different continents – ranging from the rural population in Sembene's native Senegal to the art-house cinema-goers in the West – have precisely been 'entertained' by resistant, politically radical films. Of more general importance is the fact that postcolonialism has historically been both an analyis of, and hopefully a mode of, resistance: consequently, any shift away from resistant discourses or politicized critique represents the abandonment of one of the major justifications for postcolonial studies. To argue this is not, however, to claim resistance as some ahistorical essence of postcolonialism, nor to suggest that just because we analysed resistance in the past we must continue to do so in the future. Rather, the need for it is at least as pressing as ever. As Benjamin would say, 'the enemy has not ceased to be victorious', so: Why would we want to surrender the right to resist? Indeed, faced with phenomena such as 'roll-back', as Walden Bello explains it, 'the structural resubordination [of the South] to the North via the dismantling of the economic role of the state' (1999: 70), where the relations between northern state and southern non-state/'failed' state mimic those of colonial dependency and domination, how would we *not* want to be resistant; what would be more important than resistance to these forms of resuscitated oppression?

In fact, the postcolonial field (or what some might regard as that field) continues to generate new discourses of resistance. Decoloniality, for example, as articulated by Walter Mignolo and his collaborators (2007), is a resistant and critical approach which stresses its indigenous or subaltern origins and agenda, though it wants to indicate its specificity through its perceived difference and distance from postcolonialism. As categorized by Mignolo, postcolonialism supposedly springs from Lacan, Derrida and Foucault, mediated via Said, Bhabha and Spivak. Decoloniality, on the other hand, claims descent from Cesaire, Fanon and Cabral, Gandhi and DuBois, as well as from indigenous movements. There is much one could say about the strategic rejection of postcolonialism, and the construction of these carefully opposed models of western abstract theoreticism, and non-western engaged activism, but at the very least it is an interesting gesture of appropriation to take some of the most radical thinkers in the postcolonial canon and claim that they were never postcolonial in the first place.

In the context of what has just been outlined, whether we have indeed reached the stage of *The Last Resistance* (2007), as Jacqueline Rose entitles her most recent book, seems unlikely, since neither the need for resistance, nor the willingness of groups and individuals to engage in resistant acts (nor the corresponding willingness of academics and cultural producers to chronicle that resistance) has disappeared. (Rewriting this essay in the period following the bloody Israeli war of Christmas 2008 against Hamas and the civilian population of Gaza, it is hard to imagine that we could be anywhere near the last resistance, however much we might wish for the need for such resistance to be removed.)

A second area where postcolonialists are told their energies would be better employed is globalization. Remarkably, globalization is still routinely represented, or, more importantly perhaps, represents itself, as the newest Big Thing, a completely different mode of existence for the modern world, whereas it is arguably simply the latest mask or configuration of something with which we are already all too familiar: the globalizing of the capitalist mode of production; and, as such, we find ourselves once again facing Benjamin's 'always-new in the context of the ever-same' (1997: 72). As a result of its supposed paradigm-shifting newness, various academics have argued that we should switch our attention from an outmoded postcolonialism to a more relevant globalization.

In terms of the relation of postcolonialism to globalization, a few very brief thoughts: First, does this constitute a rerouting? Arguably not, given that postcolonial studies has been concerned with the phenomenon since at least the early 1990s. Second, it is not clear in what way work done under the rubric of globalization constitutes the kind of superseding of postcolonialism which some have claimed. Third, an important aspect of the relationship of postcolonial studies to globalization is the question of how the former approaches the latter analytically (again, the question of *how* we do what we do), whether, for example, it develops a trenchant critique of unfettered capitalism, or prefers to celebrate the pleasures of Bhabha's cultural hybridization and Appadurai's border-crossing free flows of mediascapes, ethnoscapes, financescapes and the like. Finally, should we in fact be less, rather than more, concerned about it, given the possibility that we are currently facing globalization in retreat, rather than relentlessly expanding, as Walden Bello argues:

> In fact, globalisation has not only 'stalled', [...] it is going into reverse. And it is not just the key institutions of global economic governance such as the World Bank, the World Trade Organisation (WTO) and the IMF that are in crisis but the deeper structures and processes of what was formerly seen as an inevitable phenomenon. What was seen, by many people on both the left and right, as the wave of the future – that is, a functionally integrated global economy marked by massive flows of commodities, capital and labour across the borders of weakened nation-states and presided over by a 'transnational capitalist class' – has retreated in a chain reaction of economic crises, growing inter-capitalist rivalries and wars.
>
> (2006: 1346)

The disasters of the current conjuncture – the 'credit crunch', spiralling insolvencies and unemployment, the spectre of global financial meltdown – may indeed signal, as some optimistically claim, 'the end of capitalism as we know it'. On the other hand, Marx noted that capitalism was a system predicated on crisis, and its ability not only to survive crises but to draw strength from them was one reason for its longevity – so perhaps we should not get too excited just yet.

In a different context, Neil Smith has argued that we are currently in 'The endgame of Globalisation' (2006) – globalization here construed as the third moment in an unfinished US project for global dominance, most recently promulgated by George W. Bush and the neo-cons. Like its economic variant, this political project may not have entirely run out of steam, though the election of Barack Obama may signal its suspension for the foreseeable future. Both examples do, however, suggest that these forms of globalization may not automatically be where postcolonialists might wish to (re)direct their attention.

Having said that, there might indeed be elements of globalization we might want to look at: the *Amnesty International* report for 2007, for example, talks about the creation of a 'global climate of fear', needing to be tackled by the formation of 'global solidarity' – a somewhat utopian-sounding entity, perhaps, but not therefore inappropriate, as we shall see in a moment. One aspect of that climate of fear is the global training, maintenance and export of state-sponsored terrorism, particularly by the US: training carried out in centres such as the infamous School of the Americas; 'maintenance' for bodies as various as SAVAK in Iran, the Contras in Nicaragua, and the Taliban in Afghanistan; while its current strategy of global export includes illegal arrests, secret 'rendition' flights, 'outsourced' torture, 'disappearances'.

We live in a world still under the shadow of George Bush's War on Terror – perhaps better understood as a War of Terrorisms. The dominant popular image here is of terrorism as the unjustifiable, seemingly inexplicable, actions of inhuman individuals, perhaps in the shape of Palestinian suicide bombers, or murderous groups, such as Al Qaeda. Routinely missing from this picture is the question of state terrorism. That absence is not, however, accidental, because in a world where the principal perpetrators of terrorism, and the greatest killers by far, are states, arguably the most culpable state, the US, officially defines terrorism as carried out only by 'sub-statals' – individuals, groups and organizations – and not by bodies like itself. That represents an interesting ideological reversal, in view of the fact that historically, terror (usually capitalized as Terror) was principally an instrument of state control, most notably in the extreme conditions of the French and Russian revolutions.

In the colonial context, violence, including in the form of terrorism, is simultaneously part of the repertoire of anti-colonial struggle and the essence of colonial power. In Sartre's succinct formulation in *Colonialism and Neocolonialism*, 'Colonial aggression is internalised as Terror by the colonised' (2001: 145). In something like an appropriate prefiguring of today's privatizing and outsourcing of terror, colonial Terror was often carried out by private (colonial) companies, especially when there were natural resources to be exploited. All the empires seem to have had their share of this privatization of terror, though that did not involve them giving up on their own larger-scale forms. From a perspective which is not postcolonial but which echoes many postcolonial analyses, especially Fanon's, Herman and O'Sullivan in *The 'Terrorism' Industry* (1989) differentiate between Primary and Secondary terrorism. The former consists of the processes of colonial invasion and oppression, as well as the continued economic and political domination it involves. The latter is the resistance to oppression on the part of the colonized, in the absence of available alternatives.

Although there may indeed be, as Fanon (1990) famously argued in *The Wretched of the Earth*, reciprocity in the patterns of violence in the colonial sphere, there is never anything resembling parity or equality. The asymmetry of colonial terrorism is famously, and with impressive clarity, set out in Pontecorvo's film *Battle of Algiers* (1966). When the recently-captured *Front de Liberation Nationale* (FLN) leader Ben Mhidi is paraded before the press before being taken away for his 'suicide' at the hands of the French army, one journalist asks him whether he isn't ashamed to be using women's baskets to transport bombs, to which he replies: 'You give us your bombers [which have been napalm-bombing undefended Algerian villages] and you can have our shopping baskets'.

Terrorism has historically been rooted in local contexts and struggles, but is currently globalizing (and as such it represents another aspect of globalization which postcolonialists need to take account of). In particular, it makes use of effects of globalization, such as developments in communications and travel, as well as increased ease of access to information, materials, skills-training, funding and volunteers. At the same time, and as a direct result of this, the structure of the terrorist group, especially Al Qaeda and its nameless off-shoots, has 'globalized', or at least internationalized and decentralized, in ways not previously seen.

One of the areas in which groups like Al Qaeda have functioned successfully has been the visual media, and the latter in turn represents an extremely rich field much in need of postcolonial analysis. There are a number of separate-but-connected visual archives here: for instance, photographs from the global South (and very much not just the much-feted work of individuals like Salgado); television programmes; cartoons, especially perhaps political cartoons, with a figure like the murdered Palestinian Naji Al Ali as exemplary; and last, but certainly not least, postcolonial film. The latter is a huge field, but still neglected in various ways. Astonishingly, it remains the only major area of postcolonial cultural production which struggles to be recognized as such, as work in film studies continues to privilege the traditional categories of auteurs, nations, and regions. There are one or two books, such as *Postcolonial Images* (Armes 2005) and *Postcolonial African Cinema* (Murphy and Williams 2007), which attempt a partial rectification, but the field conspicuously lacks anything resembling the necessary, urgently-needed overview.

Within the postcolonial domain, one of the slowly emerging archives is that of Palestinian film. That it is not usually analysed in terms of postcolonialism is part of a larger problem, not cinematic this time, but resulting from the general absence of questions of Palestine from the postcolonial agenda. This absence is remarkably difficult to understand (How can we *not* be working on Palestine?), other than perhaps as one of the triumphs of the Israeli propaganda machine in convincing postcolonial scholars that they are not in fact witnessing a particularly brutal, if belated, form of colonialism. Whether we see it as akin to South Africa's 'colonialism of a special type' in its superimposition of two populations claiming the same land (as well as in the current Israeli moves, via the illegal Separation Wall, to produce something like Bantustans for the Palestinians), or whether we take it as the last gasp of classic nineteenth-century colonialism (and Theodor Herzl, founder of Zionism, was much impressed by Cecil Rhodes's approach to colonizing Africa), as postcolonialists we are faced with, and are not analyzing – with occasional honourable exceptions – the worst example of colonialism in the modern world. Time to reroute.

The easy part of that rerouting is that contemporary Palestinian culture offers a rich and growing resource for postcolonial analysis. The wealth of cultural production spans the written and the visual. Poetry is perhaps the best-known, with Mahmoud Darwish preeminent, though figures like Fadwa Tuqan and Mourid Barghouti have international reputations. In fiction there are novelists and short story writers ranging from the older generation which includes Ghassan Kanafani (assassinated by the Israelis in 1972) and Emile Habibi, to the emergent writing by women like Liana Badr and Sahar Kalifeh. The visual encompasses the dramatic images of Naji Al Ali, the powerful installations of Emily Jacir, and the diverse forms of film making practised by Michel Khleifi, Elia Suleiman, Hani Abu Assad and Tawfiq Abu Wael, recently joined by Annemarie Jacir as the first Palestinian woman director of a feature film.

A more difficult aspect is constituted by the ethical scandal that Palestine represents. In a poem like 'I talk too much', Darwish gently highlights the failure of the well-intentioned in the west to do more than applaud the claims of dispossessed Palestinians:

> I ask 'Is it true, good ladies and gentlemen, that the earth of Man is for all human beings as you say? In that case
> Where is my little house, and where am I?'

> (2003: 13)

Insofar as postcolonial studies has tackled ethical issues, it has often had recourse to the work of Emmanuel Levinas. However, Levinas's refusal to accord Palestinians the status of neighbour or Other (before whom one must maintain a position of responsibility and trembling openness), as well as his defence of Jewish exceptionalism (which blocks any hope for justice – one of his key terms – for Palestinians) represents a major problem in this area. Arguably, what is needed here is something like the materialist (and anti-colonialist) ethics which Sartre was developing in the 1960s (see Williams forthcoming). Levinas would certainly not agree with Darwish's contention: 'From this day on, he who does not become Palestinian in his heart will never understand his true moral identity' (Darwish 2002c), but we may well choose to. At the very least, Darwish's statement carries echoes of Said's highlighting of the importance of 'universalising the struggle', both as part of the task of intellectuals generally, and in terms of the paradigmatic status of Palestine in the contemporary moral and political landscape.

How do we get from the seemingly utterly dystopian current condition of the Palestinian people to thoughts of utopia, our final area of suggested rerouting in this rapid survey? Indeed why would we want to bother with utopia in the first place, if, as John Gray (2008) has argued, the term is now utterly outmoded, comprehensively discredited by the tyrannies perpetrated in its name. It is certainly true that – for those of a sufficiently sceptical frame of mind – any theory (postcolonialism included) can be considered as discredited by its flaws and its failures, and the question then arises for its adherents: repudiate? reroute? or even, reroot? The general acceptance of utopianism as a failed project would then be one reason for its absence (again, exception made for rare examples such as Bill Ashcroft's article in this volume) from the postcolonial agenda.

One kind of postcolonial response to 'why Palestine? why utopia?' would be in terms of understanding postcolonialism not as in any sense an achieved condition, but rather (as argued, for instance, in Childs and Williams 1996) as an 'anticipatory' discourse, looking forward to a better and as yet unrealized world by contrast from one where colonialism has not been eradicated – both what we could call 'actually existing colonialism', as in the case of Palestine, as well as the legacies and after-effects of colonialism in those notionally independent nation states that continue to suffer forms of neo-colonialist and imperialist domination. Insofar as utopia is a category grounded in the pursuit of human freedom, then it is not difficult to discern utopian foundations – the 'outlines of a better world' in Bloch's words which provide the title for this paper – in so many of the anti- or post-colonial projects: national liberationist, Pan-African, Tri-continental and more, which strove to fashion a better future for their own oppressed people, and others, across the twentieth century.

Another way of understanding the relevance of the utopian here would be via Adorno's contention in *Minima Moralia* that 'consummate negativity, once squarely faced, delineates the mirror-image of its opposite' (Adorno 1974: 247), where the 'consummate negativity' of Israeli oppression might lead the Palestinians to begin to imagine a more utopian future. More important than Adorno here, however, is someone who Adorno said inspired him (though it may be difficult to see that in their respective philosophical styles), namely utopia's greatest philosopher, Ernst Bloch.

In his enormous three-volume work *The Principle of Hope* (1986) Bloch analyses the notion of a 'utopian function' as universal human attribute; and sees utopian imaginings contained in a wide range of human praxis, creative culture, beliefs and so on. However, although the fashioning of utopias may in itself be a welcome human capacity, not all utopias point in the same direction or have the same political or social content, and Bloch was always aware of the possibility (even likelihood) of the 'bad' utopia, the deformed or deluded version which offered no liberation. An extreme example of the latter is Nazism, in which Bloch is still able to discern a utopian dimension, though it is clearly not a utopia you would want to embrace. Despite this, Bloch is clear that such deviations in no way discredit the idea of utopia, and should not stop the engaged pursuit of those elements acting towards the creation of a genuinely utopian future. This divergence or opposition of utopian formations allows us to envisage what Althusser might have called 'class struggle at the level of [utopian] theory', where 'Our' utopia fully postcolonial, believing that Another World is Possible, takes on 'theirs': capitalist, militaristic or religious fundamentalist.

Far from being merely the day-dreaming and vacuous wishing some see it as, for Bloch utopia is above all a practical project: 'concrete utopia'– as opposed to the abstract utopia of the day dream – is something which has to be built. 'Expectation, hope, intention towards possibility that has still not become; this is not only a basic feature of human consciousness, but, concretely corrected and grasped, a basic determination within objective reality as a whole' (Bloch 1986: 7). In this process, small-scale utopian projects function as both images and building blocks for the more fully-realized utopia being constructed. Two very different examples, both in terms of their relation to the postcolonial as well as their scale and ambition, are the West–East Divan Orchestra, founded by Edward Said and Daniel Barenboim, a utopian cultural project aiming at a utopian political future; and the new social movements such as the World Social Forum, with global-utopian ambitions, but working at the local level, too.

Although the suggestion here is that postcolonial studies has paid insufficient attention to the question of utopia, in a very recent book quite the opposite claim is made. Here, postcolonialism in general is vitiated by its utopian 'futurism', which, since it is apparently only able to imagine a future from which problems and conflicts have almost magically disappeared, is in the position of finding itself unable 'to learn from the actual disorderly processes of negotiating and overcoming difficulties' (Salzman and Divine 2008: 51). That might begin to constitute a serious charge, were it not for the fact that the principal 'postcolonial' theorists discussed are David Harvey (representing 'civilizational utopianism'), Hardt and Negri ('obscurantist utopianism'), and Walter Mignolo ('primordial utopianism') – the first three hardly known as representatives of the postcolonial, and the fourth, as already mentioned, strongly opposed to it in the name of decoloniality. In the face of similarly impoverished understandings of postcolonial studies, it remains important to assert that the most important routes taken in the field have precisely begun in understandings of 'the actual disorderly processes of negotiating and overcoming difficulties', and will surely continue to do so. For Bloch, at least, liberation movements thrive on a combination of the 'old' positions (with echoes of Trotsky, perhaps), and the utopian: 'The good New is never that completely new. It acts far beyond the daydreams by which life is pervaded and of which the figurative arts are full. All freedom movements are guided by utopian aspirations' (Bloch 1986: 7).

Central to the praxis of fashioning the utopia is pedagogy, the production of 'educated hope' [*docta spes*]:

> Everybody's life is pervaded by daydreams: one part of this is just stale, even enervating escapism, even booty for swindlers, but another part is provocative, is not content just to accept the bad which exists, does not accept renunciation. This other part has hoping at its core and is teachable.
>
> (1986: 3)

Postcolonial studies certainly has its part to play in the articulation of a positive pedagogy, that of a practical, resistant, 'concrete' hoping.

In *Minima Moralia*, Adorno remarks that 'Hope is soonest found among the comfortless' (1974: 223), and a remarkable example of that, which brings together a number of the issues raised in this paper, is the work of Mahmoud Darwish. Following his return to the West Bank in 1995 after years in exile, Darwish, facing the 'consummate negativity' of daily life under Israeli rule, developed a mode of writing which he saw as more defiantly hopeful than his earlier work, which appeared characterized not by despair but by the absence of definite hope. One of the extreme examples of Israeli colonial terror resulting in cultural production grounded in hope is Darwish's epic *State of Siege*, written during the brutal attacks on the West Bank in 2002 (and with a tank literally parked outside Darwish's window). Its opening stanza captures the construction of a 'concrete' hope by Adorno's 'comfortless':

> Here, at the slopes before sunset and at the gun-mouth of time,
> Near orchards deprived of their shadows,
> We do what prisoners do,
> What the unemployed do:
> We nurture hope.
>
> (Darwish 2002b)

Although the conditions for hope are obviously unpromising, the poem interrogates both them and, above all, the possibility of resistance. The two not infrequently combine in almost the only place left for Palestinians to resist – the body:

> To resist means: To be confident of the health
> Of the heart and of the testicles, to be confident of your incurable malady:
> The malady of hope.
>
> (Darwish 2002b)

At the time of the Israeli siege which resulted in the poem, Darwish was visited by a delegation from the International Parliament of Writers which included Breyten Breytenbach and Nobel laureates Jose Saramago and Wole Soyinka. In his speech of welcome, Darwish returned to the themes of resistance and hope:

> But we have an incurable malady: hope. Hope in liberation and independence. Hope in a normal life where we are neither heroes nor victims. Hope that our children will go safely to their schools. Hope that a pregnant woman will give birth to a living baby, at the hospital, and not a dead child in front of a military checkpoint; hope that our poets will see the beauty of the colour red in roses rather than in blood; hope that this land will take up its original name: the land of love and peace. Thank you for carrying with us the burden of this hope.
>
> (Darwish 2002a)

As Brecht said in a very different context: 'If you think all this is utopian, I would ask you to reflect on the reasons that render it utopian' (1973: 30).

In this combination of hope as resistance (rerooted postcolonialism) and hope as utopian function (the New, the Not-Yet of rerouted postcolonialism) there may be something like the difficult synthesis mentioned at the beginning of this paper.

For Said, however, writing in what we could call a Blochian mode: 'One must not only hope; but also *do*' (2000: 291, emphasis added). What exactly we do – and, once again, how we do that – as scholars in the postcolonial field (rerouted or not) will continue to have far-reaching implications.

Bibliography

Adorno, T. (1974) *Minima Moralia*, London: Verso.

Armes, R. (2005) *Postcolonial Images: Studies in North African Film*, Bloomington: Indiana University Press.

The Battle of Algiers (La Battaglia di Algeri) (1966) Dir. G. Pontecorvo. Written by F. Solinas.

Bello, W. (1999) *Dark Victory*, London: Pluto.

—— (2006) 'The Capitalist Conjuncture', *Third World Quarterly*, 27.8: 1345–67.

Benjamin, W. (1982) *Illuminations*, Glasgow: Collins.

—— (1997) *Charles Baudelaire*, London: Verso.

Bloch, E. (1986 [1950]) *The Principle of Hope*, trans. N. Vol. 1, Oxford: Blackwell.

Brecht, B. (1973) Plaice, S. Plaice and P. Knight, *Gesammelte Werke*, Vol. 18, "Der Rundfunkals Kommunikationsapparat; p. 129–31. Frankfurt: Surhkamp.

Childs, P. and Williams, P. (1996) *Introduction to Post-Colonial Theory*, Harlow: Longman/ Pearson.

Darwish, M. (2002a) 'An Incurable Malady: Hope', *Al Ahram Weekly*, 580, 4–10 April. Online. Available http <http://weekly.ahram.org.eg/2002/580/fr2.htm (accessed 20 June 2009).

—— (2002b) 'State of Siege', *Al Ahram Weekly*, 581, 11–17 April. Online. Available http:// weekly.ahram.org.eg/2002/581/fr2.htm (accessed 20 June 2009).

—— (2002c) 'A War for War's Sake', *Al Ahram Weekly*, 581, 11–17 April. Online. Available <http://weekly.ahram.org.eg/2002/581/fr2.htm (accessed 20 June 2009).

—— (2003) *Unfortunately, it was Paradise*, Berkeley: University of California Press.

Dirlik, A. (1994) 'The Postcolonial Aura: Third World Criticism in the Age of Global Capitalism', *Critical Enquiry*, 20.2 (Winter): 328–56.

—— (2003) 'Where Do We Go from Here? Marxism, Modernity and Postcolonial Studies', *Diaspora*, 12.3, p. 419–35.

Fanon, F. (1990) *The Wretched of the Earth*, trans. C. Farrington, Harmondsworth: Penguin.

Gray, J. (2008) *Black Mass: Apocalyptic Religion & the Death of Utopia*, Harmondsworth: Penguin.

Herman, E. S. and O'Sullivan, G. (1989) *The 'Terrorism' Industry: The Experts and Institutions that Shape our View of Terror*, New York: Pantheon.

Lazarus, N. (ed.) (2004) *Cambridge Companion to Postcolonial Literary Studies*, Cambridge: Cambridge University Press.

Mignolo, W. (2007) 'Coloniality of Power and Decolonial Thinking', *Cultural Studies*, 212.3 (March): 155–67.

Murphy, D. and Williams, P. (2007) *Postcolonial African Cinema: Ten directors*, Manchester: Manchester University Press.

Ngangura, M. (1996) 'African Cinema – Militancy or Entertainment?' in I. Bakari and M. Cham (eds) *African Experiences of Cinema*, London: BFI.

Rose, J. (2007) *The Last Resistance*, London: Verso.

Said, E. (2000) 'Humanism and Heroism (Presidential Address 1999)', *PMLA*, 115.3 (May): 285–91.

Salzman, P. C. and Divine, D. R. (eds) (2008) *Postcolonial Theory and the Arab–Israel Conflict*, London: Routledge.

San Juan Jr, E. (2000) *After Postcolonialism*, Lanham, MD: Rowman and Littlefield.

Sartre, J. P. (2001) *Colonialism and Neocolonialism*, trans. A. Haddour, S. Brewer, and T. Mc Williams, London: Routledge.

Smith, N. (2006) 'The Endgame of Globalization', *Political Geography*, 25.1 (January): 1–14.

Trotsky, L. (1966) *In Defence of Marxism*, London: New Park Publications.

Wehrs, D. (2003) 'Sartre's Legacy in Postcolonial Theory; or, Who's Afraid of Non-Western Historiography and Cultural Studies?', *New Literary History*, 34.4 (Autumn): 761–89.

Williams, P. (forthcoming) 'Sartre's *Morality and History*: Ethics for Postcolonial Times', in A. Oboe and S. Bassi (eds) *Try Freedom: Liberties and Rights in Postcolonial Cultures*.

Young, R. (2008) 'The Right to Resist', paper given at EACLALS Conference, 'Try Freedom: Rewriting Rights in/through Postcolonial Cultures', Venice, April 2008.

Section 2

Remapping the postcolonial

Globalism, localism and diasporas

8 Introduction

Cristina Şandru

The five articles included in the section on 'Remapping the Postcolonial' examine the postcolonial in conjunction with the global, the provincial/local and the diasporic, both theoretically and at a literary-critical level in texts by, among others, Ma Jian, Andrzej Stasiuk, Amitav Ghosh, Neil Bissoondath, M. G. Vassanji and Leila Aboulela.

Diana Brydon's opening essay smoothly bridges the dominant preoccupations of the first section with the major concerns in the second and third. The key question that the article poses – and in many ways the central question of the volume as a whole – is about the status and relevance of the postcolonial paradigm in a changing theoretical, political and educational landscape. The postcolonial, Brydon argues, is currently being rerouted into new spaces of thinking opened up by the accumulated 'cracks' in the modern world system imaginary, and brought into closer dialogue with the arguments of other disciplinary communities as well as different historical contexts and geographical spaces. The essay offers an overview of several such potential reroutings, both central and tangential to postcolonial studies, many of which are explored in other articles in the volume: post-apartheid and post-communist studies (see Poyner and Graham, Mather and Kolodziejczyk); Native American studies (see Madsen) and, with it, the ambivalent status of the settler postcolonial sensibility in relation to indigenous political and cultural claims (see Brydon); the 'reverse migrations' movement, its theoretical coherence undermined by the marginal and marginalized figure of the refugee (see Gikandi, Goheen Glanville), and its metropolitan diasporic communities riven by the sometimes problematic rerootings they seek to build (see Ball).

Indeed, Brydon's essay enters into fruitful dialogue with many of the concerns raised in the other articles, among which the key theme of politics and globalization, or rather, the globalizing movement of a particular type of politics (liberal), with its attendant social and cultural imaginaries. In particular, Brydon probes the crucial tensions within liberal political theory and postcolonial studies between autonomy and community, individual self *versus* politicized collective, suggesting that these are played out most self-consciously and programmatically in research and education. Highlighting the importance of pedagogical practices, she advocates 'knowledge as emancipation' and an education able to reconcile the desire for fostering individual autonomy and the responsibility to critique entrenched systems of inequality at a collective, global level. Taking up Victor Li's argument in Section 1, she suggests that postcolonial studies might attempt to supplement discreet, autonomous fields of preoccupation with more relational and transcultural forms of inquiry, whereby distinct forms of individuation and political agency can enter into dialogue. Paralleling Boehmer's own take on a similarly contentious dichotomy within postcolonial criticism (that between the aesthetic and the ethical), Brydon's essay reminds theorists and critics that only by entering into 'uncomfortable' dialogues, both within and across their own disciplines, can the postcolonial refashion itself as a 'rhizomatic' paradigm, an interpretative framework that can come to inform wider public projects such as educational policies or ethnographic and museological practices.

Brydon's concept of the 'glocal' sensibility is anticipated by Ashcroft's formulation of the 'transnation' in his essay in Section 1 and is taken up in various forms in other articles in this section. Her comment that 'it is possible to live attuned to different temporal and civilizational systems' (p. 112) is remarked upon, in a different context, in Kolodziejczyk's article, and in Anna Ball's study of Leila Aboulela's novels; both reveal the implications of this sensibility in conceptualizations of autonomy, citizenship, belonging and community.

In her provocative essay Anna Ball contends that the sensibilities and cultural practices dramatized in Aboulela's novels deconstruct most current postcolonial orthodoxies: not only are they firmly 'rooted', they are informed and guided by geographies of faith (rather than, say, cosmopolitanism) and selective localities. The focus on British diasporic Muslim communities, and their negotiation of multiple allegiances, could not be more topical; yet Ball shows how the British-Sudanese writer subverts many of the tropes of the typical diasporic text. Thus, rather than celebrating hybrid or assimilative subjectivity, Aboulela's portrayal of diasporic Muslim women is shown to work within a spatial imagination deeply rooted in the materiality, physicality and psychology of national, religious and cultural difference. The essay succeeds in reevaluating the much-discredited trope of roots, thus operating a rerouting into rerooting, as it were: roots are seen as generative networks rather than static, fixed points of reference, a necessity rather than a liability, a major component of the rhizomatic quality of postcolonial subjectivities. Ball's close reading of Aboulela teases out how allegiances built by the metropolitan sons and daughters of rerouted migrants of an earlier generation strikingly resemble those whom Gikandi identifies in various refugee communities: both groups cannot – or, perhaps, feel no desire to – partake of the ideologies and practices of cosmopolitanism. Yet, unlike Gikandi's anxious figures, Leila Aboulela's female characters *have* a choice; their identities are polycentric and their familiarity with western culture a given. It is their *conscious decision* that one aspect of their rhizomatic identity should embrace religious faith, in this case, Islam.

Anna Ball's essay anticipates routes of conversation which, perhaps among all those that Brydon enumerates, are the most difficult to travel along, for the integration of Islam within critical discourse, though advocated by moderate Muslim intellectuals, is still a no-go area in many humanistic 'progressive' subjects.

This is, therefore, a very important rerouting of the postcolonial, especially in the present context of debates about the role of religion in both the liberal secular state and in diasporic communities;[1] moreover, by engaging specifically with Islam, the article problematizes the newly erected system of easy binarisms and categorical pronouncements that have proliferated in the aftermath of the 'war on terror'.

Erin Goheen Glanville's essay on Canadian refugee fiction similarly seeks to reroute diasporic experiences by shifting the focus away from celebratory models of migrancy and hybridity back to those disempowered by global movements – the refugees and migrant workers rather than the upwardly-mobile, professional metropolitans. Echoing Gikandi's discussion in Section 1, Goheen Glanville reads refugee fiction simultaneously into and against its categorization as diaspora literature, and shows how movement and migrancy are 'constructed normativities', wholly unsuitable for the discussion of refugee trajectories. Her analysis is supported by a generically rich choice of literature, from stories (Neil Bissoondath's *On the Eve of Uncertain Tomorrows* and M. G. Vassanji's *Refugee*) and poems (Lilly Allen's 'The Refugee'), to novels (Camilla Gibb's *Sweetness in the Belly*), memoirs (Nega Mezlekia) and hip-hop songs (K'Naan's 'Soobax'). Yet the critique of 'easy diasporism' does not lead back to an undifferentiated celebration of roots; indeed, two of the texts Goheen Glanville examines engage with the oppressive conditions of 'back home' even while carving out a homeland in the new Canadian space. The illustrative stories, poems and songs do not, therefore, celebrate either roots or routes, but, rather, problematize both; indeed, they are more concerned with the obstacles that stand in the way of the refugee, those silent disavowals of colonial history that complicate the unified models of liberatory migrancy.

As Brydon remarks in her opening essay, one of the most significant 'cracks' in the modern system imaginary has been opened by the fall of the Soviet Union and the challenges – ideological as well as economic – that its aftermath has entailed. In particular, it highlights the need to reformulate neo-Marxist models of postcolonial critique to account for a post-communist set of realities and the resurgence of neo-liberalism in the former Second World. Yet concrete efforts in this sense have, so far, been few and far-between; and, with notable exceptions, relatively little account has been taken of this particular 'crack' in theorizations of the postcolonial. Two of the essays – Jeffrey Mather's on global China and Dorota Kolodziejczyk's on East European provincialism – seek to redress the balance, bringing the postcolonial onto exciting new grounds of analysis.

In his discussion of Ma Jian's *Red Dust*, a Chinese travel book of the 1980s, Mather suggests ways in which current topics in postcolonial studies can be productively used to read texts written outside the historical paradigms of western imperialism. In particular, Mather addresses issues of intellectual and imaginative resistance within the context of nationalist-communist political autocracy in China.[2] Banned in its country of origin, the book explores China's border regions in order to both define and disrupt the centre; the author, Mather argues, challenges the totalizing discourses of 'purity' and 'pollution' as well as the hegemonic official discourses of nationalism and modernity by fashioning a flexible and strategic 'travelling self' in flight from the campaign of 'anti-spiritual pollution' (read 'purification of ideological corruption') led by China in the early 1980s. Its central tropes, which incorporate Bakhtinian notes of carnivalesque subversion, revolve around various social outcasts and marginals who often function as symbolic stand-ins for exiled writers, artists and other undesirable elements of the regime. It is a fascinating article, where the centres, margins and resistances usually associated with standard postcolonial accounts are shifted and bent to reveal different kinds of 'routes', journeys taken to avoid, simultaneously, communist political persecution and the environmental ravages of global capitalism.

Finally, Dorota Kolodziejczyk's article focuses on what in Eastern Europe is usually called a 'period of transition', after the old Soviet empire has collapsed and global capitalism is seeping in – an uneasy and difficult borderzone which creates its own melancholy desires of escape, its own 'postcolonial' longings for lost spaces. The opening discussion argues for the extension of postcolonialism's theoretical boundaries and a guarded transference of its critical practices to the imaginative spaces of East-Central Europe. Tracing the complex, overlapping imperial legacies in the region, and its fraught status as a space *in* Europe, but not always *of* it, she proposes that postcolonial studies can reroute post-communist critical discourses away from a predominantly national paradigm by undertaking a comparative exploration of the region's ambivalent history and culture. Her article does precisely that: the discussion of postcolonial metropolitan writer Amitav Ghosh and contemporary Polish writer Andrzej Stasiuk takes place within the framework of what the author calls a 'translational space of comparative theorization'. What emerges is a 'cosmopolitan provincialism', a 'glocal' imaginary that eludes any one source of hegemonic worldliness (i.e. the western metropolis). Kolodziejczyk is well aware of the problematic conjoining of differential locations, perspectives, and historical experiences, but, she argues, it is precisely in such differential contexts that the political impact of translation (in its most active sense of transposition/transference) can be fully experienced.

In line with Brydon's opening essay, Kolodziejczyk thus argues for a dialogic space that is beyond the discipline as it is now conceived, but adjacent to its interests and sensitivities. The nuanced and compelling reworking of postcolonial concepts from an East-Central European context completes the 'ex-centric' views provided by the other essays in the section and highlights, once more, the need for rerouting if the discipline is to remain dynamic, flexible and, most importantly, innovative.

Notes

1   This was, in fact, one of the major themes of the most recent International PEN festival of world literature *Free the Word!* (where Leila Aboulela was also present), the opening session of which (Globe Theatre, London, 16 April) was entitled 'Beyond Faith and Reason'.
2   These are also taken up in Ma Jian's later novel, *Beijing Coma*, which has just won the TR Fyvel Book Award offered by the Index of Censorship in its recent Freedom of Expression awards ceremony (London, Tuesday 21 April 2009).

9 Cracking imaginaries

Studying the global from Canadian space

Diana Brydon

> By 'border thinking' I mean the moments in which the imaginary of the modern world system cracks.
>
> (Mignolo 2000: 23)

In *Local Histories/Global Designs*, Walter Mignolo (2000: 23) turns away from the widely accepted (within poststructuralist circles) Lacanian notion of the Imaginary (contrasted with the Symbolic and the Real) to adopt instead a usage formulated by Edouard Glissant. According to Mignolo, Glissant's imaginary signifies 'all the ways a culture has of perceiving and conceiving of the world' (in Wing 1997: 23). This definition implicitly recognizes the instituted and instituting capacity of collective imaginaries that for Cornelius Castoriadis (1981, 1991) constitutes a radical extension of autonomy beyond its liberal definitions privileging the individual self above the community. This implies definitions of culture and community as constantly under construction rather than primordial or fixed in their nature. These theorists' use of 'imaginary' points to the need for situating the terms academics employ and translating where necessary across different usages and assumptions about value they deploy. Such translation may be necessary across different geospatial locations, disciplinary formations, and frameworks of theoretical allegiance. The heightened awareness of the need for such translation is part of what is meant by the cracking of the modern world system imaginary, a cracking to which postcolonial theory has made significant contributions but which is also affecting how the postcolonial imaginary understands itself.

New spaces for thinking have been opened by these cracks. Anna Lowenhaupt Tsing calls these new spaces 'zones of awkward engagement, where words mean something different across a divide even as people agree to speak' (2005: xi). This paper considers some of the reroutings of postcolonial thought thereby opened, which in turn are reconstituting how the postcolonial understands itself. In addition to problematizing knowledge politics, cultural politics, and politics proper (especially the assumptions of liberal politics), these cracks open new possibilities for dialogue across Canadian, postcolonial and globalization studies. The aim here is not to reinforce these categories in their boundedness but rather to open each to the cross-influence of the other.

The imaginary of the modern world system has operated most strongly through national cultural imaginaries apparently supported through the capitalist structures of the world system and the logics of liberal thought. Such national imaginaries, once central in many anti-colonial liberation struggles, are now being challenged by globalizing processes. While national imaginaries still hold purchase, they are being supplemented by other forms of cultural and social imaginaries, which can operate at sub-national or supra-national levels. In a usage close to Glissant's, except that the word 'social' here replaces 'culture', with the different frameworks such a change implies, Charles Taylor describes a social imaginary as 'the way ordinary people "imagine" their social surroundings', a way of thinking that is 'carried in images, stories, and legends', which 'is shared by large groups of people', and which 'makes possible common practices and a widely shared sense of legitimacy' (2004: 23).

These are the modes of thinking students bring to their classroom encounters, modes postcolonial teachers in Canada often seek to problematize or even dislodge through our postcolonial work. To the extent that they represent the naturalization of colonial modes of thinking now adapted to endorse hegemonic assumptions about the naturalness and inevitableness of global capitalism, they are also the modes that Mignolo argues are 'cracking' as different conceptualizations of social and cultural imaginaries demand to be heard. How academics, nation-state governments, and the international system are to respond to such changes remains a matter of crucial interest in the emerging globalization debates, where postcolonial theories are often given short shrift, at best considered a minor branch of postmodern approaches and at worst either dismissed or ignored.

Accepting that many scholars today are scrambling to make sense of what these cracked imaginaries mean for how people live together and make sense of our world, this paper argues for rerouting the postcolonial into closer dialogue with the arguments of other disciplinary and interdisciplinary communities as well as with the range of views emerging out of different contexts across the world. Globalizing processes are not leading to homogenization but they are compelling the reorganization and refocusing of knowledge. Where do postcolonial studies fit in this changing landscape?

At the end of the twentieth century, postcolonial studies had emerged as an influential inter- and multi-disciplinary project, which traced its routes back to the rhizomatic interactions of anti-colonial struggle and poststructuralist theory. But in some circles there was also a sense of malaise, a worry, as articulated persuasively by David Scott (1999: 12), that in its concern with 'the decolonization of representation', postcolonial work had succeeded in altering understanding of colonialism but at the cost of suspending or deferring 'the question of the political' (14) and in particular the challenge of 'refashioning futures'. Scott locates the cracking of the modern world system's imaginary in the changed 'cognitive-political context' for postcolonial work that came about with the fall of the Soviet Union and the rise of neoliberal globalization. He sees a need for 'rethinking the claims and the categories of that very political modernity in which these hopes [for a refashioned future] found the voice – that of a morally neutral citizen-subject – in which to speak' (156–7). That morally-neutral citizen-subject is classic liberalism's autonomous subject. In arguing his case, Scott moves beyond the old debates between Marxist and poststructuralist postcolonialists, directing the tools of epistemological critique towards the task of renewing 'the theoretical question of the political' (224). This renewal requires engaging more fully with the assumptions of liberalism, beginning with its dependence on a 'self/identity that can choose to step back from its moral commitments, and through its autonomy-grounding faculty of critical reason, suspend its particularist entanglements and enter into the public space of shared political reason' (154).

Many different texts engage the questions Scott raises. Fundamental among these, for my purposes, is Duncan Ivison's (2002) *Postcolonial Liberalism*. In this study, Ivison theorizes the ways in which liberal thinking needs to change in order to respond adequately to postcolonial challenges. It is no accident, to my mind, that Ivison's book arises from his wrestling with the particular challenges posed to the Canadian and Australian nation-states through indigenous priority, survival and autonomy-claims in the current era. These are emerging as increasingly important for rethinking democracy in global times. Although Ivison addresses the work of many postcolonial scholars, he does not mention Scott's book, further testament, perhaps, to the cracks separating different fields of endeavour, many of which grapple with related questions within different frames of reference. Ivison's special attention to the claims for cultural and political autonomy and land rights for indigenous peoples in settler colony contexts places his book outside the dominant logic of a 'postcolonial exotic' (Huggan 2001).[1] Without exactly seeking to 'provincialize Europe' (Chakrabarty 2000), Ivison works with Chakrabarty's observation that European thought 'is at once indispensable and inadequate in helping us to think through the experiences of political modernity in non-Western nations' (cited in Ivison 2002: 40). From this starting point, he revisits the postcolonial challenge to liberal thinking in order to render it better able to redress historical injustice and respond to indigenous demands for more flexible and equitable governance models. For Ivison's project, there is no necessary disjunction between theory and practice. Each enables or blocks the other. They are co-dependent.

Victor Li (2005) makes the case for such a view explicit, by demonstrating the dependence of the logic of those postcolonial theorists who oppose theory and practice on a particular liberal view of autonomy as separateness that should be questioned. Citing Glissant, he suggests that

> In relying heavily on a notion of autonomy founded on difference, postcolonial theorists and their demotic opponents find themselves adopting a discourse in which identity is based on separation, demarcation, exclusion, and on contamination, a discourse of autonomy in which the other is not yet a "possible basis for agreement".

(214)

Li continues: 'Thus, in questioning the political and institutional motives of metropolitan postcolonial theory, critics such as Parry, Brennan, and During clearly seek to maintain, through the practice of separatist vigilance, what they regard as the autonomy and integrity of demotic resistance' (214). A similar belief, this time in the need 'to maintain the autonomy and purity of a freelance, exilic consciousness' (215) may be identified in the work of Edward Said (1993). In both cases, Li suggests, it might be more productive to shift attention away from this defensive understanding of autonomy as a separate domain towards more relational and transcultural forms that may be better suited to understanding contemporary conditions of neoliberal globalization. In his essay in this volume, Li turns away from a postcolonial analytics expressly devoted to identifying oppression and resistance towards an alertness to what he defines in the Hollywood film, *Cast Away*, as an, 'investment in self-reliance and self-improvement' (p. 67). To the old liberal values of autonomy as self-reliance and self-realization, as iconically represented in *Robinson Crusoe*, neo-liberal subject-formation adds an ability to embrace uncertainty and develop forms of emotional intelligence, as dramatized in *Cast Away*. Li sees this film as 'a subjective correlative of the new global economy's embrace of uncertainty as the opportunity for innovation and profit' and finds here 'the immanent disciplinary logic of capital' that Michael Hardt and Antonio Negri associate with their theorizations of an emergent kind of Empire. Through this argument, Li links the economic discourses of globalization at the macro level to the supposedly private and intimate details of the individual subject at the other end of the scale. This linkage reinforces Jane Poyner's argument, elsewhere in this volume, that 'the "dichotomy" of public/private needs reconceptualizing' (p. 187), and not just in post-apartheid South African writing, her focus, but also within the postcolonial field at large, if it is to successfully engage with the systemic violences promoted by neoliberal globalization.

Li and Poyner's suggested rerouting and broadening of the scope of the postcolonial gains credence because of several changes on the global scene:

1   the change in focus necessitated by the end of South Africa's apartheid regime;
2   the ongoing and increasing tensions between Israel and Palestine;
3   the break-up of the old Soviet Empire and efforts to reroute postcolonial thinking to address the autonomy demands of post-Communist states and their peoples;
4   increasing engagement with elements of postcolonial thinking within South American constituencies;
5   a growing self-awareness within American Studies of the ways in which the invader-settler-colony status of the United States seems complicit with its imperial roles abroad;
6   the rise of indigenous studies and the success of indigenous peoples in getting their claims legitimized at the United Nations;
7   what some have termed 'reverse colonization' and others 'reverse globalization': significant migrations to First World nations necessitating reconsideration of

the role of multicultural and multifaith communities within the nation-state; and

8   the rise to economic power of the so-called BRIC countries (Brazil, Russia, India, China) with a subsequent shifting of global power relations in other spheres, including a reinforcement of the knowledge that postcolonial studies are not a solely Anglophone endeavour.

The implications of these changes are developed in several of the articles included in this collection. Anna Ball, for example, examines the generic dimensions and geopolitical implications of the Muslim 'coming-to-faith' story, which she argues may challenge tendencies toward, homogenization of religion and of diasporic identity while rerouting the postcolonial toward, rooted forms of polycentricity. While Poyner identifies the need to rethink the public/private dichotomy and Ball, secular stereotypes of faith, Dorota Kolodziejczyk finds Eastern/Central Europe now posing 'a taxonomic and conceptual problem' to postcolonial studies as conventionally conceived, in the process demanding a new comparative perspective that can bring this territory within the horizon of postcolonial studies in the global context. Similarly, Jeff Mather argues for a postcolonial attention to China within the context of the post-communist transition and globalizing pressures. These critics are redrawing the accepted boundaries of the old postcolonial's geopolitical focus and, along with others exploring diaspora (Goheen Glanville) and queer theory (Louar), rethinking its engagements with subjectivity.

As these examples suggest, certain dimensions of these eight reroutings of the postcolonial involve increased pressures on once accepted definitions of many of the key terms of political thinking, including autonomy, democracy, and the human. Whereas settler colonies were once marginalized or excluded from discussion of the purely postcolonial, with these changes they are beginning to be seen as relevant sites for testing potential postcolonial futures. The very reasons for refusing to include Canada within dominant postcolonial imaginaries, because it did not fit the normative model established by India, for example, in this changed climate now seems an argument for more sustained engagement.[2]

As someone working on postcolonial questions within Canadian contexts, I welcome the recent turn made by some mainstream political theory to the particular challenges posed by invader-settler states for understanding the challenges of democracy today. The late Iris Marion Young (2007 [2000]) begins her book *Global Challenges: War, Self-Determination and Responsibility for Justice* with a chapter addressing 'Hybrid Democracy: Iroquois Federalism and the Postcolonial Project' in order to develop an alternative theory of self-determination which she suggests may help model new institutions of transnational governance. Carole Pateman and Charles Mills (2007) update their now classic studies, respectively, of 'the sexual contract' (1988) and 'the racial contract' (1997) to argue that 'it is virtually impossible to understand why certain patterns of deprivation, inequality, subordination, and violence persist at home and abroad without an appreciation of what has gone before', identifying this intertwined history of the sexual and racial contracts as 'a long process of European expansion into the territories of "lesser" peoples, of colonialism, slavery, and the subjection of women', a history that has not 'been at the forefront of political argument' but certainly needs to be (3). In this collaborative study, Pateman updates her earlier revision of contract theory from a feminist perspective by analysing what she terms here 'The Settler Contract', an illegitimate but powerful fiction that still carries force today. How a new democratic settlement may be negotiated with native peoples is a task she poses for political theorists, arguing that political theory must abandon its reliance on abstract starting points to embrace instead the ways in which societies were actually founded.

Each of these thinkers reengages liberal thinking about autonomy/community relations in ways concerned by their imbrication within colonial imaginaries. I find no such revisionary consciousness in Kwame Anthony Appiah's (2005: xv) return to John Stuart Mill to defend the 'conceptual resources of conventional liberal theory', but neither am I ready to abandon a belief in autonomy as 'the first of individual virtues' (Scott 1999: 154), as Scott implies we might consider doing. After spending the last seven years working on globalization and autonomy, I can see that more work is required to unpack these concepts.[3]

This brief mention of a variety of engagements between liberal political theory and postcolonial work suggests that postcolonial studies have not lost momentum but that their decolonizing energies are being dispersed within much broader fields of engagement, to the extent that in some cases a project may be informed by postcolonial thinking without actually categorizing itself as postcolonial or acknowledging postcolonial influences as such. While much work continues that is avowedly postcolonial in focus and approach, my interest here is in how critics are asking what David Slater terms 'postcolonial questions for global times' (1998). Young, Pateman, and Mills have been at the forefront of posing such questions, but they are increasingly being joined by many others across the globe. Several collaborative, interdisciplinary, and international projects with which I am currently involved are posing these questions in related terms.[4] While these are not consciously dedicated to 'provincializing Europe', they seek to advance a similar agenda albeit phrased in more forward-looking and positive terms, promoting reciprocal dialogue across the borders previously drawn between global South and global North. Parallels may also be drawn between the logics of these projects and that articulated in Phillip Darby's (2006) *Postcolonizing the International: Working to Change the Way We Are*. As he argues, 'much of the theorizing about the state system and sovereignty suffers from the neglect of extra-European factors' (20). Our projects seek to remedy these failures.

In this sense, they participate loosely in Mignolo's (2000) 'border thinking'. He synthesizes many of the insights provided by postcolonial revisionary thinking about the history that has led to what we call 'globalization' now and which blocks the move from what Mario Novelli (2006: 279) calls 'knowledge as regulation' towards 'knowledge as emancipation': a move I take to be the mandate of postcolonial studies in the schools, universities and the public sphere. Postcolonial attention to autonomy claims, discussed earlier in this paper, need to be brought into closer dialogue with educational efforts to 'unlearn' forms of 'sanctioned ignorance' (Spivak 1999: 337), understand and combat 'epistemic injustice' (Fricker 2007) and 'epistemologies of ignorance' (Alcoff 2007), and theorize 'cognitive justice' (Santos 2007b). With other educators, postcolonial work needs to question how the methods and possibly the goals of an education for autonomy need to be revised in light of postcolonial critique and cracking imaginaries.

That task is elaborated in collaborative volumes edited by Boaventura de Sousa Santos: *Another Knowledge is Possible: Beyond Northern Epistemologies* (2007a) and *Cognitive Justice in a Global World* (2007b). The introduction to *Another Knowledge* argues that the 'viability of an emancipatory cosmopolitan politics calls for adequate response to two kinds of problems which the transformations of global capitalism have brought to emancipatory struggles and to the production of knowledge relation to them'. These problems derive first from both the 'multi-dimensionality of forms of domination and oppression' and the resistances to which they give rise and, second, from the need for local actors to 'forge translocal and global alliances, which presuppose mutual intelligibility' (xxv). Noting that 'the burden of the colonial epistemic monoculture is still accepted nowadays as a symbol of development and modernity' (xxxii), they see postcolonial studies 'as a means to deal with this burden and its consequences' (xxxiv). Insofar as 'colonialism had a strong epistemological dimension', those ways of knowing must be challenged, and knowledge reconfigured, if emancipatory projects are to succeed. Santos's contribution to *Cognitive Justice* continues that argument and its focus on scientific modes of knowing to argue strongly that '[a] cycle of the hegemony of a certain scientific order has come to an end' (15).

These projects self-consciously extend the logic of Mignolo's cracked imaginary and resultant border thinking to reconsideration of what counts as knowledge, how we know, and who has the 'right to research', as Arjun Appadurai (2006) argues. By taking the notion of human rights and expanding it to include the 'right to research', Appadurai invites scholars to reroute previous postcolonial concerns with national liberation into contemporary social justice, educational, and equity movements, which operate at scales below and beyond the nation state. That challenge includes rethinking the concept of research itself, its modes and functions, who is qualified to conduct and evaluate research, and how research may function to extend other rights, including the right to participate within and to dissent from other public practices.

Appadurai argues that globalization makes research simultaneously "more valuable and more ephemeral" (167). It is also increasingly leading, in its neoliberal forms, towards a devaluing of certain forms of disinterested academic inquiry in ways that do not bode well for the broader acceptance or legitimacy of postcolonial work. For that reason, I value and endorse the principled arguments made by Satya Mohanty (2001) and other critical realists for the necessity of retaining objectivity in research and teaching as a value for which we must strive, while always recognizing the ways in which so-called objective practices are themselves always already co-implicated with subjective modes of thinking and situated within structures that make the subjective/objective binary less obvious a border than it may first appear.[5]

This essay has been written out of dissatisfaction with the current place of post-colonial studies within academic structures that I believe need to change while remaining conscious of the larger political forces that are also advocating change, but with very different agendas from my own.[6] As an institutional and pedagogi-cal initiative within educational structures, postcolonial studies has joined other theoretical approaches, winning a marginal place in the English department curriculum without succeeding in dislodging basic disciplinary assumptions about aesthetics, origins or value. At the same time, more positively, many new authors, texts and ideas are gaining critical attention, within and beyond the academy, and newer structures of attention are being enabled by diaspora, cultural, critical race, queer, and globalization studies, many of them influenced by postcolonial reroutings, as evidenced by the other essays included in this book.

The issue, as always, is: What kind of critical attention? On the evidence of this volume, the field remains as diverse as ever. Yet, as noted earlier, there is a general trend away from overarching postcolonial theories of all types (Marxist or poststructuralist) towards a renewed attention to the local, on the one hand, and reconceived notions of the global, on the other. The trend towards the local (at regional, national and sub-national levels) can take at least two forms. It can represent a turn towards an intense engagement with the particular as retaining some autonomy from global currents or it can mark a renewed awareness of how local and global are now intermeshed in ways we are still struggling to under-stand. In studying the global from Canadian space, I recognize that each locality now engages with global pressures and opportunities but the engagements occur on differently configured and often unequal terms. Scholars, as Ball suggests, are beginning to believe notions of diaspora can only take us so far in understanding this conjuncture.

For example, in discussing an African–Canadian text, I realized that a single incident might be read very differently when read through diasporic, national, or 'glocal' imaginaries. Esi Edugyan's (2004) *The Second Life of Samuel Tyne* narrates an African immigrant family's migration to a small Alberta town that was once the site of an earlier African–American migration. At a certain point in the narra-tive, the reader learns that the clocks in Samuel's house are set to indicate both Ghanaian and Alberta time. What are readers to make of this? Is it a sign of immi-grant nostalgia for a lost homeland? Samuel has no illusions about his country of origin, maintains little contact with it, and never expresses any desire to return, yet in many ways his life is deeply tied to his Ghanaian roots and its contempo-rary realities. The paired clocks remain a powerful reminder of where he comes from and the heritage he carries, however unwillingly, into his current home and his 'second life'. If they signify how the past endures into the present, how here and there are both coterminous and profoundly disjunctive, they also seem to mark an emerging 'glocal' sensibility, in which it is possible to live attuned to different temporal and civilizational systems without needing to choose defini-tively between them. Or to put this a little differently, this moment seems to signal a postcolonial condition 'distinguished by heterogeneous temporalities that mingle and jostle with one another to interrupt the teleological narratives that have served both to constitute and to stabilize the identity of "the West"' (Akhil Gupta cited in Gregory 2004: 7). Such an awareness seems similar to the 'cosmopolitan provincialism' advocated by Kolodziejczyk, which demands critical attention to time-lag as a more porous and diverse temporality including various time-frames. The human costs of being at the centre of such jostling are high yet they are the way that many live now.

Each interpretation of this detail reveals the different conclusions that might be reached by choosing to read through only one of a national, diasporic, glocal, or postcolonial frame. The more legible readings need to be challenged by the range of possible alternatives because each interpretation carries implications for how citizenship, belonging, and community are understood and whether or not theories of social cohesion or those of participatory democracy are advocated as more suitable for providing the social glue that makes nation-states function. By acknowledging the diversity of possible perspectives on this matter of the clocks, we may come to a better understanding of alternatively positioned ways of knowing in our interconnected world. Such questions loom large for current Canadian debates about multiculturalism and indigenous autonomy claims: the two fields of theory and practice where postcolonial thinking seems most relevant to Canadian life and where it has prompted substantial postcolonial attention.

This paper argues that decolonizing thinking needs to inform reading, research, teaching, and public projects in modes appropriate to their wider dissemination. If that means departing from the language of current postcolonial expression, then what results may not prove recognizable as postcolonial but that is surely not the issue. Sneja Gunew notes: 'whereas postcolonialism almost never makes the daily press in Canada and Australia, debates around multiculturalism constantly erupt; but in academic conferences the situation is reversed' (2004: 39). From my experience, this observation requires qualification. Postcolonialism, albeit in declining fashion, may seem to carry greater weight in literary and cultural academic circles, but multiculturalism attracts far greater attention within the social sciences: within the academy, the public sphere, and policy circles. Surely that is because multiculturalism has an active policy presence, at least in Canada and Australia, whereas the policy implications of postcolonial modes of thinking have attracted far less attention. One of the few areas where postcolonial studies may be seen to carry fairly direct policy implications is in the educational field, as this essay has argued. Curriculum, pedagogy, and research may all be productively rethought through postcolonial engagements. Public education beyond the schools, particularly within the field of museum studies, has also experienced some postcolonial influence, but even here the results are mixed.

My city, Winnipeg, is in the process of establishing a Human Rights Museum, a partnership involving three levels of government and the private sector, which poses many of these questions in very concrete ways. It too proposes to read the global from Canadian space.[7] It has already attracted controversy. Whose stories will be told in such a museum and how will they be told? Are indigenous and postcolonial perspectives likely to be welcomed? How will the museum balance competing claims to attention and deal with advocacy movements of various kinds? How will it deal with the two types of 'epistemic injustice' identified by Miranda Fricker (2007)? A Museum of Human Rights enters the complex terrain of both 'hermeneutical injustice', 'when a gap in collective interpretive resources puts someone at an unfair disadvantage when it comes to making sense of their social experiences' and 'testimonial injustice', which 'occurs when prejudice causes a hearer to give a deflated level of credibility to a speaker's word' (2007: 1). How fully will the museum's organizers and curators respect Seyla Benhabib's reminder: 'Once we name "genocide" as the supreme crime against humanity, we move in a new normative universe' (2006: 73). The museum has an educational mandate directed at schoolchildren and the general public. It is not yet clear how any potential university input might be framed. The 'Video Tour of the Museum', which was available on the official website in late 2007 but has since been removed, provided an instructive example of a nationalist pedagogy rerouted into a global discourse. Elements of this remain in the museum's Vision statement, which sees the museum as 'an iconic symbol of Canada – something as dramatic and inspiring as the Guggenheim Museum in Bilbao – a magnificent structure, encasing a world-class experience that will be a true testament to the importance Canada, as a nation, places on human rights'. The headings listed under the Purpose statement indicate it will serve as 'a centre for learning', 'a forum for dialogue', 'a home for our stories', 'a place for heroes', and 'a catalyst for action' (Canadian Museum for Human Rights website).

The challenge of how to translate postcolonial thinking into speech that might be heard and acted upon within such fraught public contexts is daunting. As Simon Featherstone (2005) acknowledges, much postcolonial thinking has been dedicated to the politics of museums and 'postcolonial public memory' (173). Some interventions have been made and, in some cases, perhaps 'Europe' has been 'provincialized' in ways productive for emergent imaginaries. But, as Pauline Wakeham (2008: 66) suggests, even self-conscious museological self-reflection may dissimulate 'its ongoing relationship to colonial knowledge/power systems' and '[w]hen the concepts of corporeality and affect are invoked in the context of museum space, thorny and complicated questions of contingency and agency arise' (68). The museum is proud of its location at the Forks, a traditional meeting place for native peoples, yet native peoples apparently were not consulted about building upon this site, which is also an important repository of their material history.

What is remembered and what is authorized in the name of human rights and humanitarian causes is becoming a major issue for the postcolonial field today. To the extent that human rights claims depend on the autonomy claims of persons and communities, the narratives of human rights seem to be embedded in the same liberal discourses that worried Scott and prompted Ivison to theorize a postcolonial liberalism capable of redefining the relations between individual and group rights in the Canadian context. Joseph Slaughter focuses 'on the shared image of the human person and its development in the *Bildungsroman* and in human rights legislation' to argue that 'Human rights law and the *Bildungsroman* are consubstantial and mutually reinforcing [...]' (2007: 4). From his study of this process, he concludes that 'our reading acts have implications not only for the imagination but the legislation of an international human rights community' (328). The various projects considered in this paper involve reading acts that redefine the scope and meaning of the cultural today, bringing it more closely into dialogue with the political, and, in the case of Slaughter, with the legal. Each of these moves, largely cultural in their provenance but political in their implications, continues the postcolonial project of addressing the 'powerful conventions of thinking [that] get in the way of research' on global interactions (Tsing 2005: 3). This paper has addressed some of those conventions, arguing that postcolonial thinkers need to continue to question the operative assumptions, including those built into the language of politics and culture, which collectively guide disciplinary inquiry, while also developing better ways of collaborating across disciplinary and geopolitical divides to construct imaginaries better suited to the challenges of the new normative universes we are entering.

Notes

1 For a valuable extension of Huggan's argument into the material history of authorship, see Brouillette (2007).
2 See, for example, the grudging, but still largely uncomprehending mention of Australia, New Zealand and Canada in Ania Loomba (1998: 14). Couze Venn (2006: 24) provides a similarly perfunctory stab at addressing the challenge settler-invader colonies make to postcolonial identity categories in a somewhat more generous spirit, acknowledging some contributions from Australia, New Zealand and the United States but showing no awareness of Canadian work.
3 The 'Globalization and Autonomy' project was a Major Collaborative Research Initiative, headed by W. D. Coleman and funded by the Social Sciences and Humanities Research Council of Canada. I am grateful to the SSHRC for the funding received as we worked, and continue to work, on this project. Further research for this paper also benefited from funding, in part, from The Canada Research Chairs programme.
4 In addition to 'Globalization and Autonomy', mentioned above, these include a project that has grown out of that work, also led by W. D. Coleman, 'Building South–North Dialogue on Globalization Research'; the Ford-Foundation funded 'Building Global Democracy', headed by Jan Aart Scholte; work on 'Critical Literacies' with a team of scholars led by Lynn Mario Menezes T de Souza and Walkyria Monte Mor in Brazil; and work on 'National and Global Imaginaries' with colleagues at the University of Manitoba, enabled through funding from the Canada Research Chair's programme.
5 For more on these questions, see the Book Review Forum in *Victorian Studies*, 50.4 (Summer 2008) discussing Daston and Galison (2007). The titles of two of these essays draw attention to the linkages between a liberal self and liberal ways of knowing that Scott and Santos seek to challenge: Amanda Anderson's 'Epistemological Liberalism' (658–65) and Theodore M. Porter's 'The Objective Self' (641–7).
6 I discuss current attacks on the humanities in 'Do the Humanities Need a New Humanism?' forthcoming in Kamboureli and Coleman, and the changing contexts of higher education more generally, in another article, 'Globalization and Education: Reconceiving the Mission, Working Toward Cognitive Justice', delivered at the conference, 'The Scope of Interdisciplinarity', University of Athabaska, Edmonton, in October 2008.

7 The Museum began as a private sector initiative to launch a Holocaust Museum, led by a wealthy local family's Asper Foundation. It has evolved into the Canadian Museum for Human Rights, recently becoming the first museum project, based outside the national capital, to be partially funded by the federal government without being administered through Heritage Canada.

Bibliography

Alcoff, L. M. (2007) 'Epistemologies of Ignorance: Three Types', in S. Sullivan and N. Tuana (eds) *Race and Epistemologies of Ignorance*, Albany: State University of New York Press.

Appadurai, A. (2000) 'The Right to Research', *Globalisation, Societies and Education*, 4.2: 167–77.

Appiah, K. A. (2005) *The Ethics of Identity*, Princeton: Princeton University Press.

Benhabib, S. (2006) *Another Cosmopolitanism: The Berkeley Tanner Lectures*, with responses from J. Waldron, B. Honig, and W. Kymlicka, R. Post (ed), Oxford: Oxford University Press.

Brouillette, S. (2007) *Postcolonial Writers in the Global Literary Marketplace*, London: Palgrave Macmillan.

Canadian Museum for Human Rights. Online. Available http: <http://www.canadian-museumforhumanrights.com> (accessed 23 March 2009).

Castoriadis, C. (1981) 'From Ecology to Autonomy', *Thesis Eleven*, 3: 8–22.

—— (1991) *Philosophy, Politics, Autonomy*, D. A. Curtis (ed./trans.), New York: Oxford University Press.

Chakrabarty, D. (2000) *Provincializing Europe: Postcolonial Thought and Historical Difference*, Princeton: Princeton University Press.

Daston L. and Galison P. (2007) *Objectivity*, Brooklyn: Zone.

Darby, P. (ed.) (2006) *Postcolonizing the International: Working to Change the Way We Are*, Honolulu: University of Hawaii Press.

Edugyan, E. (2004) *The Second Life of Samuel Tyne*, Toronto: Alfred A. Knopf.

Featherstone, S. (2005) *Postcolonial Cultures*, Edinburgh: University of Edinburgh Press.

Fricker, M. (2007) *Epistemic Ignorance: Power and the Ethics of Knowing*, Oxford: Oxford University Press.

Gregory, D. (2004) *The Colonial Present*, Oxford: Blackwell.

Gunew, S. (2004) *Haunted Nations: The Colonial Dimensions of Multiculturalisms*, London: Routledge.

Huggan, G. (2001) *The Postcolonial Exotic: Marketing the Margins*, London: Routledge.

Ivison, D. (2002) *Postcolonial Liberalism*, Cambridge: Cambridge University Press.

Kamboureli S. and Coleman D. (eds) (forthcoming) *The Culture of Research in Canadian Universities: Literary Scholars on the Retooling of the Humanities*, Edmonton: University of Alberta Press.

Li, V. (2005) 'Toward Articulation: Postcolonial Theory and Demotic Resistance', in P. McCallum and F. Wendy (eds) *Linked Histories: Postcolonial Studies in a Globalized World*, Calgary: University of Calgary Press.

Loomba, A. (1998; rev. ed.) *Colonialism/Postcolonialism*, London: Routledge.

Mignolo, W. D. (2000) *Local Histories/Global Designs: Coloniality, Subaltern Knowledges, and Border Thinking*, Princeton: Princeton UP.

Mills, C. W. (1997) *The Racial Contract*, Ithaca: Cornell University Press.

Mohanty, S. P. (2001) 'Can Our Values Be Objective? On Ethics, Aesthetics, and Progressive Politics', *New Literary History*, 32: 803–33.

Novelli, M. (2006) 'Imagining Research as Solidarity and Grassroots Globalisation: A Response to Appadurai (2001)', *Globalisation, Societies and Education*, 4.2: 275–86.

Pateman, C. (1988) *The Sexual Contract*, Stanford: Stanford University Press.

Pateman, C. and Mills C. W. (2007) *Contract and Domination*, Cambridge: Polity.

Said, E. W. (1993) *Culture and Imperialism*, New York: Knopf.

Santos, B. de Sousa (ed.) (2007a) *Another Knowledge is Possible: Beyond Northern Epistemologies*, London: Verso.

—— (2007b) *Cognitive Justice in a Global World: Prudent Knowledges for a Decent Life*, Lanham: Lexington.

Scott, D. (1999) *Refashioning Futures: Criticism after Postcoloniality*, Princeton: Princeton University Press.

Slater, D. (1998) 'Post-colonial Questions for Global Times', *Review of International Political Economy*, 5.4: 647–78.

Slaughter, J. R. (2007) *Human Rights, Inc. The World Novel, Narrative Form, and International Law*, New York: Fordham University Press.

Spivak, G. C. (1999) *A Critique of Postcolonial Reason*, Cambridge, MA.: Harvard University Press.

—— (2003) *Death of a Discipline*, New York: Columbia University Press.

Taylor, C. (2004) *Modern Social Imaginaries*, Durham and London: Duke University Press.

Tsing, A. L. (2005) *Friction: An Ethnography of Global Connection*, Princeton: Princeton University Press.

Venn, C. (2006) *The Postcolonial Challenge: Towards Alternative Worlds*, London: Sage.

Wakeham, P. (2008) *Taxidermic Signs: Reconstructing Aboriginality*, Minneapolis: University of Minnesota Press.

Wing, B. (1997) 'Translator Introduction and Glossary', in E. Glissant (ed.), *Poetics of Relation*, Ann Arbor: University of Michigan Press.

Young, I. M. (2007 [2000]) 'Hybrid Democracy: Iroquois Federalism and the Postcolonial Project', in *Global Challenges: War, Self-Determination and Responsibility for Justice*, Cambridge: Polity.

10 'Here is where I am'

Rerooting diasporic experience in Leila Aboulela's recent novels

Anna Ball

In the landscape of postcolonial diaspora studies, the recent novels of Scottish–Sudanese author Leila Aboulela present something of a conundrum. Her novels *The Translator* (1999) and *Minaret* (2005) both display an acute awareness of the transitional complexities of space, belonging and identity entailed in the diasporic experience; concerns which are perhaps unsurprising, given that Aboulela, the daughter of Sudan's first female demographer, was born in Khartoum and has subsequently moved between Egypt, Jakarta, Dubai, London and Aberdeen (Sethi 2005). The vast backdrop of (dis)location that informs Aboulela's writing seems to point towards the deterritorialized cartographies of the increasingly 'borderless world' often configured by postcolonial theorists (Miyoshi 1993: 726). Yet the textual landscapes of Aboulela's novels conjure diasporic landscapes formed not in the interstices, on the move or in the margins, but born out of the secure boundaries of faith-based community and identity, in which the establishment of roots – those constructs of essence, origin and belonging so frequently the subject of deconstruction – are posited as central to the diasporic experience. Aboulela's work therefore invites the postcolonial theorist not only to challenge the associations of rootedness with mental and spatial restriction, but to turn their attention towards questions of faith-based identity and community, and in so doing, to move towards the more nuanced and attentive conceptualization of Islamic faith and Muslim identity which, this chapter will suggest, must surely form an increasingly important direction in contemporary postcolonial scholarship.

How, then, might the complex and multiple resonances of religious geographies and identities be represented? It is, in fact, possible to turn to that much-discredited trope of the root as a motif for the Muslim subject's diasporic experience, as one which suggests both transition and ideological grounding. In an interview in 'The PostColonial Critic', Gayatri Spivak voices her concern with the idea of roots: 'If there's one thing I totally distrust, in fact, more than distrust, despise and have contempt for, it is people looking for roots. Because anyone who can conceive of looking for roots should, already, you know, be growing rutabagas' (Harasym 1990: 93). Spivak's views are no doubt intended somewhat lightheartedly, but her views reflect a broader concern with the concept of roots within postcolonial studies. As Erin Goheen Glanville outlines in her chapter on Canadian refugee fiction elsewhere in this section of the volume, postcolonialism has quite rightly long been suspicious of essentialist notions of origin, belonging and belief – they are, after all, the myths around which colonial power is constructed. Yet it might also be possible to appropriate Spivak's ironically organic image of those searching for roots as growing rutabagas (or what is more usually called swede in the UK) in order to suggest the root less as a static point of origin and more as a generative network. To return to the Greek root of the term 'diaspora', after all, takes us to the terms 'dia', through, and 'speirein', to scatter, evoking the idea of scattering, seed-sowing and the continual, transitional growth of roots as implicit within diaspora itself (Brah 2002: 18). Indeed, while Deleuze and Guattari are resistant to parallels between the rhizome and the structure of the root, there are nevertheless similarities between the generative rootings in faith of Aboulela's characters and the way in which rhizomes produce their own agglomerative 'maps' of experience: 'A rhizome ceaselessly establishes connections between semiotic chains, organizations of power, and circumstances relative to the arts, sciences, and social struggles' (Deleuze and Guattari 2004: 8), they write, in a statement which could just as well be applied to postcolonial studies itself. Indeed, it is significant that 'rhizome' is originally a botanical term which refers to a stem that burrows into the earth and produces roots. To describe Aboulela's diasporic novels as narratives of Islamic rootedness is not, therefore, to negate the transitional qualities of her works; rather, it is to recognize the generative quality of her characters' Muslim identities within their self-constituting landscapes of faith, diaspora and identity.

These generative rootings become immediately evident from the clearly delineated geographies of each novel. Both *The Translator* and the later *Minaret* trace the relocation of female subjects from Sudan to the UK, but their faith-based trajectories are very different. Sammar, the protagonist of *The Translator*, is born in the UK, raised in Sudan and later immigrates to the UK with her husband, who is soon after killed in a car accident. Isolated and in mourning in Aberdeen, she comes to work as a translator for a Scottish academic in Third World studies, Rae. He is the author of texts such as *The Illusion of an Islamic Threat* and, the reader is told, centres his own research around what he states is the little-made link between Islam and anti-colonial resistance. Here, Aboulela constructs an interesting alignment of socio-political approaches towards Islam with a postcolonial commitment to dispelling neo-Orientalist thought. While this, in one sense, conjures a sympathetic cultural environment in which a 'meeting of minds' can take place between Sammar and Rae, it also dramatizes the potential clash of secular and faith-based critical approaches, which is played out in the novel when Sammar and Rae fall in love. Despite his knowledge of Islam, Rae is initially unwilling to convert and Sammar, unwilling to compromise, returns to Sudan. Rather than this clash of world-views proving terminal, however, Rae subsequently undertakes what is described as a deeply personal spiritual journey, leading to his eventual conversion and their marriage. Despite Sammar's border-crossings, then, her commitment to Islam provides a constant backdrop to the novel. It operates as a territory that Rae, rather than Sammar, the western

academic rather than diasporic subject, must gradually move to root himself
in spiritually as well as academically, constituting on Aboulela's part a 'subtle
exercise in counter-acculturation' (Nash 2002: 30). Sammar's rootedness therefore offers her a mode of resistance and serves to guide her through the cultural
conflicts that she experiences during her travels. It is no accident that the novel
opens with Sammar sitting in the Winter Gardens, reading the species origins
of the tropical plants in the glasshouse which have also been uprooted but have
again set down their roots in order to flourish; a deeply symbolic gesture towards
the natural and generative need of all living things to find a terrain – whether
literal or spiritual – in which to root themselves, and so to grow.

In the later novel *Minaret*, the diasporic experience is once again 'rerouted'
through the protagonist's journey from Sudan to the West, which, rather than
forming a 'clash of cultures' or of civilizations, entails her conversion to Islam.
Aboulela therefore conjures a neat act of textual resistance to the reductive notion
of Islam a religion of 'the East', locating it instead as a global faith that speaks
to many different forms of cultural identity and experience. Like *The Translator*,
Minaret is also a 'coming-to-faith' story, but the journey here is Najwa's, who, as
the daughter of a disgraced Sudanese minister, is exiled to the UK after the coup
that sees her father executed. Najwa's conversion is therefore obliquely related to a
condition of postcoloniality. Najwa's narrative sees her move from a westernized,
decadent and corrupt 1980s Khartoum, where she goes clubbing to a soundtrack
of the Bee Gees while her brother acquires a drug habit, to her exile in Britain
where what she describes as her 'coming down in the world' (Aboulela 2005: 1)
eventually leads her to a life of social and faith-based submission to Islam as she
roots herself among the feminocentric community of the Regent's Park mosque.
In this sense, her diasporic narrative reverses the exilic narrative trajectory of a
journey from securely rooted national belonging into marginality, assimilation
or hybridity. Instead, Najwa moves from a realm of western-influenced privilege
into the parameters of the Muslim community, in which she must learn to locate
herself responsibly. This struggle is dramatized when Najwa, now in her thirties,
finds work as a maid for a wealthy Arab family in London and falls in love with
the family's teenage son, himself a devout Muslim. While both novels sketch out
paths of spatial transition, their geographies are ultimately constructed around
what is suggested as both a local and global, universal and personal landscape of
faith – a kind of Islamic humanism that her characters either remain rooted in or
learn to root themselves within.

Aboulela appears conscious of the challenge that this faith-based rooting
poses to postcolonial theory, and this appears in her subtle subversion of tropes
often invoked in the theorization of diaspora. *The Translator* is, after all, a novel
whose title refers to a concept frequently drawn on to suggest the mutational and
transitional qualities of diasporic experience by Bhabha, for instance, who invokes
the Third Space at 'the cutting edge of translation and negotiation' (1994: 39) or
by Chambers, for whom 'to translate is always to transform [... and] involves a
necessary travesty of authenticity or origins' (Chambers 1994: 4). This celebration

of translation as a model for diasporic experience appears akin to the model of the 'transnation' explored by Ashcroft in the first section of this volume. Yet while Islam is portrayed as a global community, Aboulela contests its configuration as a fluidly 'transnational' belief system that can be rendered immediately transparent according to a range of cultural codes. We see this in the way that translation is figured as something that incites distance and departure from a source of origin within the novels, specifically within a religious context; 'meanings can be translated but not reproduced [...] much is lost', Sammar states in *The Translator*, evoking the Qur'an as an example (Aboulela 1999: 124). She goes on to describe the Qur'an as both a hybrid and unique text in which certain 'truths' remain embedded: 'For the Arabs who first heard it', she tells Rae, '[the Qu'ran] was something new and strange, neither poetry nor prose, something they had never heard before. When the early verses of the Qu'ran were recited, many people were crying from the words and how they sounded' (124). Not only the text and its message are deemed to hold essential truths in Sammar's description of it here, but so is its very language, and indeed the spiritual and mental response that it inspires.

There is something untranslatable and innate about the nature of faith, then, and with this in mind, Sammar's response to Rae's marriage proposal, written formally on his behalf by a Muslim friend, is significant. Aboulela writes that Sammar 'was going to write two letters in two languages. They would say the same thing but not be a translation' (190). Her refusal to translate can be read as a commitment to the distinctness of cultural codes. The wording of Sammar's response to Rae is equally concerned with rootedness: 'Please come and see me', she writes from the Sudan, continuing the letter with the words, 'here is where I am' (191). Sammar's untranslated and definitive location of herself within the geographies of diaspora reflects her rootedness within what is described as the specific 'place of Allah's mercy'. So, too, does it also reflect Rae's own observation that while Islam is not 'tied to a particular place', 'the spiritual path' is 'a lonely thing [...]. Everyone is on his own in this' (202). Both Rae's internalization of diasporic experience and Sammar's definitive self-location therefore point towards the individual rooting of the Muslim subject within his or her own faith-based geographies.

Geographies of faith are also evoked in *Minaret*, whose opening scene conjures both the locatedness and universality of Islam for the diasporic subject. As Najwa walks through early morning London in Autumn and catches sight of the minaret of Regent's Park mosque, this symbol of the call to prayer conjures a vivid awareness of the sights, sounds and atmosphere of London rather than Khartoum in Najwa: 'I have never seen it so early in the morning in this vulnerable light [...]. Now (London) is at its best, now it is poised like a mature woman whose beauty is no longer fresh but still surprisingly potent' (Aboulela 2005: 1). Najwa feels herself firmly rooted within both the London landscape and Islam, then. She is, however, aware that the British-Muslim community is far from homogeneous, and her own location within it is distinct as a first-generation immigrant. She notes, for example, that the young Muslim girls who have been brought up in Britain puzzle her while she also admires them:

> They strike me as being very British, very much in London. Some of them wear hijab, some don't. They have an individuality and outspokenness I didn't have when I was their age, but they lack the preciousness and glamour we girls in Khartoum had.
>
> (Aboulela 2005: 77)

Najwa's class-position and indeed her newfound religiosity are also sources of tension with the wealthy Arab family she comes to work for, who, unaware of her privileged upbringing, view her suspiciously in contrast to the PhD-educated, liberal outlooks of the other women in the family. The daughter and son of the family demonstrate the complexities of faith-based subject-positions in particular. While the daughter, Lamya, has been born in Khartoum, she lives separately from her husband and, as her younger brother Tamer tells Najwa disapprovingly, smokes and drinks. In contrast, Tamer, while born in Oman, has spent longer in the UK and relishes the intellectual debate – both surrounding Islam and Middle Eastern politics – that he finds at his local mosque. The sense in which Najwa conforms more readily to Tamer's views of ideal female behaviour is perhaps one of the reasons that Najwa and Tamer find themselves drawn to each other; but so is the similar nature of their beliefs. Najwa is confronted with the question of whether to pursue the relationship, and in so doing, to affect Tamer's relationship with his family, and her decision to encourage Tamer to pursue his studies rather than their romance is a key turning point in the novel, demonstrating Najwa's spiritual maturity through her ability to place others first, and so to root herself within broader structures of community. Aboulela therefore resists the homogenization of the Muslim or diasporic community, but she does suggest the possibility of drawing a sense of connection with others based on a commonality of belief and behaviour. Rootedness, as Aboulela demonstrates continuously throughout her work, is not so much about staying put as branching out and forming connections with others.

There are also hints that Najwa's Islamic rooting is a problematic stance within the London landscape, however. She is the subject of an Islamophobic attack as she travels home on a bus from her mosque, as three young, possibly drunk, men abuse her verbally and throw a bottle of soft drink over her, an incident that goes ignored by the bus driver. Given the novel's setting in a post-9/11 London landscape, however, the incident acquires significance not so much due to its occurrence as to its elision within the plot. Rather than it forming a focal point in her story, Aboulela refuses to imbue it with a broader political symbolism and so to reduce Najwa to a 'cipher' for London's Muslim community. The immense distress caused to Najwa as an individual emerges in the poignant understatement of her thoughts: 'I blink and that's uncomfortable because my eyelashes are twisted and stuck together [from the soft drink]. I didn't know that eyelashes could ache' (Aboulela 2005: 81). Set within a social climate raw to the possibility of

Islamophobia, the understatement of Aboulela's narration can be read as subtly resistant to the governmental discourse that would, ironically, be reiterated only a month after the publication of the novel in June 2005, with the occurrence of the London Bombings in July of that year. Both Tony Blair in 2005 and Gordon Brown on the two-year anniversary of the bombings in 2007 spoke of the 'battle for hearts and minds' that they had planned for the Muslim community, in a typically double-edged move which at once signalled a desire for inclusion and assimilation, while also differentiating the Muslim community as one in need of direct address and intervention in the aftermath of terrorist attacks (Blair 2005, Brown 2007). While acknowledging the forms of discrimination to which her characters are vulnerable, Aboulela refuses to engage in reductive politicization of her character's experiences, just as she refuses to homogenize her own vision of the British Muslim community.

Indeed, Najwa is imbued with the power to negotiate her experiences largely through the firm rootings that she acquires through the support of the women at her local mosque, and in this sense, her coming to faith is something of a feminocentric journey. Significantly, Najwa describes her conversion as a form of self-location, stating:

> My guides chose me [...]. The words were clear, as if I had known all this before and somehow, along the way, forgotten it. Explain to me why I am here, what I am doing. Explain to me why I came down in the world. Was it natural, was it curable?
>
> (Aboulela 2005: 240)

Najwa hints at the possibility of an innate propensity for Islam, but it is unclear whether this is a product of her identity as a Sudanese subject or a more universal potential. She states at one stage that when she is among the women in Regent's Park mosque, she feels as though she were back in Khartoum, despite the fact that she was not a practicing Muslim when she lived there; yet the novel states at another stage that 'there's so much more to Khartoum than Islam' (244). Faith is not necessarily fixed within a geographical space; it is a question of imagined geography. Yet the question of gendered identity is one that is altogether more firmly rooted in Islam for Aboulela – to such an extent that she barely touches upon the issue of *hijab*, which has drawn such close attention from postcolonialists, feminists and the media alike. She describes Najwa's adoption of the *hijab* while in London quite simply as a gesture towards modesty and a marker of her femininity, hinted at in her observation that she likes the way her friend wears her *hijab*, 'confident that she has the kind of allure worth covering' (77). This confidence in the naturalness of veiling is also reflected in Najwa's thoughts when she finally adopts it: 'Oh, so this is what it was all about; how I looked, just how I looked, nothing else, nothing non-visual', she thinks, when she notices how 'all the frissons, all the sparks' from male attention around her die away (247).

The apparent simplicity of Aboulela's vision of female Muslim identity might appear reductive to many postcolonial feminist theorists accustomed to engaging in more nuanced analysis, but, in another sense, it is this very simplicity of her commitment to Islamic rootedness which constitutes the daring of Aboulela's work. Sammar's earlier statement, 'here is where I am', is symbolically reiterated by Najwa in her direct and self-assured adoption of the *hijab*; an act that is carried out by choice, and which acts as an expression of her own spiritual development. In her and her characters' refusal to justify their faith-based subject-position, Aboulela constructs statements of difference that cannot be easily co-opted by integrationist models of British diasporic community. The challenge faced by postcolonial theorists is to resist responding to such statements of faith as simply fundamentalist or essentialist; for while Aboulela's stance is firm in its beliefs, it is also a moderate religious stance inflected by a social awareness of class, ethnicity and culture. In this sense, her committed assertion of moderate Islam operates as an important move against the homogenization of the religion, at a time when reports of extremism and radicalization seem to steal the limelight.

The stance adopted by Aboulela in her novels can be related a number of discourses that might prove productive for postcolonial theorists of diaspora to reflect upon. Aboulela's recognition of the ways in which faith is shaped and developed in relation to the shifting diasporic landscape – and in particular, her recognition that it is possible to 'come to Islam' within the West itself – echoes the work of the moderate Islamic scholar Tariq Ramadan, whose recent work *Western Muslims and the Future of Islam* propounds the usefulness of *ijtihad*, literally 'effort' or critical interpretation of the Qur'an, in order to offer a means of contextualizing the role of Islam among the Muslim diaspora in the West (2004). So, too, does Islamic feminism offer a critical model which has, according to Miriam Cooke, 'allow[ed feminists] to balance their religious, specifically Islamic loyalties, with other allegiances, initiating new forms of conversation across what were previously thought to be unbridgeable chasms' (Cooke 2000: 177). Cooke posits what she terms 'multiple critique' as a practice which, unlike identity politics, 'allows for contradictions that respond to others' silencing moves', and ultimately works towards enabling 'principled and strategic alliances and networks' (177) among subjects implicated in a variety of discourses. The critical approaches of both Ramadan and Islamic feminists demonstrate that it is possible to combine consideration of belief with critical enquiry, and indeed reveal the question of religious faith to be an important construct within the mesh of subject-positions occupied by the diasporic subject. Indeed, Anouar Majid extends this analysis to suggest that an integration of Islam into critical enquiry might serve to build a powerfully non-Eurocentric mode of analysis, which, rather than focussing on (and often unduly celebrating) the gradual dissolution of subject-positions into modes of polymorphous identity, instead turns towards a recognition of what he terms 'polycentricity'; the recognition of many co-existent focuses of identity and culture (Majid 2000: 152). Among others, Islam might form one of these foci; yet while acknowledging the notion of a rooted subjecthood, it acknowledges the intricate situational dynamics that the individual nevertheless occupies.

Majid's concept of 'polycentricity' offers further insight into the complexity that lies beneath Sammar's deceptively straightforward statement: 'here is where I am', in *The Translator*. Sammar's self-locational utterance seems at first to be an uncomplicated assertion of her rootedness in Islam. Yet Sammar is, in fact, positioned within a number of discourses at this point, which render her rooting polycentric. She is at once the diasporic subject returned to her homeland, Sudan; but she is also emotionally displaced from all that has become precious to her in Aberdeen. She has just received Rae's proposal of marriage, and so is positioned as the heroine within the western romance tradition; yet this proposal also signals Rae's conversion, reversing the Orientalist tradition whereby the male subject is the bearer of knowledge and civilization, recasting Rae and Sammar within a diasporic Muslim feminist reversal of the romance tradition (Nash 2002, Smyth 2007). As such, Sammar's self-location is deceptively simple, actually comprising a vast network of subject-positions inflected through her identity as a diasporic Muslim subject. What remains at the core of these experiences, though, is Sammar's faith, which remains pivotal within the narrative and indeed her diasporic experiences. In this sense, the faith-based rootings of Aboulela's characters prove generative, producing alternative cartographies that reinscribe and overwrite the official limits of national space, and relocate their inhabitants from the margins to the centre of community and belonging.

While these rootings appear to have an affirmative quality within Aboulela's texts, it is nevertheless clear that rerooting religion within theorizations of diaspora poses a radical challenge to postcolonial enquiry. It requires, after all, that the postcolonial theorist confront what some hold to be an association of religious faith with essentialism; something which has tended to align religion with the possibility of dogmatic approaches to identity, and hence with discourses of sexism, racism and fundamentalism that must understandably be avoided by the postcolonialist. It also demands that the postcolonialist must, on the one hand, avoid responding to the complex dynamics of religious belief with an empty and uncritical cultural relativism, while on the other, must be careful not to resort to the brand of secularist scholarship that, as Anouar Majid notes, has 'increased the remoteness of Islam [...] thicken[ing] and intensif[ying] the opaqueness of a Muslim subjectivity shrouded in a different "regime of truth"' (2000: 3). It is precisely this kind of 'neo-Orientalism' to which postcolonial studies must be attentive and resistant; partly, as Robert Spencer's chapter suggests elsewhere in this volume, by recognizing the multiple citizenships of what Spencer understands as the cosmopolitan subject, but which can equally be applied to the female Muslim subjects of Aboulela's novels, who exist within diasporic, national, religious and gendered communities alike. Yet, in addition to resituating religious identity within the remit of existent postcolonial enquiry, it is also necessary to place it within the expansionist project identified by Patrick Williams in this volume, in which he urges increased attention to contemporary imperialisms, the 'war on terror' and notion of the 'clash of civilizations' as sites of postcolonial enquiry; discourses within which Islam has served a number of political ends, and which therefore demand critical attention. If the realm of religion is an unfamiliar territory for the postcolonial, then the territories of coerced hearts and minds are only too familiar, and ways of analyzing and critiquing the problematic discourses currently in circulation around the Muslim communities within the UK must surely become an urgent aim within postcolonial discourse.

Aboulela's novels therefore raise the question of faith as one that must be considered increasingly central, not only to diaspora studies, where its relation to immigration, assimilation and the already troubled model of multiculturalism needs to be traced, but also to postcolonial studies more broadly, within the landscapes of a contemporary Britain where religion is playing an increasingly politicized and formative role. This proves challenging because it requires a return to the 'roots' of postcolonial and diaspora studies, in every sense. It is clear that, while the notion of 'roots' may have become unfashionable in theorizations of identity and diasporic experience, they nevertheless reveal the networks of stability and nourishment that a rooting in religious belief and community may offer the diasporic subject. A return to roots is, ironically, one of the ways in which the notion of the postcolonial must therefore 'reroute' itself, if it is to respond to the pertinence, and possibilities, of religion as a further axis of diasporic experience and route of postcolonial enquiry.

Bibliography

Aboulela, L. (1999) *The Translator*, Edinburgh: Polygon.

—— (2005) *Minaret*, London: Bloomsbury.

Bhabha, H. (1994) *The Location of Culture*, London: Routledge.

Blair, T. (2005) 'Full Text: Blair Speech on Terror at Labour Party National Conference', *BBC News*, 16th July. Online. Available http: <http://news.bbc.co.uk/1/hi/uk/4689363.stm> (accessed 17 January 2009).

Brah, A. (2002) *Cartographies of Diaspora: Contesting Identities*, London: Routledge.

Brown, G. (2007) 'Interview by Andrew Marr', *BBC Sunday AM*, 7th January. Online. Available http: <http://news.bbc.co.uk/1/hi/uk_politics/6241819.stm#us> (accessed 17th January 2009).

Chambers, I. (1994) *Migrancy, Culture, Identity*, London: Routledge.

Cooke, M. (2000) 'Women, Religion and the Postcolonial Arab World', *Cultural Critique*, 45: 150–84.

Deleuze, G. and Guattari, F. (2004) *A Thousand Plateaus: Capitalism and Schizophrenia*, London: Continuum.

Falah, G.-W. and Nagel, C. (eds) (2005) *Geographies of Muslim Women: Gender, Religion, and Space*, New York: The Guilford Press.

Harasym, S. (ed.) (1990) *The PostColonial Critic: Interviews, Strategies, Dialogues*, London: Routledge.

Majid, A. (2000) *Unveiling Traditions: Postcolonial Islam in a Polycentric World*, Durham: Duke University Press.

Miyoshi, M. (1993) 'A Borderless World? From Colonialism to Transnationalism and the Decline of the Nation-State', *Critical Enquiry*, 19: 726–51.

Nash, G. (2002) 'Resiting Religion and Creating Feminised Space in the Fiction of Ahdaf Soueif and Leila Aboulela', *Wasafiri*, 35: 28–31.

Ramadan, T. (2004) *Western Muslims and the Future of Islam*, Oxford: Oxford University Press.

Sethi, A. (2005) 'Keep the Faith', *Guardian Unlimited*. Online. Available http: <http://books.guardian.co.uk/departments/generalfiction/story/0,,1499352,00.html> (accessed 9 January 2009).

Smyth, B. (2007) 'To Love the Orientalist: Masculinity in Leila Aboulela's *The Translator*', *Journal of Men, Masculinities and Spirituality*, 1: 170–82.

11 Rerouting diaspora theory with Canadian refugee fiction

Erin Goheen Glanville

Roots, I sometimes think, are a conservative myth, designed to keep us in our place

(Salman Rushdie)

To be rooted is perhaps the most important and least recognized need of the human soul

(Simone Weil)[1]

The recent rerouting of the postcolonial canon to include diaspora theory and literature from settler colonies presents a productive challenge for English departments: diaspora's awkward categorization as a geographical subset of postcolonial studies, alongside area literatures ('South Asian', 'African', etc.), highlights the limitations of national categories. The significance of this diasporic graft has been noted in the recent addition of 'diaspora' to The Postcolonial and Postimperial Literature and Culture Web site and in the subsection on diaspora in the new chapter 'ReThinking the PostColonial' in the 2002 edition of *The Empire Writes Back.* The historical intersection of diaspora and postcolonialism is apparent in migrations of European colonialists, forced migrations of the slave trade, and dispersed communities of indentured labourers. For more recent diasporas, usually associated with metropolitan centres, refugees, and immigrant-movements, the theoretical intersection between diaspora and postcolonialism hinges on discussions of identity: postcolonial analyses of hybridity join social science studies of diasporic identification in challenging essentialisms. Diasporic paradigms, as Rushdie's quote used as an epigraph suggests, have been a helpful way of recognizing the political agency of refugees, since they trouble the ideas of citizenship and national belonging and offer to the non-citizened the freedom to be 'out of place'.

Yet many diaspora scholars and authors, not directly invested in postcolonial and anti-colonial concerns, have celebrated migrancy as the new norm, loosening 'postcolonial' from its historical framework. In much the same way that the anti-colonial forerunners of postcolonialism are a useful sustained pressure on postcolonial studies, refugee literature provides an important adjustment to diasporic celebrations of movement and displacement, reminding readers of the unevenness of access to global migration. This essay echoes Gikandi's injunction in his own article in Section 1 to turn our attention to the numerous forms of underprivileged diasporic being, to those who find themselves in the midst of a global space they cannot relate to, let alone feel cosmopolitan in. By focusing on refugee narratives, I wish to reroot diaspora studies in postcolonial concerns for justice without losing the diasporic critique of the nation-state paradigm. Refugee characters are less concerned with the essentializing nature of rootedness, less celebrative of routes, and more concerned with the obstacles that keep them from rerooting themselves. Or, to use another metaphor, it is not the attachments to home that concern refugee characters in Canadian literature, but rather, the dramatic consequences of various 'reroutings', among which are the loss of home and their desire to be *at* home.

The productive dialogue between diaspora theory and postcolonial literary studies has been going on for almost two decades now. Yet delimiting the field of diaspora studies is especially difficult on account of its wide-ranging disciplinary methods, which encompass an eclectic mix of theoretical texts by scholars in Anthropology, Sociology, Cultural Theory, International Relations, Globalization, History, and English, and even a few who actually identify themselves as Diaspora scholars. Interestingly, neither *The Johns Hopkins Guide to Literary Theory and Criticism* (1993, 2004) nor *Key Concepts in Cultural Theory* (1999) feature entries on diaspora studies. Nonetheless, it has been consolidated as a recognized field of research with the founding of *Diaspora: A Journal of Transnational Studies* by Khachig Tölölyan in 1991, with the 2003 publication of *Theorizing Diaspora: A Reader*, and by the establishment of institutions and programmes focused on diasporic issues, such as the Centre for Diaspora and Transnational Studies at the University of Toronto in 2005.

Though authors such as Paul Gilroy and Robin Cohen have continued to write since the 1990s, very little has been done recently to theorize diaspora studies. Instead, the authors who originated the field have continued writing on a variety of related topics: race (Floya Anthias), multiculturalism (Paul Gilroy), cosmopolitanism (Robin Cohen), and surveys of specific diasporas (Donald Akenson, Rey Chow). A cursory review of the recently published texts that turn up in a library catalogue search with 'diaspora' as a keyword reveals few outright theorizations of the concept and many sociological studies of specific ethnic or racial diasporas. Perhaps having wrested approaches to ethnicity from their dependence on national borders, diasporists now explore the de-nationalized diasporas through transnational lenses. For some critics of the ahistorical nature of the field, this is a turn in the right direction. In their introduction to *Theorizing Diaspora*, Jana Evans Braziel and Anita Mannur argue that theorizations of diaspora 'must emerge from this [accumulation of political, sociological, anthropological, historical, and literary scholarship on specific diasporic communities], rather than purely postmodern theoretical abstractions of displacement and movement' (2003: 12). Yet many scholars have found the theorization of displacement to be productive in resisting nation-state sovereignty that is protected at the expense of human freedom for movement.

For poststructuralist-inflected postcolonial and diaspora theory, migrancy provides a model for resisting essentialism and cultural nationalism, and hybridity and plurality can challenge monolithic cultures and religions. Concluding *Culture and Imperialism* with a discussion of the way movement destabilizes imperialism, Said writes:

> insofar as these people [refugees, migrants, displaced persons, and exiles] exist between the old and the new, between the old empire and the new state, their condition articulates the tensions, irresolutions, and contradictions in the overlapping territories shown on the cultural map of imperialism.
>
> (1993: 332)

Part of the productive capability James Clifford sees in diaspora is that 'the nation state is subverted by diasporic attachments which construct allegiances elsewhere' (Anthias 1998: 566). Paul Gilroy agrees when it comes to cultural production: 'Whether their experience of exile is enforced or chosen, temporary or permanent, these intellectuals and activists, writers, speakers, poets, and artists repeatedly articulate a desire to escape the restrictive bonds of ethnicity, national identification, and sometimes even 'race' itself' (1993: 19). Those restrictive bonds are brought into relief by 'travel, migration and movement', which 'invariably bring us up against the limits of our inheritance' (Chambers 1994: 115). Chambers reminds us not to forget the 'real differences between forced movement and exiles of individuals and peoples' and 'that diffuse sense of mobility that characterizes metropolitan life, charted in the privileged channels of movement', but he does not address these real differences (28). Instead he reiterates that the gaps between the two types of movement provide room for critiquing the national idiom.

Inadvertently then, within diaspora theories, the refugee joins a host of other migrants caught up in transnational movement. In the rest of my essay, I will be looking at a number of generically different texts about refugee experiences, written by Canadian diasporic writers: two short stories, 'Refugee', by M. G. Vassanji, and 'On the Eve of Uncertain Tomorrows', by Neil Bissoondath; Camilla Gibb's international bestselling novel, *Sweetness in the Belly*; the poem 'The Refugee' by Lillian Allen, and 'Soobax', the hip hop hit by Toronto-based Somali refugee, K'Naan. If one were to read M. G. Vassanji's short story 'Refugee' (1992) as paradigmatic for the liberating potential of diasporic movement, the position between nations of the protagonist, Karim, would simply represent the possibility for thinking outside of the nation-state paradigm and the importance of crossing boundaries in pursuit of non-essentializing identities. Yet the picture that emerges from Karim's constant 'routing' is not hopeful. The state of limbo Karim most often finds himself in is characterized by a sense of shame at what he feels is a betrayal of his home, of his family, and of himself. In transit, he is extremely uncomfortable with himself, seeing himself in the mirror and realizing that he is 'dressed all wrong', that he stands out 'like a sore thumb', and that he is 'shrunken and small in this strange, alien environment' (1992: 116). Having come from a small town, he has been uprooted and thrown into the disorienting world of global travel and feels 'crowded and without meaning' when faced with questions about his legal status (118). One of the reasons why he feels this way is because he cannot maintain a sense of integrity about who he is and where he has come from. The effects of popular culture and colonial myths on Karim's self-image are also closer to the heart of Vassanji's story: Karim's careful attempts to blend in have gone to waste as he realizes that the western styles he picked up from the media are no longer chic (117). The shame he feels that his culture, family, and country have been unable to prepare him for this modern place is debilitating. He is consistently interpreting this new world through the lenses of television shows, movies, and stories he has consumed from the West, and these lenses turn out to be taken from glasses that have been discarded by the western world he encounters. He uses expressions that are outdated; sees a man who walks 'like cowboys walk in movies' and so feels like the 'Indian' who is hunted, primitive, and evil; interprets a German civilian as if he were a villain in a spy movie; and worries that he might meet a ghost or a vampire and be murdered (117–122). He lives in a half fictional, half historical reality that has been made into entertainment by western storytellers and finds that his earnestness makes him seem outdated in the world of global travel. Thus questions of ongoing colonial influence and the legitimacy of supranational organizations such as the UN Refugee Agency make this story less about an enchanting ex-centric character and more about the unevenness of contemporary global movement.

The key texts in diaspora theory are optimistic, but their portrait of the 'exile' or refugee is somewhat troubling. In some cases not only are the crucial distinctions between forced and voluntary exile collapsed, but 'the refugee' (definite article) seems to be dangerously close to becoming a general metaphor and figurehead for the postmodern condition of migrancy. Clearly I am not the first to comment on this: in the recent edition of *The Empire Writes Back*, a new subsection on the relationship between postcolonialism and diaspora comments that some scholars 'have raised concerns that [the desire to disrupt the "fixity of colonizer-colonized binaries"] emphasizes a notion of the "liberated" subject not accessible to the larger body of ex-colonized "subjects-in-place"' (219). Simon Gikandi, in his essay in this volume, challenges postcolonial theories of cosmopolitanism to refocus on refugees, whose experience is in stark contrast to that of the academic elite which theorizes from positions of privilege. Zygmunt Bauman's well-known distinction between tourists and vagabonds in *Globalization: The Human Consequences* (1998) is similarly helpful. For refugees, being in migration often means being a subject-in-place in a refugee camp or some other place where movement is impeded. Theory therefore needs to be grounded in written and spoken, public and personal narratives of specific transnational movements, not on some abstract conception of liberatory migration and uprooting. For Joaquin in Bissoondath's 'On the Eve of Uncertain Tomorrows' (1991), ex-centric spaces such as La Barricada, a café and meeting place for Latin American migrants, are not liberating. He admits that he 'would not come here if he felt he had a choice' because the place reeks of despair (15). Instead, he longs for the 'banality' of a simple domestic life, for normality (23). How does one bring this literary representation of an individual's experience of being a refugee into conversation with a theorized diaspora paradigm?

Khachig Tölölyan finds the humanist offshoot of diaspora theory to be of immense value, but also briefly registers a similar concern with its levelling influence: 'This is a reduction of diaspora, which occurs when the ideas of identity and subjectivity produced by a theory-inflected investigation of texts is projected upon the *social* text of diasporas' (1996: 28). The stories that theories tell have the potential to overwrite the stories refugees tell. Like Joaquin, who experiences the logic of Canadian refugee law as imposed on, rather than emerging from, his refugee experiences, refugee narratives can be silenced by the application of theoretical templates, and their potential to refresh the enclosed space of academic literary knowledge production can be extinguished. How might Canadian literary representations of refugee experiences speak back to a diasporic theoretical focus on routes in opposition to roots?

Camilla Gibb's best-selling novel *Sweetness in the Belly* (2005) illustrates the tension between Rushdie's and Weil's quotes in this article's epigraph and leads the reader to understand that its characters desire both new roots and the revitalization of old roots. It tells the story of Lilly, a girl who is orphaned in Tangier and eventually finds herself in London, refugee-ed by the Ethiopian crisis of the 1970s. Lilly's parents were hippy nomads, travelling through Africa in the bliss of freedom from obligation and attachment, certain that roots were a conservative ideology. Having been refugee-ed as an adult, Lilly describes her childhood as 'a series of aborted conversations, attachments severed in the very same moment they began' because of her parents' abhorrence of roots (10). 'You put roots down and they'll start growing', her father warns her. Her obvious question is 'But why is that so bad?' And his answer is that roots make travel painful and that it is better to focus on the present journey than on the past. Even the structure of the book belies his attempts to demolish roots: Lilly's present situation in London is spliced with accounts of her history in Ethiopia. The cumulative effect is a picture of the trauma of her insufficiently rooted past as inseparable from her current situation of simply being *en route*. Not until she finds the strength to root herself in a new place, which is exemplified by her willingness to find a new apartment and decorate it and to enter into a romantic relationship, does her character seem at peace (Gibb 2005: 402). The irony she realizes is that her own parents' roots are actually in England and that their death was precipitated by their attempts to raise money to go 'home'. Twisting her father's earlier warning to demonstrate the inevitability of rootedness, she comments, 'You put roots down, they'll start growing' (401). The necessity of those roots for her health and functioning is so obvious by this point in the novel that one need not even ask if rootedness is a good or a bad thing. To have healthy roots in a new place is to be at home; to have healthy roots in an old place is to enrich that home even further. As Anna Ball points out in her essay on Scottish–Sudanese author Leila Aboulela elsewhere in the volume, the freedom of rootedness can in effect enable creativity.

The intertwining here of 'roots' and 'home' is crucial Olive Senior has described home as 'a place where there is a condition of resonance, or sound returned; that is, a place where you speak to a community and it speaks back to you' (2005: 37). Like a gourd that resonates because it is being 'spoken to' by the stones shaken inside of it, home is where you find yourself in genuine dialogue with a place and its community. The question of home and belonging is a vexed one for refugees who find themselves stuck between their global and local identities as they seek asylum in the Canadian context. Home is 'back there', but can no longer be home; this new place of residence and its community may not be desired as home or be willing to open itself up to the asylum-seeker. Lillian Allen's poem 'The Refugee' describes the silence that greets one asylum seeker's appeal for refuge and for community, and the way that the stonewall of silence – 'no one appeared/or dared to care/for the solitary heart/that paced the night' – stretches his nerves, until he snaps in the taut vacancy of response, jumping from his balcony to the relief of death ((1993) 73–4).

If his loneliness is not enough to prove he was not at home, the aftermath of the asylum seeker's death is projected in the poem's final stanzas through an unresolved rhythm and rhyme: 'nothing resolved/a few problems got solve/ two months rent defrayed/the credit companies got swayed/on his apartment a sign says/Now Renting' (72–3). All that is left in his departure are concerns for credit card loans and the temporary vacancy of a landlord's income generator. The resonance between any Canadian community and this refugee is minimal, and what resonance exists speaks only to the use value of the body in matters of money. His death does not involve an uprooting that is painful for others around him; he is not leaving a home behind. The plunge he must take to the ground from his apartment balcony is the cruel distance he must bridge to impact the local place he inhabits, and the hard concrete of the city proves impenetrable.

Though Karim's story ends before he reaches Canada, one wonders if a similar fate awaits him there. On the train in Germany, he notices that 'around him, everyone else sat composed into this stillness, belonging to it' while he feels strange to it (Vassanji 1992: 121). He has come 'from a sitting-room full of family in Dar into this utter, utter loneliness under an alien sky', feeling out of touch with his own face and hoping even to be sent back home (126–7). Vassanji's 'Refugee' demonstrates a prior concern as well: the inaccessibility of Canada to lower class African refugees. In a recent CBC news piece about refugees and 'illegal' immigrants in France, a French-speaking refugee was asked why he would not come to Canada since France is so unwelcoming. 'Because Canada is hard to get to', he responded simply. The body of water that separates Canada from the majority of refugees in the world is a natural restriction on asylum seekers, allowing Canada the luxury of select generosity. Even as diasporic readings of refugee experiences do appear to empower refugee-ed subjects who have been silenced 'because they do not possess the "proper" political subjectivity (i.e. state citizenship)', diasporic paradigms must be supplemented with a realization of the material power that national borders and nation-state mechanisms maintain (Nyers 2006: 16). As Clifford has remarked, 'recurring announcements of the obsolescence of nation-states in a brave new world of free trade or transnational culture are clearly premature' (1997: 9). Refugee stories inflected with diasporic consciousness do resist, among other things, the essentialism of cultural nationalism, and a diaspora paradigm allows us to celebrate the resilience of refugee-ed people and recognize the political legitimacy of civic action by non-status people. But refugee narratives also point to the need for reworking both present and past national homes, without directly challenging the legitimacy of the nation-state.

One alternative is to express the refugee's position between nations as the potential to aid each nation's pursuit of justice rather than as the impetus for de-nationalizing politics. The poetry of K'Naan, a Toronto hip hop artist and refugee from Somalia, exemplifies this kind of position. His first popular song, 'Soobax' (2005), was born out of his desire to speak to the warlords of Somalia 'directly' and ask them to account for their violence against their people. In personal interviews, he also addresses the racism that he and friends have experienced at the hands of police officers in the West. K'Naan demonstrates a commitment both to his roots in Somalia and to his new home in Canada. Somalia becomes almost mythic in his lyrics: the cradle of civilization, he calls it, a nation of poets who need to stand up to the gunmen that have been holding their nation hostage.

Being rooted in a nation can actually increase a person's ability to pursue justice. Nega Mezlekia, in his memoir, notes the differences between living under the democratic government of Canada and living under the military junta of Ethiopia. The continuing metaphor throughout is of Ethiopia, his homeland, as a hyena eating its own children 'at an alarming rate' (2000: 162). Interestingly, he suggests that Canada does not need to become more hybrid, just more aware and considerate of the rest of the world (350). Refugee artists and authors remind us that national and cultural borders are not the source of exclusion in and of themselves; critiques must also look to the spirit in which those borders are maintained and to the lines between privileged and underprivileged peoples as those distinctions are written into state processes.

I would argue that if diaspora theory is to be helpful for understanding and empowering refugee-ed writing in Canada it needs to broaden its analysis beyond critiquing nation-state mechanisms and the state sovereignty paradigm, and address the question of the daily obstacles to rerooting that Canadian texts show refugee-ed characters facing. In *Mistrusting Refugees*, E. Valentine Daniel and John Chr. Knudsen suggest that 'the various stages in the refugee's life cycle, which threaten life with radical discontinuity, are stages in which "trust" is placed on trial. The vindication of trust depends on the creation of meaning' (1996: 4). Such is Karim's experience; he cannot connect the new things he is experiencing with anything familiar and thus ends up distrusting the very person who could assist him. He is unable to read the instructions for the phone, and, when a man offers to help him place the call, Karim 'would not give the man the number he had been trying to call. He had heard too many stories of betrayal, arrived with too many warnings' (Vassanji 1992: 119). Though he has not experienced this betrayal himself, he knows that to be a refugee is to distrust everyone around you.

While Karim finally finds home in a community of non-status migrants who give him their full trust in solidarity as 'illegals', Joaquin in 'On the Eve' has the opposite experience. The torture and betrayal that mar his past keep him from connecting with the other refugee claimants with whom he shares a house. They each keep to themselves: 'Joaquin prefers it this way – life has taught him that the friendliest smile may conceal the sharpest teeth' (7). He refers to his housemates variously by their nationalities or ethnicities. 'The Vietnamese couple' he describes as 'restless', 'watchful', and 'hard-eyed in the way of the ravenous' (6). Over breakfast, 'The Sikh' nods to him but does not speak. The heaviness of the overcast weather mirrors the heaviness of a house filled with distrusting silence, and the space between distrusting people dampens the life in Joaquin. Lack of trust makes putting down roots a risky process.

A lack of supportive community and social networks is what drives Tere, a mother who frequents the same café as Joaquin, over the edge to attempt suicide. Dropped into an apartment with two children and without any instructions or communication about practicalities, Tere is so unprepared for the life she will be living that she uses the legs of her dining room chairs to start a fire in the middle of her living room. She wishes to return to her country so that she can have the social support of her family, but she knows that her children have no future there (Bissoondath 1991: 17). She is unable to root herself without her community, and loneliness overwhelms her. Even appointed support networks can fall through. Mary Jo Leddy, founder of Romero House, a home for refugee-ed people in Toronto, Ontario, tells the true story of Medhanit whose claim was denied because 'she seemed confused and uninformed about the political situation in Eritrea' (1997: 113). Knowing Medhanit was well-connected to the opposition party in Eritrea and that her return meant she and her children would likely be taken hostage and tortured, Leddy listened to the tapes of Medhanit's hearing. What Leddy discovered was the snoring of a sleeping lawyer and the fumbles of a poor translator, and so she and a volunteer lawyer began working on preventing Medhanit's deportation.

In each of these examples, the importance of building human communities on the basis of trust is key for the health of new roots. Even when refugees are offered support through government or volunteer networks, they can still face the prominent obstacle of being expected to 'perform refugeeness'. The concept of refugeeness is found in the belief of citizens and governments that the constructed political category of 'refugee' is natural and names a certain kind of person. As Nyers writes, 'the politics of being a refugee has as much to do with the cultural expectation of certain qualities and behaviors that are demonstrative of "authentic" refugeeness (e.g., silence, passivity, victimhood) as it does with legal definitions and regulations' (xv). The necessary performance of silence, passivity, and victimhood is what compels Karim to consider giving himself up to police officers in Germany and what drives Joaquin to depression and inertia. In Bissoondath's story, Amin is cheerfully sure that his tomorrow will come and that he will become Canadian because he exudes the 'genteel poverty' and 'summoned ebullience' that he thinks he needs to succeed. But his claim is overturned despite his real need for refuge. Joaquin's scarred hands and body become his largest asset in Canada. His lawyer's pornographic gaze on the signs of his torture create in him an odd double-consciousness, aware of the fact that he has been refugee-ed even as he is performing 'the refugee' in order to be acknowledged. He knows that in order to be accepted in Canada he must present himself as someone who will not rock the boat, as someone to be pitied and in desperate need of help. Yet, on the streets, he finds that the moment when he most belongs is the moment when his scarred hands hold back the bleeding of Tere's wrists. His ability to confidently act has produced in him a sense of at-homeness in this city:

> He feels less distant from these people now, strangers become a little less strange not through any act of their own but – in a twist he cannot understand – through an act of *his* own: in this city, he has helped save a life.
>
> (1991: 22)

Noticing the signs of domesticity around him, he desires the feeling of simply being at home. But both his need to be a political and social agent and his need for community go against the performance of refugee-ness that he knows will prove he is a refugee: being a passive, fearful, but brave individual.

Karim is a slightly different case in that he does not strictly fit the UN definition of a refugee, but will most likely succeed in his claim because he knows how to perform refugee-ness well. When he first arrives in Germany his protective mantra, repeated to anyone who approaches him, is 'I am a refugee; I am a refugee' (Vassanji 1992: 118). The self-alienating performance that both characters are forced into is what blocks them from becoming full participants in the new places to which they travel. How does one make a resonant home when silence and passivity are part of the requirement for staying? K'Naan is an example of one refugee-ed artist who refuses to perform refugeeness. His popular 'Soobax' music video features dancing, singing, ululating refugee-ed communities, looking straight into the video camera and demanding that they be listened to and recognized as lively culturemakers and as political actors. 'You cripple me, you shackle me, you shatter my own future in front of me', he tells the Somali gunmen and the western powers that have ignored his country's issues. 'Soobax' (come out with it), he tells his listeners, and face what is being done to the people of Somalia. All the while he is surrounded by the energy of dancing crowds of Somali refugees in Nairobi where the video is set. He is not alone; he is not passive. He does not ask for help; instead, he demands justice from local powers (the gunmen of Somalia) and from global powers (western countries), but also demands that the unique power of refugee-ed people to lobby for justice both locally and globally be recognized.

Although I have argued for the recognition of forced exile and of the simultaneous loss of roots and impediments to rerooting that occur in refugee migration, K'Naan and refugee artists like him remind us that life can grow in blocked passageways. The liveliness, the civic participation, and the active nature of refugeeed communities in Canada are clear indications of the possibilities for rerouting life around the blockages. In the end we must remember that there is no such thing as a typical refugee story, so diverse are the paths of human diasporas. One of diasporic literature's contributions to postcolonial studies is the expansion of readers' imaginative horizons regarding who refugee-ed people are and what their migration stories have to tell us. This essay aims to be precisely such an attempt to hear more clearly the narratives of those dispossessed and uprooted in Canada. Creative stories of the kind I have been looking at facilitate a communal resonance to the tangible experiences of human beings who have been refugee-ed; they can remap diasporic experience as a struggle towards belonging that is obstructed by a much broader set of circumstances than a simple story of collusion with/antagonism against the nation-state could indicate. Placing these narratives in dialogue with diaspora theory highlights once more the importance of literature to the diasporic off-shoot of the postcolonial – which has been predominantly routed through discussions of cultural theory – and provides a much-needed return of the postcolonial to the stories lived by the contemporary disenfranchized.

Note

1 I need to acknowledge Steven Bouma-Prediger and Brian J. Walsh (2008) who first compared these two authors in *Beyond Homelessness*.

Bibliography

Allen, L. (1993) 'The Refugee', *Women Do This Every Day*, Toronto: Women's Press: 73–4.

Anthias, F. (1998) 'Evaluating "Diaspora": Beyond Ethnicity?', *Sociology*, 32.3: 557–80.

Ashcroft, B., Griffiths, G. and Tiffin, H. (2002) *The Empire Writes Back: Theory and Practice in PostColonial Literatures*, London: Routledge.

Bauman, Z. (1998) *Globalization: The Human Consequences*, New York: Columbia University Press.

Bissoondath, N. (1991) 'On the Eve of Uncertain Tomorrows', in *On the Eve of Uncertain Tomorrows*, Toronto: Penguin Books: 1–26.

—— (1994) *Selling Illusions: The Cult of Multiculturalism in Canada*, Toronto: Penguin Books.

Bouma-Prediger, S. and Walsh, B. (2008) *Beyond Homelessness: Christian Faith in a Culture of Displacement*, Grand Rapids, MI: Eerdmans Publishing.

Braziel, J. E. and Mannur, A. (eds) (2003) *Theorizing Diaspora: A Reader*, Malden, MA: Blackwell Publishing.

Chambers, I. (1994) *Migrancy, Culture, Identity*, London: Routledge.

Clifford, J. (1997) *Routes: Travel and Translation in the Late Twentieth Century*, Cambridge, MA: Harvard University Press.

Cohen, R. (1997) 'Classical Notions of Diaspora: Transcending the Jewish Tradition', *Global Diasporas: An Introduction*, Washington: University of Washington Press: 1–29.

Daniel, V. E. and Knudsen, J. C. (eds) (1996) *Mistrusting Refugees*, Berkeley: University of California Press.

Gibb, C. (2005) *Sweetness in the Belly*, Anchor Canada.

Gilroy, P. (1993) *The Black Atlantic: Modernity and Double Consciousness*, Cambridge, MA: Harvard University Press.

K'Naan (2005) 'Soobax', *Dusty Foot Philosopher*. Online. Available http: <www.knaanmusic. com> (accessed June 2007).

Leddy, M. J. (1997) *At the Border Called Hope: Where Refugees are Neighbours*, Toronto: Harper Collins.

Mezlekia, N. (2000) *Notes from the Hyena's Belly: An Ethiopian Boyhood*, Toronto: Penguin.

Nyers, P. (2006) *Rethinking Refugees: Beyond States of Emergency*, New York: Routledge.

Said, E. (1993) *Culture and Imperialism*, New York: Vintage.

Senior, O. (2005) 'The Poem as Gardening, the Story as Su-Su: Finding a Literary Voice', *Journal of West Indian Literature*, 14.1–2: 35–50.

Tölölyan, K. (1996) 'Rethinking Diaspora(s): Stateless Power in the Transnational Moment', *Diaspora*, 5.1: 3–36.

Vassanji, M. G. (1992) 'Refugee', *Uhuru Street*, Toronto: McLelland & Stewart Ltd: 116–29.

12 Ma Jian's *Red Dust*

Global China and the travelling-self

Jeffrey Mather

Postcolonial theory has taken many directions in China over recent decades, and has increasingly become subject to a number of pressing questions about its relevance and effectiveness. Rey Chow (1997) has expressed scepticism towards the idea of postcolonialism, arguing that its terminology and approach are inappropriate in the context of China and can lead to monolithic understandings of Chinese nationalism. Arif Dirlik (1997) has stressed the influence of global capitalism in China, and the ways in which global trends and transnational flows have challenged us to move beyond postcolonial models and frameworks. Anfeng Sheng (2007) has pointed to the translations and critical misuses of postcolonial theory in China, arguing that while the translation of important postcolonial texts into Chinese has elicited provocative questions about China's 'third world' status or its relationship with the history of Western imperialism, such postcolonial accounts often ignore the history in which the theories themselves were written, and tend to reinforce the binaries of East and West along with essentialist notions of Chinese identity. Ben Xu (1995) has been even more disparaging towards postcolonial theory as it has been used with regard to China, suggesting that critical engagement with the postcolonial, along with other 'posts' such as postmodernism and poststructuralism, has – despite the oppositional veneer – been ultimately complicit with the politics of the state, reflecting an inherent conservatism in post-1989 (Tiananmen Square protests) scholarship in China.

Yet some of these critics also express hopefulness towards postcolonial studies and the critical perspectives that it may open to cultural and literary studies. In Sheng's assessment, postcolonial criticism need not dwell on the pernicious effects of Western imperial history and can be applied to China's own national context:

> postcolonialism should not only be used to attack the Western hegemony in defense of any version of nationalism or essentialism. The problems within the national boundary are perhaps equally, if not more, important and urgent to resolve with the international ones.

(2007: 136)

Similarly, Xu contends that the postcolonial can offer ways of thinking beyond the language of essentialism, expressing an 'ethic of opposition'. Xu defines postcolonialism, therefore, as 'a moral imperative, that is, in opposition to cultural violence exemplified by language, philosophy, science, or ideology that can be used to perpetuate and legitimize tyranny, domination, and injustice' (1995: 16). 'It is not', Xu contends, 'something intrinsic to the object of its opposition (the West, the nation-state, universalism, etc.) that marks out the discursive practices of the postcolonial but the oppositional way in which the practice is deployed' (125).

This essay shows that a postcolonial perspective can indeed provide a productive and politically engaged way of reading literature and history, interrogating national boundaries, and questioning essentialist identity politics in the context of modern China. Elsewhere in this collection Dorota Kolodziejczyk seeks to widen the scope of postcolonial debates by discussing various ways in which postcolonial theory can acquire meaning and usefulness in the context of post-communist Eastern Europe. Postcolonialism, according to Kolodziejczyk, can be used not only to articulate questions of imperial history and anti-imperial struggle, but also to theorize, and in some senses liberate, literature from nationalist paradigms. In a way that is germane to Kolodziejczyk's discussion of Eastern Europe's 'postcolonial' status, this study will question what it means to be 'postcolonial' during a period of 'post-communist' transition in China. The particular focus of this discussion is Ma Jian's *Red Dust*, a semi-autobiographical travel book that describes the journeys through China of a dissident writer and artist during the 1980s. This article will throw light on the history that informs *Red Dust*, examining how Ma's text writes back to the disciplining and alienating effects of a repressive communist nationalism.

Red Dust is an outsider's text, both in terms of its subject matter and its general readership. The book has sold more in English translation than in the original Chinese (it appeared under a pseudonym in China, heavily censored, and with only very limited distribution). In the West the book has sold well, and it received a Thomas Cook Travel Book Award in 2002. Ma, who now lives in London, has also received critical acclaim for his other books, most recently *Beijing Coma* (2008), which offers a detailed account of the Tiananmen Square student uprising during the summer months of 1989, recounted from the early twenty-first century perspective of a comatose student who was shot during the protests. Similar to Ma's later writing, *Red Dust* is a book of political discontent and restlessness, exploring themes of physical incarceration and bodily entrapment in order to expose a history of ideological repression. In *Beijing Coma*, the narrator Dai Wei becomes a metaphor for China's inner knowledge of, yet inability to speak out about, the Tiananmen events. *Red Dust* anticipates this later work, but inverts the metaphorical terms of the body: rather than explore the inner consciousness of a bed-ridden patient, it documents the outward movements of an artist on the run.

Red Dust begins six years after the death of Mao Zedong and the end of the Cultural Revolution. The widespread paranoia, violence and hysteria that swept through China during the 1960s and 1970s had largely subsided with Mao's passing and the imprisonment of the Gang of Four, but *Red Dust* recounts another history of ideological tyranny that is less well known. During the late 1970s Deng Xiaoping's 'open-door' policy and Four Modernizations (of the economy, science and technology, culture, and the army) changed the face of the country, bringing a flood of foreign investment into areas that were deemed Special Economic Zones. Consequently, during the late 1970s foreign goods – including books, music, and luxury items – found their way into China, either through official channels or via black market networks. However, with the exception of a few brief moments of liberalization, cultural and political expression remained closed and controlled.

Red Dust is set during the Anti-Spiritual Pollution Campaign, a conservative measure implemented by the communist leadership during the fall of 1983 that was aimed at counteracting the pernicious effects of 'foreign culture' on Chinese society. Although the Campaign itself was short lived (it lasted only 27 days), its official focus on intellectual and artistic matters synthesized larger social and political tensions during the post-Mao period. Wendy Larson and others have shown that the Anti-Spiritual Pollution Campaign was the first movement of its kind in China to spend a significant portion of its energy on literary matters, which included a broad range of moral, philosophical and social issues (Larson 1989, Gold 1984, Liu 2001). During this period, literature was viewed as central in promoting a healthy, 'harmonious' society. At the highest level of government, Deng Xiaoping was quoted as blaming the existence of 'spiritual pollution' on artists and writers, whom he viewed as 'deprecating Chinese tradition' in favor of the 'modernist schools', and blindly imitating foreign culture. Party propaganda Chief Deng Liqun described 'spiritual pollution' as forms of expression that included obscene, barbarous or reactionary materials; vulgar taste in artistic performances; indulgence in individualism; and statements that ran counter to the country's social system (Gold 1984: 957).

The conservative backlash that caused Ma and other writers and artists to be suppressed during this period was in many ways a fearful response to the increased availability of foreign literature and popular culture during the early 1980s; however, the crackdown against 'spiritual pollution' was also meant to silence more troubling theoretical views which began to emerge during the late 1970s. In various newspapers and magazines, intellectuals and government officials debated fundamental questions about the place of Marxism in modern Chinese society. Perhaps most prominent was Wang Ruoshui, the editor of the Party newspaper *China Daily News* (*Renmin Ribao*), who contended that 'alienation' – rather than being the result of a decadent capitalist system, as Marx had suggested – could also take place under socialism.

Through the form of a travel book, *Red Dust* similarly challenges many of the tenets of imposed and heavily policed communist orthodoxy, articulating several ways of resistance against the ideological colonization of intellectual and creative expression in an ostensibly 'modern' and 'open' China. Ma describes the days before the campaign in terms of a growing hopefulness among artists and writers. He writes of his underground meetings with artists and poets, of how he and his friends would hold secret parties where they would listen to the banned Taiwanese singer Deng Lijun, discuss art, and occasionally converse with disguised foreign journalists. But this is a world continually under scrutiny. Windows are kept shut, despite the stifling and humid Beijing summer weather, for fear of being over-heard by neighbours or local police. The flat is a dissident space, but one that is constrained – and contained; it is, in a sense, a microcosm of the country as a whole, teeming with such pockets which, however, never come together. 'China', Ma prophetically states, 'feels like an old tin of beans that having lain in the dark for forty years, is beginning to burst at the seams' (2002 [1987]: 6). The forty years, of course, refers to the period of communist rule, and is particularly poign-ant when we consider that it was written only one year before the protests and subsequent violence that took place in Beijing during the summer of 1989.

As a propagandist for the Party, Ma travels around the country taking pictures that document China's industrial rise under socialism. His photo-graphs, however, end up being criticized and deemed unpatriotic. Soon after, his personal life and his acquaintances with other artists and writers also begin to raise suspicions. Under pressure from officials at work, and after several inci-dents of police interrogation, Ma flees Beijing and undertakes a long pilgrimage around the country.

In many ways *Red Dust* draws on a long tradition of travel in the classical Chinese tradition: as an exiled artist figure, Ma's story resonates with earlier Chinese narratives of romantic wandering, spiritual uncertainty, lyricism, and loss.[1] This Chinese tradition of travel is clearly apparent as Ma refers to classi-cal figures and texts throughout his travels (in *Beijing Coma* his narrator's favorite book is a travel text of sorts, the ancient and esoteric *The Book of Mountains and Seas* [*Shanhai Jing*]). Yet similar to Gao Xingjian's Nobel prize-winning novel of the same period, *Soul Mountain* (1989), Ma also seeks inspiration from and adapts non-Chinese literary sources in provocative ways. While Gao looked to French modernist and existential writing, Ma is primarily influenced by American litera-ture. Early into *Red Dust*, Ma refers to Salinger's *The Catcher in the Rye* (1951), an emblematic novel of alienation in mid-twentieth-century America. Later on he takes Whitman and Kerouac as models, fashioning himself, with his long hair and unkempt appearance, as a beatnik or hippie traveller celebrating the open road. Finally departing from Beijing, he writes:

> I have left my job and packed a change of clothes, a notebook, two bars of soap, a water bottle, a torch, a compass, two hundred yuan, a wad of rice coupons, my camera and Walt Whitman's *Leaves of Grass*. My old life recedes into the distance and my heart races with the train as we rattle towards China's far west.
>
> (Ma 2002; [1987]: 61).

Ma also describes himself as the first reader of a translated edition of Ginsburg poetry; the poems, teeming with anarchic energy, also simultaneously highlight the relative ease of living in America, for, as Ma remarks, political opposition, economic deprivation or artistic 'dissidence' mean altogether different things in the US and China. Ma establishes some critical distance between his own experi-ence as a dissident writer in China and the American counter-culture tradition, contrasting his very real despair with Ginsburg's relative freedom to express political disaffection:

> … Ginsburg can sing out of his window in despair, he can cry all over the street. That sounds like heaven to me. He implies that a country is not fit for humans to live in. Well, he should live in China for a month, then see what he thinks. Everyone here dreams of the day we can sing out of our windows in despair.
>
> (171)

The influence of Ginsburg and Whitman also pervades the way in which Ma expresses bodily needs and desires. Similar to Whitman's moments of spontaneous sexual expression in *Leaves of Grass*, Ma's journey is infused with a sense a longing, and throughout he recounts moments of sexual adventure.

Ma was certainly not the only Chinese writer of this period to look to Whitman for inspiration. Ning Wang has described the influence of Whitman on several important twentieth-century Chinese writers: 'His democratic spirit and pioneering sense of aesthetic adventure inherent in his poetry were translated into a forceful stimulus for the nascent Chinese literature' (2004: 119). Wang goes on to argue provocatively that Whitman's influence on Chinese writers should not be viewed as a gesture towards a Romantic age of American writing, but that a reading of Whitman's modernist elements, his stylistic heterogeneity and disruptive politics, can lend new perspectives on comparative readings of modern Chinese literary history. Indeed, one must not forget that Whitman was a rebellious figure whose works were banned in nineteenth-century America for their 'inappropriate' sexual content. In Ma's text, Whitman's influence can be understood in close intertexual terms: Whitman's free-verse finds a parallel in Ma's unstructured and eclectic travel text, but, just as importantly, Ma's unruly disregard for socially prescribed tenants of decency and morality in literature can also be traced back to Whitman's reckless and spontaneous treatment of sexuality in *Leaves of Grass*.

Yet Ma's interest in pushing the limits of 'acceptable' literary expression is also articulated through a realist style that focuses on the mundane, grotesque, and everyday functions of the body. While the official discourses of the regime are articulated along the lines of purification and moral cleanliness, Ma brings his story down to the level of bodily excrement. In the opening pages of the book he describes the public latrines in Beijing:

> The men squatting over the holes puff steam into the air like warm teapots. My neighbour Old Liu shakes his dick dry. 'Eaten yet?' he says. 'Yes, thanks.' When I see his face I always think of his daughter's long teeth.
>
> I stand at the urinal. The graffiti scribbled on the wall a few days ago – 'Mount that piece of flesh, squeeze into her thighs, up and down we go, it's just like paradise!' – is now hidden under a layer of whitewash. Outside the chicken-wire window a stack of wooden planks is propped against the wall. Women shout in the toilets next door. I can hear the clink of their metal

buttons and belts. A song blares from the nearby street stall. 'Tibetans stop drinking barely wine and churning butter tea, and cry with tears of joy at the sight of the People's Liberation Army ...'

I push through my gate. The yard is strewn with fallen leaves and pigeon shit.

(50)

Here Ma challenges the official discourses of cleanliness and moral purity by subversively portraying the humanity and normality of so-called dirtiness. The propaganda on the radio, which describes the Tibetans as happy comrades, giving up their local culture, and welcoming the PLA draws attention to the imperialist underpinnings of the totalizing idea of a pure Chinese society, even while the whitewashed graffiti contrasts with the surrounding earthiness and the pigeon shit spread everywhere (a recurring image in his urban descriptions), revealing the misplaced priorities of the campaign. In many ways Ma's bodily aesthetic may be seen in terms of Mikhail Bakhtin's 'grotesque body', celebrating primary needs (eating, drinking, urinating, sex) and revealing the human connection with the cycle of life. At the same time, however, such 'grotesque realism' can also upset and in some cases symbolically reverse social hierarchies, profanely denigrating what is sacred or official (Bakhtin 1993 [1941]). Bakhtin describes how the medieval carnival in France and elsewhere in Europe provided a setting for such grotesque, earthy, and profane images and themes. The carnivalesque as a literary mode, according to Bakhtin, functions in a similar way by overturning ideas of high culture, inverting social hierarchies, and allowing 'unacceptable' voices to be articulated in 'polyphonic' and 'dialogic' terms. Ma's interest in the corporeal and the grotesque reveals precisely such a carnivalesque tactic of subversion.

Anthropologist Mary Douglas has also written on the ways in which bodily excretions, dirt, and fears of disease can mark the limits or uphold the ideals of a social body. Douglas writes,

Any structure of ideas is vulnerable at the margins. We should expect the orifices of the body to symbolise its specially vulnerable points. Matter issuing from them is marginal stuff of the most obvious kind. Spittle, blood, milk, urine, faeces or tears by simply issuing forth have traversed the boundary of the body. So also have bodily parings, skin, nail, hair clippings and sweat. The mistake is to treat bodily margins in isolation from all other margins.

(1966: 121)

The relative cleanliness of cultural and physical boundaries, their 'constructedness', is explored as Ma exposes, and in some sense celebrates, the filthiness of his travel experience:

Last night I felt no compunction about squeezing my fleas in front of the Tianjin tiger-skin trader. I even got used to him spitting sunflower-seed husks onto the floor. I have taken to squatting on street corners munching raw tomatoes and ambling through town with my trouser legs rolled up, just like all the other peasants drifting through China trying to pick up work.

(107)

In a particularly powerful passage, he visits a leper colony and confronts those who have been ostracized, virtually forgotten, and deemed unclean by the rest of society. Here Ma finds more outcasts: the diseased, similar to the exiled artists and writers Ma meets along the way, represent the disordered and the contaminated, and by crossing the boundary into the leper colony he reveals the humanity and utter harmlessness of people who have lived their lives in isolation from the rest of the social body.

It is important to understand that the Anti-Spiritual Pollution Campaign, despite its intellectual and literary framework, had very real and, indeed, deadly, effects. During this period, the government introduced a widespread campaign to clean up crime, with a particular focus on pornographic or sexually lewd behaviour. Thomas Gold has pointed out that in the fall of 1983 alone 6000 criminals were publicly executed (Gold 1984: 950). Such executions figure in Ma's story as he describes public notice boards, which list capital offenses such as distributing pornography or seducing young women. He then vividly describes a young man being dragged off for execution (Ma 2002 [1987]: 159–60).

Ma writes against such physical incarceration and ideological disciplining of human bodies. In some cases, his descriptions take on a comic dimension. For example, visiting friends in Chengdu, he is told about the fate of an alleged 'sex maniac' friend, Qu Wei, who was thrown in jail for seven years; among other things, he was accused of selling playing cards which depicted nude women. The individual cards ended up dispersed throughout the city, but the authorities eventually tracked them down, with the exception of two that were bought by a long-distance truck driver. 'If they had retrieved the full pack' his friend explains, 'he might have got away with two years' (150). His friend goes on to elaborate on the nature of Qu Wei's crimes:

> 'It wasn't just the cards though. He was also accused of holding private parties, dancing cheek to cheek, watching obscene videos, performing foreign sexual acts and perverting an innocent policewoman.' Everyone laughs.
> 'I wouldn't mind perverting a policewoman,' He Liu says. He pops a clove of garlic in his mouth and slowly spits out the skin.
>
> (150–1)

It is unclear what 'foreign sexual acts' might be, but they could include homosexuality, which many official sources of the time claimed did not exist in China, and thus must have been foreign in nature. The laughter that follows the list of Qu Wei's offenses is clearly an expression of rebellion against such absurd laws, a liberation of sorts, at least at a rhetorical level, for the language used in the passage mocks various shades of official terminology. Yet such humour – in Freudian terms – can also mask powerful unconscious emotions such as aggression and hostility, revealing the danger, vulnerability, and desperation of the situation. It reminds one of the widespread use of political jokes in most countries behind the Iron Curtain, where the only relatively 'safe' means for the individual was to laugh in the face of authority – in private, of course, and using as much circumlocution as possible.

Travel, of course, can provide another way to hide, avoid, or assuage unruly or unpleasant emotions. In an entirely different context, Denis Porter offers a compelling psychoanalytic interpretation of European travel writing and the desire for distance amongst colonial travellers. Travel, in Porter's terms, can function as an Oedipal 'flight from paternal repressive power' (1991: 149). In the case of Ma's travel narrative, the flight away from the political patriarchy of the communist leadership can be thought of in similar psychoanalytic terms. Initially, Ma's disavowal of the material world and the journey itself takes on a spiritual dimension. In political trouble, deserted by his wife and cut off from contact with his daughter, he intends his journey to lead ultimately to Tibet, and his hope is that Buddhism will heal his damaged soul. His title, *Red Dust*, is a reference to the fog of material illusion through which an aspiring Buddhist must find his way. As far as possessions are concerned, he comes close to the Buddhist ideal. His cheap rubber-soled shoes wear out, addresses are washed off the paper when he falls in a river, and his only permanent possession is his camera. Yet the spiritual journey is revealed, at the end, as futile. For Ma, the worship of the Buddha bears all the signs of the fervent religiosity that inspired Mao's cult of personality during the Cultural Revolution. His attraction towards the Buddha is finally revealed to be a displaced desire for meaning and acceptance; when he encounters an enormous Buddhist statue in Gansu, he writes, 'I look at his face again and suddenly it reminds me of Mao Zedong. I drew the Chairman's portrait hundreds of times from primary school to middle school. The more I study Amitabha the more he resembles Old Mao' (Ma 2002 [1987]: 96). Later, near the end of the book, Ma's dissatisfaction with religion comes full circle as he writes, 'Is the Buddha saving man, or is man saving Buddha? From now on I will hold no faith. I can only strive to save myself. Man is beyond salvation' (319). As their iconography uncannily merges, Mao and the Buddha can be viewed as authoritative father figures, and as symbols that dictate the terms of national and individual identity.

In Lacanian terms, we might think of the 'Name-of the Father' and the ways in which a patriarchal ideal can play a central symbolic role in the structuring of language and the human psyche. Without such a figure, or with the loss of such a figure, the symbolic order would become chaotic and fragmented. In some sense, such a disordered and fractured idea of subjectivity and meaning is reflected in the text of *Red Dust*. While dealing with physical boundaries and peripheries, Ma's travel book is itself generically 'marginal'; it is a text 'under pressure', and one that is occasionally fragmented. Events are hung together, and exposed – there are interspersed passages of poetry, letters, and journal entries. Suggestively, each chapter begins with a map of the author's route, but the map is a scrap torn out of a larger piece. The book is divided into fragments, and the image of a torn map of China presents a country that is far from being the unified glorious nation of communist propaganda. Indeed, such generic instability in the travel text can also be understood in relation to the larger crisis of identity and subjectivity resulting from the shifting social and economic landscape that Ma describes (which compounds and reinforces the already existing distortions of public and personal identity during hard-line communist decades). Thus the journey that began as a pilgrimage becomes a melancholic attempt to decode the contradictions of 'market socialism' and find a place for the individual in the newly emerging economic, and indeed symbolic, order.

Although this essay has discussed Ma's text so far in terms of its rather focused resistance to the ideological colonization impregnating all levels of individual and public life under the communist system, *Red Dust* also seeks to come to terms with the emergence of larger global capitalist forces. Geographer David Harvey, writing on the global neoliberal turn in cultural and economic policies during the 1980s, views China as a key player in this shift to privatized capital and neoliberal economic policies during this period, referring to Deng Xiaoping's reforms as 'privatization with Chinese characteristics'. He writes of the Chinese economic reforms of the 1980s in terms of how they

> managed to construct a form of state-manipulated market economy that delivered spectacular growth (averaging close to 10 per cent per year) and rising standards of living for a significant portion of the population for more than twenty years. But reform also led to environmental degradation, social inequality, and eventually something that looks uncomfortably like the reconstitution of capitalist class power.
>
> (2005 [1987]: 122)

Such changes led to massive shifts in human geography as well; China, in Harvey's description, has become a country in flux:

> There currently are 114 million migrant workers but the government predicts the number will rise to 300 million by 2020 and eventually to 500 million. Shanghai alone has 3 million migrant workers; by comparison, the entire Irish migration to America from 1820 to 1930 is thought to have involved perhaps 4.5 million people. This labor force is vulnerable to super-exploitation and puts downwards pressure on the wages of urban residents. But urbanization is hard to stop and the rate of urbanization stands at something like 15 per cent.
>
> (127)

The very structure of Ma's travel writing, like the restlessness of the author, speaks to (and of) the itinerant condition of modern China. As so many people move to the cities in search of a better and more prosperous life, Ma moves in the opposite direction, travelling into the western provinces and remote regions, often describing the economic constraints and impoverishment that many face there. The author speaks not as an aspiring cosmopolitan sophisticate, but as just one of the many migrants in a country searching for meaning.

Elsewhere in this collection, Victor Li discusses how global forces can discipline and transform the individual subject along neo-liberal lines. In Li's assessment, notions of self-reliance and the 'enterprise of oneself' help to create 'flexible' and ultimately disciplined neo-liberal subjects. Although the historical context of China in the 1980s would have its own particular way of articulating the 'disciplinary logic of capitalism', there is nevertheless a sense in Ma's text of neo-liberalism's encroachment. Throughout his travels Ma contrasts rural squalor with the development of urban centres and Special Economic Zones. Such transformations are apparent in Shenzhen, for example, where thousands of foreign companies have opened businesses, factory leaders are now called 'managers', and employees wear suits and ties to work (Ma 2002 [1987]: 71). Ma's dishevelled appearance and rejection of material and monetary values, therefore, need to be viewed not only in relation to his resistance against the official discourses of purity, but also against this emerging 'corporate' China which seeks to establish new forms of governmentality and normative values for individual subjectivity.

The problems of a modern 'privatization with Chinese characteristics' are also brought into sharp focus in Ma's description of the landscape. He writes, 'The waters of the Yangzi look tired and abused. When man's spirit is in chains, he loses all respect for nature' (2002: 163). He continues,

> When the poet Li Bai travelled down this stretch of river during the Tang dynasty, he wrote of coloured clouds above the Yangzi and monkeys wailing from the banks. Today the monkeys have been replaced by fertiliser plants and cement factories that pollute the river with yellow waste. Where the green slopes have been cut away, the earth shines like raw pigskin.
>
> (161–2)

By drawing attention to such environmental damage and pollution, Ma not only reveals the misplaced priorities of the campaign against spiritual pollution, but he also exposes the unsavory result of rapid capitalist development and urbanization.

At the end of *Red Dust* the anti-Spiritual Pollution campaign is over, but Ma notes with cynicism that it will only be a matter of time until the next campaign begins.[2] So finally, after three years of travelling, posing as a journalist, and avoiding the authorities, the author is safe to return home, but it is a homecoming that is more of a resignation than a celebration. The periphery, which could be a potential source of romantic and spiritual inspiration, has proven to be a defining reality, and the centre itself, an unfamiliar ground. In travelling through China's border regions, as far as Hainan, Qinghai and Tibet, the outer limits have become a kind of home, and the artist's dissident space on Naxiao Lane in Beijing becomes increasingly unreachable, and in some ways undesirable. The narrator – part exiled Tang poet and part displaced beatnik – is a hybrid of sorts, a flexible 'travelling-self' that takes many different kinds of 'routes', and along the way dramatizes the alienating and fragmenting effects of ideological repression on the individual.

Although much has changed in China over the thirty years since *Red Dust* was written, writers and artists continue to have their work censored by the government or policed by their own internal sense of acceptability. The prominent writer Yan Lianke, several of whose works have been banned, has described the insidious nature of self-censorship and the ways in which it can drain artistic passion and critical sharpness (Gupta 2008, Watts 2006). Literary and cultural critics in (and of) China face similar challenges, both internal and external, as they confront sensitive and often risky political and cultural questions. Postcolonialism has been defined in many different ways over the past decades, but, irrespective of which interpretation one favours, and the problematic issues raised by 'travelling theories', 'rerouting' the postcolonial must surely begin with recognizing all marginal (and marginalized) texts, beyond institutionally prescribed canons or governmentally sanctioned frameworks. Texts of the 'periphery' – those that have been ignored, repressed, or cast aside, not merely those emerging from a geographically subordinated nation – can suggest new ways of interpreting the ethical and political questions that emerge out of our global present. Ma's outsider view of China offers an 'ex-centric' perspective of his country's transition from a communist state to a complex global capitalist configuration; the restlessness and boldness of its critical perspectives suggest ways in which the field of postcolonial studies can absorb and modulate contextually 'difficult' positions, thus preserving its theoretical mobility, its interdisciplinary character and, ultimately, its very critical import.

Notes

1 For an excellent collection of translated classical Chinese travel writing, see Strassberg (1997). Strassberg's introduction also provides a cogent overview of how ideas of travel in classical Chinese literature differ from European traditions of travel writing.

2 A recent example of repression of free speech in China, one that echoes with the anti-spiritual pollution campaign of the 1980s, is the ongoing anti-vulgarity campaign launched in early 2009, which led to the shutting down of hundreds of 'lewd' websites and blogs. While many of these sites were obviously pornographic, some of them contained politically sensitive content about Tibet, Taiwan, Charter 08, or other 'taboo' topics. In a way that resonates with Ma's strategies of debasement, humour, and evasion. Chinese bloggers responded by creating parody websites and videos about the 'Grass Mud Horse' (*Cao Ni Ma*), an imaginary creature which appears innocent enough, but whose name in Mandarin has a strong phonetic resemblance to a particularly vulgar expletive. Since its conception, the 'Grass Mud Horse' has attracted millions of hits, and numerous other mythical animals, whose names also suggest profane double entendres, have since been created. While such puns may have a childish quality, they ultimately reflect the ways in which censorship laws themselves are often crudely drawn and demeaning.

150 Jeffrey Mather

Bibliography

Bakhtin, M. (1993 [1941]) *Rabelais and His World*, trans. H. Iswolsky, Bloomington: Indiana University Press.

Chow, R. (1997) 'Can One Say No to China?', *New Literary History*, 28.1: 147–51.

Dirlik, A. (1997) *The Postcolonial Aura: Third World Criticism in the Age of Global Capitalism*, Boulder, Colo.: Westview Press.

Douglas, M. (1966) *Purity and Danger: An Analysis of Concepts of Pollution and Taboo*, London: Routledge & Kegan Paul.

Gold, T. (1984) '"Just in Time!": China Battles Spiritual Pollution on the Eve of 1984', *Asian Survey*, 24.9: 947–74.

Gupta, S. (2008) 'Interviews with Li Rui, Mo Yan, Yan Lianke and Lin Bai (translated by Xiao Cheng)', *Wasafiri*, 55: 28–37.

Harvey, D. (2005) *A Brief History of Neoliberalism*, New York: Oxford University Press.

Larson, W. (1989) 'Realism Modernism, and the Anti-"Spiritual Pollution" Campaign in China', *Modern China*, 15.1: 37–71.

Ma, J. (2002 [1987]) *Red Dust*, trans. F. Drew, London: Vintage.

Porter, D. (1991) *Haunted Journeys*, Princeton: Princeton University Press.

Sheng, A. (2007) 'Traveling Theory, or, Transforming Theory: Metamorphosis of Postcolonialism in China', *Neohelicon*, 34.2: 115–36.

Strassberg, R. (ed.) (1997) *Inscribed Landscapes: Travel Writing from Imperial China*, Berkeley: University of California Press.

Wang, N. (2004) *Globalization and Cultural Translation*, Singapore: Marshall Cavendish Academic.

Watts, J. (2006) 'Censor Sees through Yan Lianke's Guile', *The Guardian*, 9 Oct.: 25.

Xu, B. (1995) *Disenchanted Democracy Chinese Cultural Criticism after 1989*, Ann Arbor: University of Michigan Press.

13 Cosmopolitan provincialism in a comparative perspective

Dorota Kołodziejczyk

Recent debates on the dwindling resources for comparatism in postcolonial studies call for a questioning of both its disciplinary boundaries and the consequences of its ostensibly global horizons. That postcolonialism has become a globally inflected critical practice hardly needs corroborating; a range of theorists have discussed (often critically) the field's affinity to globalization studies. Thus Simon Gikandi, even while acknowledging the crucial contribution of such critics as Arjun Appadurai or Homi Bhabha to the articulation of 'cosmopolitan subjectivities' borne of postcolonial migrations, issues a warning against modes of reading that continue to privilege 'familiar tropes of postcolonial theory' such as hybridity or transgression, obliterating the 'unfamiliar, but equally powerful local scenes of being and belonging' (2001: 639). In the first section of this volume, he reiterates and extends this idea by locating the marginal figure of the refugee at the centre of global cosmopolitanism. Timothy Brennan articulates a similar critique, seeing cosmopolitanism as the dominant ideology of the diasporic elite, 'less an expansive ethos than an expansionist policy' (1997: 55). In her efforts to endorse a new understanding of comparative literature whose foundational ethos should be of reading closely in the original, G. C. Spivak elaborates a notion of 'planetarity' as a difference-sensitive mode of being in the world that refuses to yield to the flattening effects of global systems (2003: 71). The metaphor of the good translation that never exhausts difference reverberates here with Brennan's critique of 'cosmo-theory' as a translation whose goal is to co-opt difference.

Given the critical remarks above, what can be said about the export conditions for theory, or, returning to Said's connected remark: How does a theory travel? How to translate so as to avoid, as Spivak warns, the generalized 'translatese' that makes all categories easily exchangeable, because devoid of their specific (linguistic, cultural, artistic) idiom (Spivak 1993: 182)? How to preserve the unfamiliar aspect of the local, as Gikandi advocates, in the all too-easily exchangeable categories of globalized postcolonial theory? These are some of the larger theoretical questions that my essay seeks to address, with a view to offering a model of comparative analysis that would avoid the pitfalls of generalized (and levelling) transference. Such a model, moving beyond postcolonialism's founding dichotomy 'centre/periphery' into a more diffuse imaginary of routes, is clearly required by the contemporary spatiality of 'the world in pieces' (Geertz 2001: 218).

In other words, if we are to engage with and transform the current shape of the postcolonial, we need to search for a dialogic space that is beyond the discipline, but adjacent to its interests and sensitivities.

The eastern side of the former Iron Curtain divide is such an adjacent 'beyond'. In the following, I propose to examine the possibility of rerouting postcolonial studies to an area that has been so far largely absent from postcolonially-inflected studies of globalization processes. Eastern/Central Europe[1] poses both taxonomic and conceptual problems: while it is geographically part of the continent, it often functions as a space of indeterminate otherness, a kind of unacknowledged heterotopia. A region with a long and disparate experience of subjection to (mostly) European empires and, after 1945, to the geopolitics of the Cold War, Eastern Europe reveals exclusion mechanisms fundamental for Western Europe's self-definition. The prevalent concept of 'core Europeanness', originating in studies of the continent's political and cultural history (see 'Introduction' to Davies 1996), assumes that it has fringes; these latter often become an object of corrective or normative discourses. Thus, Eastern Europe's nations and ethnic groups are 'minor' or 'mixed', its existence as a community of nation-states historically tenuous, its nationalisms more aberrant and pathological than western ones. Lagging behind Europe in modernization, wavering between populist nationalism and liberal pragmatism, and, most symptomatically, longing for the status of 'proper Europe', the equivocal position of Eastern Europe calls for a theorization that would take into account its history of subjection to foreign rule as one of the most crucial factors for its ambivalent status as a periphery. Postcolonial critical practices may be seen as a potential route to the development of such a theorization. Such a rerouting would also enhance the scope of postcolonial theory to an area where it can meet, and thus conceptualize, its borders.[2]

The former Second World has been largely bypassed by the sweep of theorization of which postcolonialism is such an active agent. The region, however, is busily reconceptualizing itself through a range of cultural and literary theories, unbeknownst to a large degree to the alleged 'owners' of theory – western metropolitan academic centres. The debates on the condition of postcoloniality of the ex-Soviet and Eastern bloc countries have been going on for nearly two decades now; the attempts to redefine the dissident and resistance agency of national literatures of Eastern and Central European countries according to postcolonial paradigms have also been a subject of scholarly consideration, from outward claims of the postcolonial status of many, if not most, Eastern European literatures and cultures, to the less declarative deployments of postcolonial theory to anti-communist resistance literature and discourse, as well as post-communist transition processes (see, among others, Cavanagh 2003, Bakuła 2006, Janion 2007). Quite apart from helping to articulate the historical complexities of subjection, postcolonial studies has a remarkable potential to reroute the revisionary trend of post-communist discourse from a predominantly national paradigm and inspire, as it has manifestly done so, a new historiographic and cultural imagery that encourages an exploration of the region's ambivalent self-positioning vis-à-vis Europe. Challenging the Eurocentric forms and significations of cosmopolitanism, postcolonial studies fosters a new understanding of periphery which, among others, actively reimagines itself in a politics of provincialism.

The scope of this essay is therefore to explore the tangential relation of the Eastern European problematic to postcolonial studies, with a view to sketching a comparative perspective that will enable a reading in differential contexts – national, transnational and postnational – of texts that ostensibly have little in common, but which, on close examination, reveal a shared imaginative space, rhetoric and narrative agency. Within this comparative excursus I will discuss two authors whose work intimates a transnational (and translational) space that is often acutely critical of global relocations and flows. This is achieved through an imagery of peripheral locations as modalities of being in the world. The punning interplay of roots and routes renders here a constitutive metaphorics of the dynamic relation between location and mobility, where both categories inhere in each other and may become indistinguishable. In the work of Amitav Ghosh, an Indian diasporic writer, and Andrzej Stasiuk, a Polish novelist and travel writer exploring Eastern European provinciality, transnational narratives of the local can be seen as cutting across and into the imagery of globalization, challenging and modifying at the same time various tropes of the postcolonial. It is particularly interesting how this internal otherness within Europe – its Eastern European counterpart, or, as it has been sometimes theorized, its 'close other' (see Brubaker 1996, Offe 1996), conjures itself as Western Europe's phantasmatic alterity, and how this phantasm renders cosmopolitan Europe parochial through a playful and self-mocking ideology of provincialism. Both authors thematize issues related to globalization, such as translocations (tourism, labour flows, diaspora), borderlessness and the instability of borders, metropolitan *versus* provincial spaces. Reading Amitav Ghosh and Andrzej Stasiuk comparatively, I intend to trace in their writing the ideology and imaginary of cosmopolitan provincialism – such representations of the local, peripheral and non-metropolitan that demonstrate its agency in transnational connections.

Both authors develop a genre that can be provisionally called the 'narrative of the local'. 'Place', especially when its provinciality is staked to confront the pressing current of globalization, is much more than a structural prerequisite for a story and becomes a relational category premised on a dynamic of border-crossing, geographically, but also between histories, philosophies, sciences, technologies and, last but not least, letters. Such narratives of the local activate in the process of border-crossing a distinctive form of worldliness that I propose to link with two concepts of cosmopolitanism: Arjun Appadurai's 'grassroots cosmopolitanism' (2001: 3) and Bishnupriya Ghosh's 'literary cosmopolitics' (2004). In both categories cosmopolitanism is envisaged as a localizing practice, either a 'globalization from below' for Appadurai, or, for Ghosh, as various strategies of narrative restoration of the vernacular defying the uniformity of globalization (153). Narratives of the local elaborate a cosmopolitical agency by bringing the local to bear on other locations, showing how these reveal their interconnectedness through various forms of mobility. The cosmopolitan provincialism that the sub-genre highlights thrives on the disjunctures inherent in its constitutive antithesis: it seeks to reveal alternative modernities within the hegemonic narrative of modern Europe; it calls for an exploration of the imaginative and critical potential of the developmental time-lag embedded in these alternative modernities; finally, it encourages the rethinking of the narrative mode as instrumental in nation-formation and acknowledges that the novel's international form precedes and conditions the national. The narrative of the local thus contributes to an emergence of a literary transnationalism very similar to that theorized by Ashcroft elsewhere in this volume.

Since his first phenomenal novel, *The Circle of Reason* (1986), a story of how passions of artisanship interlace with those of rationalism, Amitav Ghosh has successfully woven the cosmopolitanism of the novelistic genre with the 'local knowledge' (Geertz 1983) indispensable for a writer focusing on the problem of rooted and diasporic states of being in their antithetical coexistence. His novels work out patterns of the global/local interaction, where the global – modernization, industrialization, the march of capital and warfare in their imperial and counter-imperial guises – pressures local forms of governmentality, local social structures, cultural specificity, and work practices. In delineating post-national forms of identity in diasporic motion, Ghosh shows how these forms expose the tenacity of local formations (cultural, historical and social) which always bear traces of prior transfers across cultures and languages. An in-depth knowledge of infinite forms of artisanship, manufacturing and work traditions has in his novels a direct bearing on the imagery of the local. *The Circle of Reason* represents Ghosh's fascination with the genius of human industry that belies the division of man and the machine, and proposes to imagine an alternative beyond the capitalist alienation of labour. Here the 'genius' is rerouted to its roots in Latin and transferred back to provide the central trope of the novel – the 'ghost in the machine' (Ghosh 2005: 133–49). Playing on the apparent dissonance between the machine and the realm of the spiritual, Ghosh challenges the foundational dichotomy between science and magic (Khair 2003a: 147). The place, always framed in his novels in a broader geopolitical context, is a composite local knowledge made up of daily rituals, work patterns, and production traditions, a knowledge combining the materiality of the local and the *unheimlichness* of its often haunting vernacular.

Andrzej Stasiuk, a Polish novelist and essayist[3] is an incorrigible partisan of Eastern European provincialism, which he traces passionately in the most peripheral regions of the Carpathians in two best-selling travelogues, *Jadąc do Babadag* [*Driving to Babadag*] (2004), and *Fado* (2006). The mountain range functions in his writing as a transnational and transhistorical space running across some seven state borders and uniting diverse nationalities and ethnicities which he refers to, quoting Hannah Arendt, as the 'belt of mixed population': 'lurking from behind fences are Germanized Poles, Polonized Ukrainians, this whole borderland hybrid, this golden dream of believers in multiculti' (Stasiuk 2004: 22). This mosaic of the perennial borderland is, however, a faded imprint of imperial European history enforcing its hegemony but also losing its definiteness here, rather than an Arcadian site of transnational conviviality. Such modern fancies as the nation lose their contours of historical absoluteness in this transnational border region and become only faint traces of a distant, partly imaginary, centre: 'To live in the Carpathians is to remember that citizenship and nationality had a minor significance here' (66).

The transnational space of the Carpathians lends itself in Stasiuk's travelogues to the steady tone of nostalgia. This self-mocking, strategically deployed tone, frames the Carpathians in a temporality of belatedness and separateness. Travelling pointedly off the main routes, Stasiuk journeys through a palimpsest of historical and literary narratives, and recounts the feeling of entering a temporal loophole at moments of an intensified experience of the local, when, for instance, he reaches a Hungarian village celebrating Franz Josef's birthday at the end of the millennium, an event of drunken nostalgia spectral in its carnivalesque absurdity. Yet belatedness does not save the Carpathians from the encroaching forms of late modernity hailing from cosmopolitan Europe. Off the main roads, Stasiuk still notes the distant buzz of motorways charting routes of global tourism: 'Somewhere on the right was Histria: the Greeks, ruins, marble columns, 7th century BC, but I didn't care for that [...]. The minaret in Babadag was austere and simple [...]. I felt the continent end [...]' (186). Stasiuk elaborates an ethos of the provincial that challenges with enduring resolve the aggrandized self-image of Europe: 'We are strangers here, coming from the outside, from countries of which Europe is little aware and which it perceives as a threat rather than a part of itself' (2006: 80). Parodying the aloofness of the West through an apocalyptic vision of the new barbarians invading the old continent only amplifies the burlesque effect of Eastern European self-absorbed and melodramatic transnational provincialism.

The narrative of the local, always inscribed in both authors' writing in a broader geopolitical framework, engenders a specific, self-ironic metaphysics. Just as the ghost dwells in the machine in *The Circle of Reason*, so does it dwell in place, because both Ghosh and Stasiuk seek to restore in their narratives a *genus loci*, a unique spirit of the place inhering in the rich material texture of the local. The *genus loci* unravels itself through the narrative process in a poetics of return, abating its inevitably nostalgic tone with the ironical self-reflexivity of the narrative voice – that of a passionate archivist searching alternative modalities of knowledge or a traveller in the provincial where he can experience the transience and insubstantiality of history. In Stasiuk's travel writing the provincial regions of Eastern Europe mark the end of European history and the continent's oblivious disappearance into nothingness – not because nothing ever happens there, but because big history has always been rolling over Eastern Europe, hardly ever acknowledging its participation in the process. As a reaction, Eastern Europe mistrusts the solidity of history and treats it as just another tale to disbelieve in. Whether it is a Polish, Romanian, or Hungarian provincial town that is being depicted, it dwells in the time-defying present familiar even if the narrator has not been there before:

> I should have stayed in Huşi. Now I have to imagine I will come back there. Best of all, in the autumn, when leaves fall down, to look for a confirmation

of all those conjectures [...]. Bacteria, gravitation and humidity – these are the elements of being in my part of the continent. [...] In the end, it turns out one seeks only what one has already seen.

(Stasiuk 2004: 277–8)

In the narrative of the local the sense of belonging can only be retrieved in the narrative process and is a matter of imaginative reconstruction through memories, fantasies, archives of other stories, more than an identification with a place one experiences physically as home. For example, in Ghosh's *Shadow Lines* the narrator identifies with the memories of his uncle Tridib to such an extent that he does not need to mention his own name even once, so inessential is it to his desire to reconstruct, and thus continue as his own innermost experience, Tridib's finely detailed, private topography of London. In *A Hungry Tide*, the two protagonists have to relive the troubled history of the village in the Sundarbans, completing by narrative proxy the unfinished story of the previous generation that involves them as sort of extraneous protagonists. In *The Circle of Reason*, the randomness of human life experienced by the protagonist Alu as a violent uprooting from memory and language to the point of autistic incommunication can be overcome by way of narrative restitution. The only object that links Alu to his perished past, the sewing machine, becomes a miraculous tool of fate operating through the 'ghost in the machine'. His uncle Balaram's passion for disinfection, infectious in its obsessiveness, drives Alu, now in his charismatic stage after the rescue, to turn the Souq – the shanty-town of illegal workers – into a utopian commune free of the germs of private money. After another apocalypse descended on the innocently unaware commune by state forces, Alu manages to run away to Algeria, where, in a situation of complicated displacement – in a desert, in the house of Indian doctors of the local hospital who somewhat absurdly decide to stage a piece of an Indian classic epic – Alu finds in Mrs. Verma's bookcase *The Life of Pasteur*, a copy of which he studied as a boy in the village of Lalpukur. The seemingly random pattern of events is finally woven into a narrative causality by the fine thread of the travelling book. It returns Alu to his past, to the heritage of his uncle's passion for disinfection as the epitome of Reason. The book becomes a home of sorts for Alu, more durable than the real one, because connecting generations with a passion that cannot perish; a very precarious home indeed, as it has sent generations off the trodden routes into the border area where reason and madness blur into each other. The book recovered in an African desert through a transgenerational and transcontinental detour helps Alu restore his lost and confused sense of the self. It becomes possible only as an imaginative reconstruction of the lost sense of rooting, and only with an awareness that rooting will inevitably be an effect, and cause at the same time, of various diasporic routes.

Both Ghosh and Stasiuk chart in their narratives a transnational space that stands revealed in locations seemingly fixed and enclosed in their unchangeability. The sites that may seem to function as counterpoints to globalization are themselves products of border crossing and diasporas (Dixon 2005: 11) that are transhistorical in the sense that they pluralize history, opening it for the spatial dimension of human mobility. In *The Circle of Reason*, the border village Lalpukur is anything but a solid settlement accrued in the course of generations. Inhabited by refugees from the time of Partition whose homes had to be left behind the newly established border, Lalpukur receives another wave of refugees from across the border of what is now Bangladesh. 'Wars keep people busy' (Ghosh 2005: 59) – new trade routes follow the refugees immediately, and the new spirit of enterprise emerges amidst the melancholy of the older refugees and despair of the current ones in the village. Anything local turns out to be the product of a dynamic diasporic mobility. When Alu starts his apprenticeship with Shombhu Debnath, the loom divulges to him the whole world of languages and work traditions that run across nations and continents. Shombhu Debnath, teaching Alu to weave, transfers this expanse of migratory patterns of invention and human industry to his apprentice:

> The machine, like man, is captive to language. [...] Shombhu Debnath squats by the loom with Alu beside him. [...] He opens his mouth, he would speak, but lo! The loom has knotted his tongue. So many names, so many words, words beaten together in the churning which created the world: Tangail words, stewed with Noakhali words, salted with Naboganj words, boiled up with English (picked up who knows where in his years of wandering). Words, words, this village teems with words, yet too few to speak of the world and the machine. Such wealth and such oppression: to survive a man must try twice as hard, pour out words, whatever comes his way, and hope.
>
> (73)

The multilingualism of the loom renders the place always already translocal. History does not proceed from the rootedness of the nation to transnational and postnational mobility. Speaking in tongues, the loom creates a history woven like a cloth – routed in many directions, premised on a patterned interweaving of languages that makes it nothing less but a dynamic, performative translation. In Stasiuk's *Driving to Babadag*, an inter-lingual dialogue poses no problems to the cosmopolitan provincials of the Carpathian ridge: 'The driver of the white van spoke without stopping and didn't worry at all that we did not understand a word. We also spoke. He listened attentively and answered in his own language' (2004: 69). Adequate translation is not a requisite for communication across languages. It is, rather, a trans-lingual mutuality based in the sense of belonging to an imaginary community of a benign, now deceased empire. The provincial relativizes the idea of the nation-state in its anarchistic disbelief in the factuality of something that is in this region only a shifting reality, tenuous in its appeal when juxtaposed with the mythic power of empire:

> A dreamy state with vague politics and history as sand dunes [...] an empire with an imprecise number of provinces, an empire on the move, marching on, obsessed with an idea of expansion and cursed with amnesia which does

not allow it to remember its lands, peoples, and capital cities, and for this
reason it has to start anew every day [...].

(281)

The almost limitless liminality of the border positions the local at the intersection
of fiction, fact and fantasy, and calls for envisioning this erratic and inconsequen-
tial area as some recalcitrant provincial cosmopolitanism. The local is anarchistic,
because it resists the reductive logic of the state and disregards its politics of
homogenization. The borderland – be it the transnational space of Eastern
European provinces or the Souq in al-Ghazira, a makeshift settlement of illegal
workers in the Gulf – resists a completed narrative; its inherent diversity pertain-
ing to population, geography, history, even temporality, does not add up to a
totality. Or, rather, the structure of the narrative has to be carefully rethought.
The narrative can still wield the power to unify contingencies, but only on condition that its apparent naturalness in plotting life is put into doubt and its rhetoric
fully disclosed.

In *The Circle of Reason* it is only the rhetoric of fiction, prefigured by the alternative narrative power of the loom, and by the ex-territorial rooting power of the
travelling book, that is able to sustain the fragile continuity of the self. History,
by contrast, is a narrative of destructive power; in order to survive, one needs
a fiction to secure the continuity of one's being. For the villagers of Lalpukur
their memories of the country they had to leave behind constitute the most
substantial reality. Any rooting is only a transient moment of translocal mobility,
a contingence of history that imagination turns into a myth of necessity.

Such imaginary reconstructions of the self are a source of agency that is denied
to those reduced by history to mere existential randomness. In a playful, ironical,
yet very sensitive merging of the border between reason and unreason, or rationality and its apparent other, madness, Ghosh opens up an uncanny space in which
these categories remain in a dialectical tension yet cease to be contradictory in
relation to each other. Balaram's passionate love for rationality that he transfers
onto his adopted nephew, Alu, launches a narrative that reroutes reason from its
roots in the West and proposes, instead, a story of reason's paradigmatic exter-
ritoriality, metonymically symbolized by the travelling book *The Life of Pasteur*.
The book travels from hands to hands across generations, linking apparently
random characters in a narrative of the fated hereditary pursuit of reason which
always presents itself magically with its other, the irrational. Such moments of
the charismatic onset of (un)reason result from an uncompromising fidelity to
the local – always a cluster of culturespecific behaviours erupting in the most
unexpected places on diasporic itineraries. The dynamic of reason and irration-
ality enables the agency of those who are bound together in their condition of
subalternity.

The Circle of Reason represents the subaltern as the condition of discontinuity and
disjuncture in one's life narrative; in other words, as the failure of life's narrativity.
The cosmopolitan provincialism developed in this novel represents this precarious
state in which the vernacular no longer finds a safe abode in the local history and

culture, but is set on a diasporic journey that exposes it to constant translations and displacements. To grasp the vernacular in its protean changeability requires a truly global generic consciousness premised on the imperative to perform perpetual revisions of the novelistic tradition across cultures and languages. Ghosh invests in the narrative anamnesis, realized through the accumulative form of the epic format of the novel. Scattered and lost elements of the narrative are threaded together by the naming power of the loom; rooted in place by the drifting reason that is nothing more than a mythic home; and consolidated by a rhetoric of subtle metafictional iteration of the central metaphor of the loom that combines worldliness and locality. Tying all separate strands of the narrative together reroutes the displaced protagonist home. It is, in fact, not so much a return as a new route of migration, a new story to weave – the itinerary of home-coming is primarily that of the self finally restored to memory: to language and its ordering narrative power.

In contrast to Ghosh's efforts to restore the fraying patterns of migratory life to the carefully scrutinized rigours of the novel as a unifying narrative form, Stasiuk explores the condition of narrative failure generically inherent in the travelogue that develops as narrative amnesia – the narrator realizes that storytelling is, in essence, about remembering, but in his case the purpose is not to retrieve facts from memory, but to show how time conquers memory. He is tempted occasion-ally to start a story that could develop into a novel, but the provincial regions of Eastern Europe yield only fragments of potential events which fade away before any plotline can be drawn, and everything remains in the sphere of conjecture (2004: 22–3). Going back in time to gather scattered events will not accumulate into a story, and especially not into a history. In contrast to the sanctioned histo-ricity of 'proper Europe', Eastern European peripheries make possible only a spatialized narrative freed from the rigours of temporality and from the impera-tive of a *telos*: 'A long narrative of the spirit of the age seems here an idea that is as pathetic as it is pretentious, like a novel written according to rules. Paroxism and boredom rule interchangeably in those parts' (59–60). The travelogue makes it possible to narrate Eastern Europe as an expansive amnesia that renders aspi-rations at a big history contained in nationalist historiographies of the 'Romania Mare, the Great Serbia, Poland from Sea to Sea' nothing more than 'the marve-lously foolish fiction of those lands' (42). Explicitly fascinated with the defiant passivity and indeterminateness of the provincial, Stasiuk pursues his ideology of narrative failure in writing that is self-consciously inconclusive, loosely structured, spiralling in repetitions, and sketching faint routes of transnational and transhis-torical *leitmotifs*. The traveller's imagination in Stasiuk's writing is prompted by maps, themselves products of palimpsestic charting across historical discourses, and autobiographies of writers from the region.

Any comparative reading engages in similarities and incommensurable areas of the text alike. Bringing Ghosh and Stasiuk together shows how texts represent-ing different genres and situated in different cultural locations can share a crucial commitment to imagine a diverse, multidirectional world in which the dynamic of roots and routes confuses the ordering power of the state and the uniformity of globalization. The new spatiality acknowledging the local is itself a result of diasporic movement, and it does not supplant historical thinking. Quite the opposite, the project of cosmopolitan provincialism that I have been tracing in both authors sustains a strong historical awareness challenging the kind of historical thinking that monopolizes historicity for a restricted area of Europe. The idea owes much to Dipesh Chakrabarty's injunction to provincialize Europe – to show how Europe functions as an implicit subject in social sciences and history especially, and how this specifically western idiom translates into other, non-western, non-European uses and changes in the process.

This is how cosmopolitan provincialism emerges in a comparative reading of narratives of the local as necessarily a paradox: the local proves the inevitable immanence of history and geography and dislodges claims to transcendence. Just as reason does not arrive from anywhere specifically, but is always a local, even if itinerant, practice, so is theory, as discursive practice meant to determine how we position ourselves in the world. Returning to the constitutive problem of how to include Eastern Europe into the horizon of postcolonial discourse, it should not be a territorial annexation but an exercise in comparativism. It is perhaps impossible to entirely avoid a representation in which the periphery – the local and the provincial – will not have the role of an 'economic image function' (Brennan 2005: 101). One should realize, however, that charting theory onto a new map starts a process of rethinking and interrogation that is routed in both directions. Eastern Europe can find in the postcolonial a repository of new articulations for itself, as long as the mode of application will be closer to translation rather than copying from a matrix. Andrzej Stasiuk is only one of the many writers in Eastern Europe reconsidering the 'lesser' status of the region and operating such a rearticulation. Comparative literature operating within the postcolonial horizon promises a critical practice whose method is translation rather than grafting – preserving the local complexity of the original while making it available in other tongues and theories.

The loom in Ghosh and trans-border multilingual trade in Stasiuk are such constitutive figures of 'dislodging translation', a practice at the core of cosmopolitan provincialism and which places both authors askance the global/local polarity. It belies an opinion that globality supersedes the local – it is not only that the local in its specific version of the provincial shows how globalization flows across the local, but also how the provincial routes a carnivalesque diversion from the global, and how it fosters its own, one would like to say, indigenous cosmopolitanism, claiming worldliness in the classical Saidian sense. In Amitav Ghosh's writing the local reflects the paradoxical condition of the novel: it is the consequence and, concurrently, the cause of the global dynamic, just as the novel is both international in form and 'founded upon a myth of parochiality [...] a place named and charted, a definite location' (Ghosh 2003: 294). In Andrzej Stasiuk, Eastern European melodramatic provinciality, with all its paroxysms of neglect, turns out in the final, absurdly eschatological vision of new barbarians invading old Europe in a ludic conquest, to be the final rescue from the demise brought upon the continent by the completed process of global standardization.

Notes

1 Although Eastern Europe and Central Europe are two distinct geopolitical categories, I will use the category of 'Eastern Europe' in the rest of this essay in order to underscore Stasiuk's insistence on the region's unfamiliar otherness in relation to Western Europe.
2 See studies deploying postcolonial discourse to the analysis of post/communism and Eastern/Central Europe, in a broad spectrum of ideological positions and engagements with postcolonial theory, e.g. Todorova (1997); Thompson (2000); Dušan and Savić (2005); Chernetsky (2007); Korek (2007); Kovačević (2008).
3 Translations of Stasiuk into English: *White Raven* (Serpent's Tail, 2001); *Tales of Galicia* (Twisted Spoon Press, 2003); *Nine* (Harcourt, 2007). All translations in this essay are mine.

Bibliography

Appadurai, A. (2001) 'Grassroots Globalization and the Research Imagination', in A. Appadurai (ed.) *Globalization*, Durham and London: Duke University Press: 1–21.

Bakuła, B. (2006) 'Kolonialne i postkolonialne aspekty dyskursu kresoznawczego' [Colonial and postcolonial aspects of the borderland discourse], *Teksty Drugie*, 6: 11–33.

Brennan, T. (1997) *At Home in the World: Cosmopolitanism Now*, Cambridge and London: Harvard University Press.

—— (2005) 'The Economic Image-Function of the Periphery', in A. Loomba, S. Kaul, M. Bunzl (eds): 101–22.

—— (2006) *Wars of Position: The Cultural Politics of Left and Right*, New York: Columbia University Press.

Brubaker, R. (1996) *Nationalism Reframed. Nationhood and National Question in the New Europe*, New York: Cambridge University Press.

Cavanagh, C. (2003) 'Postkolonialna Polska. Biała plama na mapie współczesnej teorii' ['Postcolonial Poland: the blank space on the map of contemporary theory'], *Teksty Drugie*, 2/3: 60–71.

Chernetsky, V. (2007) *Mapping Postcommunist Cultures: Russia and Ukraine in the Context of Globalization*, Montreal & Kingston: McGill's Queen's University Press.

Davies, N. (1996) *Europe: A History*, Oxford: Oxford University Press.

Delaperrière, M. (2008) 'Gdzie są moje granice? O postkolonializmie w literaturze', [Where are my frontiers? About postcolonialism in literature], *Teksty Drugie*, 6: 9–19.

Dixon, R. (2005) '"Travelling in the West": The Writing of Amitav Ghosh', in T. Khair (ed.): 9–35.

Dušan, B. and Savić, O. (2005) *Balkan as Metaphor: Between Globalisation and Fragmentation*, Cambridge, Mass.: MIT Press.

Geertz, C. (1983) *Local Knowledge: Further Essays in Interpretive Anthropology*, London: Basic Books.

—— (2001) *Available Light: Anthropological Reflections on Philosophical Topics*, Princeton: Princeton University Press.

Ghosh, A. (2005, [1986]) *The Circle of Reason*, Boston and New York: Houghton Mifflin Company.

Ghosh, B. (2004) *When Borne Across: Literary Cosmopolitics in the Contemporary Indian Novel*, New Brunswick: Rutgers University Press.

—— (2003) *The Imam and the Indian Prose Pieces*, Delhi: Permanent Black.

Gikandi, S. (2001) 'Globalization and the Claims of Postcoloniality', *South Atlantic Quarterly*, 100/3: 627–59.

Janion, M. (2007) *Niesamowita Słowiańszczyzna* [The Uncanny Slavic], Kraków: Wydawnictwo Literackie.

Khair, T. (2003) 'Amitav Ghosh's *The Calcutta Chromosome*: The Question of Subaltern Agency', in T. Khair (ed.): 142–61.

—— (ed.) (2003) *Amitav Ghosh: A Critical Companion*, Delhi: Permanent Black.

Korek, J. (2007) *From Sovietology to Postcoloniality. Poland and Ukraine from a Postcolonial Perspective*, Huddinge: Södertörn Academic Studies 3.

Kovačević, N. (2008) *Narrating Post-Communism*, London: Routledge.

Loomba, A., Kaul, S., Bunzl, M., Burton, A. and Esty, J. (eds) (2005) *Postcolonial Studies and Beyond*, Durham and London: Duke University Press: 9–35.

Offe, C. (1996) *Varieties of Transition. The East European and the East German Experience*, Cambridge: Polity Press.

Spivak, G. C. (1993) *Outside in the Teaching Machine*, London and New York: Routledge.

—— (2003) *Death of a Discipline*, New York: Columbia University Press.

—— (2008) 'Komparatystyka ekstremalna', trans. D. Kołodziejczyk, Wrocław: *Recykling idei*, 10: 130–35.

Stasiuk, A. (2004) *Jadąc do Babadag*, Wołowiec: Wydawnictwo Czarne.

—— (2006) *Fado*, Wołowiec: Wydawnictwo Czarne.

Thompson, E. M. (2000) *Imperial Knowledge. Russian Literature and Colonialism*, Westport, Conn., London: Greenwood Press.

Todorova, M. (1997) *Imagining the Balkans*, Oxford: Oxford University Press.

Literary reroutings

Ethics, aesthetics and the
postcolonial canon

14 Introduction

Sarah Lawson Welsh

This final section explores the multiple ramifications of the disjunction between the aesthetic of the literary and the ethical-political drives of postcolonial studies, addressing the question posed by Elleke Boehmer's opening essay: In what sense can postcolonial writing be political *and* aesthetic, both at once? Boehmer suggests that, although there can be no clearly defined postcolonial aesthetic, postcolonial texts should be approached in aesthetic as well as politically-engaged terms, if only to highlight the ethical impact that appropriately used forms (modes, stances, sets of motifs) can generate.

It is, in many ways, a 'daring' position. A centuries-old debate defines the aesthetic more generally as a philosophical response to works of art and the evaluation of different types of perceptual experience or, as in Boehmer's essay, as a consideration of the formal characteristics and qualities of literary texts (the aesthetic as poetics). But, despite an impressive roll call of thinkers (Plato, Aristotle, Kant, Hegel, Heidegger, Croce, Benjamin, Adorno, Eagleton), the current status of the aesthetic in the literary is not high. As Boehmer notes, the category of 'the aesthetic', and critical readings which privilege the aesthetic qualities of postcolonial literary texts, are either elided or else seen only in opposition to texts and readings which more clearly privilege the 'engaged', politicized or ethical nature of postcolonial literary production. This tension prevails despite a number of influential thinkers arguing, after Marx, for a more complex and imbricated relationship between the aesthetic and the political: the 'aesthetication of politics' (Benjamin 1968) and, more recently, 'the ideology of the aesthetic' (Eagleton 1990). Indeed, the Adornian notion of the aesthetic being always already ideological is acknowledged by both Boehmer (172) and Poyner (183) in their essays. In the western academy at least, readings of literary texts primarily in terms of their aesthetic qualities have arguably not been in vogue since the New Criticism of the 1930s to 1950s, so far-reaching have been the effects of the theoretical turn, and, in particular, the influence of post-structuralism, in literary studies. Indeed, as Bennett *et al.* note,

> the aesthetic is itself often qualified by the modifier 'merely' or 'purely' to indicate [...] a despised sphere of social irrelevance, the fussiness of the often-denigrated aesthetes, or [...] the purity and autonomy of a realm of

freedom and disinterestedness (as envisaged by Kant, for example) where pleasure and a liberated imagination can roam.

(2005: 2)

The latter Kantian position, as Boehmer suggests, presents a particular sticking point for ethically grounded postcolonial criticism in its seemingly problematic take on aesthetic judgements as purely subjective, a matter of the imagination rather than understanding; moreover, Kant's formulation of aesthetic satisfaction as 'purely disinterested' and therefore theoretically universal, seems, likewise, to contradict postcolonial studies' stress on cultural specificity and the impossibility rather than possibility of 'freedom and disinterestness' of this kind. Within post-colonial studies, aesthetic considerations in the analysis of literary texts have implicitly been considered a western 'middle-class' indulgence, and there has been a reluctance to approach the postcolonial *literary* text primarily *as writing*, rather than as some kind of a 'tract' or 'manifesto' for a higher ideal. Boehmer's questions are therefore both timely and important. Must an interest in historical context preclude the demands of literary form? Is a literary text (whether postco-lonial or otherwise) reducible to historical, social or political frames of reference, or do considerations of generic voice and connotative language play a significant part in how texts construct their meanings *within*, but not exclusive to, these frameworks?

Boehmer considers 'rerouting' or 'revision' as a way out of the critical *cul de sacs* of 'repeating on the present'. Her article traces the decades-long debate between the political and the aesthetic in postcolonial studies, itself an extension of earlier disputes about the 'engaged' or, contrariwise, purely aesthetic, function of literature. From Kant through Adorno to Gikandi, Parry and Young, through writers as diverse as Ben Okri, Derek Walcott, Achmat Dangor and Yvonne Vera, Boehmer teases out what a postcolonial aesthetic might be – or, indeed, whether it *can* be at all. As Patrick Williams argues of the need to defend older positions, including this 'ideologically suspect category of the aesthetic', the 'call for the elaboration of a postcolonial aesthetics could be seen both as something of a rerouting, and also as a rerooting' (87). Likewise, in tackling the conten-tious opposition between the aesthetic and the ethical in postcolonial criticism, Boehmer's essay takes up Diana Brydon's call in this volume for theorists and critics to enter into '"uncomfortable" dialogues both within and across their own disciplines can the postcolonial refashion itself as a "rhizomatic" paradigm, an interpretative framework that can come to inform wider public projects' (Sandru, p. 102).

The subsequent essays in this section take up some of the possibilities thrown open by Boehmer's essay and its initial question of how an ethical stance might be embodied within an aesthetic. In their different ways, the contributors to this section also respond to Robert Spencer's call in this volume for a critical practice that takes seriously George Steiner's insight that '[t]o read well is to take great risks. It is to make vulnerable our identity, our self-possession' (44). As Boehmer suggests, it is only by embracing (rather than evading) the problems and potentialities of the aesthetic that the ethical and political objectives of postcolonialism are to be fully realized.

Nowhere is the question of how the ethical is embodied *within* aesthetic forms more relevant than in historical contexts of trauma. And if the question of whether any more poetry can be written after Auschwitz resounded with a particularly dreadful impact at the end of the Second World War, then post-apartheid South-Africa poses a similar question today. Jane Poyner's and James Graham's essays both interrogate the extent to which it is possible to invest in ethically post-apartheid literary texts. Thus, Poyner's essay argues that, despite a marked 'inward' turn of much post-apartheid fiction, and a proliferation of autobiographies and confessionals, the need to rediscover and bear witness to a suppressed and censored past is as urgent as ever. Drawing on several South-African novels (Coetzee's *Disgrace*, Achmat Dangor's *Bitter Fruit*, Nadine Gordimer's *The House Gun* and Phaswane Mpe's *Welcome to our Hillbrow*), Poyner explores fictional representations of the Truth and Reconciliation Commission (TRC) and public notions of truth-telling and confession. She points to the need to 'reroute' and reconceptualize the private/public dichotomy – now that the limitations of protest literature are apparent – and shows how these novels offer an implicit critique of the TRC and public notions of truth. What they propose, she suggests, is a new ethical investment of the private as a corrective by which to critique and reform the public domain. The literary ceases to be merely a politically invested 'weapon of struggle': rather, in the canon of much post-apartheid fiction, it becomes an aesthetic-ethical position which can effectively 'speak the truth to power'.

A rather different ethical investment – that of a postcolonial social ecology – is identified by James Graham in his analysis of Nadine Gordimer's *Get a Life*. Drawing on Huggan and Tiffin's (2007) definition of a postcolonial environmental ethic (reimagining the nature of the human and the place of the human in nature), Graham examines the political sense of representation to which he contrasts the aesthetic mandate to represent the environment or social group in language. Alert to the new interface between postcolonialism and environmentalism, Graham contends that Gordimer's problematizing of 'people-centred environmentalism' has implications for the interdisciplinary aspirations of postcolonial studies and signals a welcome decoupling of globalization from what he tentatively identifies as an alternative social ecological vision to that of neoliberal development.

Deborah Madsen's essay widens the scope of enquiry to the US and to the disciplinary fields of American Studies and American Ethnic Studies, in which the 'place of postcolonialism is conspicuous by its absence' despite the fact that 'its relevance is hard to miss' (206). Madsen takes as her textual locales the Hollywood film *Crash* (2004) and selected poems by Anishinaabbe writer and scholar Gerald Vizenor, in order to discuss the implications of different theoretical conceptualizations of US national and ethnic identity. These include the figure of the "un-American" (the individual who is *in* but not *of* America), the diasporic citizen of questionable national affiliation', Michael Novak's notion of the 'unmeltable ethnic' (1972) (e.g. the Native American), and Aihwa Ong's concept of the 'Flexible Citizen' (1999). Madsen demonstrates the role that Postcolonial Studies has played in rerouting American Studies away from its roots in US nationalism and the white nation state; her argument raises some important questions about the ethics and future of American Studies and other nation-based academic disciplines when held in tension with currently hegemonic transnational, cosmopolitan models of literary study (see Ashcroft, Gikandi, Spencer in this volume).

Madsen's essay complements Nirmala Menon's call for a more provisional, contingent and nomadic textual canon. In Menon's essay on the postcolonial canon, the larger ethical-political investment of the discipline is scrutinized, including its assumed representativity of postcolonial literatures. Menon critiques the silent identification of postcolonial literature with a body of works which are predominantly written in English, to the exclusion of the rich vernacular literatures of the diverse multicultural, multilingual spaces of Asia and Africa. This, she contends, not only limits an understanding of postcolonial subjectivities, but also perpetrates yet another kind of 'epistemic erasure', even more disabling for being effected in the name of these very subjectivities. Menon recommends that the discipline widens its theoretical and critical approaches to encompass literatures written in different languages, and modulates its discussions of hybridity, cosmopolitanism or subalternity in accordance with these texts' own engagements with them.

Louar's article reroutes the now familiar postmodernist approach to interrogating marginality by reflecting on postmodernism's blindness to and neglect of the intersecting marginalities of postcolonialism and sexuality, an area of critical concern inaugurated by Frantz Fanon in his 1952 *Black Skin: White Masks*. She argues that the 'ways in which various politics of identity – queer and post-colonial criticism – have pervaded literary studies under the aegis of politically subversive theoretical discourses' have ironically foregrounded 'a fundamental conflict between singular, discrete, individual marginal experiences and the identity categories and configurations established by these very discourses' (236). Louar recognizes that the epistemological and political project of queer theory has always involved an entanglement of the aesthetic and the political; as a result, the mapping and discussion of the discursive construction of colonial sexualities has only occurred in the most limited ways (e.g. in terms of sexual tourism and male queer 'othering' of the cultural other from a European perspective). Moreover, it has meant that the imaginary communities (white, black, queer, straight) constructed by such theoretical discourses have repeatedly excluded certain artistic individuals according to differing ideological and cultural codes of 'outsidership'. Louar's focus is the much-neglected Algerian poet Jean Senac, assassinated in Algier in 1973, whose mentor was Albert Camus. She enquires into this neglect by contrast to the canonization by postcolonial critics of, among others, fellow queer writer Jean Genet, who was also engaged in radical political activities. Louar attempts to reroute theory in the direction of the affective as she posits a new critical category of the 'unrequited lover' closely linked to the land as a new model of subjectivity, and offers in her reading an alternative to both the colonial/postcolonial and queer narratives of Jean Senac.

Bibliography

Benjamin, W. (1968) 'The Work of Art in the Age of Mechanical Reproduction', in *Illuminations*, New York: Harcourt, Brace & World.

Bennett, T., Grossberg, L. and Morris, M. (eds) (2005) *New Keywords: A Revised Vocabulary of Culture and Society*, Oxford: Blackwell.

Eagleton, T. (1990) *The Ideology of the Aesthetic*, Cambridge, MA: Blackwell.

Huggan, G. and Tiffin, H. (2007) 'Green Postcolonialism', *Interventions*, 9.1: 1–11.

Trotsky, L. (1966, [1926]) *In Defence of Marxism*, New York: New Park Publications.

15 A postcolonial aesthetic
Repeating upon the present

Elleke Boehmer

The task of rerouting involves not only a remapping but also a revision (a redoing as well as a new way of seeing) of what we take as read in our practice as postcolonial critics. If we assume this to be the case, then a central concept we might want to revise, to look at again, and attempt to make more transparent, is the too-little-examined notion of a postcolonial aesthetic. Driving this contention is, at one level, the awareness that 'postcolonial aesthetic' represents nothing less than a contradiction in terms, perhaps even an oxymoron. Insofar as *the postcolonial*, always a contentious term, is used to refer not merely chronologically but politically, and is taken to designate writing in opposition to empire and its oppressions, then there is little sense in which postcolonial writing can be both political *and* implicated in a (purely) aesthetic stance.

A crucial way of rerouting or reexamining the postcolonial therefore would be for those of us designated as critics of postcolonial literature to set aside the 'issues' that tend to define the postcolonial, and interrogate what its aesthetic, or its literariness, might in fact consist in. This, then, means asking what makes up the singularity of the postcolonial artefact. Is there something intrinsically postcolonial about certain kinds of writing *qua* form, about their structures of feeling or the modes of attention they invite; about certain inflections of voice or certain tropes and uses of trope? Or is a postcolonial aesthetic – if it exists – always to be understood with reference to some real world out there, separate from the artefact?

John Keats is one of those who in his letters memorably evoked the disinterestedness of the aesthetic by saying that he hated poetry 'that has a palpable design upon us'. Yet there is a whole host of postcolonial texts, many of which are critically deemed evocative, moving, beautiful, that manifestly have a 'palpable design upon us' not so much through their evocativeness as through the message they are trying to transmit whether stylistically or otherwise. In postcolonial writing and criticism, as this implies, a purely aesthetic approach or theory has to date often been considered a western, middle-class indulgence. This, then, is one way through which the postcolonial has repeated upon the present (to refer to my title): in its hostility to matters 'solely aesthetic'. The second edition of the Routledge *Post-Colonial Studies Reader* (Ashcroft *et al.* 2005) typically refers postcolonial representation to 'issues and debates': globalization, the environment, resistance, diaspora. There is no overt mention of an aesthetic discernible.

And yet, as is manifestly clear from our practice, postcolonial critics do rely on a generally unacknowledged notion of an aesthetic – what we might call an aesthetic in so many words – when we speak of postcolonial literature, or of the singularity or particularity of the writing we're interested in. Most typically, and here is another repetition upon the present, we invoke the polyglot layerings and cross-cultural mixings of postcolonial writing as tracking the standard-issue cross-hemispheric, migrant or postcolonial experience. In such cases, a mimetic aesthetic, if nothing else, is involved: an aesthetic that is deemed to reflect a certain postcolonial cultural politics or condition.

Given this tacit acknowledgement, would it not give greater clarity and salience to our work, and a more powerful understanding of postcolonial *writing*'s significance to the task of rerouting the discipline, if we more *boldly* considered, in theoretical-aesthetic and not only political terms, what a postcolonial aesthetic might entail? Indeed, it might help to shed light on the politics of the postcolonial text if we looked more closely at its generic and stanzaic forms, as a critic like David Scott of *Conscripts of Modernity* suggests, as when he discusses the tragic mode of much postcolonial discourse (Scott 2004).

At base, what we are dealing with here are the connotations of both the programmatic and the reductive that to date tend to attach to the concept of a postcolonial aesthetic – and this awareness of the concept's limitations then generates a range of important questions. Is what we name a postcolonial aesthetic no more than a reiteration of tried and tested humanist assumptions about literature dressed in a late colonial guise – assumptions concerning its inherent yet universally accessible meaningfulness; concerning its capacity to elicit a cathartic or ethical response? Alternatively, are there particular modes, stances, or sets of motifs that could be characterized as peculiarly or typically postcolonial, yet are not entirely circumscribed by their real-world reference? Or, again, do we need a specialized critical vocabulary to speak of specifically postcolonial texts? Thinking strategically, if we were able to formulate, even just in a preliminary way, the notion of a postcolonial aesthetic, if we were able to establish postcolonial aesthetic protocols, this would assist in legitimating the study of postcolonial writing *qua* writing, as not simply reducible to testimony, tract, or manifesto.

I do not have critical or theoretical rabbits up my sleeve, in the sense of full or satisfactory responses to those questions with which I began. Instead I aim to retrace the polarities of certain well-known debates about the aesthetic *and* the postcolonial (or indeed the aesthetic *versus* the postcolonial), in order finally to assess whether, on balance, that *and* represents a legitimate, even legitimating, connection. Is it, alternatively, no more than a formal bridge between two concepts in irreconcilable and universalizing contention? Throughout, I take the term 'aesthetic' broadly speaking as referring to a concern with the form and structure of a work of art over its raw content, or with form as a critical part of its content. The phrase 'postcolonial aesthetic' therefore implies the privileging, for example, of the work's generic aspects and connotative language. Above all, it implies a concern not to read that work only with orientation to other frames of reference, historical, social, or political, but on its own terms, as insisting on its own particular modes of attention.

Strictly speaking, that is to say, if we speak in ways tending in the direction of one of the most influential, rigorous western theorists of the aesthetic, Immanuel Kant, the aesthetic denotes 'an analytic of the beautiful'. This of course famously stands as the title to the opening of his *Critique of Judgement* (Kant 1951: 1–12; Cavell 2002: 73–96). The aesthetic, in other words, involves an understanding of the perception of harmonious or beautiful form in an artwork, that may or may not coincide with cultural or authorial intentions, but in any case is perceived to transcend them. It may further designate what Kant might have called the purposiveness of a work's form, outside of concepts or sensations inhering to it: that is, how the work presents itself as beautiful, though without any representation of goal or end. The Kantian aesthetic also signifies or points to – and this is a area most problematic for postcolonialism – a universality of the judgement of taste. In other words, to experience a subjective pleasure in the beautiful implies at the same time a participation in a universal capacity to experience, and then an ability to talk and adjudge of this feeling, in a way that transcends cultural-political co-ordinates and determinations.

The recourse to the *a priori* and the universal, while closely associated with Kant's philosophy, covertly or overtly underlies the greater majority of aesthetic speculations and statements, postcolonial or otherwise. So, having noted the often problematic, culturally enmeshed tendency of the aesthetic to invoke universal categories of judgement, it is worth challenging it with an important reminder from Theodor Adorno, a theorist equally preoccupied with aesthetics, if from a rather different theoretical and ideological perspective than Kant. Writing about cultural mass production in the essay 'The Schema of Mass Culture', Adorno makes the sober observation that any claim to aesthetic autonomy rests upon an untruth. In the realm of aesthetic image-consciousness, he persists, universality 'remains allied to ideology' (Adorno 2004: 63–4). Susan Buck-Morss and Simon Gikandi in their fascinating investigations of the *interestedness* of enlightenment discourse – of its social and political determinations in slavery – would no doubt agree (see Buck-Morss 2009). It is between these two poles of speculation – of the aesthetic as autonomous, in-and-for-itself, and the aesthetic as deeply complicit – that this essay will oscillate.

Turning now to the political: quite *contra* the transcendence associated with certain versions of the aesthetic, *political* writing by contrast never loses sight of ideology. To generalize for the sake of the argument, openly political, post-colonial work undertakes, without apology, to be ends-directed, programmatic, instrumentalist, didactic, intent on direct impact. It is dedicated, in the words of postcolonial critic Benita Parry, to 'reclaiming community from the fragmentation and denigration attendant on colonialism' (2004: 10). It is tasked with reconstitution. It is therefore very far from being preoccupied with an aesthetic as such. Insofar as the postcolonial can be taken to signify a political commitment to some form of struggle and as allied to the traditions of anti-colonial resistance (Young 2001), a simultaneous commitment to an aesthetic is understandably viewed in some postcolonial circles as a distraction, an unaffordable indulgence. It is true of course that virtually all writing from situations of crisis, in the words of the Palestinian writer Hassan Khader, encounters an extreme, practical difficulty in finding distance, in making the bridge into the aesthetic and the universal, or '[surviving] the transplant into another consciousness' (Soueif 2006: 326).

In a nutshell, the postcolonial aversion to, or circumspection around, the aesthetic has to do with political and also national and cultural allegiances. Indeed, the majority of postcolonial writers are read with reference to a national matrix: the writing is deemed to mirror a foundational national identity in some clear and even obvious way (Ramazani 2006: 332–59). The circumspection grows especially acute where the aesthetic is regarded not as well-made expression or as a precise framework of perception that may however, as a spin-off, serve the postcolonial cause, but *rigorously*. It becomes acute if the aesthetic is seen, whether antagonistically or sympathetically, as something that does not refer beyond itself; that is irreducible to anything outside of the work. Maurice Blanchot expressed this pure inwardness, this pure circularity of the art work in these suggestive ways in the essays that make up *The Space of Literature* (1955): 'nothing', he wrote, 'is ever made of being'. 'One never ascends from the world to art', therefore art is dissimulation only superficially. 'To write is', he further said, 'to withdraw language from the world' (Blanchot 1982: 47, 48, 26).

Or, to turn from a French structuralist theorist to a writer who attempts from within his own creative practice to outline a poetics, Ben Okri in his *A Way of Being Free* (1997) sees a similar remove between the artwork and the world. Note, however, that in the essays which comprise *A Way of Being Free*, Okri is never interested in talking about a *postcolonial* poetic or even, unless glancingly and aphoristically, an African poetic. For him a poetic is idealized, transformative, searching; it is not to be pinned down by epithets like African, postcolonial, Commonwealth. In this Blanchot would concur, as, too, would Okri's fellow postcolonial writer and crusader for various aesthetic affiliations with the English literary tradition, Derek Walcott (whom Okri discusses in this collection). Okri further concurs with Blanchot in regarding song and metaphor as distant from 'the unyielding world', as continually moving beyond the known, working through mystery and transgression. Poets, contends Okri, setting himself against wishful firebrand Shelley, 'are not the unacknowledged legislators of the world', which to him implies endorsing the world's present form. Driven by human suffering, they instead strive to *remake* the world. Their poetics, or indeed their aesthetic, requires poets to participate in the desire 'to be transformed into something higher', yet this aesthetic is not revolutionary in the sense of changing the world (Okri 1997: 1, 25, 63). To this Okri crucially adds – and it is notable that he is still talking about the poet in the most generic of terms – that poets *therefore* are inevitably, though not dutifully, on 'the side of the greatest good, the highest causes, the most just future' (3, 6). It is something within art, not outside it, that produces this striving for justice. The question invoked by these contentions is how an ethical stance might inhere to, or be embodied within, an aesthetic, or a tradition of dissent within a generic form, and whether this might be deemed postcolonial – though, as previously observed, Okri himself would resist any such identification.

Depending on which side of the fence one stands, the coupling of *postcolonial* with *aesthetic* by now begins to appear either deeply abstruse, or deeply suspect, or both. So far, however, I have looked at the concept in abstract and general terms. To gain some more immediate, concrete purchase on what the term *postcolonial aesthetic* might signify, it is worth now proceeding deductively, even pragmatically. It is worth asking whether it is possible, for example, *deductively* to identify a piece of writing as postcolonial according to certain structural, generic and, perhaps above all, discursive features which it bears. Stanley Cavell usefully reminds us that aesthetic judgement refers to what we are able to say about art, how it encourages us to say these things, and how we justify our choices to each other (2002). On this basis, it might be possible to analyze a text as unfolding a certain postcolonial rhetoric, or as *practising* a postcolonial aesthetic.

But, then again, as my phrasing might imply, it may not be possible to pose, let alone answer, such a question about practice without specifying a text's context, the geographical and historical co-ordinates that inform and motivate that practice. The real-world reference points are again unavoidable. Moreover, references to informing context inevitably also raise issues concerning the nature of the postcolonial in that context: how typical is it? Insofar as it produces certain distinctive or generic features, how representative is it? We may want to go to the extent of asking, for example, whether there is a regional writing, or even a period writing, say, the post-independence writing of the 1960s, that might generate a more characteristic postcolonial aesthetic practice than writing emanating from other kinds of location. Is there a postcolonial writing to which the label *aesthetically postcolonial* might stick more closely? In such cases the inclusiveness of chronologically based definitions of the postcolonial becomes problematic. Though some postcolonial writings might be regarded as more typical, more definitive and form-giving of the postcolonial condition than others, surely *no* world writing dealing with anti- and postcolonial dilemmas, whether in one of the former colonial languages, or in a vernacular, can legitimately be excluded from our postcolonial category? In this regard, it is now widely recognized that postcolonial writing in English is writing from around the world, produced since about 1947, in some cases earlier, and emanating from a host of different cultures and communities. It is writing dealing in one way or other, obliquely or directly, with the experience of being colonized.

Even so, identifications based on reading practice remain potentially productive of a sharper understanding of a till-now theoretically inconceivable postcolonial aesthetic, so it is worth suspending that postcolonial inclusiveness for a moment and returning to the overarching question. Our search is for an aesthetic method that might allow us to refer to some of the different types of postcolonial writing as characteristically and hence recognizably postcolonial; as preoccupied with a shared, even if widely disseminated, aesthetic. Is there present in the writing, say, a set of refractions of the raced body, or a shared and distinctive mode or mood, like Kwame Appiah's pessimism as articulated in his well-known essay, for example, or the anti-heroism isolated by John Thieme when discussing Naipaul (Appiah 1990: 336–97; Thieme 1987)? Might there be evidence of a common approach to mythmaking or remythifying, to 'redreaming' the world through local myth, as in the many regional versions of postcolonial magic realism, from Vikram Chandra through to Zakes Mda? Alternatively, postcolonial writing, especially from conflict zones, may coalesce in particular around expressions of valediction and mourning, as Ahdaf Soueif says of Palestinian writing. Here, worlds are vanishing in front of people's eyes, destruction seems irrational and widespread, feelings of loss are extreme. In literature, she and others suggest, writers feel bound to reinvent and reinscribe mourning rituals for their communities (Soueif 2006: 324–30; see also Durrant 2005).

For most writers and critics, to bring the words postcolonial and aesthetic together will at once conjure up certain connotations, perhaps of hybridity and in-betweeness, possibly also of sly civility, postmodern slippage and breakage, of writing back – all of them in their ways repetitions upon the present. Canonical postcolonial theory, most notably that associated with Homi Bhabha, gives us a clear guide to the salient features we are looking for: what it is within the art that does postcolonial and historical *work*, what practice bears the deepest imprint of the collisions of the colonial encounter (Bhabha 1995). To give just one example, at once lucid and yet typical, consider this sentence from Shalini Puri's 2004 study of what she calls 'the Caribbean postcolonial': 'discourses of hybridity have offered a rhetorical clearing space for assertions of Caribbean [...] identities' (2004: 44). For her, it is hybridity that most clearly identifies a postcolonial, or in particular Caribbean, aesthetic. But this identification also excludes a great deal of work. One can doubtless make an equally convincing postcolonial case for writing that is openly combative rather than subtly hybrid. Or for writing that is not so much subtly hybrid or openly combative as involved, say, in performing the colonized body, or as preoccupied with weaving myths of the past for the postcolonial present. These are surely not to be excluded from the category of works that convey a postcolonial aesthetic or carry out a postcolonial aesthetic practice?

Still thinking pragmatically, one could argue it is the *language* of postcolonial writing that embodies more or less what we mean when we refer to a postcolonial aesthetic. Certainly language use involves practice, and provides grounds for concreteness and some objectivity in our terms of aesthetic judgement. The postcolonial critics Jean-Marc Moura in *Exotisme et lettres francophone* (2003), and Ismail Talib in *The Language of Postcolonial Literatures* (2002), for example, foreground the post-imperial struggle with voice and language as the *defining* feature of a putative postcolonial writing. Here the voice of the oppressed finds expression in the mutated language of the oppressor. For critics like Talib, postcolonial literatures in the once-European languages (English, French) contend with the dominance of these languages as the linguistic vehicles of empire, by subverting the languages from within. Moreover, in the case of writers from strongly oral cultures, the dominant language is infused with the rhythms of local orature. A text deemed most pleasing or achieved or singular with regard to this version of a postcolonial aesthetic, therefore, would be that which most successfully, movingly, harmoniously, interrogated and integrated the language of the former empire in these various ways.

That said, it is worth pointing out that even the linguistic formulation of a postcolonial aesthetic is based on a restricted set of characteristics and prioritizes certain kinds of language use over others. Such a formulation would ultimately operate in prescriptive and reiterative ways, privileging heterogeneity over homogeneity. And to say as much as this does not yet begin to address the cultural and institutional contexts where such formulations originate. Seemingly, we cannot get around the problem of the coercive *a priori* in defining a postcolonial aesthetic – perhaps because there is an implication of hierarchy in any aesthetic definition. Once again we find ourselves up against the strategic but problematic inclusiveness of the category of the postcolonial. More fundamentally, to bring out a difficulty which underlies that inclusiveness, we find ourselves up against the irrefutable fact that the postcolonial entails a definition drawn not from the *work* but the *world*; that it first and foremost denotes history, not aesthetic form. This difficulty pinpoints why it is that postcolonial critics committed to diversity and democracy have generally, and no doubt wisely, steered clear of dealing with a postcolonial aesthetic *per se* at all. It would appears to imply not only a political distraction but also a complicit diktat.

To illustrate this general avoidance of the aesthetic in postcolonial criticism, we need look no further than any recent catalogue of postcolonial publications from a 'postcolonial friendly' publisher like Routledge – though I might equally mention Oxford, Duke, Manchester, Johns Hopkins, and so on. In the recent catalogue which I consulted (for 2007), titles and blurbs consistently referred the work and the artist to the post-imperial world, or trans-world. To cite a typical handful: *Writing across Worlds, After Empire, Postcolonial London, Nationalism and Post-Colonial Identity*.[1] From the point of view of these books, the catalogue tells us, writing is a means of making crossings, or of coming to terms with the loss of empire, or of expressing cultural histories of resistance in London, or alternatively the role of culture in nationalism. But, joining the crowds of critics who since the 1970s and the demise of New Criticism have turned their backs on any reference to the text-in-itself, these books, the blurbs suggest, make only the most tentative, qualified references to style, imaginative transformation, generic choice, singular language, modes of poetic attention. As for the word 'aesthetic' – as in the *PostColonial Studies Reader*, it is avoided at almost any cost.

It remains important of course not to lose sight of the sheer variousness of the work that we designate as postcolonial and onto which we are seeking to pin a still-hypothetical 'postcolonial aesthetic', even as it insists upon the difficulty of doing so. I turn now to three extracts from three recent postcolonial texts. All were published in the twenty-first century, all are decisively postcolonial, indeed post-millennial, in terms of chronology, yet all are resolutely diverse in their preoccupations. However, in relation to the plastic concept of a postcolonial aesthetic, it is productive to think not only of their many differences, but also, at the same time, of the possible ways in which these three texts might be seen as participating heterogeneously and yet collectively in some postcolonial aesthetic. The method I am suggesting for arriving at a clearer understanding of an irreducibly postcolonial aesthetic, in other words, at this point remains advisedly deductive and *a posteriori*. In this I am myself repeating upon the present. Any number of postcolonial critics deploy the same self-undoing technique in order to discuss postcolonial issues, juxtaposing work from different contexts and communities in comparative readings that harness together under one theme or title postcolonial writers from vastly different cultures.

My first extract is from Manju Kapur's *Home* (2006), the chronicle of three generations in the life of an extended Delhi family of cloth merchants. The novel, which is quietly realist, could be called a feminine *A Suitable Boy*, though it is built up out of repeated searches for suitable marriage partners, not just the one singular and definitive one. Throughout the novel social details are carefully observed and recorded. At certain points the individual occasionally seeks to define him- or herself against the group, but is all too soon subsumed by the relentless onward flow of life.

> The patriarch was dead, and all connected to the family came to condole. Many cloth traders and relatives near and distant gathered at the Karol Bagh house to pay their respects to a man who had embodied all the virtues of the old-fashioned bania, honest, sincere, industrious, whose love had held the entire family together through trials and disagreements. During his entire life he had made no enemies, the many tears shed for him were ample testimony to that.
>
> The family couldn't believe he had gone so soon. He had not troubled them enough, in itself an indication that he was free from the cycle of death and rebirth, all his bad karma expiated during six months of suffering.
>
> His wife wept ceaselessly. She had been twelve, he fifteen, when they married, and now, after sixty years, she was alone. 'Why, why,' she wailed, 'why did he have to go before me? Why did I have this misfortune? Kill me,' she begged her sons, 'kill me so I may go to him.'
>
> (120)

Moving back slightly in time, the second extract is from Achmat Dangor's *Bitter Fruit* (2003), a cynical and realist, if somewhat programmatic, post-apartheid novel preoccupied with the necessary processes of making 'accommodations' in relation to the past, and with the hard lessons of learning to be ordinary again.

> He grieved. He had lost Mireille and was alienated from his mother. She gave him fearful looks, constantly fighting back her tears. Soon, however, the whispering came to an end, a new and irresistible tension filled their lives, a force outside of their private lives, a fleeting moment when history became utterly important, inescapable, and compelling. Nelson Mandela became President, and the word 'freedom' took on an almost childlike meaning, so magical was its effect. Mikey heard Mam Agnes say, 'We're free,' when Mandela stood up to take the oath, her voice hoarse, filled with tenderness. Then, aware that Mikey was watching, she quickly reverted to her old, disbelieving self, her joy pressed like a dead flower between her unsmiling lips.

Still, Mikey could not believe the euphoria that swept through his family, cool Uncle Alec and laconic Grandpa Jackson, cold Gracie and an increasingly self-contained Lydia, their usual crusty suspicion of life's good intentions flung aside like an unfashionable worn-out coat. Until that enchanting April passed, and autumn came and the winter suddenly, and only Silas was left to walk about with a new sense of pride.

(38)

The third extract is from Yvonne Vera's poetically charged and elegiac *Stone Virgins* (2002), a short novel that cryptically charts outrages perpetrated upon civilians during the undeclared civil war in western Zimbabwe in the early 1980s. The prose is marked throughout by its preoccupation with reinvented rituals of mourning.

It is true, everything else in Gulati rots except the rocks. On the rocks history is steady, it cannot be titled forwards or backwards. It is not a refrain. History fades into the chaos of the hills but it does not vanish. In Gulati I travel four hundred years, then ten thousand years, twenty more. The rocks split open, time shifts and I confess that I am among the travellers who steal shelter from the dead.

(95)

Looking at these three extracts alongside one another, juxtaposed, strong differences almost immediately emerge, or radiate forth. Respectively, one is mutedly realist, strongly informed by the cyclical temporality of generation. The second is bitterly realist, with something of a Keatsian 'design upon us', sombre about the delusions of revolutionary romance; the third poetically mournful, imbued with an epic sense that history, or the past, is eternally present in every moment. Despite the largely superficial similarities of realism, the differences of form and style between the three texts are palpable. The most prominent element which links them, and which might allow us to speak of all three as postcolonial, refers in each case outside of the work. All three novels comment on and reflect elegiacally upon the societies and the histories of loss from which they rise. Yet, as I have tried to demonstrate by quoting at length, it would be extremely difficult if not impossible to isolate in these three works, even if we were able to look at them in full, and side-by-side, *aesthetic* features in common which might invite and justify the label postcolonial. Although they do all participate in a valedictory mode, they do not noticeably share a formal language of mourning or elegy.

By probing the doubtful salience of aesthetic approaches to, and concepts within, postcolonial writing, I have fetched up with a cluster of open-ended questions and suggestions, and few, if any, points of resolution. It is clear that the concept of a postcolonial aesthetic brings into tension – if not into crisis – what we mean when we seek greater-than-subjective standards of judgement when approaching literatures that rise out of the blood and mire, as Yeats might have put it, of oppression and struggle. What then might a postcolonial aesthetic signify if it is to avoid the charge that, no matter how responsibly framed, it represents exclusion and insidious evaluation, the reimposition of a so-called disinterested but in fact always imperializing western poetic? That it produces, yet again, the reiteration of tried and tested humanist definitions in a late colonial guise?

Ben Okri, with his attention to the forms of beauty that emerge even out of day-to-day suffering, or to the Fanonian 'occult sphere' where the people dwell, exercises, in his own particular poetic language, precisely such concerns (Fanon 1986 [1961]: 43). Okri is specifically interested in a poetics, one might even say an ethics, which emanates from outside the work of art, from the world, from people's suffering, yet which only finds adequate expression, which can only be realized, within the art work. The latter is the domain in which this poetics achieves its transformative potential. For Okri, there is evidently something within the aesthetic that for the reader bridges and links together the material and the transcendent. This may be the same impulse that Adorno perceived when he spoke of the *forceful* construction of texts – their forceful, even purposive conflict with life – as allowing them to rise above and overcome their social and economic predetermination (Adorno 2004: 72, 77).[2] This suggestion of a mediation or calibration between work and world appears to lead us away from a too hermetic and inward definition of the aesthetic, offering us something more productive than the contradictory divide or oxymoron that the term 'postcolonial aesthetic' otherwise seems to impose.

To address this, it is helpful to turn to a critical consideration of postcolonial close reading from Ato Quayson, in a study that confronts precisely this kind of question. In *Calibrations* (2003), he attempts to theorize how we read or understand 'the structures of transformation, process, and contradiction' which inform not only literature but also society. For Quayson, not the 'literary-aesthetic domain' alone, as he calls it, but the social or social realm, too, is 'produced' or 'configured': the aesthetic and the social are involved in one another's production, linked through a structure of 'interacting thresholds and domains' (Quayson 2003: xiii, xvi). To him, a way out of the postcolonial versus aesthetic divide lies in seeing the social not as a primary determinant of the aesthetic, but as intricately intercalated with it, in such a way that the aesthetic equally prepares us to read the social as the social the aesthetic. Paradoxically, Quayson's way out is more concerned with the world than the text, and therefore cannot be used to produce a closer understanding of a postcolonial aesthetic as such. He is also not particularly concerned with privileging the postcolonial aesthetic domain over any other, though he *does* refer to postcolonial cultures as being by necessity particularly preoccupied with 'a mediation between terms and discourses', and hence with calibrations. Where Quayson is illuminating is in his repeated emphasis on the textual element as the 'threshold' of particular problems or enigmas, and not as the 'disclosure of a discrete social or cultural verity as such' (xv, xxii).

Quayson's formulations are allied not only to those of Raymond Williams, whom he acknowledges, but also Said, whom he does not. Yet Said's thoughts about the simultaneous worldliness and shapeliness of texts, though apparently more conventional, are equally preoccupied with what Quayson terms 'the great dialectic of acquisition and representation' in texts (xxxiii–xxxiv, 59, 63). It was also Said who helpfully argued in *The World, the Text and the Critic* (1984) that we cannot have solidarity (postcolonial or otherwise) before criticism, by which he means aesthetic criticism, because criticism is productive of the meanings and values we must live by. Texts are not mere symbols of something else, but 'deviations from, exaggerations and negations of, human presence [...] phenomena of excess and rupture' (Said 1984: 23, 28, 147).

Drawing together these various materialist and post-materialist critical observations and suggestions, the following proposal can be tentatively formulated. *Perhaps* there is that within a postcolonial aesthetic that clarifies or sheds light on the postcolonial condition, be it hybrid or manichean, though without necessarily setting out to do so, without overt intention, without set and specific interest. There is that within an aesthetic that we might call postcolonial that draws in the postcolonial world, imbibes its affect, and constellates and reconstellates its meanings through our reading of it, our participation in it. It may be this that Quayson was suggesting in his discussion of the particular in art as a threshold of meaning always opening out to other levels. By this token we might even venture to say that there is that within an aesthetic which we might want to call postcolonial, that catalyses a post-humanist or non-western humanism, though again this effect is largely incidental – the process plays itself out with mostly unanticipated consequences.

What a post-humanist humanism and consequence-less process might entail has for the present to be the subject of another chapter. In this essay, I point to what a postcolonial aesthetic might *do* rather than define what it *is* – indeed it may *be* nothing at all. The postcolonial aesthetic, then, is *in* language rather than *of* language; it requires participation from readers; it draws us into a process that makes possible certain kinds of postcolonial understanding. Books, suggests Hanif Kureishi throughout his biography of his father *My Ear at his Heart* (2004), allow us to ask questions of the final *unknowability* of other human beings. Perhaps that is ultimately all we can say about a postcolonial aesthetic. Like other kinds of aesthetic, it allows us to interrogate, and, as compensation to our questioning selves, tell stories about, the mystery that is not so much the Other, generically speaking, as the ultimately unknowable other human being.

Notes

1 For rhetorical effect I only cite titles at this point. Full references are listed at the end of the essay, in Bibliography.
2 Adorno writes: 'Certainly every finished work of art is already predetermined in some way but art strives to overcome its own oppressive weight as an artefact through the force of its very construction'.

Bibliography

Adorno, T. (2004) 'The Schema of Mass Culture', *The Culture Industry*, ed. J. M. Bernstein, trans. Nicholas Walker, New York and London: Routledge.

Appiah, K. A. (1990) 'Is the Post- in Postmodernism the Post- in Postcolonial?', *Critical Inquiry*, 17/2 (Winter): 336–97.

—— (1992) *In my Father's House: Africa in the Philosophy of Culture*, London: Methuen.

Ashcroft, B., Griffiths, G. and Tiffin, H. (eds) (1995; 2nd edn 2005) *The Post-Colonial Studies Reader*, New York and London: Routledge.

Bhabha, H. (1995) *The Location of Culture*, New York and London: Routledge.

Blanchot, M. (1982, [1955]) *The Space of Literature*, trans. A. Smock, Lincoln and London: University of Nebraska Press.

Buck-Morss, S. (2009) *Hegel, Haiti and Universal History*, Pittsburgh: University of Pittsburgh Press.

Cavell, S. (2002) 'Aesthetic Problems of Modern Philosophy', in *Must We Mean What We Say?* Cambridge: Cambridge University Press: 73–96.

Dangor, A. (2003) *Bitter Fruit*, London: Atlantic Books.

Durrant, S. (2005) 'The Invention of Mourning in Post-Apartheid Literature', *Third World Quarterly*, 26.3: 441–50.

Fanon, F. (1986, [1961]) *The Wretched of the Earth*, trans. C. Farrington, London: Penguin.

Gilroy, P. (2004) *After Empire: Melancholia or Convivial Culture*, London: Routledge.

Kant, I. (1951) *The Critique of Judgement: The Critique of Aesthetic Judgement*, trans. J. H. Bernard, New York: Hatner Publishing Co.

Kapur, M. (2006) *Home*, London: Faber.

McLeod, J. (2006) *Postcolonial London: Rewriting the Metropolis*, New York and London: Routledge.

Mondal, A. A. (2003) *Nationalism and Post-Colonial Identity: Culture and Ideology in India and Egypt*, London: Routledge.

Moura, J. (2003) *Exotisme et lettres francophone*, Paris: Presses Universitaire de France.

Nasta, S. (ed.) (2004) *Writing Across Worlds: Contemporary Writers Talk*, New York and London: Routledge.

Parry, B. (2004) *Postcolonial Studies: A Materialist Critique*, New York and London: Routledge.

Puri, S. (2004) *The Caribbean Postcolonial: Social Equality, Post-nationalism, Cultural Hybridity*, Basingstoke: Palgrave Macmillan.

Quayson, A. (2003) *Calibrations: Reading for the Social*, Minneapolis: University of Minnesota Press.

Ramazani, J. (2006) 'A Transnational Poetics', *The Author* (March): 332–59.

Said, E. (1984) *The World, the Text and the Critic*, London: Faber.

Scott, D. (2004) *Conscripts of Modernity: The Tragedy of Colonial Enlightenment*, Durham and London: Duke University Press.

Soueif, A. (2006) *Mezzaterra: Fragments from the Common Ground*, London: Bloomsbury.

Talib, I. (2002) *The Language of Postcolonial Literatures*, New York and London: Routledge.

Thieme, J. (1987) *The Web of Tradition: The Use of Allusion in V. S. Naipaul's Fiction*, Aarhus: Dangaroo.

Vera, Y. (2002) *The Stone Virgins*, Harare: Weaver Press.

Young, R. J. C. (2001) *Postcolonialism: An Historical Introduction*, Oxford: Blackwell.

16 Rerouting commitment in the post-apartheid canon

TRC narratives and the problem of truth

Jane Poyner

In recent times cultural commentators have endeavoured to gauge the reroutings in South African fiction now that apartheid is over. Under apartheid, South Africa was, in the words of Njabulo Ndebele, 'a very *public* society. It is public in the sense that its greatest aberrations are fully exhibited. [...] It is totally heroic' (4–50). J. M. Coetzee's novel *Age of Iron* ([1990] 1991), set during the waning yet most virulent years of the Afrikaner National Party, succinctly captures this lack of privacy when the protagonist Mrs Curren's house is being ransacked by detectives. Rifling through her letters, one of the policemen tells her, 'This is not private, Mrs Curren. [...] Nothing is private any more' (157). Similarly, challenged by Mrs Curren for losing parental authority of her activist child, Florence responds: 'It is all changed today. There are no more mothers and fathers' (36). Necessarily lessening the distance between artistic expression and public intellectualism, the apartheid condition forced even the most reluctant novelists to engage with the public domain. Questions of aesthetics and litera-ture's capacity for interiority, it seemed, were to be set aside for the more pressing needs of politics. Indeed, such needs may account for the neglect, identified by Elleke Boehmer in this volume, of the category of the aesthetic in postcolonial studies. A number of progressive critics, notably Ndebele, Nadine Gordimer, Coetzee, Lewis Nkosi and Albie Sachs, warned that in South Africa this led to a debased and didactic form of literature. For Ndebele, '[t]he entire ethos [of committed literature] permits neither inner dialogue with the self, nor a social public dialogue. It breeds insensitivity, insincerity and delusion' (50). Critics like David Attwell and Michael Chapman, however, have shown that such a position itself represents a 'critical orthodoxy' (Attwell 2005: 177) that overlooks the complexities of literature that, whilst committed, at times also reveals a distinct African modernism and that is capable of combining self-reflexivity with political critique.

Yet with the demise of apartheid some critics have speculated on whether the 'subject' of South Africa is now over. Rob Nixon suggests that writers feel out of place in the social and cultural arena: 'They have gained key freedoms but lost, in the process, the very stresses that fuelled their creativity' (64). Tested against the emergent fictional genre of the TRC (Truth and Reconciliation Commission) narrative, it is my contention that literary commitment continues to energize this new body of writing, but that it has been rerouted inwards towards self-censorship and ethico-political responsibility. It is clear that the public sphere shapes and defines our private identities, but post-apartheid fiction reveals that the private can serve productively as a corrective to the public, suggesting that the 'dichotomy' of public/private needs reconceptualizing. The imagined world of the novel, because it belongs to another mode of discourse, circumvents the kinds of pressures that can, for instance, compromise received notions of public intellectualism.

It should not be surprising that, with the demise of apartheid, novelists and writers have been enabled to reroute their creativity. The new political climate, for instance, has facilitated a *critical* discourse on an environmental ethic in Nadine Gordimer's novel *Get a Life* (2005), James Graham argues elsewhere in this section, an ethic which heretofore Gordimer had rejected as a vehicle of racial oppression. The end of the struggle has enabled writers to turn their gaze to the private sphere, to reflection and self-questioning, which may account for the proliferation of confessional novels. Although South Africa has a long history of 'truth and confession' represented in the genre of autobiography, as the novelist Phaswane Mpe has argued (Attree 2005: 144), this confessional turn has gathered pace, post-1994. In line with an Adornian aesthetic that, as Boehmer suggests, is always already ideological I argue that the very literariness of the TRC narrative, specifically in the expression of interiority, illuminates the socio-political critique such a narrative embeds.

In 'Memory, Metaphor, and the Triumph of Narrative' (1998), Ndebele changes tack by welcoming the restorative function of narrative. He suggests that in South Africa today 'there may be an informal truth and reconciliation process under way among the Afrikaners' (24), which he sees reflected in recent Afrikaner fiction. (Of course, the TRC itself employed narrative and the act of telling for purposes of (self-) healing that would pave the way for nation-building.) Whilst Ndebele regards Afrikaner TRC narratives as therapeutic mechanisms for overcoming personal guilt and complicity, my focus is rather different: the TRC narratives I analyse here are representative of a category that, rather than uncritically employing the TRC's procedures, *unsettles* the boundaries between private and public to explore the ways in which the TRC erroneously transposed the private sphere of truth-telling and forgiveness to the public domain of law and justice. TRC narratives reveal that, in looking for moral (private) truths, the TRC obscured the everyday reality of apartheid oppression.

The discourses of truth and reconciliation invoked by the TRC have been called into question by numerous political commentators. Most have noted that confession usually belongs to religious discourse in which the confessant's ultimate goal is absolution granted by God. Benita Parry, for instance, comments upon the 'atmosphere of euphoric Christian revivalism' that she believes tainted the hearings (Parry 2004: 188), whilst Jacques Derrida has suggested that 'when Desmond Tutu was named president of the Truth and Reconciliation Commission, he Christianized the language uniquely destined to treat "politically" motivated crimes (an enormous problem ...)' (2001: 42). Derrida delineates the realms of judgement, that falls within the remit of the State, and forgiveness, which only the individual can grant (44). In the ethical economy of forgiveness the state 'has neither the right nor the power' to forgive because 'forgiveness has nothing to do with judgement' (43). Similarly, Holiday is troubled by the collapsing of the categories of the private and the public on religious grounds. The religious formulation of forgiveness is concerned with an 'inner moral life' which cannot by its very nature be regulated by public bodies: 'forgiveness, by reason of its conceptual dependence on remorse, must be an intensely personal, even a private matter' (1998: 55–56). It would be germane to ask how the two notions of confession, those of the private (religious, secular) and public (institutional) domains, can be usefully and indeed credibly brought together, which is effectively what the TRC strove to do.

According to Mamdani, who has been one of the TRC's most consistent and incisive critics, it was the main part of the Commission rather than the Amnesty Committee which had the power to delimit its narrative of truth, and this was where the TRC's real power lay. Mamdani distinguishes between individual and institutional truths, the former resisting truth to power whilst the latter collapses truth with power. The TRC relied upon institutional and therefore politically compromised truths, compromised because of their very limited time frame (2000: 176–7). The Commission was born of political compromise and, whilst compromise in the political sphere was a necessary evil (South Africa's fledgling democracy was built on the back of a negotiated political settlement between two opposing parties), political compromise under the auspices of the TRC became a moral compromise which 'obscured the larger truth', and this could not be justified (177–8). This larger truth is the systemic violence perpetrated in apartheid's name – segregation, the criminalizing of miscegenation, the implementation of the Pass Laws and so on – that had a direct impact on every black individual in South Africa.[1] In other words, the marginalized majority was not accounted for by 'gross violations of human rights'.

Established novelists like Athol Fugard, Mandla Langa, Sindiwe Magona, and those who didn't cut their teeth during apartheid like K. Sello Duiker, Phaswane Mpe, Ishtiyaq Shukri, have implicitly critiqued the TRC hearings and public notions of truth, as well as the less than bright 'rainbow nation'. I briefly discuss four TRC narratives here: Gordimer's *The House Gun* (1999), Coetzee's *Disgrace* (1999), Dangor's *Bitter Fruit* (2004 [2001]) and Ndebele's *The Cry of Winnie Mandela* (2003).

In *The House Gun*, the central motif, the 'house gun' presents violence in 'domesticated' form, symptomatic of the violence that is a scourge on the 'rainbow nation': 'A house gun – kept like a house cat: a fact of ordinary life' (271). The plot revolves around a young middle-class white man, Duncan, who in a jealous rage shoots an ex-(male) lover whom he finds having sex with his girlfriend. The gun is to hand, suggestive of the normalization of violence in the post-apartheid state, and it is this fact that the young black lawyer, Motsamai, uses in Duncan's defence. Departing from the chronological sequencing of events characteristic of the realist mode that typifies much of Gordimer's early work, and inverting the stereotyped assumptions about violence in present-day South Africa, the narrative circles forensically around the 'truth' of Duncan's story. In a novel in which little actually happens, we experience through this painstaking exhumation of truth his parents Harald's and Claudia's very private anguish over the shooting – there is no doubt over the young man's guilt – which allows Gordimer to move the discussion of 'truth' into the private, familial sphere. Here, Duncan ponders mockingly on the question of remorse, and on his parents' attempt to comprehend his crime:

> [...] my poor parents, do you want your little boy to come in tears to say I'm sorry? [...] Shall I be a civilized human being again, for the one, and will God forgive and cleanse me, for the other. Is that what they think it is, this thing, remorse.
>
> (Gordimer 1999: 281)

By invoking religion, Gordimer alludes to a key flaw of the TRC in its use of religious discourse in the spheres of politics and law – the charge frequently laid at Tutu's feet. Duncan recognizes the banality to which confession and accountability have been reduced under the auspices of 'Justice': that saying sorry in contexts such as this – Duncan's trial but also, by analogy, the Truth hearings – is inadequate recompense for the crimes committed both outside and under apartheid.

From the outset, the novel unsettles boundaries of private and public. We enter the story with Duncan's parents, Harald and Claudia, sitting cocooned from catastrophe that always until now happened elsewhere, watching images on the TV of 'Bosnia or Somalia or the earthquake shaking a Japanese island [...] whatever were the disasters of that time' (3). Implied in these words is the privilege accorded white (liberal) South Africans, privilege that allows Claudia and Harald to separate their own cosy world from that of the violence of South Africa that heretofore has left them untouched. Later they realize that

> [...] they were invaded by a happening that had no place in their kind of life, the kind of life they believed they had ensured for their son. (A liberal education – whose liberalism did not extend to admitting blacks, like Motsamai, they realized now.)
>
> (69)

Duncan's crime shakes Harald's and Claudia's belief systems to the core. Whilst they 'have never belonged in the public expression of private opinions, which [Harald] supposes is the transformation of opinions into convictions' (134), their experiences in the court and their relationship with Motsamai force them to revise their world view as they are obliged to confront the reality of the past of apartheid and the 'now' of the 'new South Africa'. Harald understands that his son cannot be above the law yet begins to doubt his own religious belief and, in the process, to recognize that the expression of remorse – a moral conviction – is beyond the jurisdiction of the law. Here Harald's thoughts are conveyed through an indirect focalizer: 'No confession (already made), repentance in exchange for forgiveness possible. So much for the compassion of Harald's God' (105). The realization of Harald and Claudia, arrived at through the process of soul-searching with which the crime forces them to engage, is that they have been beneficiaries of the apartheid regime all along and that they no longer can preserve themselves from this fact. Privacy in this novel is closely associated with the politics of white liberalism, of 'turning a blind eye', and this is the politics that Harald and Claudia must reconcile.

Any sense of redemption offered by the text lies in what Clingman identifies as a new mode of communication in post-apartheid South Africa, located through 'oscillation' (Harald and Claudia) and 'triangulation' (Harald, Claudia and Duncan) of voice and consciousnesses. The narrative opens moments before Duncan's friend Julian intrudes upon the couple with the news of the murder. Harald and Claudia are seated in front of the television: 'He, she – twitch of a smile, he got himself up with languor directed at her and went to lift the nearest receiver' (3). This oscillation is linked closely with the narrative's introspective mode and effects a 'collective', 'collaborative' sharing of the burden of the knowledge of Duncan's offence. Clingman argues that '[o]*scillation* becomes a less sharp, in its essence a more *forgiving*, mode of representation; for Gordimer's work it becomes a different version of perception and – in its deepest sense – communication in South Africa' (149). In so much as the use of the interior monologue in postcolonial literature (for example, James Joyce's *Dubliners*) represents the exercising of an embryonic citizenship constitutive of nation-building (Kiberd 2008), then in this novel a conjoined mode of indirect discourse, even expressed as 'he/she', suggests the kind of shared responsibility of beneficiaries of the regime that would furnish the ground for a more just, 'reconciled' society.

If *The House Gun* closes on this note of redemption, Coetzee's novel *Disgrace* (1999) paints a profoundly bleak picture of the 'new South Africa' through the controversial depiction of black-on-white rape in which the 'trial' scene is presented as an analogy of the TRC. The unsavoury protagonist Professor David Lurie is brought before a disciplinary committee at the university where he works to answer publicly for an illicit affair with one of his female students Melanie, who by apartheid designation is 'coloured'. Significantly, the affair is mirrored in the text by the rape of Lurie's daughter Lucy by three black intruders to Lucy's farm. The culmination of Lurie's involvement with Melanie is a sexual encounter that he recognizes as 'Not rape, not quite that, but undesired nevertheless' (25). In this way Lurie is held accountable by the text for his actions. Lurie refuses to make the public apology required of him by the committee, to 'express contrition'. Instead he interrogates the question of sincerity in confession: 'I have said the words for you ['It was wrong, and I regret it'], now you want more, you want me to demonstrate their sincerity. [...] I plead guilty. That is as far as I am prepared to go' (54–5). Rejecting the authenticity of quasi-religious confession in the public sphere, Lurie is propelled into a journey of self-discovery and personal atonement which, nevertheless, is also revealed to be morally bankrupt: he visits Melanie's family home and, in an act of what Graham Pechey calls 'grotesque obeisance' (2002: 81), kisses the feet of her father, all the while secretly lusting after Melanie's even more beautiful sister, the aptly named Desiree.

Like all 'TRC narratives', this is a novel that is about 'coming to terms': Lurie struggles to find his place in the 'new South Africa' which has rendered him, in the terms of the new masculinities engendered in the novel, marginalized by his black neighbour Petrus. It is also about Lurie coming to terms with his sense of self, to face his inner demons which in part hinder his opera project, *Byron in Italy*. Whether, ultimately, Lurie is able to say sorry with conviction or sincerity is subject to doubt, though Coetzee certainly gestures in this direction. First, Lurie learns through processes of identification and empathy to give voice to the Teresa character in his opera rather than the salacious Byron with whom he first identifies. Nonetheless, the self-oriented motive of this gesture is itself questionable; he can only subdue his violent rage against the child-rapist Pollux through Teresa, '[t] hat is why he must listen to Teresa. Teresa may be the last one left who can save him' (209). Second, he gives up the sick dog with which he has formed a particularly intimate bond for euthanasia. However, one might conclude that Lurie's failure to atone for the affair signals that this is also a novel about saving oneself.

A particularly troubling aspect of the novel is Lucy's rationalization of the rape, that she is 'prepared to do anything, make any sacrifice, for the sake of peace' (208), including tolerating the presence of Pollux, the child rapist, and marrying Petrus, his uncle. Purposefully moving the story from the public to the private sphere, she tells her exasperated father: '[...] what happened to me is a purely private matter. In another time, in another place it might be held to be a public matter. But in this place, at this time, it is not' (112). Despite perversely sacrificing her rights as a woman in the name of reconciliation, Lucy takes charge of her story from her father (who, after all, admits to the near rape of Melanie), and in the process 'decommodifies' her body from the system of patriarchal exchange. She also acknowledges the need for nation building that could be hindered by the damaging effects of what Lucy Graham identifies as the discourse of 'black peril' that is particular to South African history and for white racists is evidenced in the prevalence of rape at the current time (Graham 2003: 434–5). Lucy's claim that her story is private signals her recognition that individual stories like those heard by the TRC tended to obscure the larger truth of oppression of the marginalized majority, the mundane everyday reality of apartheid. Lucy makes this abundantly clear when she alludes to the question of reparations and tax collection. This is the story of black dispossession from the land and from employment rights. Of course, she is dealing with common criminals and her implicit allusion to them as representative of South Africa's dispossessed and disenfranchised is therefore problematic.

Bitter Fruit by Achmat Dangor responds to the controversy that *Disgrace* has sparked. In *Bitter Fruit*, which Boehmer refers to as 'a cynical and realist if somewhat programmatic post-apartheid novel' (xxx), it is a black woman, Lydia Ali, who is raped by a white policeman, Lieutenant du Boise. Through her political activist husband Silas, who liaises for the new government with the TRC, the narrative records the pain and repression of her story experienced by the couple and the process of healing through which they both pass towards their private, marital 'reconciliation' (the marriage ultimately breaks down). Whilst guilt is a common theme in recent white writing, it is the black Silas who experiences guilt in *Bitter Fruit*, forced to listen helplessly as his wife is raped. In *Disgrace*, Lurie is ignominiously locked in a lavatory and can do nothing as he hears his daughter being attacked by the three men. Importantly, both novels stage questions about new masculine subjectivities, post-apartheid. Indeed, Lurie in *Disgrace* identifies his daughter's raped body as 'booty, war reparations [...] in the great campaign of redistribution' (176) and Lydia, speaking about her rape, rebukes Silas: du Boise 'took your woman [...] I became his property, even my screams were his instrument' (17).

Confronted by her husband with the until now unspoken story of her rape, Lydia smashes a bottle and walks upon the crushed glass, in order, we assume, to transfer the psychic trauma of rape onto the physical pain in her feet. Following Lydia's hospitalization, Silas is also admitted, with a suspected heart attack. Here, he imagines how gender relations have altered, post-apartheid, in a sardonic critique of the concept of sincerity and the problematic use of the religious discourses of confession and forgiveness by the Commission:

> He would atone, as soon as he was dressed, for having spoken to [the nurse] so sharply [...]. Things have changed; in the old days, his behaviour would have earned him a scolding. [...] No need for all that now, this new liberated Age of Truth and Confession. He rehearsed how he would say, 'I'm sorry for being rude,' and she would smile and say, 'It's alright, Mr Ali,' and he would go away feeling virtuous.'
>
> (Dangor 2004 [2001]: 95)

The triteness and banality with which truth and confession are presented sits uncomfortably with the distressing story of Lydia's rape; truth and confession, over articulated and expressed without conviction, the text implies, are rendered meaningless during this period.

Silas, Lydia and Mikey – the progeny of Lydia's rape – all struggle with the need to remember and the need to forget. Here Lydia reflects on the family:

> We'll learn, all of us, to live in our spheres of silence, not saying the unsay-able, denying everyone the pleasure of seeing us suffer the divine virtue of the brave new country: truth. We have to learn to become ordinary, learn how to lie to ourselves, and to others, if it means keeping the peace.
>
> (138)

Not only do the family have to reassess their 'heroic' apartheid existence, but we see that truth and reconciliation, as Mamdani points out, are predicated on compromise.

As in the case of Harald and Claudia in *The House Gun*, the private world of Silas and Lydia's marriage is punctured by events from outside. Du Boise, the policeman who raped Lydia nineteen years earlier in the knowledge that Silas was an ANC activist and has applied for amnesty at the TRC hearings, resurfaces at the local supermarket. Experiencing the return of traumatic memories, Silas has already been anticipating 'run[ning] into someone from the past, someone who had been in a position of power and had abused it' (4). The narrative quickly sets in process discourses of accountability and responsibility, but these are immediately undermined by the interjection of Silas' voice over that of an omniscient narrator:

> Good men had done all kinds of things they could not help doing, because they had been corrupted by all the power someone or something had given them.
>   'Bullshit,' Silas thought. It's always something or someone else who's responsible, a 'larger scheme of things' that exonerates people from taking responsibility for the things they do.

(3)

So whilst the omniscient narrator tries to rationalize responsibility on the national-political plane, Silas brings it into the sphere of personal responsibility, little knowing that in the course of events he will have to take responsibility for his own sense of guilt: on a private level his guilt that, hearing his wife being raped, he wept for himself and his own sense of emasculation, and collectively, his guilt for the failings of the new dispensation. Ironically, whilst attending to the national-political plane, the omniscient narrator in fact obscures the responsibility of the perpetrators of violence and the beneficiaries of the regime. The expletive that interrupts Silas's narrative draws a line under this particular kind of myth-making which let such individuals off the hook.

The narrative attempts to restore Lydia's agency through her diary entries, and it is here that her religiosity is tested. Ultimately, she suffers a loss of faith in the concept of confession, as Helene Strauss has argued (2005 n.p.), be it religious or of the secular variety practiced at the TRC hearings. The words of Lydia, functioning here as focalizer, recall the satirical tone employed in *The House Gun* and *Disgrace* to point up the quasi-religious spirit of the TRC hearings: 'Confess your sins, even those committed against you [...] but confess it once only' (127). Immediately following his mother's private revelations, of which as readers of a diary we are privy as intrusive observers, Mikey is described as absorbed not in 'the vast fiction of great histories' which previously inspired him, but in the private tragedy of his conception recorded in his mother's diary.

Ndebele's *The Cry of Winnie Mandela* (2003) invites us with 'Let's begin' to enter the mythical framing device of Odysseus's Penelope-in-waiting who, in Ndebele's novel, is the archetypal submissive wife, 'so loyal and so true' (2), and who resides at '*the centre of a great South African story not yet told*' (1; original emphasis). This is the story of Everywoman. The stories of the four 'descendents' of Penelope, recounted in Part One, are South African women's everyday stories of waiting for husbands who, for reasons spanning economic migrancy to political activism, never return. In Part Two, on the initiative of Mamello, the women decide to play a game in order 'to go beyond [their] conversations' (43), in the process establishing a feminized public sphere based on the traditional Zulu codes of the *ibandla* (public gathering). The game requires the women to offer supplications or 'confessions' to a fifth, elected member of the *ibandla*, Winnie Mandela, who qualifies for the group because she 'waited too. The only difference between us and her is that she waited in public while we waited in the privacy of our homes, suffering in the silence of our bedrooms' (44).

Within the bounds of the *ibandla* and represented in the confessional and performative qualities of the narrative, the game amounts to an informal and Africanized 'truth and reconciliation commission' through which Ndebele strives to disentangle the shortcomings of the real TRC: that it was ill-equipped to address the stories of everyday suffering engendered by apartheid and colonialism before it, including Mandela's own, and that it therefore sanctioned a mythologized or distorted truth. The truth that the TRC was *not* furnished to tell, for instance, is that Mandela is the 'child' (134) of the apartheid system. In its opening pages the novel couches itself in terms of the courtroom scenario and the dangers of 'unfair' judgement (Penelope has been wrongly accused by her neighbours of infidelity) (3), thus preparing the ground in Part Two for Mandela's notorious appearance at the TRC hearings at which she was accused of being nothing more than 'an unprincipled and unblushing liar' (2003: 77). (In real life, of course, Nelson Mandela cited Winnie's infidelity during his long years of absence as part of his grounds for divorce.)

The diptych patterning of the text – the 'private' myth of the biddable wife versus the 'public' myth of Winnie Mandela – paves the way for a corrective 'public space' to the TRC in which a strategic 'rediscovery of the ordinary' is set in place. Although Ndebele's particular rediscovery relates to cultural production, it has wider applications in the public sphere, combating political posturing and what Gordimer, writing in the context of writers' freedom, refers to as 'conformity to an orthodoxy of opposition' (Gordimer 1988: 106): commitment to any set of politics is in danger of fostering an uncritical mindset which threatens the very notion of free speech. Invoking Zoë Wicomb's South African novel of reappraised resistance, *David's Story* (2001), life under apartheid was 'reduced [...] to one long scream' (73). Under the egregious oppression of apartheid, language lost its nuanced and critical edge and, in the hands of Mandela, the novel suggests, it became corrupted. The smoothed-over language of political rhetoric, like the self-confessed 'language of theatrical gesture' learned by Mandela (Ndebele 2003: 132), flies in the face of Edward Said's category of the public intellectual, 'whose whole being is staked on a critical sense, a sense of being unwilling to accept *easy formulas, or ready-made clichés*' (1994: 23; emphasis added).

Within the safe limits of a female *ibandla* that serves as the novel's alternative TRC, and through a contrived 'rediscovery of the ordinary' that turns upon the problem of empty political rhetoric, the narrative endeavours both to unravel the complexities of a woman who was the product of an extreme situation and to illuminate the everyday oppression of ordinary women in the marital home.

Tacitly invoking Fanon's thesis on the hazards of neo-colonialism that threatens any postcolonial project of nation-building, Mamello inveighs Mandela with the salutary words, 'You become the most dramatic, most visible manifestation of the culture of political posture that may have had its use at a particular point in time, but which now bedevils our ability to recognize the real needs of a new society' (73). Mandela's involvement with the *ibandla*, Mandela concedes, has awakened a self-awareness, but one which she lacks the linguistic or critical tools to analyse. She experiences the shock of the full historical perspective to which the *ibandla* gives her access: 'Your voices have brought me into that state of being in which I can see something in me deeply, but find I lack the language or other means to express it' (104). We encounter a woman unschooled in the nuanced language from which the crude political education into which she was thrown as Nelson's lover excluded her.

Mamello recalls that the confession Tutu manages to elicit from Mandela at the TRC hearings lacked sincerity. Rather than truths revealed, this was a case of the 'victory of image and posture' and 'technical victories and technical innocence' that 'characterise [...] courtroom procedure' (75). The TRC, born of a spectacular apartheid society, relied upon distorted language and thus distorted truths. (Despite the fact that in real life Mandela was implicated in a string of crimes including the high-profile murder of Stompie Seipei, Mamello's suspicion of judicial process is problematic. She looks to the TRC for moral truths rather than justice, a strategy which compromised the success of the TRC.) In the spirit of public debate, Mara gives a more celebratory verdict: the TRC was 'not so much about judgement, but about *the process of formulating judgement*. It was about reconstituting *the public domain through social insight*' (86; emphasis added).

It is here that the narrative and Ndebele's rediscovery of the ordinary converge, for it is the *process* of arriving at a moral outcome that Ndebele's strategy of rediscovery promotes. Like Mannete, whose belief in Christ shows her the difference between a 'moral outcome' and the journey or 'process' arriving at it (97), Mandela remains deeply suspicious of the moral outcome of the TRC, namely reconciliation; yet she too, like Mara and Mannete, believes in the efficacy of the process itself:

> I will not be an instrument for validating the politics of reconciliation. For me, reconciliation demands my annihilation. No. You, all of you, have to reconcile not with me, but with the meaning of me. For my meaning is the *endless human search for the right thing to do.*
>
> (Ndebele 2003: 137; emphasis added)

Mandela recognizes the burden of mythologizing that she has accrued, and points up the danger of taking the heroic stories of the few as a beacon of reconciliation. In fact, the 'me' to whom she refers, as in the model of moral conversion of which Coetzee writes in his essay 'Confession and Double Thoughts' (1985), is the true or private self that the community of women have helped reveal, rather than the 'false' self of public posturing, signified by 'the meaning of me'. Reconciliation, being necessarily compromised as Mamdani argued, would mean papering over the more nuanced true self that Mandela has only now discovered.

The true-self/false-self dialectic is signified in the text by Mandela's narrative itself fragmenting into two, into her private or 'true' self and her public persona or 'false' self (false because 'public' in the context of Mandela conjures notions of political posturing). It is her true (private) and false (public) selves that Mandela invokes when she declares that she 'too will speak to Winnie' (111). Mandela takes herself on a journey of 'self-reconciliation' (to be mirrored by the women and by Penelope as hitch-hiker at the end of the narrative) to her old home in Soweto to experience through this private/true self the life that the public/false self lived, believing that 'if one's very life becomes a weapon of resistance, something designed to negate repressive intent [...] is there a point at which self-negation becomes a permanent feature of identity' (114).

In the tradition of committed writing, contemporary South African novelists have pointed out the need both to bear witness to the past in order to build a better future, and also to regard the promises of truth and reconciliation in the 'rainbow nation' with a politically urgent and measured scepticism. Literary reroutings in South Africa today do not signal a complete break, politically or aesthetically, with the past. Such a move would wilfully ignore Frantz Fanon's prescient warnings about the pitfalls of national consciousness: that without due diligence the new postcolonial regime is in danger of slipping quickly back into the malpractices of the old. Functioning as critics of the echelons of power, such novelists expose the misappropriation of the private in the public by the TRC by parodying discourses of truth and reconciliation in the private familial or religious sphere. The TRC wrongly conflates private and public; yet, ironically, it is through the private sphere that such novelists reflect upon and engage with the procedures of the TRC.

Acknowledgements

This essay is a revised revision of 'Writing Under Pressure: A Post-Apartheid Canon?' (2008), *Journal of Postcolonial Writing*, 44.2: 103–14.

Note

1 I use black in the politically inclusive sense.

Bibliography

Attree, L. (2005) 'Healing with Words: Phaswane Mpe Interviewed by Lizzy Attree', *Journal of Commonwealth Literature*, 40.3: 139–48.

Attwell, D. (2005) *Rewriting Modernity: Studies in Black South African Literary History*, Scottsville: University of KwaZulu-Natal Press.

Chapman, M. ([1990] 1996) *Southern African Literatures*, London and New York: Longman.

Clingman, S. (2000) 'Surviving Murder: Oscillation and Triangulation in Nadine Gordimer's *The House Gun*', *MSF*, 46.1: 139–58.

Coetzee, J. M. ([1990] 1991) *Age of Iron*, London: Penguin.

—— (1992) *Confession and Double Thoughts* (1985), *Doubling the Point: Essays and Interviews*, D. Attwell (ed.) MA: Harvard University Press.

—— (1999) *Disgrace*, Secker & Warburg.

Dangor, A. (2004 [2001]) *Bitter Fruit*, London: Atlantic.

Derrida, J. (2001) *On Cosmopolitanism and Forgiveness*, Thinking in Action, London and New York: Routledge.

Gordimer, N. (1988) *The Essential Gesture: Writing, Politics and Places*, S. Clingman (ed. and intro.) London: Jonathan Cape.

—— (1999) *The House Gun*, London: Bloomsbury.

Graham, L. (2003) 'Reading the Unspeakable: Rape in J. M. Coetzee's *Disgrace*', *Journal of Southern African Studies*, 29.2: 433–44.

Holiday, A. (1998) 'Forgiving and Forgetting: the Truth and Reconciliation Commission', in S. Nuttall and C. Coetzee (eds).

Kiberd, D. (2008) 'Edward Said and the Everyday', The Edward Said Memorial Lecture, University of Warwick.

Mamdani, M. (2000) 'The Truth According to the TRC', in I. Amadiume and A. An-Na'im (eds) *The Politics of Memory: Truth, Healing and Social Justice*, London and New York: Zed.

Ndebele, N. (1994) *South African Literature and Culture: Rediscovery of the Ordinary*, Manchester: Manchester University Press.

—— (1998) 'Memory, Metaphor, and the Triumph of Narrative', in S. Nuttall and C. Coetzee (eds): 21–8.

—— (2003) *The Cry of Winnie Mandela: A Novel*, Banbury: Ayebia Clarke.

Nuttall, S. and Coetzee, C. (eds) (1998) *Negotiating the Past: The Making of Memory in South Africa*, Oxford: Oxford University Press.

Parry, B. (2004) *Postcolonial Studies: A Materialist Critique*, London: Routledge.

Pechey, G. (2002) 'Coetzee's Purgatorial Africa: The Case of *Disgrace*', *Interventions*, 4.3: 374–83.

Said, E. (1994) *Representations of the Intellectual: The 1993 Reith Lectures*, London: Vintage.

Strauss, H. (2005) 'Intrusive Pasts, Intrusive Bodies', *Postcolonial Text*, 1.2: np.

17 From exceptionalism to social ecology in Southern Africa

Isolation, intimacy and environment in Nadine Gordimer's *Get a Life* (2005)

James Graham

In recent years the traditionally anthropocentric orientation of postcolonial literary criticism has been questioned by those calling for a more eco-critical appreciation of colonial and postcolonial conditions and cultures (O'Brien 2001, Nixon 2005, Mukherjee 2006, Huggan and Tiffin 2007). This essay explores both the possibilities and the problems posed by this rerouting in a reading of Nadine Gordimer's 2005 novel *Get a Life*. It begins by discussing the changing form of South African environmentalism, the novel's central frame of reference. In the years since apartheid ended in South Africa, the politics of conservation – previously seen as complicit with apartheid ideology – have been rerouted by a range of protest groups and campaigning organizations in what has come to be known as the movement for environmental justice. In a manner consonant with the way the post-apartheid texts discussed by Jane Poyner elsewhere in this volume unsettle the boundaries between public and private, *Get a Life* explodes the 'myth' of South Africa's political, cultural and environmental exceptionalism[1] through an intensely private drama that simultaneously gestures towards a new kind of political philosophy in southern Africa: social ecology (Bookchin 2005). However, heeding Elleke Boehmer's call for a greater appreciation of the aesthetic in postcolonial literature in this volume, this essay argues that the literary treatment of social ecology in *Get a Life* – specifically, the narrative's self-conscious attention to the limits of discursive knowledge in comprehending the alterity of nature – purposefully contrasts the ethical demands of ecology with the political challenges of social justice intrinsic to this form of environmental activism. In doing so it enables a timely, critical appreciation of the tension between the political and ethical in the emerging interdisciplinary field of postcolonial ecocriticism.

In her 1984 review of J. M. Coetzee's novel *The Life and Times of Michael K*, Nadine Gordimer was critical of what she perceived to be a flight from South African reality through pastoral allegory. The 'idea of gardening' in that novel is treated as a retreat from urgent politic imperatives. The novel's pastoral impulse amounted, at best, to an ethical orientation that was out of place and time during the interregnum in South Africa. But with the publication of her latest novel, *Get a Life*, just over twenty years later, it seems that post-apartheid South Africa might finally have become the right place at the right time for this idea to become, as she might put it, more relevant (see Gordimer and Clingman 1988). Where *The Conservationist*, Gordimer's Booker prize winning novel of 1974, viewed the practice of conservation as a symptom of social inequality, as a 'surplus' effect of white bourgeois liberalism in apartheid South Africa (Clingman 1986: 145), *Get a Life* offers a much more sympathetic exploration of environmental activism. It is the story of one man's attempt to comprehend the ecosystem he inhabits, to work out how best to take responsibility for its survival: not so much a Voltairean 'idea of gardening' as what Graham Huggan and Helen Tiffin have elsewhere described as a 'postcolonial environmental ethic' (2007: 6). What might have changed in the intervening years to warrant this seeming rerouting from the political to the ethical in Gordimer's fiction?

As a literal reading of Gordimer's review of Coetzee's *The Life and Times of Michael K* infers, conservation and environmental policy were seen by many of those opposing South African apartheid 'as an explicit tool of racially-based oppression' (Macdonald 1998: 74). All too often the practice of conservation and the social engineering of the colonial and apartheid states went hand in hand. The Betterment schemes of the 1940s, for example, sought to introduce 'villagization, fencing, the separation of arable land from grazing' for the rural black population, leading to the displacement of 'millions of people' (Beinart 2001: 135) on the land. Despite these oppressive measures subsequently proving 'highly effective in mobilizing rural communities against the state' (332), the state of the environment itself did not become a major rallying point for the protest movements of the 1970s and 1980s. Yet by the time of the democratic transition in the early 1990s, South African environmentalists now argue, something of a cultureshift had taken place. Resistance to government conservation policies was modified by the desire to make environmental justice an aspect of the ongoing liberation struggle. David Macdonald (1998) argues that

> Many South African unions, community organizations, NGOs and political parties which had previously rejected or ignored environmental debates [...] now developed sophisticated environmental positions [...] Once 'the environment' is redefined to include the working and living space of black South Africans it quickly becomes apparent that environmental initiatives are akin to other post-apartheid, democratic objectives.
>
> (74)

Founded in Johannesburg in 1988, the NGO Earthlife Africa provided the catalyst for this 'rainbow coalition' (Cock and Koch 1991) of activist groups, rerouting the nascent movement for environmental justice in South Africa around 'the need for a "people-centred" interest in the environment while being alert to both South Africa's colonial legacies and its peripheral position within a globalised economy' (Vital 2005: 298). Moving into the twenty-first century, environmental justice has become an increasingly important aspect of political struggle in South Africa (Cock 2004). Major campaigns revolve around: the development of a new nuclear reactor at Koeberg in the Cape (Earthlife Africa Cape Town); the human displacement and environmental devastation of the Eastern Cape through the Coega industrial development zone (Bond 2002); the commercialization of conservation with the expansion of the tourist industry for the purposes of economic uplift and development;[2] the impending energy security crisis, threatening bioregional and geopolitical stability through dam building and water privatization (International Rivers Network); and the persistent pressure for land reform and redistribution – to 'restore the land', as one pioneering collection of essays puts it (Ramphele *et al.* 1992). It is in the intertwined contexts of post-apartheid national development, regional geopolitics and a complex family drama, then, that Gordimer's latest novel explores environmental activism. It is on this point, however, that Gordimer's engagement with the environmental justice movement can be read as more than a matter of contextual convenience. In the particular way it presents eco-crisis in the southern Africa region – as a highly subjective, anthropocentric experience of a society undergoing major changes – *Get a Life* lends its weight to the movement for environmental justice while implicitly questioning both its ethical precepts.

The novel begins with an ecologist, Paul Bannerman, being quarantined in his parent's home having becoming radioactive following treatment for thyroid cancer. He finds solace in their garden – the garden he grew up in as a child – as he struggles to come to terms with his dependency and the infantilization it brings. There, in that allusive pastoral refuge, he reflects at length on the irony of his fate. He has become radioactive and isolated from his nuclear family while pursuing a number of environmental campaigns, one of which is to stop the development of the Koeburg pebble bed Nuclear Reactor. Compared with the catastrophic toxic threat the reactor poses, the immediate fallout from his own contamination is richly suggestive. It recalls, albeit in a different context, that of Jack Gladney in Don Delillo's *White Noise*.[3] Nature has revenged itself capriciously on one of its own; yet, in the work Paul so ardently wants to return to, it still calls to him. To play along with the text's own allusions to the pastoral traditions of English literature, it is as if the Ancient Mariner was in fact an Ancient Ornithologist, and his crime against nature all the more tragic for it. And so, living out his quarantine in the symbolic garden-idyll of the western imagination – what the eco-critic Jonathan Bate has in a more general context described as Schiller's 'childlike age of man' (2000: 73–75) – Paul finds himself in an exceptional situation. It is a state of existence that returns a new consciousness of the natural world he works to conserve, but which also transforms his sense of social being: his understanding of himself through family and friends as well as of nature itself.

The early parts of the narrative present us exclusively with Paul's consciousness of his quarantine. No doubt this is at least partly intended to ironize what Rob Nixon (2005), in his important essay on the growing dialogue between environmentalism and postcolonialism, calls the 'centuries-long English tradition of *hortus conclusus*, the enclosed garden' (240).[4] Given Gordimer's abiding Luckácsian preoccupation with the individual as a social being, with literary characters as 'the bearers of a socially transmissible truth' (Lazarus 2004: 623), marrying this pastoral conceit to a solitary consciousness – which also happens to be embodied in a white, middle-class, male human the colonial subject redux – is clearly intended to court contradiction. The deployment of Gordimer's trademark free-indirect narrative style, where the thoughts of others – his wife, mother and son, the black housekeeper and his black colleague – intermittently take narrative precedence, further disrupts the narrative and so the subjective authority and integrity of this central character. The focal narrative space also moves from the childhood garden to a zoo and a nature conservation park, where Paul takes his family, towards the end of the novel. This transition, from an idealized Eden to spaces of conservation but also commercial spectacle, offers a telling contrast. These aspects of the narrative generate something like the 'kind of environmental double consciousness' that Nixon identifies as a feature of what he calls the 'postcolonial pastoral' (239).

Postcolonial pastoral, Nixon argues, is 'writing that refracts an idealized nature through memories of environmental and cultural degradation in the colonies' (239). Though not the kind of metropolitan text that Nixon specifically has in mind, *Get a Life* nonetheless advances these concerns in the challenge it presents, as one reviewer puts it, to the kind of post-apartheid 'progressivism which brashly overrides the past and insists on starting from today, on grounds both human and ecological' (Stevenson 2005). Unlike Nixon's synoptic overview of postcolonialism's environmentalist rerouting, however, *Get a Life*'s specific focus on southern Africa enables Gordimer both to historicize and critique the politics of universalism that are elided in this reviewer's seemingly straightforward identification of 'grounds both human and ecological' in postcolonial writing.

The ambivalent nature of the novel's greenness in this respect therefore provides the critical focus of this chapter. On the one hand, the environmental concerns of *Get a Life* are broadly consonant with the emerging eco-critical rerouting of postcolonial writing. In particular, the novel seems to advance Huggan and Tiffin's 'postcolonial environmental ethic' in its 'reimagining and reconfiguration of both the nature of the human and the place of the human in nature' in a way that lays bare the complicity of these universals in southern Africa's history of imperial, colonial, racial and economic projects of domination (2007: 6–7). On the other hand, however, the novel quite deliberately tests the limits of this ethic within a relatively narrow social horizon. The cosmopolitan world of activists, advertising executives, lawyers and tourists in *Get a Life* is not so far removed from the social milieu of Gordimer's most powerful apartheid era novel, *The Conservationist*. The major difference is that in the more recent novel, the social, cultural and economic effects of globalization are taken to amplify the contradictions and complicities that this social group encounter and embody. My contention, then, is that the extent to which the novel problematizes South Africa's specific kind of 'people centred' environmentalism – even as it self-consciously participates in the very same discourse – has important implications: in

terms of the trajectory of Gordimer's work at one level, and for the interdisciplinary aspirations of postcolonial studies at another.

In what follows I outline the twofold nature of *Get a Life*'s engagement with
green ideas in the South African context of the environmental justice movement.
First, the novel dramatizes the personal and the political stakes involved in representing the environment – that is, in speaking or acting for nature as well as the
different human communities exposed to what historians have now categorized
as 'environmental injustice' (Jacobs 2000). Second, at a more formal level, the
narrative reflects on the capacity of scientific discourse, as well as its own literary
medium, to represent the alterity of nature. It questions the extent to which such
discursive modes of representation can ever capture or comprehend the inner-
life of other species, their non-human being, in- or for-themselves. And, equally
importantly, it explores what kinds of violence such efforts involve (epistemological but also, in the 'real' referential world of the text, ecological). Yet by no means
does *Get a Life* damn the South African project of 'people-centered' environmentalism. Quite the opposite. Uniting both of these perspectives is the possibility of
a politics that might *act upon* an ethical awareness of the relation between what we
might call, following Bookchin, first (endogenous) and second (human-created)
nature (2005: 11).

The exploration of this possibility and its attendant dangers – so central to
mainstream ecocriticism – is that aspect of the 'eco-poco' dialogue, I want to
suggest, which *postcolonial* ecocriticism has yet to theorize adequately. While I
am in agreement with the emerging anthropocentric consensus behind both
Huggan's and Tiffin's 'green postcolonialism', for instance, *Get a Life* is replete
with contradictions that emerge when the thinking behind this consensus is faced
with the complexity of a specific society struggling to respond to the challenges of
social and environmental inequality in an era of globalization and with many of
the scars of the colonial and apartheid eras still discernible. In this way *Get a Life*
expands our appreciation of what Neil Lazarus has described, in his reading of
Gordimer's 1998 novel *The House Gun*, not just as damaged forms of subjectivity
in southern Africa but 'damaged forms of *intersubjectivity*' (2004: 622).

It is not simply the immemorial rift between nature and culture that Paul
Bannerman's contamination throws into relief, so much as the way that those he
is in contact with relate to the world through one another and the worlds they
create *for* one another. His micro-environmental crisis becomes an existential
one and quickly spreads through his family. Just as his isolation forces him to
come to grips with a new, more complex sense of being in the world, so, too,
does it compel in his wife, mother and father a newfound awareness of their
interdependency. Having taken it for granted for so long, the survival of the
bourgeois 'nuclear family' in the new South African society is revealed to be
every bit as precarious as the fragile ecosystem Paul defends. The Bannerman
family is dependent on each other, but these relationships are themselves
contingent within much broader social and environmental relationships. These
are presented in the novel as a series of intertwined macrocosms: the legal and
political systems of South Africa at one level, specific ecosystems and bioregions

at another, and the preying capital of the global economy, committed to what Paul sees as 'Destructive Development' (Gordimer 2005: 92) in southern Africa, encompassing them all.

Hovering on the periphery of the global economy but orientated by its 'western' aspirations (Lazarus 2004), the South African government has committed the country to a neoliberal development model prepared to sacrifice indigenous environmental resources to multinational commercial exploitation (Bond 2002). It is on the back of anticipated economic boosts from international investment, however, that the government proposes to redress the enduring inequalities of the past. Resisting this kind of 'Destructive Development' is therefore far from straightforward. Not only do the environmental activists Paul works will have to divorce conservation from its heritage of complicity in unjust social policies and racist ideology, they also have to prove the social and political – which increasingly means *economic* – benefits of their approach to communities with quite different interests. So who they prove this *to* is thus deeply problematic. Should their work raise awareness *within* these local communities (to galvanize grassroots resistance), or are they more concerned with gaining national and international attention (to effect change from above)? In their campaigning do they speak in the name of nature or of those inhabiting the given environment?

These questions indicate the extent to which a postcolonial environmental ethic is subject to the politics of representation in different spheres. Or rather, the fact that these characters are compelled to view and experience the environment through the seemingly discrete spheres of first and second nature, indicates the core problem faced by those advocating this critical position. In the novel these issues are foregrounded through different aspects of the narrative style. We find a constant tension, for instance, between the political meaning of representation – that is, of characters speaking or acting *for* nature or in the environmental interests *of* a given community – and the more philosophical sense of representing nature or a social group in language. It is through the second sense of representation that a transformed understanding of the individual's place in the world is most consistently expressed.

The narrative is interspersed with Paul's consciousness of naturein-itself, yet the latter is invariably mediated by his professional, scientific knowledge of a given environment. He frequently muses on the enchanting endogeny of the Okavango delta in Botswana, for example, yet 'he realized he knew too abstractly, himself limited by professionalism itself, too little of the grandeur and delicacy, cosmic and infinitesimal complexity of an eco-system as complete as this' (Gordimer 2005: 90). It would seem that it is only in his exceptional isolation in the childhood garden that nature can be experienced and evoked without such mediation:

> The garden is where the company of jacaranda fronds finger the same breeze that brushed the boy's soft cheek, where caught in peripheral vision a cent's worth of never-exterminated snail moves by peristalsis over a stone, there is the wise presence that changes the solitude of monologue into some kind of dialogue.
>
> (55)

This certainly reads like the poetic ecology, the *eco-poeisis* championed by mainstream eco-critics, but there is an ironic undertone that invites a more circumspect reading. The passage is self-consciously Romantic. Paul considers the experience a 'dialogue with questions; or answers never sought, heard, in the elsewhere' (54). It is a quintessentially Wordsworthian 'mute dialogue' (Bate 2000: 75) with nature; one that, in the view of an eco-critic such as Jonathan Bate, might mark the possibility of a poetic relation to nature's alterity, of creating a dwelling place within it.

Yet time and again in the novel the possibility of such eco-poetic intersubjectivity, realized poetically through the free-indirect style narrative, is confounded by a number of 'reality' checks. These typically stem from the pressing social and environmental issues facing the characters in their fictional world, but which also have recognizable corollaries in the referential context of early twenty first century southern Africa. The proliferating national and transnational nature reserves and wildlife parks, passionately promoted to tourists by Paul's wife and her advertising agency, offer a pertinent example. When Paul considers these constructed and commercialized spaces of conservation, there is a distinctive caesura in his thought:

> These places stimulate life in the wild for indigenous animals who would otherwise not survive industrial and urban expansion; the territory bought by what is known as the leisure industry is land where the equally indigenous people were driven out by conquest of old colonial wars and exchanges of papers and possessions for paper money [...].
>
> (Gordimer 2005: 56)

His train of thought is ambivalent, moving from his natural impulse towards the conservation of habitats and species endangered in the onrush of colonial modernity and post-apartheid national development, to the uncomfortable knowledge that the same spaces often have a fraught social history: of people who have been removed from their territories by force in the first instance, and by more insidious forms of coercion – economic and legal – in subsequent years. And, in this instance, an ideology of conservation is identified as being complicit in past, but also, it becomes apparent, *present* social injustice.

This précis of the conservation-as-development dilemma highlights how inevitable the instrumentalization of nature becomes when, as a motor of land restitution and wealth redistribution, conservation is married to social justice. Yet this is the intractable anthropocentric compromise that postcolonialism insists upon in its engagement with environmentalism. What is intriguing about *Get a Life* in this respect is that Gordimer does not offer a grassroots perspective on this dilemma. She does not transport us to a world where cosmopolitans and activists actually encounter (and so might be transformed by) other experiences of subsistence, survival and local developmental projects in the way that, say, Amitav Ghosh does in his novel *The Hungry Tide* (2004). For the postcolonial eco-critic Pablo Mukherjee (2006), Ghosh's novel, plotted around themes of conservation, natural disaster, and personal transformation in the Sunderbans Delta, 'is primarily engaged in displacing metro/cosmopolitanism with a historically differentiated refugee condition as the paradigm of postcoloniality. It writes a natural history of the migrant refugee and critiques instrumentalist "environmentalism"' (157). Gordimer, by contrast, seems more interested in *exposing* the contradictions faced by exactly this kind of project in southern Africa: for being *inherently* cosmopolitan rather than *displacing* cosmopolitanism *per se*. The social and ethical parameters of 'environmental justice' are explored through the intermeshed perspectives of Paul Bannerman and his close social circle, for whom transnational mobility and personal health-care and security, while threatened by South Africa's social problems, are nonetheless taken for granted.

Just as these characters are invariably at a social remove from the environments they think about and discuss, Gordimer is at pains to draw attention to the way nature is mediated differently by the scientific and literary discourses available to this group. Whereas Ghosh's cosmopolitans, to use Mukherjee's (2006) example once again, relearn 'the lessons of inhabiting [...] through their encounters with radically different texts and contexts – songs, folk tales, folk theatre performances, oral historical narratives, and, above all, the complex networks of everyday lives that they briefly share with the migrants and refugees' (152–3), the un- or relearning undergone by characters in *Get a Life* is primarily occasioned by social and environmental interactions *within* their own social milieu (even when the novel does reflect on issues of race and cultural difference within that milieu – see Rose 2006). This difference in social context is also expressed by differences in literary form.

In contrast to Ghosh's lucid realism, Gordimer's free-indirect narrative is syntactically challenging and self-consciously prolix. The literary effects are quite different. Whereas Ghosh's characters come to understand a 'universal solidarity' (Mukherjee 2006: 156) through sharing their ways of seeing, being and telling in a specific bioregion – made possible by the heteroglossia of Ghosh's realist style – the awe and reverence Paul holds for nature, his incomprehension before it, is not so much shared as *intensified* by *Get a Life*'s more radically decentred narrative. This intensification is most keenly felt when Paul and his wife Berenice take their family to the zoo towards the end of the novel. Observing the zoo's pair of nesting Eagles, Paul notes that

> the language of the pamphlet in hand fails to represent the being of the withdrawn black entity on the bed of dead wood and the other disappearing off into the sky and returning in the guise of a menace or as deliverance of omniscience, as the surveyors' plans and the reports he writes fails to represent the Okavango or the Pondoland dunes.
>
> (Gordimer 2005: 167)

In close proximity to it, Paul can *apprehend* the being of the Eagle. But, like the Okavango and Pondoland eco-systems, it cannot be represented by language in a way that brings it under his power. Ultimately, it is not reducible to scientific knowledge; it cannot be discursively *comprehended*. Despite his time spent on field-trips in wilderness areas, despite communing and interacting with many people with a different way of relating to their environment, there seems no other way (aesthetic or experiential, cultural or practical) for Paul to approach nature. And yet despite this – in fact precisely *because* Paul is left so mute and impotent before it – we are left with the abiding impression that nature can retain its alterity, that it can survive, while still existing in a world irrevocably altered by, and indeed *for*, humans. But the question Gordimer leaves us with is: For how long, given the myriad social, economic and geopolitical pressures in southern Africa?

Whereas, in Mukherjee's analysis, *The Tide Country* expresses a universal solidarity between people through their shared relation to a specific environment, *Get a Life* reminds us of the ethical limits to this anthropocentric ideal. In other contexts this universal solidarity does not always emerge from, or lead to, an ideal symbiosis of human needs with ecological sustainability. At root, this universality inevitably privileges social justice over the utopian possibility of human and non-human intersubjectivity. While Paul seems to embody a deconstructive and above all *ethical* attitude in the episodes where he apprehends the alterity of an ecosystem or species, the narrative juxtaposes such moments with the urgent economic and political pressures that circumscribe and threaten the very survival of the same (especially if the species happens to be human). Against his inability to discursively comprehend nature, Paul, like his colleagues, *is* prepared to transform such ethical values in order to act for the environment at a political level. One such colleague, the former incarcerated MK[5] cadre Thapelo, is politically pragmatic in his bid to prevent the government from licensing mining rights on the Wild Coast to an Australian corporation and approving a new super-highway through the region.

Contrary to Paul's growing conviction that the campaign should be fought under economic criteria – conservation safeguards tourist income – Thapelo argues that 'pleas for beauty destroyed in these issues are regarded as going soft, just sentimental objection to progress' (85). A harder-hitting campaign, by contrast, entails politicizing the local community:

> I'm talking about the Amadiba, my brother, they're living on the Wild Coast, five communities, not so? Go for *them* [...] Need to make them shout. Loudly. All stops out. Rally the traditional leaders; the government has to hear them; you know it's policy, government's having to recognize right now all kinds of questions on land distribution rights.
>
> (85)

But it turns out that the Australian multinational is one step ahead of Thapelo. It is already in the process of securing a deal with a black empowerment company that represents the interests of the Amidaba, presenting them with a 15 per cent share in the dunes mining project. Both the precious ecosystem *and* the rights of its human inhabitants to it – treated by all parties, it seems, as an economic resource rather than for its intrinsic ecological and cultural value – are delivered to global capital in a rapprochement between customary authority and the national elite.

With their political approach gazumped at the grassroots level, Paul decides to mobilize international support by upping the media coverage of the campaign. But by doing this he has to acknowledge that his activism is now little different from the work of his advertising executive wife: that it had 'now desperately become like any other publicity campaign' (146). Nature's antithesis, the language of commodification and consumerism, is deployed in order to protect nature. But before Paul comes to this conclusion, however, he insists upon a distinction between the absolute values of the 'individual' and the relative values of the 'world'. 'What is this all about?' he says,

> but an obvious matter of the incompatibility between the advertising industry and environmental protection. Two clichés. *So what?* Can't even call it by its true name. Irreconcilability. Because the world, in distinction from the individual, has no absolutes, there's a mix that goes along prescriptively with the mixed economy.
>
> (58)

His subsequent capitulation to the promotional culture of the advertising industry suggests that, subsequent to South Africa's post-apartheid embrace of a neoliberal development policy, ecological value has become entwined with – if not yet entirely subordinated to – the *economic* imperatives of social justice. His 'absolute' individual values are transformed in this context, yet they do so in a way that does not challenge the 'prescriptive' norms of the 'mixed economy' which is proving so destructive. And this despite his experience in the enclosed garden having intensified his sense of 'the world' as constituted by the relative values of first and second nature – and where, in the spectre of nuclear contamination, the latter threatens to destroy the former irrevocably.

Gordimer is fascinated by this contradiction. We find it reflected in the family drama in the various attempts to reconcile personal and professional interests. The ripe irony of Paul's marriage to Berenice, for example – ecologist and advertising executive – is paralleled in the relationship between his mother, a human rights lawyer, and her estranged husband, a businessman turned global-tourist. Despite inhabiting different value-systems at the professional level, both son and mother nonetheless find common ground at a personal level. They share a 'dedication beyond the personally intimate, of belonging to the condition of the world. Justice. The survival of nature' (141). The family's transformation following Paul's contamination – he comes closer to his wife, her colleagues and friends; his father leaves the family to travel in Latin America; his mother adopts an AIDS orphan – is a relatively sympathetic study of the way national politics (especially surrounding personal responsibility) as well as the cultural and economic forces of globalization, are shaping liberal, middle-class South African sensibilities with regard to the environment. At the same time, *Get a Life* also offers a sharp critique of how the movement for environmental justice in South Africa is – inevitably – compromised by those same sensibilities and subject positions (at least insofar as Gordimer views the movement, at any rate).

The problem Gordimer broaches is not simply how to reconcile the need to protect invaluable ecosystems with the imperative for social justice in southern Africa. The situation is complicated in that the environmental justice movement is subject to a matrix of national and international law, the local and national interests of marginalized communities, and above all, it would seem, the pervasive influence of global capital. As the novel's focalizing consciousness, Paul never questions or elaborates on what he describes as the 'prescriptions' of the 'mixed-economy' in all this. At an individual level, the novel seems to say, such contradictions can be worked through as a responsibility *for* the world. But if such individual commitment relies on a transformed consciousness of the alterity of (first) nature, it also rests on the acceptance of a seemingly unchallengeable socio-economic world (second nature). In this way *Get a Life* participates in the rerouting of environmentalism in southern Africa – from the unjust conservation practices of a land apart to the social ecology of a transnationally active and globally conscious environmental justice movement. At the same time, however, an appreciation of the literary treatment of these issues in the novel sees an important (though by no means *negative*) critique emerge: of the ethical contradictions faced by such movements at one level, and of the ecocritical rerouting of postcolonialism at another.

Notes

1 As Jane Poyner (following Neil Lazarus) puts it, this myth is 'the illusion that South Africa, perceived from within as "western", is free from the problems of neo-colonialism that have plagued other nations on the continent' (Poyner).
2 The problem of tourism-driven development provides the backdrop to two celebrated novels by Zakes Mda, *The Heart of Redness* (2000) and *The Whale Caller* (2005).
3 As with Paul Bannerman's contamination, Jack Gladney's exposure to the 'airborne toxic event' sees his body 'penetrated and reclaimed by the ecosystem' (Kerridge 1998: 192). But whereas in Delillo's novel 'environmental crisis confronts postmodernity with another sort of totality, the global ecosystem' (191), in *Get a Life* Gordimer is more concerned with exploring the complicity and contingency of individuals within different systems that, in line with her avowed humanism, mediate a social ecology.
4 The politics of the *hortus conclusus* in *Get a Life* and Gordimer's late apartheid era novel, *My Son's Story* (1990), are discussed at greater length in an excellent review article by Jacqueline Rose (2006).
5 MK is the common abbreviation for Umkhonto we Sizwe – the name of the ANC's militant wing during the apartheid era.

Bibliography

Bate, J. (2000) *The Song of the Earth*, London: Picador.
Beinart, W. (2001) *Twentieth-Century South Africa*, Oxford: Oxford University Press.
—— (2003) *The Rise of Conservation in South Africa: Settlers, Livestock, and the Environment 1770–1950*, Oxford: Oxford University Press.

Bond, P. (2002) *Unsustainable South Africa: Environment, Development and Social Protest*, London and Pietermaritzburg: Merlin and University of Natal Press.

Bookchin, M. (2005) *The Ecology of Freedom: The Emergence and Dissolution of Hierarchy*, Oakland: AK Press.

Clingman, S. (1986) *The Novels of Nadine Gordimer: History from the Inside*, London: Allen & Unwin.

Cock, J. (2004) 'Connecting the Red, Brown and Green: The Environmental Justice Movement in South Africa', Centre for Civil Society, Durban, University of KwaZulu-Natal, School of Development Studies: 1–34.

Cock, J. and Koch, E. (1991) *Going Green: People, Politics and the Environment in South Africa*, Cape Town and Oxford: Oxford University Press.

Earthlife Africa Cape Town. http://www.earthlife-ct.org.za/.

Gordimer, N. (1974) *The Conservationist*, London: Jonathan Cape.

—— (1984) 'The Idea of Gardening', *New York Review of Books*, 31: 3 and 6.

—— (1990) *My Son's Story*, London: Bloomsbury.

—— (1998) *The House Gun*, London: Bloomsbury.

—— (2005) *Get a Life*, London: Bloomsbury.

—— and Clingman S. (eds) (1988) *The Essential Gesture: Writing, Politics and Places*, London: Cape.

Head, D. (1998) 'The (im)possibility of ecocriticism', in R. Kerridge and N. Sammells (eds) *Writing the Environment: Ecocriticism and Literature*, London and New York: Zed Books, 27–39.

Huggan, G. and Tiffin, H. (2007) 'Green Postcolonialism', *Interventions*, 9.1: 1–11.

International Rivers Network. http://www.irn.org/

Jacobs, N. (2000) *Environment, Power and Injustice: A South African History*, Cambridge: Cambridge University Press.

Kerridge, R. (1998) 'Small Rooms and the Ecosystem: Environmentalism and Delillo's *White Noise*', in R. Kerridge and N. Sammells (eds) *Writing the Environment: Ecocriticism and Literature*, London and New York: Zed Books, 182–95.

Lazarus, N. (2004) 'The South African Ideology: The Myth of Exceptionalism, the Idea of Renaissance', *South Atlantic Quarterly*, 103.4: 607–28.

Macdonald, D. A. (1998) 'Three Steps Forward, Two Steps Back: Ideology and Urban Ecology in South Africa', *Review of African Political Economy*, 25.75: 73–88.

Mda, Z (2000) *The Heart of Redness*, Oxford: Oxford University Press.

—— (2005) *The Whale Caller*, London: Viking.

Mukherjee, P. (2006) 'Surfing the Second Waves: Amitav Ghost's Tide Country', *New Formations*, 59: 144–57.

Nixon, R. (2005) 'Environmentalism and Postcolonialism', in A. Loomba *et al.* (eds) *Postcolonial Studies and Beyond*, Durham and London: Duke University Press.

O'Brien, S. (2001) 'Articulating a World of Difference: Ecocriticism, Postcolonialism and Globalization', *Canadian Literature* (Autumn), 170/171: 140–58.

Ramphele, M., McDowell, C. and Cock, J. (eds) (1992) *Restoring the Land: Environment and Change in Post-Apartheid South Africa*, London: Panos.

Rose, J. (2006) 'A Use for the Stones', *London Review of Books*, 20th April (np).

Stevenson, J. (2005) 'Cast out of Eden', *The Observer* 13th November, 16.

Vital, A. (2005) 'Situating Ecology in Recent South African Fictions: J. M. Coetzee's *The Lives of Animals* and Zakes Mda's *The Heart of Redness*', *Journal of Southern African Studies*, 31.2: 297–313.

18 Un-American exceptionalism in the disciplinary field

From unmeltable ethnics to flexible citizens

Deborah L. Madsen

From its beginnings in the mid-twentieth century with the foundational work of scholars such as R. W. B. Lewis (1955), Henry Nash Smith (1950), Leo Marx (1964), and Perry Miller (1956), American Studies as a discipline has been concerned with the processes of Americanization to which predominantly European migrant communities have been subject. Migration and westward expansion provided, from the 1970s, a focus for a revisionary discourse of US nationhood and foreign empire-building in the work of scholars like Richard Drinnon (1980), Annette Kolodny (1975, 1984), and Richard Slotkin (1973, 1998 [1985], 1992), work which formed the basis for more recent studies of US imperialism at home and abroad by Amy Kaplan (2002), Donald Pease (1994), John Carlos Rowe (2000), and others. Much of this latter scholarship has illuminated the complex and pervasive ways in which the ideology of white supremacy has affected US foreign policy as well as domestic politics. As Reginald Horsman shows in his study, *Race and Manifest Destiny: The Origins of American Anglo-Saxonism* (1981), an ideology of Anglo-Saxon supremacy has structured the emergent US national identity through patterns of immigration (and restrictions on entry to the US by certain national and ethnic groups) and the discourses that name ethnic immigrant groups. This line of inquiry has taken American Studies out of the realm of domestic US concerns and into the field of transnational cultural studies. In the US context, transnationalism is often construed as the study of US imperialism in its various guises: cultural, economic, political, and military. The place of the postcolonial is conspicuous by its absence in American Studies but its relevance is hard to miss.

This article addresses the role that Postcolonial Studies has to play in the rerouting of American Studies away from its roots in US nationalism, and so complements Nirmala Menon's call (in this volume) for a more provisional, contingent and nomadic textual canon. While Menon's discussion remains largely grounded in national literatures, her argument supports a further call for disciplinary de-nationalization. Postcolonialism offers an intellectual perspective that is necessarily cross-national and comparative; thus, postcolonial scholars have developed strategies for discussing issues and concepts such as exile, displacement, diaspora, migration, nationhood, and hybridity that enable us to cut through the pervasive and obfuscating American ideology of white supremacy to see what is at stake when we study the nation on its own terms. What we see clearly from a postcolonial perspective is the ethical dimension of an academic discipline that places US nationalism at its centre and takes the white nation state as its fundamental organizing principle. It may be objected that, in fact, American Studies has grown and diversified to a point where it is no longer a single discipline, and the field of American Ethnic Studies could be invoked as evidence of this plurality. However, the organization of Ethnic Studies into hyphenated sub-disciplines, which replace nationalism as the object of study with cultural nationalisms, intensifies this ethical issue. By pursuing a 'mono-hyphenated' understanding of ethnicity, the sub-disciplines of American Studies such as Asian-American, African-American, and Hispanic-American Studies replicate patterns of white supremacy by conflating identity with putative origin, affiliation with filiation, cultural difference with racially marked difference. A refusal of multiple ethnic and national identifications is structurally inscribed in the sub-disciplines of Ethnic Studies and this refusal reproduces existing structures of power and control that are grounded in the white nation state.

It was in the latter half of the last century, as American Ethnic Studies developed out of the Civil Rights movements, that these hyphenated fields of study emerged, motivated in part by the desire for redress, for recognition of and compensation for historical injustices. American Ethnic Studies have, consequently, been organized along broadly nationalistic, though hyphenated, axes. The naming remains unchanged despite widespread consensus that these hyphenated cultural categories are dangerously misleading. The hyphenation of ethnic identity implies a double locatedness: the hyphenated subject is situated both in the US and also in Asia, or Africa, or Latin America. The effect of hyphenation is to create a subject position that is split between the categories of native and foreign, 'here' and 'there'. This can be a perilous situation, as Chinese-Americans discovered in the wake of the 1882 Chinese Exclusion Act when they were refused reentry into the US after travelling to visit their families in China, or as American citizens of Japanese descent discovered in 1942 when they were forcibly removed from their homes and detained for the duration of the war in the Pacific.

Central to understanding such events is the figure of the 'un-American' – the individual who is in America but is not of America: the diasporic citizen of questionable national affiliation and loyalty. The following discussion is structured around the film *Crash* (2004) and this figure of the 'un-American', the diasporic citizen of doubtful loyalties. In this film, the figure of the threatening unassimilated migrant is represented in the person of the Iranian shopkeeper, Farhad (Shaun Toub). In *Crash* every character is shown to be ambivalently racialist, at turns sympathetic and hostile to others, with the exception of the Iranian who is demonized in the film. Before turning to the implications of this figure of the un-American or the 'unmeltable ethnic', the question must be asked concerning the ethnic group that is not included in this film portrait of multicultural Los Angeles. This question reveals a glaring absence: the absence of Native peoples. This is both a substantive and structural omission. Thematically, the plot addresses conflict and violent tensions among the 'multicultures'; structurally, the film focuses on the multicultural city that is populated overwhelmingly by migrants of various kinds. So we might ask: 'Are Native American Indians "multicultural"'?

Native Americans, in important respects, constitute the very first threateningly unassimilated group ('unmeltable ethnics') in US history. The un-American is not necessarily a migrant to the United States but is always a discursive product of migration histories that cannot escape the here/there binary. Thus, the Native American stands as the paradigmatic un-American: a member of a community that is disrupted by mass inward migration, who occupies a geographical position that is territorially American but a subject position that is in a complex and problematic tension with the demands of the emergent multicultural settler nation. I am aware that many indigenous groups resist inclusion in the category of the 'multicultural' and for good reason. But such hostility may point to the inadequacy of current understandings of the potential of multiculturalism to deliver social justice rather than the complete uselessness of the concept. One such inadequacy is the identification of the 'multicultures' with immigrant cultures and a narrow understanding of what constitutes a migrant. *Crash* offers a useful focus for exploring some of these issues, centred as it is upon immigrants – whether they came to the US voluntarily or, in the case of African-Americans, perhaps not. I say 'perhaps' because increasing numbers of US migrants of African ancestry are not descended from slaves but from more recent migrations. One thinks of the recent debate over the 'African-Americanness' of the US President Barack Obama. However, the position of Native Americans as belonging to domestic-dependent nations raises the issue of whether the move from tribal to US territory (such as from the reservation to the city) constitutes 'migration'.

In both his critical and creative works, the Anishinaabe writer and scholar Gerald Vizenor has repeatedly imaged urban Indians as migrants. The poem 'Family Photograph', from Vizenor's collection *Almost Ashore* (2006), reads the figure of the poet's father, Clement Vizenor, as 'a native immigrant / moved to the city' (9). Here, migration is the move from the White Earth Reservation in northern Minnesota to the city of Minneapolis. This poem brilliantly interweaves the tribal with the colonial interventions of the US in a sequence of objective correlatives such as the opening images: 'my father / clement vizenor / was a spruce / among the trees / a native / by totems // corded for pulp / by federal / indian agents' (6). The image of the totemic tree as his father raises the question of which – the tree or the man, or indeed the totemic tribal culture – has been pulped by federal Indian agents. But this is a question that answers itself as soon as it is expressed. The poem concludes:

> clement vizenor
> holds me
> in a photograph
> that winter
> almost a smile
> a new spruce
> among the bricks

paint cans
half white earth
the other
native immigrant
moved to the city
and lost at cards
(9)

Here, the father is figured as 'a new spruce', a new creation though one defeated by the evil gambler of tribal myth, now ambiguously hybrid (to continue the botanical metaphor): 'half white earth / the other / native immigrant'. Indeed, this hybrid quality is clear in an earlier poem entitled 'The Last Photograph', also written in response to this image, included in *Interior Landscapes: Autobiographical Myths and Metaphors* (1990):

my father
holds me in the last photograph
the new spruce
with a wide smile
half white
half immigrant
he took up the cities and lost at cards
(31)

Clement's mother, Alice Beaulieu, was an Anishinaabe woman of the White Earth Reservation, who took her children with her to Minneapolis. As Vizenor writes in *Interior Landscapes*, Clement was considered a 'half-breed Indian' by the police officers who investigated his murder and his white 'half' came from his mixed-blood father. In the poem, Clement's paternal descent is described as 'half white', leaving his maternal Anishinaabe 'half' to be accounted for as 'half immigrant'. Here, migration for Native peoples is clearly related to departure (whether voluntary or not) from the tribal reservation. But does this 'half white / half immigrant' status make Clement Vizenor a hyphenated American? A Native-American-American? The 'unhyphenability' of Native Americans is suggestive of the 'unmeltable' status of Native people, and hence of their marginalization in US society, and is also indicative of the way in which the naming of the settler-nation, 'American', functions as the foundation for all hyphenated ethnic designations. Commenting on the poem 'The Last Photograph' in the context of Vizenor's autobiography, Elvira Pulitano writes:

As a 'half white,' 'half immigrant,' urban mixedblood removed to the cities at twenty three, Clement William Vizenor was imprisoned in the simulation of indianness, a misnomer, as Vizenor has pointed out, that erases a native presence while affirming a logocentric absence.

(2007: 142)

Vizenor describes, in *Fugitive Poses* (1998) how: 'Clement and his brothers, and other natives in urban areas were *indians* by simulation, transethnic by separation, but native in their stories of survivance' (51). '[T]ransethnic by separation' is certainly a better formulation than 'hybrid' to describe the double life of a subject in exile from both the White Earth Reservation and the white city of Minneapolis but who is, at the same time, 'transethnic' and a part of both worlds.

Elsewhere in *Interior Landscapes* Vizenor refers to a different kind of immigrant hybrid, the immigrant-Native mixedblood, such as the 'Norwindians' who were left out of a 1984 historical exhibition of Norwegians in America. Presumably, these Norwegian immigrants were subsumed under the label of Norwegian-Americans. Where we might expect reference to indigenous America, the point of reference for so much in US culture – from boy scouts to Walden Pond, as scholars like Philip Deloria (1999) have pointed out, we find instead that 'America-as-Europe' terminates hyphenated migrant identities. The rhetorical sleight-of-hand that substitutes Anglo-American for Native-American as the foundation of hyphenated national US migrant identities is repeated every time we talk about a hyphenated-'American' and perpetuate the erasure of Native peoples. The logic of US nationalism demands that America be identified with the United States and that a 'Native' American should be a subject born in the United States. That is, logical priority is filtered through the lens of nationalism so that 'Native' becomes synonymous with 'Nativist'. This entails the erasure of indigenous Native Americans who then occupy a place that is geographically in the United States but is not American.

The discursive matrix that positions and defines Native Americans offers the foundational instance of the 'unmeltable ethnic'. The most notorious example of this is the internment of approximately 120,000 Japanese-Americans, and some US residents of German or Italian descent, during the Second World War, under Executive Order 9066. However, the first group of suspect 'aliens' to be sequestered during military conflict was a group of more than 500 so-called 'praying Indians' who were interned on Deer Island in Boston Harbor during King Philip's War. The order for their removal was passed by the General Court in Boston in October 1675; those who survived were permitted to return to the mainland in May 1676. The notion that an entire community can be deemed a security risk has particular resonance for us today, but the logic reaches far back into the colonial heritage, producing the enduring image of the threatening unassimilated 'domestic alien'. This logic depends upon the hyphenated naming of national affiliations: Japanese- or German- or Italo-American. The hyphen indicates that culturally such migrants remain 'there' – in Japan, Germany or Italy – even though they are physically located 'here'.

The exception (which proves the rule) is the discursive placement of Native Americans. When Gerald Vizenor refers to Native Americans as *indians* (in lowercase and italicized), he is making the claim that 'Indians' do not exist. 'Indians' were invented by colonizers at the time of first contact and, like the concept of 'America' and 'Americans', the designation has no meaning for indigenous peoples who bear their own tribal names. Thus, the category of the *indian* is a simulacrum, in Jean Baudrillard's sense of the term: a copy without an original, an invention that poses as the real. As Elvira Pulitano suggests in her comment (quoted above) on the figure of Clement Vizenor, in the poem 'Family Photograph', this simulation of the *indian* is a restrictive, prescriptive stereotype. To resist the invented image is to resist the ideology of white supremacy and European cultural imperialism that it supports. In an interview with Laura Coltelli, Vizenor explained:

> Practically every tribal name is a western colonial imposition: the tribes don't speak of themselves that way, but they must, in a written language, do so. Just encountering a word is a creative act in a word war. If someone says, 'Are you an American Indian?', you have an instant word war; all you have to do is, say no.
>
> (Coltelli 195)

The language of naming, and particularly the ethnic labels applied to indigenous and migrant groups alike, constitutes an invitation to collude with the powers of white supremacy. The rhetorical slippage between 'Native' and 'Nativist' erases Native presence and instantiates the simulacrum of the *indian*. This is the exception to the rule of 'mono-hyphenation', which is essential to the process of naming and categorizing the migrant communities of the US. We see this process at work everywhere. What we do not see is evidence of multi-hyphenation, where people of multiply-mixed descent can claim a truly plural heritage.

The film *Crash* is articulated almost exclusively in terms of mono-hyphenation: Asian slaves are trafficked by a Korean man, Blacks marry Blacks; in the only instance of a mixed-race relationship, the film endorses the view of ethnic singularity. This occurs in the scene where Ria (Jennifer Esposito), the Latina detective, and her Black partner Graham (Don Cheadle), are interrupted in bed by his mother's telephone call. Ria is angry that he answers the telephone and becomes even more incensed when Graham cuts the conversation short by telling his mother that he is busy having sex with a white woman. In response to Ria's question, he confesses that he described her as white rather than Mexican because he knew it would upset his mother more. So Ria gives him a geography lesson: she points out that her father is from Puerto Rico and her mother is from El Salvador, which makes her neither white nor Mexican. However, her words are obliterated by his response: he observes sarcastically that there is then a mystery how members of such remarkably diverse cultures should come to the US and suddenly all start parking their cars on their lawns. His comment is represented as humorous and the audience is led to collude with this humour. The camera lingers in a medium close-up shot of Graham lighting a cigarette as Ria storms out of the scene, the slamming of the door punctuating his dialogue and endorsing the validity of his view of cultural homogeneity. Mexican, Puerto Rican, El Salvadorian: these migrants all become 'American' by virtue of the hyphen.

The insistence upon ethnic 'mono-hyphenation', and the misrecognition it entails, is a powerful and insidious expression of racialism that is troped throughout the film by the motif of the invisible bullet-proof cloak given by the Hispanic locksmith, Daniel Ruiz, to comfort his traumatized young daughter, Lara. He comes home from work late one night to find her huddling under her bed, made afraid by the experience of street shootings in their previous home, and unable to sleep in her new home. Her father presents her with the imaginary cloak which, he persuades her, repels bullets and will keep her safe. The symbolic significance of the cloak evokes the following quotation from Audre Lorde's autobiographical *Zami: A New Spelling of My Name* (1983) where she writes:

> ... but sometimes, I was close to crazy with believing that there was some secret thing wrong with me personally that formed *an invisible barrier* between me and the rest of my friends, who were white. [...] I had no words for racism.
>
> (66; emphasis added)

This 'invisible barrier' surrounds all the characters in *Crash*, accounting for their loneliness, violence, and desperation. As Graham, the black detective, reflects at the beginning of the film, perhaps people in Los Angeles are so atomized that they crash their cars so they can have an opportunity to touch each other. However, they do not touch each other – the Black woman Christine Thayer (Thandie Newton) in her burning car recoils in horror from the white policeman, Officer John Ryan (Matt Dillon), whom she only knows as abusive but who risks his own life to save her – because each person is involved in their own private process of what has become known as 'racial profiling'. Racial profiling, the categorizing of other people according to ethnicity on the basis of their physical somatic identity, is precisely what mono-hyphenation promotes, rendering those who are ambivalently American 'unmeltable ethnics'.

The term 'unmeltable ethnics' comes from Michael Novak's 1972 book entitled *The Rise of the Unmeltable Ethnics: Politics and Culture in the Seventies*. But Novak's 'unmeltables' are not the kinds of diasporic transnational subjects we might imagine. He writes, in terms evocative of Stanley Fish's concept of 'boutique multiculturalism', of 'weekend Italians' who drive from the suburbs to Little Italy to stock up on 'ethnic supplies' (Novak 1972: 33). Novak is at his most powerful when reporting and condemning the kinds of racialist abuse confronted by European immigrants. For example, a New York newspaper editorial from the early twentieth century put this in the following terms:

> The flood gates are open. The bars are down. The sally-ports are unguarded. The dam is washed away. The sewer is choked ... should there be [...]? the scum of immigration is viscerating upon our shores. The horde of $9.90 steerage slime is being siphoned upon us from Continental mud tanks.
>
> (quoted in Novak 1972: 117)

This same rhetoric of threat, invasion, and inundation endures and dominates the film *Crash*.

To return to the figure invoked at the beginning of this essay: the Iranian 'terrorist' – the shopkeeper Farhad (who is not given a surname) turned would-be murderer who terrorizes the locksmith's family, and the audience, in the most emotional and disturbing scene of the film. After the vandalizing of his shop, and the refusal of the insurance company to compensate him, he discovers in the trash a receipt disclosing the name of the locksmith, whose work failed to keep out the vandals. Daniel's house has already, through the motif of the invisible bullet-proof cloak, been associated with gun-related violence. All of these elements work to create a sense of suspenseful foreboding. The camera follows the gun in Farhad's hand as Daniel's car pulls into his driveway and then cuts to the interior of the house, where Lara hears her father's car and peers out of the window. While the camera cuts between interior and exterior shots, the scene is focalized through Lara and, as she sees the gun pointed at her father, she runs out the front door calling to her mother that he does not have the cloak that he needs for protection. As she leaps to cover her father, the gun is fired and Lara is shot in the back. The viewer's worst foreboding is realized. In slow motion, and with the human voices silenced, the reactions of each figure in the drama are registered: her screaming father, holding her; her weeping mother on the steps; Farhad, recoiling from the gun and the horror of what he has done. We are returned from slow motion to real time by Lara's voice and at that point we realize that she is miraculously alive. The family retreat behind their front door and we see in an overhead crane shot Farhad standing bewildered on the street, a shot that balances the opening shot into the sun, where the camera looks up at Farhad and then cuts to the gun in his hand. The scene ends with the powerful symbol of a US flag stirring in the breeze as Farhad stands immobile: the importance of this iconography is emphasized by the director's commentary on the DVD version of the film.

In this scene, the Iranian is represented unambiguously as the 'bad' immigrant, in contrast to the 'good' immigrant locksmith. The scene depicts an act of revenge for the racialist attack on his shop; however, the locksmith has withstood the racialist abuse of the district attorney's wife, Jean (Sandra Bullock), without betraying any desire for vengeance. This motivating incident, the attack on the shop, with the anti-Islamic graffiti daubed on the walls, is incomprehensible to the shopkeeper's wife, Shereen, who wonders aloud 'They think we're Arab. When did Persian become Arab?' Here we have another case of the 'invisible barrier' of racialism obscuring the recognition of what individuals actually are.

This issue of mis/recognition is especially important in relation to the role of Dorri, their Americanized adult daughter, who represents a key ambiguity. She is associated with death (she is shown in the mortuary, presenting the body of Graham's brother Peter for identification) but also with the angelic preservation of Lara's life. After his attempt to kill is thwarted by the blank bullet, Farhad claims this is a miracle, brought about by the intervention of an angel. However, it is his daughter who is responsible for the blank bullets in his gun. Dorri's purchase of blank bullets for her father's gun is ironically contextualized: the racist gun-store owner demands that she choose bullets and, when she expresses her choice by the colour of the box, asks sneeringly, 'You know what those are?'

He appears to take pleasure in selling her blank bullets. But does she know this? Does Dorri knowingly choose blanks but disdains to say so in order to keep her dignity? Or does she in fact choose according to the most appealingly coloured packaging? The interpretation of this incident – whether Dorri is duped because she is 'foreign' or whether she chooses knowingly because she is 'American' – is left to the audience, who must confront their own assumptions and prejudices in order to construct an interpretation. We must decide where the emphasis falls in Dorri's hyphenated identity: Iranian or American? Is she assimilated as an American or is she a perpetual foreigner? This is the question addressed to all potentially un-American immigrants who can be seen as 'flexible citizens' of both 'here' and 'there'.

The term 'flexible citizen' is taken from Aihwa Ong's influential book, *Flexible Citizenship: The Cultural Logics of Transnationality* (1999), where she discusses the kinds of belonging available in the contemporary global economy. For example, she describes how:

> Many Hong Kongers opted to work in China while seeking citizenship else-where. Caught between British disciplinary racism and China's opportunistic claims of racial loyalty, between declining economic power in Britain and surging capitalism in Asia, they sought a flexible position among the myriad possibilities (and problems) found in the global economy.
>
> (123)

In contrast to this representation of transnationality, the *San Francisco Chronicle* has reported, in upbeat terms, the increasing incidence of 'reverse migration' from the US to China. According to this report, wealthy Chinese-Americans are retiring to the Westernized cities of Shanghai, Guangzhou and Beijing, or are choosing to spend part of the year in China and part in the US. The reason for this return is represented as a response, not to white supremacy or racial hostility in the US, but to residual 'ethnocentrism' on the part of some 'Chinese immi-grants' (Hua 2006). What is not clear from the report is for how long these Chinese immigrants have lived in the US and, indeed, whether they were born in China. The implication of the rhetoric, however, is that these Chinese are perpet-ual foreigners in the US, just waiting for a chance to 'go home' – even if their descendants arrived in America in the 1850s.

Given these kinds of developments, Arjun Appadurai, in his essay 'Patriotism and its Futures' (1993), claims for us a utopian era of postnationalism, of free international mobility, describing the US as no longer a nation in itself but as a place of intersection, where deterritorialized transnational citizens come together in diasporic communities. In some ways, Appadurai's claims might be seen as echoing the sentiments expressed by Randolph Bourne in his 1916 essay 'Trans-National America'. Where Bourne proposes an America that permits multiple citizenship, with individuals living part-time in the US and elsewhere, Appadurai sees not multiple national affiliations, but no nationalism at all in this new era of delocalized transnationalism. He writes:

For every nation-state that has exported significant numbers of its populations to the United States as refugees, tourists, or students, there is now a
delocalized transnation, which retains a special ideological link to a putative
place of origin but is otherwise a thoroughly diasporic collectivity. No existing
conception of Americanness can contain this large variety of transnations.

(1993: 424).

However, the very impulse that brings these diasporic subjects to the US in order
to seek their fortunes, even if they are unwilling to sever cultural connections with
the homeland, is evidence of the longevity of American exceptionalism and
particularly of the economic dimension of exceptionalism, 'the American Dream'.
As Appadurai rightly points out: 'No existing conception of Americanness can
contain this large variety of transnations'. But the concept of the 'un-American',
the threatening diasporic subject who is eternally foreign because he or she
'retains a special ideological link to a putative place of origin', is grounded in an
awareness of these 'transnations' and, in part through the strategy of hyphenation,
uses this awareness to strengthen the ideology of American white supremacy.

In a direct response to Appadurai's claims, Kandice Chuh points to the availability of racialist discourses that impose upon migrants 'unmeltable' status,
excluding them even as they are rendered 'perpetual foreigners'. The metaphor
of the foreigner who refuses to 'melt' into the multicultural 'pot' is a dangerous
one. Chuh highlights the example of Japanese-Americans who were literally
'excluded' from designated geographical areas in the Pacific Northwest because
of the perception that they inhabited a 'cultural Japan' that extended across the
Pacific to the US. This is not a phenomenon specific to the US: commentators
on the global Chinese diaspora, such as Ien Ang and Wang Gungwu, point
to historical instances of pogroms against *peranakan* Chinese communities in
Malaysia and Indonesia as examples of the very real dangers of being perceived
as 'diasporic'; that is, of sustaining a cultural nationalism that is hostile to the
domestic culture of the nation of residence.

The racialist discourse of the 'unmeltable ethnic' or the subversive alien seems
to dominate the post-9/11 world, supporting a powerful regime of nationalistic
belonging and ethnic exclusion. The soundtrack to the film *Crash* emphasizes
the unavailability of belonging that is the consequence of mono-hyphenation.
Throughout, the abstract music gives the action an air of unreality which shifts
abruptly as a helicopter shot distances us from an arguing crowd, and the
Stereophonics' song 'Maybe Tomorrow' plays as the final credits roll. With the
refrain, 'Maybe tomorrow/I'll find my way home', this song expresses a yearning
for 'home' which is denied by the film's refusal to acknowledge, let alone endorse,
the possibility of multiple homes or forms of multiple transnational belonging.
While the song addresses 'tomorrow', the film narrative is largely retrospective,
showing the audience what happened 'yesterday', with the sense of ontological
finality that the past carries. The failure of the liberal multicultural 'experiment'
represented in the film therefore acquires an epistemological reality that the audience carries outside the cinema. At the same time, American exceptionalism does

offer a kind of belonging to those few who are able to revise their 'ethnic-ness' and become complicit in the ideology of American white supremacy. Nation-based academic disciplines remain ethically complicit with this exclusionary regime of nationalistic identification, so long as these disciplines do the following: replicate the discourse of mono-hyphenation; privilege subjects, textual canons, and educational courses that collude with the interests of the racialized white nation state; and refuse to engage in what Gerald Vizenor calls the 'word wars' against western colonial impositions.

Bibliography

Appadurai, A. (1993) 'Patriotism and its Futures', *Public Culture*, 5: 411–29.

Bourne, R. (1916) 'Trans-National America', *Atlantic Monthly*, 118 (July): 86–97.

Chuh, K. (1996) Transnationalism and its Pasts', *Public Culture*, 9: 93–112.

Coltelli, L. (1990–91) 'Gerald Vizenor: The Trickster Heir of Columbus: An Interview', *Native American Literatures Forum*, 2–3: 101–15.

Crash (2004) Dir. P. Haggis. Written by P. L. Haggis and R. T. Moresco, Lion's Gate Films, Bob Yaris Productions.

Deloria, P. (1999) *Playing Indian*, New Haven: Yale University Press.

Drinnon, R. (1980) *Facing West: The Metaphysics of Indian-Hating and EmpireBuilding*, Minneapolis: University of Minnesota Press.

Fish, S. (1997) 'Boutique Multiculturalism or Why Liberals are Incapable of Thinking about Hate Speech', *Critical Inquiry*, 23 (Winter): 378–95.

Horsman, R. (1981) *Race and Manifest Destiny: The Origins of American Anglo-Saxonism*, Cambridge: Harvard University Press.

Hua, V. (2006) 'Emigres Feel China's Pull: Affordable housing, food, recreation drive a trend of reverse migration', *San Francisco Chronicle*, 24 August. Online. Available http: <http://www.sfgate.com/cgi-bin/article.cgif=/c/a/2006/08/24/MNGE7KO8FJ1. DTL> (accessed 2 September 2006).

Kaplan, A. (2002) *The Anarchy of Empire in the Making of U.S. Culture*, Cambridge, MA: Harvard University Press.

Kaplan, A. and Pease, D. (eds) (1993) *Cultures of U.S. Imperialism*, Durham, NC: Duke University Press.

Kolodny, A. (1975) *The Lay of the Land: Metaphor as Experience and History in American Life and Letters*, Chapel Hill: University of North Carolina Press.

—— (1984) *The Land Before Her: Fantasy and Experience of the American Frontiers, 1630–1860*, Chapel Hill: University of North Carolina Press.

Lewis, R. W. B. (1955) *The American Adam: Innocence, Tradition, and Tragedy in the Nineteenth Century*, Chicago: University of Chicago Press.

Lorde, A. (1983) *Zami: A New Spelling of My Name*, Ithaca: Crossing Press.

Marx, L. (1964) *The Machine in the Garden: Technology and the Pastoral Ideal in America*, New York: Oxford University Press.

Miller, P. 1956. *Errand into the Wilderness*, Cambridge: Harvard University Press.

Novak, M. (1972) *The Rise of the Unmeltable Ethnics: Politics and Culture in the Seventies*, New York: Macmillan.

Ong, A. (1999) *Flexible Citizenship: The Cultural Logics of Transnationality*, Durham: Duke University Press.

Pease, D. (1994) *National Identities and Post-Americanist Narratives*, Durham, NC: Duke University Press.

Pulitano, E. (2007) 'Chances of Survivance: Gerald Vizenor's Autocritical Auto/biographies', in S. Pellerin (ed.) *Gerald Vizenor: Profils américains 20,* Montpellier: Presses de la Méditeranée.

Rowe, J. C. (2000) *Post-Nationalist American Studies*, Berkeley: University of California Press.

Slotkin, R. (1973) *Regeneration through Violence: The Mythology of the American Frontier, 1600–1860*, Middletown, CT: Wesleyan University Press.

—— (1998 [1985]) *The Fatal Environment: The Myth of the Frontier in the Age of Industrialization, 1800–1890*, Norman: University of Oklahoma Press.

—— (1992) *Gunfighter Nation: The Myth of the Frontier in Twentieth-Century America*, New York: Atheneum.

Smith, H. N. (1950) *Virgin Land: The American West as Symbol and Myth*, Cambridge, MA: Harvard University Press.

Stereophonics (2003) 'Maybe Tomorrow'.

Vizenor, G. (1990) *Interior Landscapes: Autobiographical Myths and Metaphors*, Minneapolis: University of Minnesota Press.

—— (1998) *Fugitive Poses: Native American Scenes of Absence and Presence*, Lincoln and London: University of Nebraska Press.

—— (2006) *Almost Ashore*, Cambridge: Salt Publishing.

19 Rerouting the postcolonial canon through linguistic remapping

Why remap?

Nirmala Menon

This means [...] seeing the imperial and capitalist metropolises as a specific historical form, at different stages: Paris, London, and Berlin, New York. It involves looking [...] from outside the metropolis: from the deprived hinterlands, where different forces are moving, and from the poor world, which has always been peripheral to the metropolitan systems. This need involve no reduction of the importance of the major artistic and literary works, which were shaped within metropolitan perceptions. *But one level has certainly to be challenged: the metropolitan interpretation of its own processes as universals.*

(Williams 1989: 3; emphasis added)

Before answering the question in the title, 'Why remap'?, I will first consider another question: What does the current map look like? The putative postcolonial canon includes texts from India, Africa, and the Caribbean, with new entrants from Latin America. The works of Salman Rushdie, Arundhati Roy, Vikram Chandra, Shyam Selvadurai, and J. M. Coetzee represent many postcolonial geographies, and all are written in English. I begin with the assumption that engaging with the rich literatures in diverse languages coming from different postcolonial spaces will simultaneously underscore the plurality of the discipline and open new avenues for postcolonial enquiries. Neil Lazarus charges:

To read across postcolonial literary studies is to find, to an extraordinary degree, the same questions asked, the same methods, techniques, and conventions used, the same concepts mobilized, the same conclusions drawn – about the work of a remarkably small number of writers.

(2004: 422)

I argue that, while postcolonial scholarship has successfully challenged Eurocentrism, the stagnation in critical perspectives that Lazarus talks about can be confronted if we look to the wide base of literatures available in multiple postcolonial languages. In short, it is now time to reroute the discipline into a multilingual field.

I define *multilingual* as moving beyond Anglophone and Francophone literatures to varied literatures in Hindi, Telugu, Tamil, Tagalog, and Swahili, to name just a few. I contend that discourses from literatures in different languages – both in translation and in the original – will result in a linguistic rerouting of postcolonial literary criticism. I argue for a project that seeks to enable a conversation that will expand the literary archive of postcolonial literature and allow a self-reflexive criticism of its theoretical premises. Such a conversation can also inspire new concepts in the postcolonial critical vocabulary.

Recent issues concerning postcolonial scholarship include allegations by materialist critics such as Benita Parry, Neil Lazarus, Aijaz Ahmad that the attempt to find complex nuances of interactions between the colonizer and the colonized has resulted in a rejection of dualism in all forms; consequently, postcolonial theory has delegitimized even complex models of struggle-based politics. According to Neil Lazarus postcolonial literary scholars have tended to write with reference to a woefully restricted and attenuated corpus of works *because* of the narrowness of their theoretical assumptions. In this essay I argue that, while works already in the orbit of postcolonial criticism certainly need to be looked at from beyond existing critical perspectives, the very narrowness of the range of works limits theoretical assumptions. I examine the literature of a single postcolonial state, India, to support the argument that in order for postcolonial studies to become more representative and varied, the diverse works in multiple regional languages should be included. In the interests of a more inclusive aesthetics, postcolonial studies needs to look beyond literature written in just one language – English. Lazarus examines the book *Interviews with Writers of the Postcolonial World* and asks: 'What thematic concerns, historical conditions, or existential predicaments can plausibly be said to license the inclusion of such authors as Ngugi, Ghosh, and Ihimaera under any shared rubric, let alone that of postcoloniality?' (425). This rhetorical question underscores the differences between the writers themselves and the unacknowledged disparities in their respective postcolonialities. To answer Lazarus, all the writers represent geographies that are, for varying reasons, postcolonial, and form an emerging canon of postcolonial literature representative of these places. Moreover, they all write in English.

Such a consecration of postcolonial works from predominantly metropolitan centres and by select writers has dominated the discourse of postcolonial criticism, thereby centralizing and universalizing a select genre – the novel – as representative of postcolonialism *per se*. Thus, Raymond Williams's (1989) critique of the politics of modernism for its 'metropolitan interpretation of its own processes as universals' (47) may be read as analogous to postcolonial criticism. One of Edward Said's foci in *Orientalism* is the Euro-American academy and the 'power/knowledge' axis of that institution. Initial research in postcolonial studies, including some of Spivak's less cited essays, was built on Said's formulation of Orientalism. Postcolonialism's shift to an anti-binary perspective claims a more complex analysis of fast-changing global realities. Susie Tharu, however, comments on the discipline's trajectory thus: 'Abandoning the responsibility of engaging Western power/knowledge in its entirety, the new postcolonial studies, with anthropology in the lead, has concerned itself with a problematic designed to unearth residual or continuing colonialism in the ex-colonies' (Yeager 2007: 643). I interpret Tharu's call for a return to 'Saidian history' on the part of postcolonial studies not as a return to colonial/anti-colonial binaries, but, rather, as a call for a more self-reflexive critique of the inclusions and exclusions of the field. In this essay I will take a self-reflexive look at the field of literature and the forming of the postcolonial canon.

'The Postcolonial Canon' is a difficult term. As a discipline, postcolonial literary studies challenges canons and canon-building. However, challenging the European canon does not mean that this is not perceived as exceptional. Whether we agree on the existence or irrelevance of canons, whether 'postcolonial canon' is a self-contradictory term or not, the field as currently formulated is dominated by select writers and literary works to the exclusion of other writers, works, and languages. The process of arriving at a particular selection, in turn, becomes the basis for critical analyses and conclusions about postcolonialism. Such a circular movement results in (1) an emerging postcolonial 'canon', whether we acknowledge it or not and (2) theoretical conclusions based on that narrow selection of literatures that are then extrapolated to the larger field. A few select literary texts and writers are often uncritically referred to and un-selfconsciously understood as *the* postcolonial perspective. In examining the development, formation and history of canons and canon-building, a linguistic rerouting is the key to expanding the postcolonial canon.

The *Oxford English Dictionary* (*OED*) defines the noun 'canon' as 'a body of literary works traditionally regarded as the most important, significant and *worthy of study* (italics mine), those works esp. western literature considered to the established as being of the highest quality and most enduring value' (*Oxford English Dictionary Online*). The first edition of the *OED* (published between 1884 and 1928), according to Ingrid Johnson, does 'not contain in its twenty-five listings any word approximating the modern meaning of an approved catalog of books' (42). In the earlier meanings, the 'canon' is defined as a 'collection or list of books of the Bible accepted by the Christian Church as genuine and inspired' (42). Only in 1972 was this meaning supplemented to include 'secular authentic authors'. The selectively secular emphasis in the definition of 'canon' in the late nineteenth and twentieth centuries unsurprisingly coincided with the rise of the British Empire and global power gravitating towards the European capitals of London and Paris.

The *OED* also records the changes in and expansion of the meaning of the word 'canon' brought about by intellectual debates, specifically those of feminist and postmodernist disciplines. Thus, a 1992 supplement to the definition of 'canon' is: 'A body of work considered to be established as the most important or significant in a particular field' (*Oxford English Dictionary Online*). In returning to the original discussion about the validity of a 'postcolonial canon', then, as 'canon' still means a select or exemplary collection of works in any field according to the *OED*, for my purposes I will rely on the word's expanded meaning and continue to use the term 'postcolonial canon'.

Edward Said has been one of the most stringent critics of canon-formation. Along with Foucault and Derrida, he has supported a new kind of canon that operates from 'nomadic centres' (1978: 17), provisional structures that offer new forms of continuity, vision and revision. Said's vision values the potential over the institutional and is open-ended. His proposed literary shelf resembles what Jan Gorak has termed 'a kind of mental bazaar: a place of many tongues, a variety of goods, and an endless circulation of people and goods' (1991: 215). Said's 'nomadic centres' are indicative of the way postcolonial theory and literature compelled a reexamination of assumed centres and proposed alternative centres of thought. The idea of 'nomadic centres' is compelling even though it reiterates the inevitability of 'centres', poststructuralism notwithstanding. 'Nomadic centres' can be seen as interventionist through their periodic appraisal and dismantling, so that no particular centre can claim permanence.

Postcolonial literature has now established itself as a discipline 'worthy of study'. Its theoretical structure has inevitably been developed through the conscious and unconscious formation of a postcolonial canon. It is worth recalling 'Commonwealth literature', that is, literature in English written by writers from the former colonies of Britain. Salman Rushdie, in a scathing critique of the nomenclature, noted that it is:

> that body of writing created, I think, in the English language, by persons who are not themselves white Britons, or Irish or citizens of the United States of America [...]. Not only was it a ghetto, but also it was actually an exclusive ghetto. And the effect of creating such a ghetto was, is, to change the meaning of the far broader term 'English Literature' [...] into something far narrower, something topographical, nationalistic, and possibly even racially segregationalist.
>
> (1991: 62–3)

John McLeod has commented that Commonwealth literature was 'really a subset of canonical English literature' (2000: 14). Though scholars have disputed the use of terms like 'Commonwealth literature' and 'Third World literature', when the term 'postcolonial literature' is substituted, all that has changed is the nomenclature. Rushdie's critique would still be valid. Postcolonial literature, as it is currently formulated, is a 'body of writing, in the English language, by persons who are not white Britons or white citizens of the United States' (Rushdie 1991: 62). Thus, the selection is still an exclusive ghetto under a different name.

Therefore, Said's notion of provisional and non-permanent canons can be a useful self-reflexive critical tool with which to examine the postcolonial canon. Is the narrow literary base of postcolonial theory justified? What is the range and number of works that are published over a given time period, and is that diversity reflected in theoretical representation? Can we channel such criticism to advance research in the field? What is the distribution of writers, languages, and works in postcolonialism? These are all elaborate and complex questions that will necessarily have different answers for different postcolonial spaces. For my purposes here, I will only consider the literary production in the postcolonial space of India,[1] and examine its representativeness in theory. My findings are based on an analytic study of three different scholarly journals/websites that publish critical writings in postcolonial literature and theory. I begin by plotting a graph of my findings from the Modern Language Association (MLA) Bibliography, as illustrated in Figure 19.1.

The *x*-axis (the horizontal) of the graph represents a sample for each of five different authors, while the *y*-axis (the vertical) represents the total number of critical articles found on those particular authors. The *z*-axis represents the years of their publication. For this sample, I have chosen three time periods: 1980–1985, 1985–1993 and 1994–2006.

The three chosen time periods, differentiated by the colours blue, maroon and yellow respectively, mark the shifts in critical attention that take place between those junctures. 1980 is the starting point of my investigation because it signifies the time when postcolonial studies began to attract academic attention. Acclaim of Rushdie and the popularity of other postcolonial authors accelerated that interest, and, by the early 1990s, the discipline had a firm foothold in academia. About this time certain authors, writers, and languages began to dominate the discourse and have continued to do so until the present.

In the graph below, the uneven and disproportionate concentration of a few writers across the theoretical spectrum is obvious. Of the 3,483 entries for 'postcolonial' as a category, 177 entries were about Francophone postcolonial, and the remaining 3,306 were almost exclusively Anglophone postcolonial. Of these 3,306 articles, Rushdie alone is the subject of 794 articles in the survey, and Arundhati Roy's *The God of Small Things* (1997) is discussed 67 times. Many Indian writers in English, including Gita Hariharan, Bharati Mukherjee, Vikram Chandra, and Shashi Tharoor, have also inspired a good number of articles. Critical articles about authors in languages other than English are few. As the

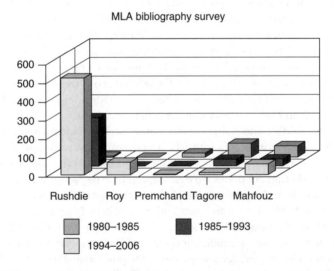

Figure 19.1 Survey of MLA Bibliography indicating scholarly articles published about these authors, 1980–2006.

graph shows, most of these articles are barely visible between the scales of 0–100; also notable is the span 1980–1985 when articles about authors in Indian languages were more numerous; they progressively declined subsequently, with the most recent from 2000–2006 nearly invisible. For example, while Tagore and Premchand have 120 and 27 entries between 1980–1985, they are virtually non-existent as subjects of articles published in the 1990s and completely disappear in the new millennium.[2]

I also analysed two other important journals of postcolonial research, *Interventions* and *The South Asian Review*, and came to similar conclusions. As in the analysis of the MLA Bibliography, the range of authors discussed was limited to postcolonial authors writing in English. Even among those, select authors and their works dominated the discourse. Rushdie and Roy together accounted for 861 articles. In other words, 25 per cent of the total number of critical articles was based on approximately four texts. I cannot imagine how the theoretical assumptions that draw from such a small corpus could be representative for very diverse and disparate postcolonial realities. Between 1983–2005, *Interventions* has had special issues devoted to (1) global diasporas and (2) postcolonial American studies. In addition, a number of recent articles focus on empire and neo-imperialism or US imperialism. Transnationalism is also a constant presence, and postcolonial theory is seen in the larger contexts of globalization, WTO, and the environment. The role of diasporas dominates the scholarly conversation; authors repeatedly mentioned include Rushdie, Achebe, and Coetzee. The issues from the mid to late 1980s contain no articles about non-English works or authors from either South Asia or Africa, arguably two of the largest postcolonial spaces.

The South Asian Review paints only a slightly different picture. The canonical bifurcation continues here with the bulk of articles focused on the same few authors and themes. Interestingly, though, the journal's issues 80, 81, and 82 have a more varied selection of topics and writers. There are articles comparing the writings of Gandhi and Tagore and an analysis of different nationalisms. The 82 issue compares Chandi Das with Dante and Raja Rao with T. S. Eliot. The 81 issue discusses E. M. Forster's *Passage to India* with Bhasa's *Pratima Natika* and the folk form of *Bhavai* and its position in Indian theatre.

In the graph in Figure 19.2, I plot the contents of the *South Asian Review*, focusing on the years 1980–2005. During the given periods, I plot the percentage of articles that discuss authors or their works in English, those that cover languages other than English, and articles that undertake a comparative analysis of both. The other languages tower is significantly higher during 1980–85 and then progressively declines, while the tower for English literally towers over the other languages during the period 2000–06.

The trend towards the domination of postcolonial works written in English begins with a shift in the late 1980s and early 1990s, an exciting time with Indo-Anglian writers 'the flavor of the era' (Jusdanis 1992); Rushdie was acclaimed, and other Indian writers in English were being noticed and read and, most importantly, winning awards. This was refreshing initially, but the recurrence of

The South Asian review

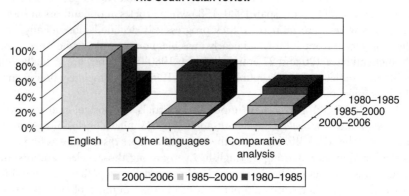

Figure 19.2 Distribution of English and other language authors and their works for the period 1985–2000.

the same writers, questions, and themes over the years gives pause for reflection: Is this interventionist field becoming more exclusive? Have we exhausted the limits of literary works and explored all the challenges of postcolonial subjectivity? A survey of major journals, articles, and theorists in the discipline in the most recent decade indicates a closing in of the discipline. The *South Asian Review* issues from 2000 onwards continue to present articles about Salman Rushdie, Raja Rao, and Arundhati Roy. They also feature the same themes, with merely a switch from the hybrid to the migrant in the 2005 special issue about 'global diasporas'.

The exclusions are even more pronounced when authors in non-English and non-languages are examined. Referring to the complexities of African postcolonialism, Mamadou Diouf charges that 'in Africa, postcolonial studies speak English, not French' (Yeager 2007: 640). Postcolonial studies should actually identify not just English or French but a host of other active languages that experience the postcolonial condition in these places. That is really the point here. Postcolonial spaces are vast and multilingual, and no single language – whether English or French – can by itself be representative of the diversity of experiences and literary forms that emerge from these places. There is a need to decentralize the different representations in order to be able to imagine the much more linguistically varied spaces in their *lived* experience.

David Damrosch observes that in 'world literature', as in some Miss Universe literary competitions, an entire nation may be represented by a single author: Indonesia, the world's fifth largest nation, is usually seen, if at all, in the person of Ananta Toer. Jorge Luis Borges and Julio Cortazar divide the honours for 'Mr. Argentina' (Damrosch 2003). This may be said of postcolonial literature as well, except that, in this case, each of the nations is represented by only a handful of writers writing in English. The representations inevitably reflect an 'othering' process. 'World literature' is a quaint and problematic term because it represents not so much the 'world', as a particular part of it: in effect, it reiterates the binary of the West and the rest. Western canonical authors are not included in this group, which is a token acknowledgement of 'other' authors from the less important parts of the 'world'. In postcolonial literature, acknowledging only writers writing in English as part of a postcolonial literary corpus smacks of an imperial influence, not a postcolonial stance. Damrosch also points to the existence of a shadow canon in postcolonial studies, including writers such as Premchand and Ghalib, whom everybody 'knows', but who are rarely discussed in print. By circumscribing its orbit to a few, select authors in a single language, postcolonial studies creates what David Damrosch calls a 'hypercanon' within the field. To account for the multilingual expansion of the canon, therefore, another category needs to be created, in this case, regional language literature from India.

The Sahitya Akademi awards for literature are instituted by the government and have gained a certain respect among writers and critical circles in India. A survey of the awards granted from 1980 to 2005 reveals that an average of 23 works in 22 different languages have won the award each year. Collectively, approximately 500 literary works written in these languages have won some literary acclaim and have been translated into other Indian and Asian languages as well as into English. Figure 19.3 presents a graph for the Sahitya Akademi awards for fiction, poetry, and criticism in five different languages. Sanskrit is included to demonstrate that, as a language less widely spoken than the others and consecrated as an exclusively religious language visible only in the areas of Ayurvedic medicine and Yoga, it nevertheless has a healthy literary production.

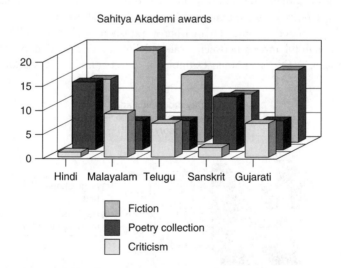

Figure 19.3 Literary production in five Indian languages, 1986–2006.

The graph is plotted with the number of award-winning works on the *x*-axis and the different languages on the *y*-axis. I have further separated fiction, poetry, and criticism. I have randomly selected five different regional languages.

To the argument that such comparative study is the domain of comparative literature departments, I contend that 'postcolonial' is, by definition, multilingual and is, thus, obliged to be comparative. So what does this survey mean for postcolonial theory? How can it be a useful resource, and can it widen our understanding of postcolonialism? Does it raise new questions that might call for new tools and methodologies? In Figure 19.4, a comparative study of the three previous graphs gives the following picture about postcolonial theory and discourse: the *x*-axis is the two comparative bars for literary production vis-à-vis their representation in postcolonial theory. The graph shows that Anglophone literary production in India is much lower than that of texts produced in the regional languages, but is disproportionately represented in the theoretical structure.[3]

The above analysis is not entirely new. Many scholars and especially many of the materialist critics have pointed out the extraordinary narrow base of postcolonial literary theory and criticism. Gayatri Spivak (1993), Neil Lazarus (2004), Benita Parry (1994), and Tim Brennan (2005) to name but a few, have consistently pointed out the need to widen the scope of the field by including writers from different languages that occupy the postcolonial space.

Such a move will open up different imaginative spaces, alternative ways of articulating and perhaps reconfiguring concepts of hybridity, nationalism, and cosmopolitanism. Tim Brennan, in a powerful critique of what he terms 'new cosmopolitan writing', points out that 'today a new literary genre is emerging that gives the impression of having been produced precisely with an eye to their postcolonialist reception' (108). It is difficult to read a work like Githa Hariharan's *In Times of Siege* and not agree with the above criticism, especially when it is compared to some of her earlier works (such as *The Ghosts of Vasu Master*, with its delightful moves between oral and literary forms). Pauline Melville's *A Ventriloquist's Tale* is another example of a self-conscious postcolonial text.

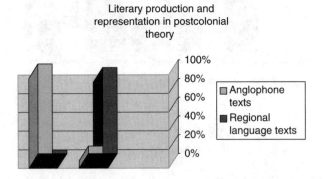

Figure 19.4 This figure is a comparative analysis of the previous three graphs.

In terms of self-referential theoretical conversations, Kiran Desai's latest *Inheritance of Loss* is identifiably postcolonial.

Gayatri Spivak refers to the shortchanging of other-language authors in post-colonial theory aptly as 'jumping over' (1993: 93). With respect to the Indian context, Spivak has been even more forthright, recognizing that

> [I]f literature is a vehicle of cultural self-representation, the "Indian cultural identity" projected by Indo-Anglian fiction, and more obliquely, poetry, can give little more than a hint of the seriousness and contemporaneity of the many 'Indias' fragmentarily represented in the many Indian literatures.
>
> (1996: 239)

For example, the novellas of Bengali writer Mahashweta Devi (like Malayalam modernist O. V. Vijayan's works) represent a subaltern consciousness that 'the modernist' finds difficult to explain or position (see *Imaginary Maps, Legends of Khasak*). From this perspective western modernity is exposed as woefully inade-quate, without the chance to romanticize the fantastic (or the mysticism of the East). These narratives dismantle binaries or certainties of any sort. What can be more postcolonial than that? Should we not know about more works that may give us more literary insight into different and diverse postcolonial subjectivities? And, while it is impossible for a handful of scholars to cover all the different languages in different postcolonial places, I suggest that we have to make a begin-ning. The larger endeavour is to initiate a postcolonial dialogue that can be taken up in Tamil, Telugu, Tagalog, Maori, or Swahili by scholars conversant in those languages.

In Rushdie's *Haroun and the Sea of Stories*, the conversation between Rashid, the storyteller, and Khattam-Shud (literally, one who finishes-off) posits that narra-tives escape control:

> 'But why do you hate stories so much?' Haroun blurted out feeling stunned. 'Stories are fun.'
> 'The world however, is not for fun,' Khattam-Shud replied. 'The world is for controlling.'
> 'Which world'? Haroun made himself ask.
> 'Your world, my world, all worlds,' came the reply. 'They are all to be ruled.
> And inside every single story lies a world, a story-world, that I cannot rule at all – and that is the reason why.'
>
> (1990: 112)

The story world, as Rushdie reminds us, has the power to move beyond texts and contexts and may be conceived in the mind of the readers, subtly transforming the way they see and perceive the world. The social and political power of stories is, of course, not always positive, hence the need to resist the seduction of seeing the text as a transparent reflection of the world. Postcolonial studies is only too aware of the colonizer's stories about 'empty continents' and 'western discoveries'. As Said explains in *Culture and Imperialism*:

> Stories are at the heart of what explorers and novelists say about the strange regions of the world; they also become the method colonized people use to assert their identity and the existence of their own history [...] nations them- selves are narrations; the power to narrate, or block other narratives from forming and emerging, is very important to culture and imperialism and constitutes one of the main connections between them.
>
> (1990: xii–iii)

Thus Said's 'nomadic canon' conveys the importance of devolving the power to narrate to different people in different times of history: that power to narrate is diminished if it is allowed to only come to light in a select few languages. This struggle between resisting seductive narratives and hearing new stories in new ways is one that counter-theories and counter-narratives have to confront. If Khattam-Shud can control the number of stories that are told and heard, theo- retically, the power of fictive subversiveness can be contained.

Reading diverse narratives from different languages will also open up the discourse on theoretical concepts. There will be narratives that address issues that have not yet been confronted in existing theoretical models, or which can be articulated differently. Reading conflicting narratives will render these models more complex and tease out some of the difficult issues when dealing with repre- sentations of different cultures.

Velutha's 'silence' in *The God of Small Things* and Saladin Chamcha's confused identity problems in *Midnight's Children* are rich literary motifs, but they are not universal representations. Intentionally or unintentionally, when every theoreti- cal concept recycles the same characters or authors, it is impossible to ignore the universalization of the particular. While my argument is premised on an example from South Asia (largely India), itself a vast literary space, such research can just as well be conducted for Africa, the Caribbean, or South American contexts. Oral literatures and their influence are a major influence in postcolonial contexts. So how does oral literature figure in postcolonial theory? Currently, it does not account for much in postulating the theoretical concepts, because it is largely unexplored. By virtue of its relative obscurity, however, it holds out an exciting potential for scholarship.[4] Multicultural texts that have been the foundation of a great deal of postcolonial theory have their uses, but such texts by themselves provide a narrow rubric when we consider all the disparate conditions of postco- loniality around the world. Deepika Bahri cautions against the exclusive nature of such 'multicultural' disseminations:

> The problem is such subjects are to speak as minorities; they are to repre- sent their communities and the victimization suffered by them in individual voices; and their texts are to be used often solo, to 'inform' students [...].

[I]t encourages students to learn about the world, often exclusively, from token fictional texts.

(2003: 73–4)

Cultural diversification of the curriculum can only be good, but we also need to be aware of its limitations in representation: those limitations and their consequences have also to be part of that dissemination.

In conclusion, I argue for a postcolonial discourse that includes texts from regional languages in India, either in the original or through translations. The canon should expand outwardly, not converge inwardly. Speaking from the perspective of postcolonial scholars committed to pushing disciplinary boundaries for reasons of representation as well as expanding horizons, Arun Mukherjee expresses this view very well:

> I think those of us who teach 'postcolonial' literatures should at least point out the absurdity of our being saddled with the responsibility of teaching about two thirds of the world that our institutional position forces us into. And we should stop making and homogenizing theories that create a 'unitary' field out of such disparate realities.
>
> (1998: 223)

Mukherjee is alluding to different postcolonial histories and their specific intersections and parallelisms. I think the same can be said with respect to languages. The term 'Postcolonial literatures' means varying literatures in a range of languages in two-thirds of the world. We should desist from projecting it as a range of monolingual narratives from these vastly disparate places.

Notes

1 India has at least 17 official languages, each of which has its own literary conventions. I plot a few samples of languages and their literature; this is indicative of a trend that may be possibly extrapolated to the remaining languages with some readjustments for every language.
2 Authors writing in any language other than English do not register on the postcolonial critical map.
3 Bar 1 is for postcolonial theory, the second comparative bar is the literary production, both approximately calculated for the years 1980–2005.
4 Dalit literature from India is an indispensable database when studying subaltern narratives. Dalit means the 'oppressed': in recent years, literature written by or about Dalit communities has established itself as a distinct and important genre that challenges and subverts dominant regional narratives.

Bibliography

Bahri, D. (2003) *Native Intelligence: Aesthetics, Politics and Postcolonial Literature*, Minneapolis: University of Minnesota Press.

Bernheimer, C. (ed.) (1995) *Comparative Literature in the Age of Multiculturalism*, Baltimore: The Johns Hopkins University Press.

Bhabha, H. (1994) 'Signs Taken for Wonders: Questions of Ambivalence and Authority under a Tree outside Delhi, May 1817', in *The Location of Culture*, New York: Routledge.

—— (2000) 'The Right to Narrate'. Online. Available http http://www.uchicago.edu/docs/millennium/bhabha/bhabha_a.html (accessed 27 November 2007).

Brennan, T. (2005) 'The Economic Image-Function of the Periphery', in A. Loomba, *et al.*, (eds) *Postcolonial Studies and Beyond*, Durham, NC: Duke University Press.

Damrosch, D. (1995) 'World Literature in a Postcanonical, Hypercanonical Age', in H. Saussy (ed.) *Comparative Literature in an Age of Globalization*, Baltimore: Johns Hopkins University Press.

—— (2003) *What Is World Literature?* Princeton, NJ: Princeton University Press.

Deleuze, G., and Guattari, F. (1987) *Capitalism and Schizophrenia*, trans. B. Masumi, Minneapolis: University of Minnesota Press.

Desai, G. and Nair, S. (eds) (2005) *Postcolonialisms: An Anthology of Cultural Theory and Criticism*, New Brunswick, NJ: Rutgers University Press.

Gikandi, S. (2005) 'Globalization and the Claims of Postcoloniality', in G. Desai and S. Nair (eds): 608–34.

Gorak, J. (1991) *The Making of the Modern Canon*, London: Athlone.

Johnston, I. (2003) *ReMapping Literary Worlds. Postcolonial Pedagogy in Practice*, New York: Peter Lang.

Jusdanis, G. (1992) *Belated Modernity and Aesthetic Culture*, Minneapolis: University of Minnesota Press.

Lazarus, N. (ed.) (2004) *The Cambridge Companion to Postcolonial Literary Studies*, New York: Cambridge University Press.

Macaulay, B. T. (2005; [1835]) 'Minute on Indian Education, February 2, 1835', in G. Desai and S. Nair (eds): 121–131.

Marx, J. (2004) 'Postcolonial Literature and the Western Literary Canon', in N. Lazarus (ed.): 83–97.

McLeod, J. (2000) *Beginning Postcolonialism*, Manchester: Manchester University Press.

Morrison, T. (1989) 'Unspeakable Things Unspoken: The Afro-American Presence in American Literature', *Michigan Quarterly Review*, 28.1 (Winter): 1–34.

Mukherjee, A. (1998) *Postcolonialism: My Living*, Toronto: TSAR.

Parry, B. (1994) 'Resistance Theory/Theorising Resistance, or Two Cheers for Nativism', in F. Barker, P. Hulme, and M. Iversen (eds) *Colonial Discourse/Postcolonial Theory*, Manchester: Manchester University Press.

—— (2004a) *Postcolonial Studies: A Materialist Critique*, New York: Routledge.

—— (2004b) 'The Institutionalization of Postcolonial Studies', in N. Lazarus (ed.): 66–83.

Roy, A. (1997) *The God of Small Things*, New York: Harper Perennial.

Rushdie, S. (1990) *Haroun and the Sea of Stories*. London: Granta.

—— (1991) *Imaginary Homelands: Essays and Criticisms. 1981–1991*, London: Granta.

Said, E. (1978) *Orientalism*, New York: Vintage Books Edition.

—— (1990) *Culture and Imperialism*, New York: Knopf.

Saussy, H. (ed.) (2006) *Comparative Literature in an Age of Globalization*, Baltimore: Johns Hopkins University Press.

Spivak, G. (1993) *Outside the Teaching Machine*, London and New York: Routledge.

Spivak, G., Landry, D., and McLean, G. (eds) (1996) *The Spivak Reader*, London and New York: Routledge.

Talib, I. S. (2002) *The Language of Postcolonial Literatures: An Introduction*, London and New York: Routledge.

Vijayan, O. V. (1995) *The Legends of Khasak*, trans. O. V. Vijayan, New Delhi: Penguin.

Williams, R. (1989) *The Politics of Modernism: Against the New Conformists*, London: Verso.

Yeager, P. (2007) 'Editor's Column: The End of Postcolonial Theory? A Roundtable with Sunil Agnani, Fernando Coronil, Gaurav Desai, Mamadou Diouf, Simon Gikandi, Susie Tharu, and Jennifer Wenzel', *PMLA*, 122.3: 633–51.

20 At the intersection of queer and postcolonial discourses

Rerouting the queer with Jean Sénac and Jean Genet

Nadia Louar

This chapter offers a narrative model that departs from the orientalist[1] practice of 'the coming out genre' in North Africa displayed in works such as André Gide's *Immoralist* (1951) and, in some respects, Roland Barthes' *Incidents* (1987), in which the relation of desire between the white man and the Arab boy is conditioned by the dynamics of power that structure relationships in their (post- and neo-) colonial world. It posits its authors as lovers rather than colonizers. Within the specific context of the French gay male relation to the Arab man, I bring forward the distinctive situation of Jean Sénac (1948–1973), one of the most problematic figures in the literary history of colonial and postcolonial Algeria, and show how the sexual identity of the poet as deployed in his work and life is uniquely entangled in his political investment in the Algerian revolution. I argue that, rather than being motivated by power, his relation to the other is conditioned by his love of the other. The rereading I undertake in this chapter opposes the subjectivity of the unrequited lover to that of the occidental sexual tourist. It proposes a new model of subjectivity, a poetic model that can translate the unique experience of the lover in its relation to the other in the context of queer and postcolonial realities.

Taking as points of reference the essay by Edward Said, 'On Genet's Late Works' (1999 [1995]: 230–43), and more recently, Ross Chamber's analysis of the gay sexual tourism of Roland Barthes (1999: 250–70), I look at the way sexual, cultural and social identities intersect in the life of Jean Sénac as opposed to the way they develop in the lives of such authors as Roland Barthes or André Gide. I oppose here primarily Sénac's and, to some extent, Genet's literary and personal routes to that of the sexual tourist uncovered by critics who are reassessing the connection between homosexuality and colonialism (Aldrich 2003, Boone 1995). I argue that, in contradistinction to the orientalist pattern these critics describe, Genet, in his final work, *Prisoner of Love* (*Un captif amoureux*, 1986), shapes himself into an empathetic witness, while Sénac becomes an unrequited lover in his poetic corpus. Although I focus here primarily on the almost unknown Jean Sénac, I will tie the poet's experience to Genet's so as to reexamine the place of eroticism in the poet's political desire for solidarity; indeed, both authors' literary and personal routes combine the sensual and the political in a unique manner.

First, I introduce the poet Jean Sénac and show how his life and work challenge contemporary discourses of identity politics, and offer a multilayered individual whose identity cannot be comprised within the clear-cut regulated politics of difference that these discourses have produced. In fact, identity politics assumes a collective identity and compels the idea of an organic political group that excludes plurality. If indeed identity politics facilitates the recognition of various subjectivities along racial, sexual, and gender lines, it does not account for identities that deviate from group norms – thus, for instance, it does not distinguish various sexual affiliations within the larger category of racial identity. As a result, the multidimensional composition of identity is obscured. In the final part of this chapter, I examine the body of work that Jean Sénac created to delineate his poetic identities and, drawing on the work of the feminist writer Gloria Anzaldúa (1987), I will bring forward a poetic model of transnational identity that travels across sexual, social, and cultural borders.

Jean Sénac was born near Oran in 1926 from an unknown father. He was of Spanish ancestry, and, like many other settlers in the Oran region of French colonial Algeria, his early years were marked by poverty, military service and bad health. After the war he became a radio broadcaster and began publishing poetry in Algiers magazines. In 1954, his first collection, *Poèmes*, was published in Paris thanks to the help of his friend and mentor, Nobel Prize writer Albert Camus. The same year marked the beginning of the eight-year Algerian war of independence, which Sénac spent in France. He resolutely and immediately took the side of the Algerians against supporters of French Algeria. In 1962 he returned to a newly independent socialist state founded on Arab-Muslim principles. He found work with the radio, continued composing his own poetry, and published anthologies of francophone Algerian writers. His violent criticism of the Algerian regime, combined with his openly homosexual poetry and life, brought him into conflict with the newly established authorities. He was assassinated in Algiers in 1973. The Algerian police who arrested, and soon released, a supposed lover of the poet, muffled his murder. Some friends and other acquaintances of the late author are still convinced that it was not, as was claimed, a crapulous and sexual crime, but a political assassination that should be read along the same lines as those of other famous intellectual agitators of his time.

Indeed, in the lineage of fascinating artists such as Pier Paulo Pasolini or Garcia Lorca, Jean Sénac's life and work are intrinsically linked to the revolutionary time within which his poetic corpus arises. The life of the writer, like Camus's, was deeply affected by the politics of his time and the task of reconciling opposed cultures. Sénac's body of work betrays the multiple influences that characterize his problematic composite identity as a French, Algerian-born, gay poet living in the young independent Muslim nation. His poetry combines his equivocal sense of belonging and is thus conceived along the twin lyrical and mystical thematic lines of Arab poetry (represented by poets such as Al-Hallaj and Abu Nuwas) and the modernist conception of poetic language as articulated by René Char and Mallarmé. The life and work of Sénac also tell the tale of a poet who envisioned himself within the tradition of gay authors from Walt Whitman to Garcia Lorca to Jean Genet.

Sénac's life, as Genet's, spanned both the French colonial period and the coming to independence of its colonies. Both writers had strong ties to North Africa and the Middle East, and engaged actively in its political causes. However, despite his sexual proclivities and his criminal record, Jean Genet became part of the French literary canon. The nomadic author had an anchor in France, and was fortunate to meet Jean Cocteau and other famous writers who zealously promoted his work and raised his status. Jean Sénac's position is, in this sense, quite different from Genet's. It is, in many ways, more poignant and more complex because he was denied his Algerian identity and was *de facto* considered part of the colonizing process. Before the independence of Algeria, the question of nationality had not mattered, since Algeria was a French colony. But in the wake of the revolution, Sénac found himself suddenly a Frenchman, whereas in his heart of hearts he considered himself to be Algerian. He consequently refused to apply for Algerian nationality considering that he had always been, and never stopped being, an Algerian.

The complexity of Jean Sénac's cultural and sexual identities reveals the contradictions at the core of identity politics as articulated in a variety of contemporary theories. More than the orphaned Genet, Jean Sénac's work and life is exemplary in this respect; he is the example *par excellence* of the 'missing in action' of identity politics. He presents us with an undefined and indefinable subject position that ethnically, and, to some extent, culturally sides with the colonizer, and ideologically and economically sides with the colonized, even while being in one way or another structurally denied by all sides. Because of his race, sexual preference and geo-political situation, Jean Sénac cannot but represent an anomaly – a deviant, literally, a queer. Very much like the Anglo-Irish Huguenot Samuel Beckett who is considered both a French and an English writer while being neither, Sénac occupied the position of being neither Algerian nor French, neither quite colonized, nor quite colonizer. In this respect, Jean Sénac embodies perfectly the postmodernist subject position that is committed to negativity, dislocation, fragmentation and ontological exile. Neither/nor, either/or, Sénac cannot be contained within specific theoretical collective denominations. His identity is kaleidoscopic.

Jean Genet and Jean Sénac have in common their rejection of French nationality. Genet spent his life travelling around the world and lived mostly in hotels, and Sénac's sense of self was undeniably informed by his sense of belonging to a much fought for independent Algeria. Both let their love for the Arab man influence their adherence to the Arab cause. Indeed, both authors allowed their sexual life to fuel their political activism. Sénac's collection of poems, *Citizens of Beauty* (1997 [1967]), devoted to the eroticism and heroism of the Algerian revolutionaries, and Genet's last *œuvre*, *Prisoner of Love*, a self-reflective account of his sexual and political engagement with the Palestinians, attest to the sexual politics at work in their literary enterprises. In both men's texts, the political always appears contiguous to the sexual. Yet neither Genet, nor Sénac, can be assimilated to the occidental cruiser or benefactor one encounters in colonial history in the nineteenth and early twentieth centuries. Their singular affinity with the Arab fighter stands outside socio-economic or political considerations; it is erotic, but not eroticized. Jean Genet expresses this distinction brilliantly in his essay about the Chatila massacre,[2] in which he theorizes on the link between revolution and eroticism:

> Is a revolution really a revolution when it does not make the faces and bodies shed the dead skin which enervates them? I am not speaking about an academic beauty, but about the impalpable – unnamable – beauty of bodies, of faces, of cries, of words, which are not dismal, I mean a sensual joy which is so strong that it tries to banish eroticism.
>
> (1997: 21)

The subversive position of both Genet and Sénac, however, leads to critical interrogations. Of Genet, Edward Said asked: 'does his love for the Palestinians nevertheless amount to a kind of overturned or exploded Orientalism? Or is it a sort of reformulated colonialist love of handsomely dark young men?' (1999 [1995]: 235) Should we ask here the same question about Sénac? The fascination of the poet for 'dark young men' is incontestable. One very explicit collection of poems entitled *The Myth of the Mediterranean Sperm* (*Le mythe du sperme méditerranéen*), written in 1984 [1967], describes his passion for the male dark body and combines the erotic fascination of the poet for his Arab 'comrade' with his political desire for Algerian independence:[3]

> Come and read, comrades!
> [...]
> criminal sexes on my skin
> drawing frescoes of chaos
> Come and see comrades,
> there is no myth as gorgeous among your whorish lives! [...]
> To ensnare me God has placed in my privates
> Adam, Jacob and Job – and the Jewish angel
> And the Arab angel.
>
> (539)

Of Genet, Said concludes that there is 'something quietly but heroically subversive about his extraordinary relationship with the Arabs'. According to the Palestinian critic:

> Genet did allow his love for Arabs to be his approach to them, but there is no indication that he aspired to a special position, like some benevolent White Father, when he was with them, or wrote about them. On the other hand, he never tried to go native, be someone other than he was. [...] He entered the Arab space and lived in it not as an investigator of exoticism but as someone for whom the Arabs had actuality a presence he enjoyed, felt comfortable with, even though he was and remained different.
>
> (1999; [1995]: 235)

This portrait of Jean Genet by Edward Said could easily be transposed to Sénac, except that the poet did not 'enter' the Arab space and never considered himself an outsider. Rather, he felt contained in, and nurtured by, his place of birth. The poet was not an Arab in the ethnic sense of the term, and yet he was Algerian. He was born and raised in Algeria and lived among the people he called his brethren of misfortune.

It would be equally wrong to see Sénac as the figure Kobena Mercer described when he distinguished between models of appropriation and expressions of political solidarity and referred to the 'white negro'.[4] According to the critic, the 'white negro' is

> like a photographic negative, [...] an inverted image of otherness, in which attributes devalorised by the dominant culture [are] simply revalorized or hypervalorised as emblems of alienation and otherness, a kind of strategic self-othering in relation to the dominant cultural norms.
>
> (1992: 207–8)

Sénac does not take on any role. His position as a French gay poet in colonial and postcolonial Algeria results in a persona that does not attempt to control or impose intellectual domination over a mythical Algeria, nor attempts to assimilate difference, but which is instead rooted in a common fate and a common struggle to undo inherited models of subjectivity and subjection.

For the past three decades, various politics of identity have pervaded literary studies under the aegis of politically subversive theoretical discourses.[5] In so doing, they have brought to the forefront a fundamental conflict between singular, unique, experiences and identity categories established by these very discourses. As we know, endemic to queer and postcolonial theories is the establishment of clear identity categories; whether contested, problematized or deemed necessary for political action, they are foundational to both discourses. Individuals have to organize themselves in order to counter discriminatory practices in society. Yet identity categories within these theoretical frameworks do not reflect actual discrete subjects, but rather *represent* in discourse a coherent group of individuals: straights, gays, colonizers, colonized, white, blacks. Indeed, the corollary problem to the construction of identity categories is that they create a communal identity theory through the assumption of shared experiences and aspirations. This is achieved at the expense of actual individuals, with the result that their multifaceted and complex identities systematically escape such distinct categories: they are effectively written out of these theoretical models. In other words, the initially subversive discourses reiterate the very models of exclusion and inclusion that they critique. They, in turn, lead to indiscriminate exclusion and inclusion.

In the following I look at the way queer and postcolonial discourses intersect in this context. It is important to recall here that identity politics 'has come to signify a wide range of political activity and theorizing founded in the shared experiences of injustice of members of certain social groups' (Heyes 2008).

As such, the epistemological and political agenda of queer and postcolonial activities, understood here as sociopolitical movements and academic practices, is not informed by a paired ethical imperative; rather, their respective projects both circumvent and intersect with each other. The emancipatory political actions of each group are indeed linked to their respective politics of subversion. Let us think, for instance about the fact that gay male theory and research have, for a long time, failed to consider the relation between the emergence of male sexual identity and the colonial enterprise. As Robert Aldrich (2003), Joseph A. Boone (1995) and Ross Chambers (1999) have demonstrated in their respective works, (homo)sexual tourism started as a colonial phenomenon. Certain colonies even became a Mecca for the gay western literati and other prominent personalities in the heyday of colonialism. Tangiers, in particular, and North Africa, more generally, became notorious for their homosexual license. Said (1979: 103), by describing the imaginary orient created in nineteenth-century European literature as 'a living tableau of queerness', could not have been closer to the truth. Some critics have recently started to uncover the relationship between colonialism and western homosexuality and investigated the sexual politics of colonial and postcolonial narratives written by occidental writers travelling to North Africa (or to the Orient). They have established a literary gay tradition that accounts for the genre of the coming out story in an overtly eroticized orient. Joseph A. Boone, for instance, has shown how the novel of homosexual awakening of the western writer abroad is encoded in the colonial hierarchy white man/brown boy (1995: 104). He takes French novelist André Gide's 1902 novel, *The Immoralist*, as paradigmatic of the homosexual version of the *bildungsroman* and demonstrates 'the unconscious colonialism involved in Gide's projection of gay awakening onto the near East' (101): 'A corollary of the occidental tourist's fantasy that all boys are available for the right price is the assumption that they represent interchangeable versions of the same commodity: (nearly) underage sex' (102).

In the same vein, Ross Chambers shows that Roland Barthes, in his posthumously published autobiographical work *Incidents*, is necessarily oblivious of the colonial aspect implicated in his sexual *loiterature*.[6] Barthes's text is structured as a diary, and *incidentally* recounts his encounters, first in Morocco, when he was young and attractive, then in a diversely populated part of Paris, now old and lonely. Ross Chambers identifies Barthes's *incidentalism* as an orientalist practice that reveals itself in his 'commoditization of relations' (1999: 253). For Chambers, 'the emergence in the west of a gay male sexual identity might be directly related to the historical apogees of colonial empires' (254). He suggests that the marginal male homosexual at home is particularly apt to put himself at the service of colonial power abroad. Such notions as *home* and *abroad*, with their corollary sense of belonging and alienation, are necessarily problematic in colonial and postcolonial times and spaces. Home is a question of perspective, and a highly charged ideological and geopolitical entity. In the context of sexual tourism, these notions are fundamental. Indeed, it is precisely because Genet feels homeless everywhere and Sénac is actually at home abroad (in Algeria) that both authors cannot be assimilated to the sexual tourists contained in the aforesaid narrative paradigms.

Even more than nomadic Genet, Sénac, an Algerian-born Frenchman, cannot be considered a tourist. Contrary to André Gide and Roland Barthes, whose sexual and literary loitering in the former French colonies amounts to some form of *sexploitation*, Genet and Sénac's routes do not follow the narrative model of the gay man in North Africa in which the power-structured relation between the white man and the brown boy is dictated by politics. The marginality of their position prevents their identification with the white master/patron. So, if indeed, as Ross Chambers argues, 'the deluded belief [...] in a possible authenticity of contact with the other within the nevertheless commoditized context of colonialism is the condition for this gay relationship' (1999: 255), then a new model of relation is necessary to reconsider the singular relationships both Genet and Sénac have established with the other.

As suggested so far, Sénac cannot be easily *identified*. The poet shapes himself through his poetry and composes himself as a man from the land in which he thrives as a poet. He conceives of himself as the offspring of the Algerian soil, shaped by its sun and its water. Sénac (1999) feels that he organically belongs to the earth that surrounds him: its heat, its sun, its beaches and its men. He adopts the sun as his signature and signs all his writings with the drawing of a shining sun. The following verses illustrate his sense of belonging:

> For we don't grow from their Gaul.
> Our ancestors were all gnawed by the sun
> and their pores punctured by the desert winds
> Contained in our bodies is their growing life.
>
> (*Oeuvres Poetiques* 277)

The vegetal, the floral and animal world play a fundamental part in Sénac's creation of his poetic identity, which he conceptualizes as taking root in the earth in the same way as a flower stalk does, and as such coming from and belonging to the ground that nurtures it. Sénac continued, despite all rejections, to declare his *natural identity* through the poetic lyrics of his love for the land and its people; and he professed his love against all human laws and political objections. After the dream of a harmonious and welcoming independent Algeria was crushed in 1961, he writes:

> This land is mine beyond its seasons
> This land is mine beyond its bitter liturgy
> Beyond its waste, its dangerous paths
> Its weary soul and its tired people.
>
> (55)

In *My People's Early Rising* (*Matinales de mon peuple*), the collection of poems written between 1950 and 1962, which can be read both as the poetic journal of the

Algerian revolution and a love letter to its people, the fate of the Algerians is viscerally embedded within the natural elements, as if these elements were the true witnesses of the ongoing violence:

> You were saying easy things;
> the hard-working woman of the morning
> the forest that grew in your voice
> its trees so thick that they tear hearts apart
> and know the full weight of song
> the warmth of a clearing for the up-right man who demands
> a word of peace
> a word of human proportions
>
> (253)

His love is asserted through his poetry and later reasserted through his self-renaming as 'Yaya el Ouahrani', Jean from Oran in Arabic. When Jean Sénac decided to take an Arabic name during the Algerian revolution, rather than conferring upon himself a symbolic title of ownership or dreaming the dream of a new man in a free Algerian land, his renaming takes the significance of the renewal of love vows. 'This land is mine', he writes, 'and I am hers' (*Cette terre est mienne et je suis sienne*). Jean Sénac was not merely a romantic poet, a political idealist or even a sensualist, he shared the struggle of his *natural* brothers and was always painfully aware of his untenable position as the following verses violently attest: 'O my people/My people lynched by my people' (*O mon peuple lynché, mon peuple par mon peuple*) (66).

In order to shed light on the critical ambiguity of Jean Sénac's identities, I now draw on the mythologies created by the famous Latina lesbian critic Gloria Anzaldúa, and discuss Sénac's position of both belonging and resistance. In her seminal text *Borderlands/La Frontera* (1987), Anzaldúa creates a poetry of resistance to oppose the patriarchal forces that have negated her multifaceted identity. She deconstructs and redefines the culturally determined roles imposed on Latina women, by rewriting the myths that have shaped their fixed identities. 'This step is a conscious rupture', she writes, 'with all oppressive traditions of cultures and religions' (1987: 82). She then constructs a new 'mythos of mestizaje' that allows her as a *mestiza* – a woman of white, Mexican and Indian descent – to identify herself as a multilayered subject and grant herself an identity that did not previously exist. In an illuminating article written on Anzaldúa's seminal text, Erika Aigner-Varoz (2000) shows how the critic 'engages in a dialectical process in order to transcend imposed conceptual boundaries that have made her an outcast' (48). Through her mythical creations, Anzaldúa 'reinterprets history and, using new symbols, she shapes new myths [...] adopts new perspectives toward the dark-skinned, women and queers' (1987: 82). She is then able to recreate poetically and politically the reality of a *Home* that was, like Sénac's, denied to her in her social and cultural world. She writes: 'And if going home is denied me then I will have to stand and claim my space, making a new culture – *una cultura mestiza* – with my own lumber, my own bricks and mortar and my own feminist architecture' (22).

Gloria Anzaldúa's position helps us envision one that transcends categorical opposition. Through her mythical recreations the multifaceted author meta-phorizes and theorizes her indefinable subject position. In a comparable manner, Sénac's poetic construction shapes his identity and recreates a poetic model of intersubjectivity, one of subjugation and seduction. Sénac poeticizes himself into a subjugated lover, simultaneously subjected and seduced by the people and the land he inhabits, and that, inversely, inhabit him. The poet uses formal literary means from various cultures and literary traditions to compile an identity that circumscribes his sense of belonging and his love for Algeria and its peowwwple. What is remarkable in the life and work of the poet is the ambivalent intermixing of eroticism in his political desire for fraternity. Sénac, like Genet, can only give his political support to the people for whom he feels an erotic attraction. Both authors' works and lives *reroute* the representations of the queer individual experience, and redefine it as travellers across identities.

In the field of identity politics, the theoretical imperative shared by Sénac and Genet is that of poetization. It is necessary to convey in a poetic language the ambiguity of this distinctive queer subject, and thus use a language that can render one's experience as lover. Through the poetic process, this experience becomes one of subjugation and seduction. The subject ultimately appears to the reader as the subjugated lover, literally reduced to love, both seducer and seduced, and whose identity comes to be defined by his love.

Notes

1 Orient in its many declinations (oriental, orientalist, orientalized, etc.) should be under-stood as theorized by Said in his seminal text, *Orientalism*, not primarily as a political or geographical actual entity, but as a western ideology that has become a site of theoretical investigation and an academic practice. Most importantly, it represents also 'Europe's [...] deepest and most recurring images of the Other' (1979: 1).

2 The Sabra and Shatila massacre was a massacre of Palestinian and Lebanese civilians carried out between September 16 and 18, 1982 by the Lebanese Forces Christian militia group in alliance with Israeli forces.

3 All translations are mine, since no translation of Sénac's work exists at this time.

4 The 'white negro', to which Kobena Mercer responds, is the phrase used by Norman Mailer to describe the posture of white individuals during the rebellion that took place within their community against middle class culture between the 1960s and 1970s.

5 Here I refer to 'reverse discourses' (in the Foucauldian sense) established by literary critics and rhetoricians such as Judith Butler on gender, Judith Alberstam on masculinity and Said on orientalism.

6 *Loiterature* (or loiterly literature) is the title of the collection of essays written by Ross Chambers in which he combines the fact of literature and that of loitering. It also includes in its definition the act of sexual cruising in the narratives of western writers chronicling or fictionalizing their trips in the former colonies, or postcolonial outposts such as in the journal of Roland Barthes in Morocco and parts of Paris, *Incidents* (1999).

Bibliography

Aigner-Varoz, E. (2000) 'Metaphors of a Mestiza Consciousness: Anzaldùa's Borderlands/ La Frontera', in *The Society for the Study of The Multi-Ethnic Literature of the United States*, 25.2: 47–63.

Aldrich, R. (2003) *Colonialism and Homosexuality*, London and New York: Routledge.

Anzaldúa, G. (1987) *Borderlands/La Frontera, the New Mestiza*, San Francisco: Spinster/Aunt lute.

Barthes, R. (1987) *Incidents*, Paris: Seuil.

Boone, A. J. (1995) 'Vacation Cruises; or, The Homoerotics of Orientalism', *PMLA*, 110.1 (January): 89–107.

Chambers, R. (1999) *Loiterature*, Lincoln and London: University of Nebraska Press.

Genet, J. (1997) 'Quatre heures à Chatila', reprinted in 'Jean Genet et la Palestine', Special issue of the *Revues d'Etudes Palestiniennes*, 21.

Heyes, C. (2008) 'Identity Politics', in E. N. Zalta (ed.) *The Stanford Encyclopedia of Philosophy*. Online. Available http: http://plato.stanford.edu/archives/fall2008/entries/identity-politics/ (accessed 15 December 2008).

Mercer, K. (1992) '"1968": Periodizing Politics and Identity', in L. Grossberg, C. Nelson, and P. A. Treichler (eds) *Cultural Studies*, London: Routledge.

—— (1992) 'Skin Head Sex Thing: Racial Difference and the Homoerotic Imaginary', in K. Mercer (ed.) *How Do I Look?* Seattle: Bad Object Choices, Bay Press.

Said, E. (1979) *Orientalism*, New York: Vintage Books.

—— (1999 [1995]) 'On Jean Genet's Late Work', in J. E. Gainor (ed.) *Imperialism and Theatre*, London: Routledge.

Sénac, J. (1954) *Poèmes*, with a preface by R. Char, Paris: Gallimard.

—— (1961) *Matinale de mon peuple*, Rodez: Subervie.

—— (1984 [1967]) *The Myth of the Mediterranean Sperm*, Arles: Actes Sud.

—— (1997 [1967]) *Citizens of Beauty*, ed. C. La Bartavelle, Rodez: Subervie.

—— (1999) *Oeuvres Poétiques*, Arles: Actes Sud.

Index